Variations on the Ethics of Mourning
in Modern Literature in French

Modern French Identities

Edited by Jean Khalfa

Volume 143

PETER LANG

Oxford • Bern • Berlin • Bruxelles • New York • Wien

Carole Bourne-Taylor and
Sara-Louise Cooper (eds)

Variations on the Ethics of Mourning in Modern Literature in French

With a preface by
Dominique Rabaté

PETER LANG

Oxford · Bern · Berlin · Bruxelles · New York · Wien

Bibliographic information published by Die Deutsche Nationalbibliothek
Die Deutsche Nationalbibliothek lists this publication in the Deutsche
Nationalbibliografie; detailed bibliographic data is available on the Internet at
http://dnb.d-nb.de.

A catalogue record for this book is available from the British Library.

Library of Congress Cataloging-in-Publication Data

Names: Bourne-Taylor, Carole, 1968– editor. | Cooper, Sara-Louise, editor.
Title: Variations on the ethics of mourning in modern literature in French
   / Carole Bourne-Taylor, Sara-Louise Cooper, [editors]
Description: Oxford ; New York : Peter Lang, [2022] | Series: Modern French
   identities, 1422-9005 ; vol. 143 | Includes bibliographical references
   and index.
Identifiers: LCCN 2021013728 (print) | LCCN 2021013729 (ebook) | ISBN
   9781789972733 (paperback) | ISBN 9781789972740 (ebook) | ISBN
   9781789972757 (epub)
Subjects: LCSH: French literature—20th century—History and criticism. |
   Bereavement in literature. | Liminality in literature. | Philosophy,
   French, in literature.
Classification: LCC PQ307.B47 V37 2022 (print) | LCC PQ307.B47 (ebook) |
   DDC 840.9/353—dc23
LC record available at https://lccn.loc.gov/2021013728
LC ebook record available at https://lccn.loc.gov/2021013729

Cover image: *L'arbre: tout un cortège de doigts et de questions à poser.*
Photograph by Emmanuel Merle.
Cover design by Peter Lang Ltd.

ISSN 1422-9005
ISBN 978-1-78997-273-3 (print)
ISBN 978-1-78997-274-0 (ePDF)
ISBN 978-1-78997-275-7 (ePub)

© Peter Lang Group AG 2022

Published by Peter Lang Ltd, International Academic Publishers,
52 St Giles, Oxford, OX1 3LU, United Kingdom
oxford@peterlang.com, www.peterlang.com

This publication has been peer reviewed.

'Le deuil oblige à dire'
     – Philippe Forest, *L'enfant éternel* (1997)

Take this moment aside
from the dailiness of the days
a block of sheer granite fallen:
run your finger on the dressing table glass
to gather a smidgen of dust
the albums I cannot open
the letters I cannot read
Not yet, I say, not yet,
now is not the time but there will be time
there will one day be time
there will be
presumably
one day
time
    – Stephen Romer, 'Not Yet', *Set Thy Love in*
      Order: New & Selected Poems (2017)

Contents

DOMINIQUE RABATÉ

Préface

In memoriam Michaël Sheringham

Avec le deuil on ne saurait en finir, malgré les injonctions qui nous sont faites d'en faire le travail, de surmonter la mélancolie qui risque de nous engloutir dans cette épreuve de la disparition des proches. Expérience chaque fois singulière, *privée* (et le mot s'entend aussitôt selon un autre sens, expérience privée du destinataire auquel on voudrait continuer de s'adresser) et commune, le deuil dérange l'ordre du temps en introduisant dans ce qui nous semblait son cours étal une faille ou un abîme.

C'est parce qu'il est une expérience intensément personnelle, qu'il renvoie à une souffrance qui semble pétrifier les mots et même les réactions émotionnelles ou physiques, que le deuil a à intimement à voir avec la littérature. Nous sommes coupés de celui ou de celle qui nous accompagnait, qui était notre interlocuteur (mental ou réel), à qui nous nous promettions de dire ceci, de confier cela ; nous sommes plongés dans une sorte de stupeur des mots trop ordinaires, dans le vide moderne des rituels sociaux qui entouraient et guidaient le congé donné aux morts. Et la toute récente pandémie du covid, en comptabilisant les décès en longues processions de chiffres, en réduisant le nombre de ceux qui peuvent prendre part aux enterrements, nous rappelle cruellement cette confiscation de l'accompagnement, l'évacuation de plus en plus sensible de la dimension partagée des deuils.

Disons plus précisément, en reprenant l'inspiration principale du volume *Deuil et littérature*, paru en 2005 dans la collection Modernités, l'expérience du deuil est intimement liée à la définition nouvelle et moderne de ce qui commence à s'appeler du terme de « littérature » comme expression personnelle, comme manière de retenir un monde que le chaos des temps fait disparaître devant nos yeux. Comme tâche interminable pour retenir ce qui ne cesse de s'effacer.

Le livre collectif qu'on va lire prolonge cette compréhension à la fois historique et esthétique du lien énigmatique et puissant entre deuil et écriture moderne, à la fois comme épreuve collective depuis le cycle des révolutions, dans le désarroi d'un dix-neuvième siècle défaisant l'ancien monde, et comme épreuve toujours singulière du survivant qui cherche à garder vif ce monde qui vient de s'abolir. Car c'est toujours un monde qui s'éteint, qu'il ait la proportion d'une société qui bascule ou qu'il soit le monde privé que tout mourant emporte avec lui. Il faut le dire : tout deuil est un appauvrissement de notre monde personnel et collectif. Un appauvrissement sans remède ni réparation, car ce qui manque alors pour toujours c'est bien la personne et tous les liens particuliers que nous avions avec elle seule, tout ce que nous pouvions projeter de conversations, de voyages, de rencontres, d'avenir possible en commun.

Écrire le deuil, retenir le souvenir le plus vivant du disparu, c'est moins protester contre cet appauvrissement que déplier à nouveau la richesse de la relation interrompue, lui donner ou redonner place et volume. On le vérifiera dans ces « variations » qui composent le chemin du livre : ce souci de l'autre qui vient de disparaître, cette attention à sa singularité qui manque justement comme singularité irremplaçable obligent à une inventivité des formes et des mots, de la langue même – quand elle retourne par exemple chez Valérie Rouzeau vers le parler de l'enfance pour rester au plus près du père, ou dans les néologismes que forgent Michel Deguy ou Jacques Derrida, ou dans le retour des mots anciens et plus simples comme celui de « chagrin » chez Barthes.

La suite des études réunies par Carole Bourne-Taylor et Sara-Louise Cooper dessine donc un nouveau chemin en renouvelant les points de vue et les œuvres envisagées. Commenter les livres de deuil oblige le critique, à son tour, à trouver le ton juste entre pathétique et analyse, entre proximité et distance, entre sentiment de l'irrévocable et appel évocatoire. Ce travail de relecture nous rappelle la préséance d'autrui, l'ouverture éthique qui préside aux œuvres littéraires, la patience attentive qu'il faut pour donner au temps sans fin du deuil son rythme et sa diction.

DOMINIQUE RABATÉ: TRANSLATION BY STEPHEN ROMER

Preface

With mourning we shall never be done, despite being enjoined constantly to 'work through it', and rise above the melancholy that threatens to engulf us in the ordeal of losing our loved ones. It is, each and every time, a singular experience, and a *private* one (in the sense also of privation, of being deprived of the addressee to whom one should like to go on talking); it is a shared experience, too – mourning disrupts the order of time by inserting into what we took for its steady passage a fissure or a chasm.

Mourning is an intensely personal experience, one that entails a suffering which seems to petrify words and even physical and emotional reactions, and this is why it has everything to do with literature. We are cut off from our companion, from the person who was our interlocutor (in mind or in reality) and to whom we were going to say this, or to confide the other; we are plunged into a kind of linguistic stupor, where the words are too banal, used to fill the modern emptiness, the social rituals that surround and ease this rite of passage. The Covid pandemic we are undergoing even as I write, by turning all these recent deaths into a series of statistics, and by limiting the numbers allowed to attend funerals, is a cruel reminder of this deprivation, and of how mourning as a shared, meaningful ritual has been palpably emptied out.

To put this more exactly, let me take as my principal inspiration the volume *Deuil et littérature*, (Mourning and Literature), which came out in the collection *Modernités* in 2005: the experience of mourning is intimately linked to the new, modern definition of what was meant by 'literature', that is, a personal expression, a way of holding on to a world the chasm of time swallows before our eyes. The unceasing task being to hold on to what unceasingly vanishes.

The volume by several hands before us extends our understanding of the mysterious and powerful link between mourning and modern writing in the context of history and of aesthetics; it is explored both as a collective ordeal since the revolutionary era, moving into the anxiety of a nineteenth-century coming apart from the old world, and as the perpetually singular ordeal of the individual survivor, seeking to keep alive the world that has just vanished. And it is indeed with the extinction of a world that we are here concerned, whether of an entire society or of the private world which every dying person takes with them. Lest we forget : every passing represents an impoverishment of our personal and collective worlds. And there is no reparation or remedy for this impoverishment, because what is lacking now and forever is indeed the person and all the particular links we had with him or her alone, and everything we might still have had in the way of conversation, travel, encounters and a shared future.

To write through mourning, to write it out, is to retain the most vivid memory of the deceased, less in an act of protest against that impoverishment than in an attempt to deploy once more all the richness of the relationship now severed, to give it or restore to it space and dimension. This is clear in all the 'variations' of this book as it progresses : the concern for the person who has just gone, the attention to their singularity which is precisely that which is irreplaceable; this demands an inventiveness in forms and words, even in language itself – hence Valérie Rouzeau, who returns to a form of babytalk in order to remain as close as possible to her father, or in the neologisms forged by Michel Deguy or Jacques Derrida, or in the re-emergence of older and simpler words, for example, the word 'chagrin' in Barthes.

The collection of papers gathered here by Carole Bourne-Taylor and Sara-Louise Cooper sets us in a new direction, by varying points of view and renewing the works under consideration. To discuss books of mourning requires that the critic, in his or her turn, strike the right tone, between pity and analysis, between empathy and distance, between a keen feeling for what is lost and a responsiveness to the power of evocation, of calling someone back. The work of re-reading here reminds us of the decorum required of the other, the ethical dimension that envelops works of literature, and the patient attention it takes, to give to the unending time of mourning a rhythm and a speech.

Acknowledgements

As editors, it is our pleasure to record our thanks to the contributors to this volume, the product of whose meticulous research you have in your hand; their enthusiasm for the project has been boundless and personally rewarding for us all, especially Dominique Rabaté for his gracious preface.

It was in September 2016, at the study day hosted by the Maison Française d'Oxford that this book was conceived. As ever, I (Carole) record the predictable support of my college, Brasenose, contributing handsomely towards the cost of publication. And to my colleague and friend, Stephen Romer, for his sensitive and accurate translation of Emmanuel Merle, as well as Yves Bonnefoy, of whom he is a leading translator. Where would any editor be without assiduous clerical back-up and persistent commitment to the nuts and bolts of production? For this, I have to thank my husband!

I (Sara-Louise) should like to thank my family for their support during this project and am especially grateful for fruitful conversations with Francesca Clara Parker and regular nudges towards completion from Lucia Beata Parker.

– Carole Bourne-Taylor and Sara-Louise Cooper

CAROLE BOURNE-TAYLOR

Introduction

Death is the ultimate alterity and the ultimate referent, inescapable in its reality and its unreality, its concreteness and its abstraction; the telos and the process, the *finale* and the *basso continuo*; unknowable yet intractable, evidential yet enigmatic: that which imparts intensity to life. The Covid-19 pandemic is the latest tragedy, on an epic scale, that has brought this paradox into sharp focus, an emotional mix exacerbated by a fraught political climate. Death has suddenly become an omnipresent and imminent possibility for each of us. Faced with the evidence of disaster, we have come to think of ourselves as both witnesses and survivors. Embedded within the pandemic is the death of George Floyd,[1] the personal tragedy a symptom of the monstrosity of endemic collective violence and a matter of global concern. This against the background of humanitarian conflicts, including the ongoing migrant crisis with its bodies washed away unmourned.[2] The pandemic may have prompted a new 'visibility' of death in the sense of its ubiquity, but the singularity of each death is eclipsed by the magnitude of the collective toll. A sense of loss that is certainly growing at an alarming rate, prompted by 'the three contemporary deaths': 'atomic; terrorist; climactic',[3] forever accompanied by the Shoah's lingering trauma of annihilation.

---

1 The death of George Floyd, as a result of police restraint on 25 May 2020 in Minneapolis, sparked a sense of grief worldwide as well as reactivating the Black Lives Matter movement.

2 Marielle Macé articulates her polemic in *Sidérer, considérer. Migrants en France* (Paris: Verdier, 2017) which argues that each single death should instantly be granted a form of public mourning, for those dead bodies are ours somehow; they are how we define (or *ought to*) ourselves as European subjects.

3 Michel Deguy, 'Les trois morts contemporaines', which is the excipient poem in *La vie subite: Poèmes Biographèmes Théorèmes* (Paris: Galilée, 2016), p. 231.

Loss, too, is carried along by a paradox: it is acute, yet diffuse; intimately felt, yet universally applicable; specific, yet all-encompassing. The particularity of loss exists against the background of its genericity.[4] What we are, what we do, what we love, is doomed to loss.[5] Loss is not only directed to what was, but also, and perhaps more poignantly, to what might have been or might never be. Longing overflows nostalgia, a feeling all the more overwhelming as it is undefinable. Imagination roams freely over the infinite hinterland of lack which trails off into a plethora of persistent phantasms, its pain being as interminable as death is sudden; an absence so intense that it may, paradoxically, take on the '*thereness* of a presence'.[6]

Thriving in that indeterminate interval between anticipation and retrospection, loss is always beyond consciousness's capability to comprehend the chasm it causes; it is experienced as an alteration of time, existence and the self, as desolation, hence the ubiquity of figures of disjunction, in congruence with a lexicon of non-adequation – 'disproportion'[7] or 'impropriété'[8] – and the recourse to a discontinuist technique. Indeed, grief has its own pace, its own tempo, out of step with any imposed cadence. The Proustian principle of intermittence and the Barthesian predilection for

---

4   Michel Picard highlights the telescoping of each loss with all the other losses in one's life in *La littérature et la mort* (Paris: Presses Universitaires de France, 1995), p. 146.

5   Christina Howells examines the imbrication of love and loss against the backdrop of twentieth-century French thought's emphasis on subjectivity and mortality in *Mortal Subjects. Passions of the Soul in Late Twentieth-Century French Thought* (Cambridge: Polity, 2011).

6   Richard Stamelman, *Lost Beyond Telling: Representations of Death and Absence in Modern French Poetry* (Ithaca, NY & London: Cornell University Press, 1990), p. 12.

7   M. Deguy, *À ce qui n'en finit pas. Thrène* (Paris: Seuil, 1995), unpaginated. If this Pascalian notion is actually omnipresent in Deguy's œuvre, Pierre Bergougnioux also submits time and space to disproportion when seeking to express the sense of disjunction between distinct existences and the impossible mourning of the original landscape, in *La Puissance du souvenir dans l'écriture* (Nantes: Éditions Pleins Feux, 2000), pp. 37–8. Emmanuel Merle's systematic use of the prefixes 'dé' and 'dis' is also symptomatic of a general sense of loss and exile.

8   Jacques Roubaud, *Quelque chose noir* (Paris: Gallimard, 1986), pp. 75–6.

idiorrhythm(y)⁹ and interstice are avatars of discontinuity, symptoms of a
loss keenly felt and at odds with norms. Inscribed in the very fabric of the
text, uncoiling its diegetic spring, rupture generates its own procedures of
resistance, facilitating the emergence of an *alternative* discourse that operates on the margins, as promoted by Abdelkebir Khatibi's pointillist poetics.

The heuristic value of mourning lies in its reactivating and re-motivating
the critical potential of literature – its writerly implications – through figuration. Outside any pre-established framework, at a loss, concepts no
longer operate at full power, whereas experience thrives, carried along by
its paradoxical expression: another experience, another language, generating each other. The neologism 'désapparition'– neither appearance of
absence nor disappearance of presence, somewhere in-between – which
Patrick Chamoiseau borrowed from Édouard Glissant, points to the possibility of expression within impossibility, the desperate effort to cling on
to appearance within a lucid confrontation with disappearance. The motif
of 'disparition' ['disappearance'], which Chamoiseau prefers to 'mort',
is inexhaustible with its Mallarmean connotations being prolonged and
dramatized by Michel Deguy as some kind of conjuring trick ('la prestidigi-
tation du deuil').¹⁰ Death, the prestidigitator par excellence, swiftly ravishes
one's beloved. In Deguy's threnody, *À ce qui n'en finit pas* [*To That Which
is Never-ending*], the metaphorical dedication to his late wife, 'à ma femme
disparue en mort' – always already 'disparue', just like Proust's Albertine,
herself a variation on Charles Baudelaire's *passante* [passer-by] – pushes
the event into the eventuality of figuration. Whilst conjuring the all too
familiar phrase, 'disparue en mer' [lost at sea], the metaphor paradoxically
fulfils its mission of poetic transfiguration, retrieval and conjuration: the
beloved is 'mise à mots' [put into words/set to poetry] rather than 'mise à
mort' [put to death]. If the adjective 'disparue' – promoted to the status

---

9   Roland Barthes, *Comment vivre ensemble. Cours et séminaires au Collège de
    France 1976–77* (Paris: Seuil, 2002), p. 37; which is echoed in his *Journal de deuil*
    (Paris: Seuil, 2009): 'Chacun son rythme de chagrin', p. 175.

10 *À ce qui n'en finit pas*, unpaginated. Similarly, *'la vie subite'* is a loaded metaphor
    playing on the cliché of 'mort subite' (sudden death), life flashing by, reworking the
    nucleus of the Baudelairean passage – the 'soudainement' tipping into the 'jamais'
    in 'À une passante', *Les Fleurs du Mal* (Paris: Garnier, 1961), p. 99.

of monostich in Jacques Roubaud's poem 'Morte' – best encapsulates the new state of his late wife,[11] it is surely because of the enigmatic, spectral and poetic possibilities inherent in this term. Marie Darrieussecq's *Tom est mort* reveals the urge to forge one's own idiolect[12] when considering the exact meaning and value of the generic term, deuil [mourning], which sits neatly within the dictionary and which, therefore, does not seem appropriate because it is at odds with one's own very unique suffering (which she refers to as '*ça*'): she calls for a word that would be for her own exclusive use,[13] to which she could give her own twist.

Figuration is what is left in loss – language's *alternative* when loss seeps into it. It is necessarily indeterminate and thwarted, yet propelled by an 'energy of despair'.[14] Utterance is compelled into being by non-being, wrenching from it its own ambiguous motivational force, drawing its figural energy from the gap between loss and its formulation.[15] The mimetic conundrum opens up figural possibilities in this linguistic game of hide-and-seek between intention and invention, compulsion and articulation. Loss reappears as grief and bereavement, one that prolongs itself as mourning; the other disappears to reappear *as other*: therein lies the paradoxical logic of writing, always at odds with its referent, always suspended between its obscure source and its elusive telos, always bound up with absence.[16] Figuration is a force of differentiation/*differantiation* that dispels ready-made discourses and defers completion; it ensures that truth overrides reference.

---

11   Roubaud, *Quelque chose noir*, p. 68.
12   Cf. Daisy Sainsbury's analysis of Valérie Rouzeau's neologizing prattle in *Pas revoir*.
13   Marie Darrieussecq, *Tom est mort* (Paris: P.O.L, 2007), p. 67.
14   Cf. Deguy's *L'Énergie du désespoir ou d'une poétique continuée par tous les moyens* (Paris: Presses Universitaires de France, 1998).
15   Cf. Laurent Jenny on 'le jeu du figural' and its 'tensional force', *La Parole singulière* (Paris: Belin, 1990), p. 23. Paul de Man construes figuration as the trope of loss, in *Allegories of Reading: Figural Language in Rousseau, Nietzsche, Rilke and Proust* (New Haven, CT: Yale University Press, 1979).
16   This conception of writing in absentia or as being bereft of its referent, as an orphan, is encapsulated by Richard Stamelman in *Lost Beyond Telling:* 'Writing is always the writing of loss', p. 17.

What transpires is the role of writing on mourning as a challenge to dominant social, economic, or scientific modes of thought – which seek to comprehend reality solely through a normative framework. An antidote to the blandness of official discourses, literature emerges as a qualitative discourse of resistance and hospitality[17] channelling its logico-aesthetic resources against reproducibility and screenization and transcending the limitations of conceptual systems. Despite different paradigms informing it, *poethical*[18] mourning is the counter-discourse (counter in its double sense of opposition and connection) par excellence, enacting *another* discourse that seeks to explore the otherness of language: in the sense of an 'autrement dit',[19] but also 'with' *and* 'for' *and* 'to' the other in a world ruled by the media with their proliferation of impoverishing or infantilizing discourses; this *other* discourse runs counter to the *doxa* of mourning – whether psychoanalytical or social – and *Doxa* more generally.[20] Mourning brings into visibility the friction between the mourner's quest for qualitative forms of thought/thoughtfulness and the demands of hypervisibility in an iconosphere saturated by cacophonic communication.

Loss and alteration are bound up with each other: the return of the past alters the present in the same way as death alters the subject. Temporal alterity is the discrepancy between events that pass temporally but not affectively: time may pass, it *will* pass, inexorably so, but the experience of being caught up in grief is equated with a time that does not pass.[21] Temporal

---

17 Of which Chamoiseau's *Frères migrants* (Paris: Seuil, 2017), Ananda Devi's *Ceux du large* (Paris: B. Doucey, 2017) and Marie Darrieussecq's *La Mer à l'envers* (Paris: P.O.L, 2019) are amongst the best illustrations.

18 Jean-Claude Pinson is one of the main theoreticians of this notion, which extends beyond poetry *per se* to valorize the existential and experiential motivations of literature. Cf. *Poéthique. Une autothéorie* (Seyssel: Champ Vallon, 2013).

19 Michael Edwards, 'Autrement dit', *Le Genre humain* 47/1 (2008), 95–105. Translated as 'in other words', 'autrement dit' preserves and highlights the idea of difference.

20 Jean-Pierre Siméon makes such a case for poetry in our world, in *La poésie sauvera le monde* (Paris: Le Passeur, 2016).

21 Dominique Rabaté's reference to 'un temps qui ne passe pas' [a time that does not pass], in Pierre Glaudes and Dominique Rabaté, eds, *Modernités 21. Deuil et Littérature* (Bordeaux: Presses universitaires, 2005), p. 320; it reads like a variation on Kristeva's description of '[u]n passé qui ne passe pas', which binds melancholy to

discordance[22] is the chiasmatic disjunction between living memories and a petrified present. Temporality is eroded and truncated, textualized as *ressassement*, which is the painful duration of grief with its interplay of recurrence and difference and 'différance'. When repetition tips into rumination, it is subsumed under the paradigm of *ressassement*[23] – which defines much of modern literature and is consubstantial with the aesthetics of variation in musically minded writers like Proust and Barthes. It is somewhere between distance and proximity, memory and oblivion, presence and absence, identity and exile, in that in-between of a polymorphous *alteration* and representational vacillation that literature can (re)imagine aborted possibilities and propose others.

Exploring the borderland between aesthetics and ethics, mourning sharpens the critical potential of literature as a practice of life – that of being a caretaker of the world and our fellow human beings. Construed as a response to loss, mourning moves in mysterious ways – unthought, unthinkable, unthought-of, even 'rethought'[24] *and* thoughtful – which all coalesce within a regime of pensiveness/attentiveness,[25] typified by the

hauntology, in *Soleil noir. Dépression et mélancolie* (Paris: Gallimard, 1987), p. 70. This motif takes on more ominous resonances within the context of crimes against humanity, with postcolonial theory being embedded within the framework of traumatic memory, with particular regards to Henry Rousso's *Le Syndrome de Vichy*. Cf. Sara-Louise Cooper's analysis of Chamoiseau's treatment of the past in this volume.

22 M. Deguy calls this hiatus 'un discord du temps en lui-même', in 'Nous nous souvenons', *Compagnies de Pierre Michon* (Lagrasse: Verdier, 1993), p. 40.

23 A tricky concept to translate with its connotations of rumination and melancholy and acquiring metapoetic value in the genre of complainte as practiced by Jules Laforgue: 'Tu te racontes sans fin, et tu te ressasses', 'Complainte d'un autre dimanche', *Les Complaintes et les premiers poèmes* (Paris: Gallimard, 1979), p. 61. Eric Benoit *et alii*, eds, establish a coincidence between the modernity inaugurated by Flaubert and anticipated by Rousseau and *ressassement*, 'Avant-dire', *Modernités 15. Écritures du ressassement* (Bordeaux: Presses universitaires de Bordeaux, 2001), p. 5; p. 11.

24 Cf. Shoshana Felman and Dori Laub, *Testimony: Crises of Witnessing in Literature, Psychoanalysis, and History* (New York: Routledge, 1992), p. xv.

25 M. Deguy, who looms large in discussions of mourning, theorizes this *'pensivité poétique'*, in *La Poésie n'est pas seule. Court traité de poétique* (Paris: Seuil, 1988), p. 92.

(lyrical) *pensivité* of a Baudelaire and his heir, the *poèthe-poéthicien* Michel Deguy,[26] who has been honing his own brand of *tristesse poétique*. *Pensivité* relies on figuration, whose inexhaustibility never quite matches the immeasurability of loss.[27] The paradigm of thinking (of or about *and* with) is encapsulated in the Deguyan double-entendre 'compenser',[28] which extends far beyond the impulse to compensate; if anything, it resists compensation, unless one regards the possibility of figuration as the counterpoint to the impossibility of mourning. In the throes of mourning, literature is conducted as a practice of thinking/thoughtfulness which persists in interrogating what it cannot possibly express, and attending to the testimonial gesture. A plea for vigilance, 'compenser' conjures up the ideal of a community of mortals that would bring otherness into the fold of togetherness, which is encapsulated in the punning neologism 'comme-un des mortels'[29] [the likeness and 'as-oneness' of mortals: our common humanity]. Watchfulness[30] is the watchword, in the form of a constantly reconducted act of watching over the other – '*penser-à*'.[31] All too aware of its insufficiency, the compulsion to think of/about the other is conflated with the imperative to think *with* the other, which conjures up the French verb 'composer avec' – not so much in the sense of coming to terms with one's loss as composing the work with *and* for the other. An ethics of alterity and relationality is inherent in Nerval's paradigmatic elegiac invocation: 'Je pense à toi, Myrtho …'[32] [Myrtho, I think of you]: a presence imaginatively

---

26   This regime of *pensivité* may be described as an epiphenomenon of *poésie pensante* or *poéthique*. This propensity for philosophizing in French poetry, at least since Baudelaire, is analysed in Joseph Acquisto's, ed., *Thinking Poetry: Philosophical Approaches to Nineteenth-Century French Poetry* (New York: Palgrave Macmillan, 2013).

27   Cf. R. Stamelman on loss being bound up with figuration in the sense of being beyond it, in *Lost Beyond Telling*, pp. x–xi.

28   M. Deguy, *Tombeau de du Bellay* (Paris: Gallimard, 1973), p. 83.

29   M. Deguy, *La raison poétique* (Paris: Galilée, 2000), p. 34.

30   'Veiller', which is ubiquitous in Deguy's *À ce qui n'en finit pas*, means 'to watch over' and 'to watch at a dying person's bedside'.

31   M. Deguy, *Desolatio* (Paris: Galilée, 2007), p. 2. This autobiographical text on love, friendship and mourning epitomizes the anticonsolatory paradigm.

32   G. de Nerval, 'Myrtho', *Chimères* (1854), in Jean Guillaume and Claude Pichois, eds, *Œuvres complètes* (Paris: Gallimard-Pléiade, 1993, III), p. 746.

recalled, a humble thought to signify absence on the site of Virgil's tomb. More poignantly though, the *raison d'être* of poetry is encapsulated in the Baudelairean proclamation of irretrievability: 'À quiconque a perdu ce qui ne se retrouve/Jamais, jamais!'[33] [Of whoever has lost that which can never be retrieved/Again, ever!']. Here, bearing witness to the loss of the old city prompts refiguration, allegorization and hospitality.[34] *Pensivité* is enshrined in Baudelaire's 'Andromaque, Je pense à vous!'[35] [Andromache, I think of you!], which breathes humanity into the grieving mythic figure and confers onto the Baudelairean address an ethical lucidity. It is the experience of loss that makes us 'semblables'[36] [like each other] and cements our fellowship: the incontrovertible truth of mortality is the ultimate criterion for our shared humanity – 'le comme-un des mortels' delineating an all-inclusive community. Each addressee in their singularity refers to a universal alterity, carries within themselves a universal victimhood: migrants, orphans, the Negress,[37] the captives, the vanquished and 'many others' – the list of those suffering from irrecoverable loss is growing every day. The stranded, suffering swan in Baudelaire's poem anchors the empathetic allegorization of human tragedy,[38] drawing attention to the porous boundaries between existential and stylistic ideals; somehow Baudelaire's

33   Baudelaire, 'Le Cygne', *Les Fleurs du Mal*, p. 95.
34   A vivid illustration of the many literary filiations which criss-cross this volume, Jacques Roubaud's appropriation of the Baudelairean hemistich – 'la forme d'une ville' (the form of a city) – is permeated by memory and melancholy, loss and longing, with a slight variation though: *La forme d'une ville change plus vite, hélas, que le cœur des humains* (Paris: Gallimard, 1999); a form of melancholic mourning, necessarily diffuse and asynchronous: Cf. Karl Heinz Bohrer, *Der Abschied. Theorie der Trauer: Baudelaire, Goethe, Nietzsche, Benjamin* (Frankfurt: Suhrkamp, 1996), pp. 181–209.
35   Baudelaire, 'Le Cygne', *Les Fleurs du Mal*, p. 95.
36   Cf. 'Au Lecteur', *Les Fleurs du Mal*, p. 6.
37   The generic or periphrastic appellation to refer to Jeanne Duval is construed by Yves Bonnefoy as a 'fundamentally poetic act', bestowing upon her the supreme gift, that is her human 'absoluteness', in *Sous le signe de Baudelaire* (Paris: Gallimard, 2011), p. 338.
38   'Tout pour moi devient allégorie' (everything becomes allegorical), 'Le Cygne', in *Les Fleurs du Mal*, p. 96.

Inconnu encompasses mortality and figuration, while the quest for l'*Idéal* has to contend with spleen and unfolds within the reality of ailing, aging and ending. Mourning contributes to turning figuration into a potent concept that teases out and reinforces, beyond any aesthetic motivation, literature's existential value.[39]

Exacerbating the rift between language and meaning, mourning relentlessly enacts its ruminative lament, mobilizing the work of memory – beyond the narrow enclosure of symbolic structures and commemorative conventions – and playing the whole scale of figuration. Thriving in breaches, relishing twists and torsions, figuration is the unexpected eloquence emerging from the impulse of silence to express suffering. If mourning has to do primarily with signs[40] it is surely because death is the ultimate metaphor.[41] Always already there as a prefiguration,[42] its radicalness prompts a multifarious figuration, which encompasses refiguration, transfiguration, configuration and disfiguration. Figuration is the very admission of the faltering of language, yet is its apotheosis: its inexhaustible and vivifying potentialities unfold in an incommensurate space of loss, a loss that is invariably experienced as excess and exile, as well as a common ground.[43] There is, of course, more to the Baudelairean homophony *cygne* [swan]/*signe* than meets the eye, but above all it signals the reappearance of the swan as an allegory of mortality; *autrement dit*, the impossibility of

39 Forms, styles, images, rhythms, which are all bound up with existence, are harnessed to an ethically orientated project carried out by and in literature. Cf. Marielle Macé's anthropology of style or stylistics of existence, in *Façons de lire, manières d'être* (Paris: Gallimard, 2011), *Styles. Critique de nos formes de vie* (Paris: Gallimard, 2016), 'Du Style!', *Critique* 752/53 (2010). This is in keeping with Barthes, who ascribes to the work an 'existential finality', in *La Préparation du roman, Cours au Collège de France 1978–9 et 1979–80* (Paris: Seuil-Imec, 2003), p. 224.

40 Patrick Marot defines it as 'un travail sur les signes', 'Deuil et métaphore', in *Deuil et littérature*, p. 105.

41 M. Deguy calls it 'métaphore par excellence', in *Figurations. Poèmes-Propositions-Etudes* (Paris: Gallimard, 1969), p. 121; it is that incommensurable 'unknowable' that gives all things 'the status of figure', p. 122.

42 Deguy, idem, p. 122.

43 Cf. Robert Harvey, *Sharing Common Ground: A Space for Ethics* (London: Bloomsbury, 2017).

description triggers the possibility of inscription – of alterity, temporality, mortality – through allegory.[44] Speaking ambivalently and elusively, differently or otherwise (*allos*), allegory is a breach in signs, the very figure of exilic existence within language. The alterity of the lost other calls for the alterity of discourse. Born out of absence and spurred by language's inadequacy, figuration contains a principle of alteration that shatters narrativity, fractures textual fabric and ruptures rhythm. Figuration is all intensity and energy, as well as hospitality, which is intrinsically 'poetic'[45] in its imaginative and altering potential; in keeping with the idea that the use of style[46] in modernity is inherently ethical in its channelling both the exploration of what was hitherto hidden and the contestation of dominant values: style points to an ethical pact.[47]

The quest for the lost other summons 'a poetic experience of language',[48] one that would not actually (or merely) aestheticize, but incessantly gesture its 'energy of despair', delineating a figurative space outside and beyond normative and consolatory models, within which mourning – pivoting on the inextricable relation between memory and history, singularity and collectivity – can be harnessed as a critical tool.

****

A number of seminal theorizations of mourning demonstrate its all-pervasiveness in a pluridisciplinary field that encompasses the politics of modernity,[49] postcolonial studies,[50] memory

44   Allegory is bound up with mortality; Stamelman names it 'the trope of death', in *Lost Beyond Telling*, p. 53.

45   'Un acte d'hospitalité ne peut être que poétique', Jacques Derrida writes in *De l'hospitalité* (Paris: Calmann-Lévy, 1997), p. 10.

46   Cf. Antonio Rodriguez, 'Le style et sa valeur éthique dans la modernité', in Florence Quinche et Antonio Rodriguez, eds, *Quelle éthique pour la littérature ?: pratiques et déontologies*. Le champ éthique 47 (Geneva: Labor et Fideson, 2007) style being not only an aesthetic norm, but also an ethical one.

47   Rodriguez, idem, p. 29.

48   J. Derrida, *Poétique et politique du témoignage* (Paris: L'Herne, 2005), p. 9.

49   Jean-Philippe Mathy, *Melancholy Politics. Loss, Mourning, and Memory in Late Modern France* (University Park: Pennsylvania State University, 2011).

50   Cf. Fiona Barclay, *Writing Postcolonial France: Haunting, Literature, and the Maghreb* (Lanham, MD: Lexington Books, 2011).

studies,[51] deconstruction and psychoanalysis,[52] with its far-reaching questioning potential being distilled into 'traumatic hermeneutics'.[53] Within
the wide and eclectic literary corpus generated by mourning,[54] life
writing – whether autofictional or *autobiopoietic*, or more overtly (auto)
biographical – has proved particularly fertile. In texts of mourning, the
logic of blurring boundaries extends to the 'je' hovering between narrator
or speaker and author – not in the sense of a biographical or psychological subject; no mere shifter either, rather a shifting subject, who tends
to relinquish any signifying authority in favour of a commitment to the
beloved.

   A nexus between memorial and textual recreation, the text of mourning
takes up the challenge of articulating the absence of the beloved by resorting
to formal experimentation, which often consists in rethinking generic

51   Cf. Henry Rousso, *Le Syndrome de Vichy de 1944 à nos jours* (Paris: Seuil, 1987);
     Marianne Hirsch, *Family Frames: Phtography, Narrative, and Postmemory*
     (Cambridge: Harvard University Press, 1997); Dominick LaCapra, *Representing
     the Holocaust: History, Theory, Trauma* (Ithaca, NY: Cornell University Press,
     1994) and *History and Memory after Auschwitz* (Ithaca, NY: Cornell University
     Press, 1998); Michel Lantelme, *Figures de la repentance. Littérature et devoir de
     mémoire* (Paris: Garnier, 2017) and the indefatigable Annette Wieviorka, whose
     numerous essays include *L'Ère du témoin* (Paris: Hachette, 2002), *Déportation et
     génocide. Entre la mémoire et l'oubli* (Paris: Hachette, 2003), *Nouvelles perspectives
     sur la Shoah* (Paris: Presses Universitaires de France, 2013).
52   Cf. Colin Davis, *Haunted Subjects. Deconstruction, Psychoanalysis and the Return of
     the Dead* (London: Palgrave Macmillan, 2007).
53   Cf. Colin Davis, *Traces of War. Interpreting Ethics and Trauma in Twentieth-
     Century French Writing* (Liverpool: Liverpool University Press, 2018).
54   Major references include: Paul Eluard's *Le Temps déborde*; Henri Michaux's *Nous
     deux encore* (1948), Philippe Jaccottet's *Requiem* (1947), *Leçons* (1969), *Chants
     d'en bas* (1974), James Sacré's *Cœur élégie rouge* (1972) and *Une petite fille silencieuse*
     (2001), Claude Esteban's *Elégie de la mort violente* (1989), Michel Deguy's *À ce qui
     n'en finit pas* (1995), Philippe Forest's *L'enfant éternel* (1997), *Toute la nuit* (1999)
     and *Tous les enfants sauf un* (2007), Camille Laurens's *Philippe* (1995) and *Cet
     absent-là* (2004), Martine Broda's *Éblouissements* (2003), Yves Charnet's *La trist-
     esse durera toujours* (2013), Jean-Michel Maulpoix's *L'hirondelle rouge* (2017), Pierre
     Jourde's *Winter is Coming* (2017), Dominique Fourcade's *deuil* (2018), Jean-Michel
     Espitallier's *La première année* (2018), etc.

boundaries between literary criticism and life-writing.[55] Composite and elastic qualities often characterize the poetics of mourning, in keeping with its tentativeness. Hybridity telescopes the construction of the text and self-(re)construction, within the intentionality of an ambiguous addressivity. The tradition of elegy and the poetic *livre de deuil* or *tombeau* is the site of endless innovation,[56] one that, in our contemporary age, tends to keep aestheticization and sentimentalization at bay in favour of disruption: anti-elegy might be a better label[57] to describe a discourse in which experience and experiment join forces to redefine the lyrical subject as an ethical subject.[58] Oulipianism turns out to be a reinvention rather than an outright rejection of lyricism.

The reinvention of the sixteenth-century genre of the *tombeau* consists in variations on voice, at least since Mallarmé, more specifically the fantasy of a 'duo' with the two almost indistinguishable voices of the mourner and their beloved,[59] as in Roubaud's *Quelque chose noir* [*Some Thing Black*] (1986) – an example of generic heterogeneity, combining fictional, poetic and meditative genres enveloped in dazzling intertextuality. In its wake, Deguy's *À ce qui n'en finit pas* (1995)[60] – labelled a threnody – qualifies as

---

55   Cf. J. Derrida, *Chaque fois unique, la fin du monde* (Paris: Galilée, 2003).

56   Cf. Jean-Michel Maulpoix's anthology, *Histoire de l'élégie* (Paris: Agora, 2018), which traces the evolution of the genre.

57   Jean-Claude Pinson's poem, 'Fin d'Élégie à Saint-Nazaire', in *J'habite ici* (Seyssel: Champ Vallon, 1990), proposes new, unexpected, trivial associations, lamenting the disappearance of a poetic genre which seems incongruous in our modern world while renewing it at the same time, p. 12s.

58   In *Témoins de l'inactuel. Quatre contemporains face au deuil* (Paris: Corti, 2007), Dominique Carlat situates texts by Barthes, Pierre Pachet, Claude Esteban, Michel Deguy within the broader context of the attempt to rethink one's relationship to memory since the Second World War – arguably the most traumatic event in French history since the Revolution – emphasizing the all-pervasiveness of mourning in poetic writing.

59   Dominique Moncond'huy, 'Qu'est-ce qu'un tombeau poétique ?', *La Licorne*, 29 ('Le Tombeau poétique en France'), 3/16 (1994), 10.

60   The revised edition of *À ce qui n'en finit pas* (nouvelle édition revue et augmentée, Paris: Seuil, 2017) implements its performativity as interminable mourning.

mourning diary, love letter, song of grief, poem, essay, tombeau,[61] 'livre-poème' (or 'poème-livre'), enlisting 'obsèques' and 'convoi' to converge in *autobiopoiesis*.[62]

Death often shapes and re-orientates the autobiographical project.[63] If diaries – such as the expanding 'Covid' brand – are contemporaneous with the event, much autofictional writing originates from a deferred relationship with History, as exemplified by Oulipian techniques of displacement.[64] The serendipitous rhyme between 'retour' and 'détour' points to an alteration of the subject, amongst other forms of alterations. Constraints – whether hyper-consciously exploited by Baudelaire and dazzingly manipulated by OuLiPo, or more loosely handled – invariably invigorate literature through the constant negotiation between chaos and control, emotion and elaborateness.

With their memorializing quality,[65] texts of mourning lead to a prob-lematization and *ipso facto* revaluation of autobiographical discourse, which, in some instances, can be labelled 'genealogical'; many *récits de vie* are *récits de*

---

61   Michel Deguy is one of the main practioners of the tombeau, as exemplified by his *Tombeau de du Bellay* and 'Tombeau de Jacques Dupin', in *La vie subite*, pp. 47–53.

62   Despite its denomination as a mere love letter, Nathalie Rheims's *Lettre d'une amoureuse morte* (Paris: Flammarion, 2000), which is haunted by a Durasian sense of loss, reads like a mourning poem or prayer within a Racinian dramaturgy, conflating the two forms of the lyrical cantata and tragic soliloquy: the result is a *tombeau* not only for the loved ones, but also for the narrator herself whose flesh bears the stigmata of her suffering. In fact, if Rheims' text is so compelling, it is be-cause a text of mourning can often be read as a love letter, all the more poignant as it is never read by its addressee.

63   Culminating in *thanatography*. Cf. Roger Laporte's *Une vie* (Paris: P.O.L, 1986), p. 542; or *autothanatography*, in Louis Marin's *La Voix excommuniée: essais de mémoire* (Paris: Galilée, 1981), p. 37.

64   Cf. Michael Sheringham, *French Autobiography: Devices and Desires – Rousseau to Perec* (Oxford: Clarendon Press, 1993), p. 320. In a different vein, Philippe Jaccottet also valorizes obliqueness in *Paysages avec figures absentes* (Paris: Gallimard, 1998), p. 22.

65   Amongst Jacques Roubaud's main preoccupations is memory, which is consubstan-tial with poetry and of which a recent example is his *Poétique. Remarques. Poésie, mémoire, nombre, temps, rythme, contrainte, forme, etc.* (Paris: Seuil, 2016).

filiation[66] engaged in an experimental and devotional search for ways to express ties to the beloved and repatriate them from oblivion. In the late twentieth century, metaliterary preoccupations receded in favour of a rehabilitation of transitivity, which Barthes himself – abjuring his structuralist credo of the gap between words and the world – came to embrace: intent on writing '*à partir d'elle*'[67] [with her in mind, originating from her], following his mother's death, he defined his fantasy of the 'Novel' as 'filial'.[68] The epistemological rift between textual structure and extratextual referentiality subsided further, in keeping with the historical turn in the 1980s, which took on its full significance in the ethical turn[69] in the 1990s, an era mourning for meaning.[70] The transitivity of bearing witness is bound up

66   Cf. Dominique Viart, 'Le récit de filiation. "Ethique de la restitution" contre "devoir de mémoire" dans la littérature contemporaine', in Christian Chelebourg, David Martens and Myriam Watthee-Delmotte, eds, *Héritage, filiation, transmission. Configurations littéraires (XVIIIe-XXIe siècles)* (Louvain: Presses universitaires, 2012). The conceptualization of filiation is a response to a mutation in French literature from the mid-1970s onwards when it became a major topos in fiction in French. The corpus includes: Simone de Beauvoir's *Une mort très douce*, Perec's *W ou le souvenir d'enfance* (1975), Annie Ernaux's *La Place* (1984) and *Une Femme* (1988), Pierre Bergounioux's *L'Orphelin*, Jean Rouaud's *Les Champs d'honneur* (1990), *Des Hommes illustres* (1993) and *Sur la scène comme au ciel* (1999), Pierre Michon's *Les vies minuscules* (1984), Leïla Sebbar's *Je ne parle pas la langue de mon père* (2003), Chamoiseau's *À bout d'enfance* (2005), Michel Séonnet's *La marque du père* (2007), Virginie Linhart's *Le jour où mon père s'est tu* (2008), Martine Sonnet's *Atelier 62* (2009), etc. which could all be subsumed under the appellation 'encres orphelines'. Cf. Laurent Demanze, *Encres orphelines, Pierre Bergounioux, Gérard Macé, Pierre Michon* (Paris: Corti, 2008).

67   Barthes, *Journal de deuil*, p. 227. This so-called 'quelque chose à partir d'elle' will turn out to be *La Chambre claire*.

68   Barthes, *La Préparation du roman*, p. 378.

69   Thinkers such as Emmanuel Levinas, Paul Ricœur, Jacques Derrida, Martha Nussbaum, Jacques Bouveresse, Cynthia Fleury, Alexandre Gefen, Sandra Laugier, Pascal Riendeau, Rita Felski, etc. have become established references in the consideration of literature as a site of ethical resistance.

70   Christian Prigent exploits the polysemy of the expression, 'en manque de sens', which encapsulates an acute sense of deprivation: both the undeniable fact (perceived as a fatality) of this lack and the act of suffering from a lack of meaning (in the sense also of suffering withdrawal symptoms) and craving it, in *À quoi bon encore des poètes* (Paris: P.O.L., 1996), p. 7.

not only with subjectivity but also with contingency, which is the intersection between ethics and aesthetics: something of our fragility and vulnerability is incorporated into discourse. Transitivity has to do with loss,
which has become the all-pervasive mood in French culture, with its proliferation of narratives of rupture and return:[71] a return to the subject and
the author – with a more acute consciousness of alterity[72] – to the story
and history, all symbiotically connected in a pluridisciplinary 'discourse
of return'.[73] A sense of things disappearing pervades much contemporary
literature[74] with its renewed emphasis on filiation (and transmission),[75]

71   Cf. Lucas Hollister, *Beyond Return: Genre and Cultural Politics in Contemporary
     French Fiction* (Oxford: Oxford University Press, 2019).

72   The return of the subject marks a return to the other, hence the 'pôle de l'altérité'.
     Cf. Michel Collot and Jean-Claude Mathieu, eds, *Poésie et altérité* (Paris: Presses de
     l'E.N.S, 1990), p. 7.

73   Lucas Hollister, p. 5. The author takes his cue from Colin Davis and Elizabeth
     Fallaize's *French Fiction in the Mitterrand Years: Memory, Narrative Desire*
     (Oxford: Oxford University Press, 2000). D. Viart had identified the prevalence
     of the trope of the return in post-1980 fiction. Cf. 'Mémoires du récit: questions
     à la modernité', in Dominique Viart, ed., *Mémoires du récit* (Paris-Caen: Lettres
     modernes Minard, 'Écritures contemporaines', 1, 1998), pp. 3–37.

74   Cf. Dominique Rabaté, *Désirs de disparaître: une traversée du roman français
     contemporain* (Rimouski: Tangence, 2015). Jean-Philippe Mathy addresses this dis-
     enchantment in *Melancholy Politics*.

75   The melancholia that pervades those writings is linked to an ethical project. In his
     'Figures de l'héritier dans le roman contemporain', *Études françaises*, 45 (2009),
     Demanze looks at the crisis of transmission in contemporary literature with regard
     to the condition of the orphan. Pierre Michon's reinvention of hagiography de-
     lineates an extinct rurality. In the mournful deplorations of Jean Clair's *Terre
     Natale: exercises de piété* (2019), loss stems from moral bankruptcy and an erosion
     of national identity. Further right on the political spectrum, Richard Millet's neo-
     reactionary chronicle of the plight of *la France profonde* – in his trilogy: *La Gloire des
     Pythre* (1995), *L'amour des trois sœurs Piale* (1997), *Lauve le pur* (2000) – smacks of
     nostalgia for an agrarian ancestry and a more classical brand of French. The ubiqui-
     tous trope of yearning for a bygone era in the age of globalization betrays a certain
     idea of France. In a very different vein, turning to the left, Deguy combines grief and
     grievance to mourn the old Paris – most notably in his *Spleen de Paris* (2001) – and
     lament the demise of culture, reduced to cultural capitalism and eschatologically
     described as 'apocalypse' and 'deluge' (*La raison poétique*, p. 140). This so-called
     'culturel' is a leitmotiv, especially in *La Raison poétique* and *Réouverture après*

which is the axis of genealogical and biographical investigation and fosters an 'ethics of restitution'.[76]

The 'ethics of restitution' relies on an ethics of transcription. The literary text engages in the fraught enterprise of restoring voice to the voiceless and metaphorizing one's own memory through that of the other. In this respect, the thriving genre of the investigation[77] – or counter-investigation for that matter – reads like a search for ethical restitution through the coalescence of personal identity and historical trauma: the mourner's desire to write proceeds from a sense that the lives of their loved ones have been silenced or sidelined, repressed or betrayed by collective memory. The sense of a broader context may be diffuse or marginally relevant, but mourning invariably points to an ethical agenda that hinges upon an intricate

---

travaux (Paris: Galilée, 2007). Informed by Guy Debord's society of the spectacle promoting ephemera and spluttering simplistic meanings and Jean Baudrillard's hyperreality, humanity has fallen prey to the idolatry of its own technologically enhanced image: uniformity engenders inhumanity. This consumer society hides a more insidious side, which Jérémie Lefebvre has anatomized in *La Société de consolation. Chronique d'une génération ensorcelée* (Paris: Sens & Tonka, 2000) with its mass-production of myths and illusions that fill the void. For thinkers of disappearance such as Deguy, these are all interrelated preoccupations, amongst which anthropomorphist humanity's estrangement from a world it has wrecked through systematic carelessness. An all-encompassing label, *Poéthique* (with which Deguy is synonymous) extends to a geopoetics of attachment or ecopoetics – which applies to Emmanuel Merle. Amongst the many reasons for the pervasiveness of the motif of disappearance in contemporary literature, there is also the instinct to insulate oneself from terroristic systems and the tyranny of hypervisibility. Chamoiseau's denigration of the destructive effects of tourism on Creole culture is on the same continuum. All these endeavours testify to a sense of unshakeable grief.

76   Cf. Dominique Viart, in D. Viart and Bruno Vercier, eds, *La Littérature française au présent. Héritage, modernité, mutation* (Paris : Bordas, 2005), pp. 91–5.

77   In *Un nouvel âge de l'enquête. Portrait de l'écrivain contemporain en enquêteur* (Paris: Corti, 2019), Laurent Demanze highlights the ethical stance of such investigators as George Perec, Patrick Modiano and Kamel Daoud, amongst many others, all cultivating an 'ethics of opacity' (p. 266; p. 277), which guarantees the integrity of the testimony by acknowledging the problematic nature of experience and its rendition.

relationality of continuities, intersections and overlaps that transcends questions of filiation.

Filiation is poised between a sense of tradition – that of the *tombeau* or elegy, for example – and a quest for experimentation. Each text of mourning gestures to its predecessors, sedimenting the commonality of the experience of loss to the extent of configuring a community of *endeuillés* [mourners].[78] The pre-text – whether an explicit hypotext or not – contributes to texturing and altering the text further. Resonating with the unconscious as well as the conscious, hypertextuality is the sign that the past is open for endless re-visitation and inventiveness.

Within such a context of memorialization and filiation, the production of literature is summed up by the concept of 'lecture-écriture' [reading-writing].[79] Texts of mourning draw incessantly on a profuse literary memory, cross hatched by filiations and affiliations – whether as exergues, epigraphs, references or quotations within the text itself. Loss can spur new forms of engagement with other mourning texts[80] whose ghostly influence testifies to the enduring status of the great spirits of literature and philosophy: Balzac, Chateaubriand and Flaubert haunt Proust[81] (whose own œuvre turned out to be an inexhaustible matrix), but significant others, such as Montaigne, Hugo, Nerval, Baudelaire, Mallarmé, Apollinaire, Césaire, Frankétienne, Barthes, Derrida, Glissant, Bonnefoy, etc. crop up in this volume. Cross-national dialogues, such as Rouzeau's translation of Sylvia Plath or the inspiration Denise Riley and Naja Marie Aidt find in

---

78 Myriam Watthee-Delmotte makes this case in *Dépasser la mort. L'agir de la littérature* (Arles: Actes Sud, 2019). Daniel Bougnoux found a 'société du deuil' when he turned his blog into a mourning diary in the aftermath of his son's death.

79 Dominique Viart, 'Filiations littéraires', in *États du roman contemporain* (Paris: Minard, 1999), pp. 114–39, more specifically the section entitled, 'Une lecture-écriture', pp. 127–31.

80 Cf. Jennifer Rushworth's *Discourses of Mourning in Dante, Petrarch, and Proust* (Oxford: Oxford University Press, 2016).

81 Cf. Mireille Naturel, *Proust et Flaubert: un secret d'écriture* (Amsterdam: Rodopi, 2007), 13. Flaubert is enlisted as a practicioner of intermittency by Andrew Gibson, *Intermittency: The Concept of Historical Reason in Recent French Philosophy* (Edinburgh: Edinburgh University Press, 2012), pp. 54–67.

Roubaud, further corroborate intertextuality's role as a site of confusing entanglements. If Emmanuel Merle's poetry bears the imprint of American literature, it also ruminates on the legacy of Paul Celan and Primo Levi. Lewis Carroll has influenced both Roubaud and Chamoiseau, who also relates to Gabriel García Márquez. This sense of a cultural heritage may be negotiated with some ambivalence by Khatibi and Chamoiseau[82] whose intertextual practices fuse fascination and alienation.[83] Yet, revenances of textual traces invariably compose a rich palimpsest, enriched by the encounter between the insurmountable trauma of the Shoah[84] and postcolonial grappling. Writing is more often than not rewriting, echoing one's predecessors and perpetuating the memory of the other even when transmission proves a fraught phenomenon. Dizzying overlaps and typological pitfalls certainly thrive in the literature of mourning. In the same way as alterity is polymorphous, so is writing – fictional and critical, archeological and intertextual.

82   Cf. *Écrire en pays dominé* (Paris: Gallimard, 1997).
83   Similarly, J. Derrida's negotiation with Augustine in *Circonfession* (1991) brings out the alienation inherent in its confessional subject.
84   Cf. the status of Perec's *La Disparition* and *W ou le souvenir d'enfance* (1975), the legacy of which is reworked by both Modiano and Christian Boltanski. That literature is bound up with revenance is truer than ever, reactivating the topos in investigations of the *années noires*, displaying a spectral imaginary that unhinges temporality. Haunting is a recurring metaphor in testimonial writing, most notably Charlotte Delbo's *Spectres, mes compagnons* (1995), Lydie Salvayre's *La Compagnie des spectres* (1997), Modiano's novels, amongst which, *Dora Bruder* (1997) and *Dans le café de la jeunesse perdue* (2007) and Gilles Rozier's œuvre, which emblematizes the 'Jewish Revival'. The abundance of 'photobiographies' in contemporary literature is also symptomatic of that impulse. In this context, it is worth mentioning Carola Hänel-Mesnard, Marie Liénard-Yéterian, and Christina Marinas, eds, *Culture et mémoire. Représentations contemporaines de la mémoire dans les espaces mémoriels, les arts visuels, la littérature et le théâtre* (Palaiseau: Éd. École Polytechnique, 2008) and Jutta Fortin and Jean-Bernard Vray, eds, *L'imaginaire spectral de la littérature narrative française contemporaine* (St Etienne: Presses universitaires de Saint-Étienne, 2013). Survivors were at a loss as to how to honour the duty to remember. Robert Antelme described his own personal experience as 'unimaginable', in *L'Espèce humaine* (Paris: Gallimard, 1957), p. 9.

The literary topos of mourning is a route into exploring relationships between the personal and the collective,[85] the contemporary and the historical, the textual and the contextual. In the shadow of 'l'Histoire avec sa grande hache' [History with a capital H/History with its big axe][86] – the Terror, the Shoah, slavery, colonialism, wars, terrorist attacks, the migrant crisis, all genocides and the *geocide* – texts process the aftermath, humbly drawing attention to their inadequacy, instability and fallibility, yet persisting in their ethical attentiveness to the other and the world.

****

This pluridisciplinary volume presents a corpus of poetic configurations of mourning ranging from post-revolutionary to postcolonial literary memorializing practices, all perpetuating a copious literary legacy while striving to activate new aesthetic and ethical possibilities for literature. The cross-cultural phenomenon of the *poethics* of mourning is a prismatic exploration of how texts, concepts, images and languages are disseminated, revealing postcolonial histories as constitutive – if often occluded – strands in national histories.

Forcing form to negotiate with experience and existence, and sign to interact with sense, mourning contributes to recasting a range of important texts – both canonical and lesser known – as well as it prompts a new interrogation of the role of literary language in a transnational world. There may be many 'ways of re-thinking literature':[87] mourning is certainly

---

85 Most vividly illustrated by two recent autofictional texts: Colette Fellous's *Pièces détachées* (Paris: Gallimard, 2017), in which the terror attack on the beach at Sousse, in Tunisia, in 2015 triggers a movingly all-encompassing meditation on loss, mourning and exile, at the centre of which is a eulogy for the father and, a homage to her literary inspirers – Flaubert, Maupassant and Proust and, more subtly, yet profoundly and creatively, her mentor, Barthes; and Philippe Rahmy's Odyssean investigation, *Monarques* (Paris: La Table Ronde, 2017), which weaves the genealogy of his multicultural family and the history of Europe and the Middle East, embedding a tribute to his father and the intriguing and tragic story of Herschel Grynszpan – a Jewish teenager who shot a Nazi diplomat in Paris in 1938 and who had haunted Rahmy for decades.

86 George Perec, *W ou le souvenir d'enfance* (Paris: Denoël, 1975), p. 17.

87 Tom Bishop and Donatien Gruau, eds, *Ways of Re-thinking Literature* (London: Routledge, 2018).

a fruitful one. In this respect, our intention is to build on, and rearticulate, some of the concerns outlined in previous studies,[88] especially the premise that writing and mourning are intertwined and can trigger a newly interrogative edge of the linguistic medium. At the junction of the individual and the collective, and bound up with the unrepresentable, literature lends itself to the articulation of an experience as shattering in its singularity as it is ritual in its recurrence.[89]

As 'the epochal marker of modernity',[90] absolutely unique, yet infinitely iterable, the 1789 Revolution ushered in a distinctively modern aesthetics of mourning, inflected by a renewed awareness of the mortality of civilizations and an ensuing melancholic strain in the relationship to the collective past – a perspective which is in congruence with the emergence of the definition of modern literature as 'an intentionally unresolved dialogue between world and word':[91] a honing of its questioning value. The Revolution – just like death itself – is a moment of rupture that pulls insistently on the present and, resisting interpretation, spurs experimentation. Hence the many attempts at unravelling the heuristic potential of the fraught evenementiality – spectacular, radical, paroxystic[92] – of the French Revolution as a composite of realized and unrealized ambitions, including re-imaginings of democratic possibilities in our own era.[93] Traces

88   Glaudes and Rabaté, eds, *Deuil et Littérature*. Other major landmarks include Cécile Yapaudjian-Labat's *Écriture, deuil et mélancolie: les derniers textes de Samuel Beckett, Robert Pinget et Claude Simon* (Paris: Garnier, 2010) and Bernadette Hidalgo-Bachs and Catherine Milkovitch Rioux, eds, *Écrire le deuil dans les littératures des XIX-XXè siècles* (Clermont-Ferrand: Presses universitaires Blaise Pascal, 2014).

89   Cf. Glaudes and Rabaté, *Deuil et Littérature*, p. 7.

90   Rebecca Comay, *Mourning Sickness: Hegel and the French Revolution. Cultural Memory in the Present* (Stanford, CA: Stanford University Press, 2011), p. 7.

91   Roger Pearson, *Unacknowledged Legislators: The Poet as Lawgiver in Post-Revolutionary France. Chateaubriand-Staël-Lamartine-Hugo-Vigny* (Oxford: Oxford University Press, 2016), p. 50.

92   Cf. Dominick LaCapra, *History and Its Limits: Human, Animal, Violence* (Ithaca, NY & London: Cornell University Press, 2009), p. 93.

93   Most notably Sophie Wahnich, *La Révolution française n'est pas un mythe* (Paris: Klincksieck, 2017); Robert T. Denommé and Roland H. Simon, eds, *Unfinished Revolutions: Legacies of Upheavals in Modern French Culture* (University

and renascences proliferate in post-revolutionary literature, whose power of remanence is attuned to the all-pervasive phenomenon of *revenance*[94] – a more acute and emotionally charged consciousness of mortality. A vast nineteenth-century corpus tapped into an imaginary of spectrality,[95] as illustrated by the phantasmagoria of *morts-vivants* and ghosts that emerged from the Revolution. As temporality is reconfigured as spectrality, the '*disparu*' is textually converted into a '*revenant*' whose alterity is inviolable.

Poised between presence and absence, '*revenance*' is a variation on both, a 'semi-presence', mapped onto the indeterminacy of the past which not only differs from the present, but also causes the present to differ from itself.[96]

Park: Pennsylvania University Press, 1998); Sylvie Aprile, *La révolution inachevée 1815–1870* (Paris: Belin, 2015). Worth mentioning, too, despite its altogether different perspective is Laurent Jenny's analysis of metaphorical transfers between literary innovation and political revolution, in *Je suis la révolution* (Paris: Belin, 2008).

94 Cf. Daniel Sangsue, *Fantômes, esprits et autres morts-vivants. Essai de pneumatologie littéraire* (Paris: Corti, 2011), p. 357. Revenance thrives in poetry: Hugo's *Contemplations* (1856) and Mallarmé's unfinished *Pour un Tombeau d'Anatole* (posthumously published in 1961), a cross between a poem and a play overflowing with tears. This text features in Richard Stamelman's 'Le poétique et l'expérience de la perte', in Jean-Michel Maulpoix, ed., *Poétique du texte offert* (Fontenay & St Cloud, MN: ENS, 2002), pp. 25–55.

95 In the wake of Jean-François Hamel (*Revenances de l'histoire. Répétition, narrativité, modernité* (Paris: Minuit, 2006)), D. Sangsue has been forging his own version of 'hantologie' [hauntology] (J. Derrida's punning neologism in *Spectres de Marx. L'État de la dette, le travail de deuil et la nouvelle Internationale* (Paris: Galilée, 1993), p. 31; p. 89) in the form of 'pneumatologie', which he develops in *Fantômes, esprits et autres morts-vivants. Essai de pneumatologie littéraire* (2011) and *Vampires, fantômes et apparitions: nouveaux essais de pneumatologie littéraire* (Paris: Hermann, 2018), studies of the widespread phenomenon of revenance in the nineteenth century, renewing the way death is processed in the aftermath of the Revolution. Cf. Also Kate Griffiths and David Evans, eds, *Haunting Presences: Ghosts in French Literature and Culture* (Cardiff: University of Wales Press, 2009). Baudelaire and Flaubert feature prominently in Sangsue's latest book, as they did in Ross Chambers' *Mélancolie et opposition. Les débuts du modernisme en France* (Paris: Corti, 1987) and Dolf Oehler's *Le Spleen contre l'oubli, juin 1848, Baudelaire, Flaubert, Heine, Herzen* (Paris: Payot, 1996). In *Haunted Subjects*, Colin Davis defines the ghost as 'a figure of the other, of the strange and the stranger, of that which in me is other than myself and that which outside me is more than I can know', p. 76.

96 Hamel explains the mechanism of this discontinuist memory, op. cit., p. 201.

Intermittency and multiplicity characterize spectrality, which, enacting some form of continuity – albeit within a perforated chronology – is construed as ethical in its preserving not only what was, but also what could, might or should have been, what is and what will be; and in cultivating a spirit of alertness to otherness.

I. Unmournable Revolutions

The inaugural essays on the aftermath of the French Revolution under the Restoration and the Haitian Revolution as an unwriteable, unmournable version of the Revolution are predicated upon the role of unresolved mourning in their analysis of the rippling legacy of 1789, and a conception of time as being entwined with the experience of loss.[97] The 1804 Haitian Revolution – more radical, yet completely silenced[98] – is thus figured not as supplemental to the history of the French Republic, but rather as interwoven amongst the many threads of repressed possibilities that are still haunting our modernity: an example that sheds light on the endless entangled and messy negotiation between national, imperial and postcolonial forms of mourning.[99]

97   This is covered thoroughly in a number of studies, amongst which: Philip Knee, *L'Expérience de la perte autour du 'moment 1800'* (Oxford: Voltaire Foundation, 2014), which consists in an exploration of the post-revolutionary void, highlighting the link between history and consciousness and the centrality of the notion of heritage; Glaudes and Rabaté, 'Introduction', *Deuil et littérature*, pp. 7–12 (p. 8); Emmanuel Fureix, *La France des larmes. Deuils politiques à l'âge romantique (1814–1840)* (Paris: Champ Vallon, 2009); and Sangsue, *Fantôme, esprits et autres morts-vivants*.

98   Cf. Michel-Rolph Trouillot, *Silencing the Past: Power, and the Production of History* (Boston: Beacon Press, 1995). Victor Hugo's novel and Lamartine's play, respectively *Bug-Jargal* (1826) and *Toussaint Louverture* (1850), are set in Saint-Domingue (Haiti's pre-revolutionary name) during its Revolution.

99   David Geggus addresses the two Revolutions' contemporaneity and 'intertwined narratives', in David Patrick Geggus and Norman Fiering, eds, *The World of the Haitian Revolution* (Bloomington: Indiana University Press, 2009), p. 3.

In 'Impossible Mourning: Funeral Orations for Louis XVI (1814–1815)', Benjamin Thurston explores the status of the Revolution as bequeathing a complex legacy of suppressed and belated mourning to subsequent generations. This inbetweenness is symptomatic of an unrepresentable and irreparable trauma. Before it was expunged from the list of national festivals by Napoleon, January 21 (*2nd Pluviôse* of the Republican Calendar) was dedicated to the 'just punishment' of the King and to an oath of hatred of royalty. To mourn the death of Louis XVI during the Restoration was to simultaneously experience a long-repressed mourning and to attempt to erase the memory of a sacrilegious festival. Thurston highlights the stakes involved in the representation of the regicide/deicide in the royalist imagination from 1815 onwards by means of an original analysis of contemporary speeches, funeral orations and plays, all competing for some new, yet aporetic, expressivity: that a loss of such magnitude should be reduced to a mere funeral thought amidst chaotic funeral rites was bound to hinder any notion of mourning. The death of the king turned out to be a palimpsestic phenomenon, with history being constantly rewritten in a multiplicity of ways, drawing upon political turmoil and its accompanying literary modes. The confusion that ensued was exacerbated by the perceived insufficiency and obsolescence of both the lexicon of repentance and the gestural paraphernalia of traditional mourning to convey the trauma of January 21; commemorative practices were themselves shattered by the undecidability of the status of death, of *this* particular death. The grieving French struggled to understand the meaning of sacrifice, atonement and forgiveness, while seeking to orientate themselves by the deceased figures of ancient or recent history – Jesus, Charles I. Thurston ventures that this may be a desperate and repeatedly renewed attempt at self-exorcism on the part of the French, to bury once and for all this king who is never done with dying.

The post-traumatic symptoms of revolutionary Terror – which finds in disfiguration an eloquent manifestation[100] – will never cease to be elucidated.[101] Rather than its being cast as the archetypal terrorism, the

---

100 Cf. The scene of the two disfigured effigies, in Chateaubriand, *Mémoires d'Outre-Tombe*, Tome I (Paris: Gallimard, La Pléiade, 1957), p. 171.

101 In *La Discordance des temps: Une brève histoire de la modernité* (Paris: Armand Colin, 2011), Christophe Charle undertakes to show the inexhaustible legacy of the Revolution with its endless diffraction in the arts.

irrepressible and impossible history of the Revolution is construed as a conundrum that exposes the fallacy of mourning rituals and favours figurations that strive to grapple with its radicalism.[102] Constantly liable to intrusions, the despair of 1793 is distilled into Sophie Cottin's sanguinary romanticism of pathos,[103] with its staging of a Racinian sense of relentless fate within symbolic landscapes of tombs and funerals. But such monumental metonyms of conventional mourning and memorialization seem to act as a foil to a more subtle and oblique form of mourning. A popular novelist of the Revolutionary and Napoleonic periods, Cottin, like other female contemporaries, has been relegated to oblivion. Amongst the early romantic themes that thrive in a tempestuous landscape, mourning looms large alongside the exploration of the self, madness and melancholy. In *Claire d'Albe* (1799), *Malvina* (1801), *Amélie Mansfield* (1803), *Mathilde* (1805) and *Élisabeth ou les exilés de Sibérie* (1806), Cottin's female characters – whose plight is consonant with trauma theory[104] – are seen as recovering from trauma and/or rebelling against oppression through their interacting with deathscapes: mourning is somehow construed as a means of gaining liberty. In a world overshadowed by the trauma of the revolutionary upheaval, as well as patriarchal restrictions, Cottin injects into the sentimental some implicitly political meaning,[105] revalorizing grief as a means of recovery. This novel interpretation of sentimental fiction turns it into a gendered form of defiance in keeping with a Kristevean conception of mourning as spurring expressive forms.

The collapse of the old order opened the floodgates to a more than problematic representational impulse, often filtered through masochistic

---

102   The dysphoric expressivity of elegy contributes to explaining its omnipresence in the Restoration. Cf. Pierre Loubier, *La voix plaintive – Sentinelle de la douleur. Élégie, histoire et société sous la Restauration* (Paris: Hermann, 2013).

103   Cf. Jean Gaulmier, 'Sophie et ses malheurs ou le Romantisme du pathétique', *Romantisme* 3 (1971), 3–16.

104   Cf. Cathy Caruth, *Unclaimed Experience: Trauma, Narrative, and History* (Baltimore, MD: Johns Hopkins University Press, 1996) and Laurie Vickroy, *Trauma and Survival in Contemporary Fiction* (Charlottesville: University of Virginia Press, 2002).

105   In keeping with Katherine Astbury's analysis in *Narrative Responses to the Trauma of the French Revolution* (Oxford: Legenda, 2013), p. 5.

self-scrutinization. In the aftermath of the Revolution[106] a wretched Chateaubriand grasped history's inevitability and swiftness, with its concomitant questioning of identity.[107] Embodying the gap between the past and the future,[108] he poured into his *Mémoires d'outre-tombe* [*Memoirs from Beyond the Grave*] (1850) a sense of loss at a time of crisis. All those staples of the romantic lexicon – loss, isolation, longing, nostalgia, melancholy,[109] ennui, spleen, alienation – coalesced in a magnified 'mal du siècle' in models of sorrow-laden lyrical textuality from Hugo[110] and Lamartine to Baudelaire – albeit with a more ironic twist – and beyond.

The picture of post-Revolutionary mourning is certainly messy. Examples of the trauma of history creeping into literature include

106 Cf. Gail M. Schwab and John R. Jeanneney, eds, *The French Revolution of 1789 and Its Impact* (Hofstra University, 1995). Katherine Astbury, *Narrative Responses to the Trauma of the French Revolution* is a study of the traumatic effects of the Revolution on literature. Julia V. Douthwaite, *The Frankenstein of 1790 and Other Lost Chapters from Revolutionary France* (Chicago: University of Chicago Press, 2012), which is an attempt to read history through literature. Claude Simon's *Les Géorgiques* (Paris: Minuit, 1981) offers a compelling illustration of the fracture that the Revolution is, and its various re-enactments throughout history. In *Le XIXème siècle à travers les âges* (Paris: Denoël, 1984), Philippe Muray describes mourning as 'the religion of the century', as a shorthand for romanticism, p. 44.

107 Philip Knee analyses Chateaubriand as emblematic of an 'historical self-consciousness', i.e. a self who is inseparable from his historicity: cf. 'La dissolution du conflit dans *l'Essai sur les révolutions de Chateaubriand*', in Frédéric Charbonneau, ed., *Histoire et conflits* (Québec: Presses de l'Université de Laval, 2007), p. 95. Marc Fumaroli's *Chateaubriand, Poésie et Terreur* (Paris: Éditions de Fallois, 2003) captures the friction between modernity and antimodernity, p. 9.

108 Cf. François Hartog places Chateaubriand between old and new Regimes of historicity, hailing him as an inspirer for the very concept of the 'regime of historicity', in *Régimes d'historicité. Présentisme et expérience du temps* (Paris: Seuil, 2003). Symbolically, 1789 can be construed as separating two regimes of historicity, ancient and modern, a major crack in time, opening the modern regime of historicity, in fact the emergence of History itself.

109 For P. Glaudes the 'interminable' nature of romantic mourning is symptomatic of 'incurable melancholy', 'Nécropolis: Les romantiques et le deuil', in *Deuil et Littérature*, p. 24.

110 Evocations of the Revolution punctuate Hugo's œuvre, amongst which *Le Dernier Jour d'un condamné* (1829) and *Quatrevingt-Treize* (1874).

Baudelaire's morbid and macabre phenomenology of damnation – lachrymose or graphically haemorrhagic[111] – which accommodates ghastly
motifs of torture and dismemberment.[112]

Writing mobilizes all its resources: funeral orations on the one hand,
the highly personal and confessional tone in poetry and prose, diaries and
memoirs, on the other hand, all bearing witness to a generational malaise
summed up by Musset's *Confession d'un enfant du siècle* [*Confessions of
a Child of the Century*] (1836).[113] A far cry from the trope of the melancholic hero in the literature of that time – typified by Chateaubriand's
Atala (1801) and *René* (1802) and Senancour's *Obermann* (1804) – Claire
de Duras's *Ourika* (1823) gives the marginalized and oppressed Other the
power to generate another discourse, another truth, a female version of
the melancholic malaise for which Chateaubriand is famous: 'un autre
mal du siècle',[114] which, echoing Cottin, anticipates George Sand's second
edition of *Lélia* (1839).

An historical shadowland, haunted by gothic topoi, romanticism
hinges upon the paradox of disenchantment/re-enchantment with its
multifarious manifestations. Nerval's fertile epithet 'inconsolé' [disconso-
late][115] conjures up a shadowy, neurotic subject, whose traumatic loss is forever enclosed in a spectral past; a subject fundamentally abandoned, astray
and altered; disinherited, deprived and disillusioned. In 'El Desdichado',
an accumulation of moribund motifs, grammatically heterogeneous predi-
cates and nebulous references contributes to linking identity and alterity
through figurality. Figuration is another language, the language of otherness or the otherness of language, a disorganized discourse; a subversive

---

111   Cf. Ève Morisi's *Capital Letters. Hugo, Baudelaire, Camus, and the Death Penalty*
       (Evanston, IL: Northwestern University Press, 2020), pp. 116–17.
112   Cf. Morisi, ibid., p. 71; p. 104.
113   Deborah Jenson's wide-ranging *Trauma and Its Representations: The Social Life
       of Mimesis in Post-Revolutionary France* (Baltimore, MD & London: The Johns
       Hopkins University Press, 2001) provides a historicization of romanticism as post-
       traumatic symptom.
114   Chantal Bertrand-Jennings, *Un autre mal du siècle. Le Romantisme des romancières
       1800–1846* (Toulouse: Presses Universitaires du Mirail, 2005).
115   Nerval, 'El Desdichado', p. 645.

strangeness with an affinity to the spectral. By promoting the chimera as a pivot for figuration, Nerval's poetics of disconsolation[116] posits loss as a prerequisite for poetry,[117] whose privilege is to tune in to an elusive and voiceless other. Foregrounding its existential – if not autobiographical – and memorial[118] quality, romantic lyricism is symbiotically elegiac. The memorializing impulse inheres in the address to the absent other. The *primum mobile* of this new lyricism is the crisis of the subject, who, de-centred, fulfils himself/herself as another.[119] A legacy of romanticism, the tensional notion of 'lyrical subject'[120] swings between the two poles of ref-erentiality and fictionality, subjectivity and alterity, thus prompting a shift within lyrical enunciation. Taking his cue from Hugo, Baudelaire injects into the personal and elegiac lyricism of the romantics a good measure of de-personalization, which is forcibly dramatized by a string of desubjectifying

116 The disappearance of archeological vestiges and cultural traditions exemplifies the fact that mourning is foundational to Nerval's endeavour: a general sense of loss that encompasses transcendence and the other/the mother. Cf. Dagmar Wieser's *Nerval: une poétique du deuil à l'âge romantique* (Geneva: Droz, 2004). As the translator of Nerval's poems (including 'El Desdichado') into German, Paul Celan significantly underscored the imagery of mourning, twisting and inflecting it to cast the widower as an orphan, thus bringing to the fore what is repressed in Nerval's poem. Celan maximizes the speaker's inconsolability by placing the entombed speaker in the clutches of an incurable melancholy, which is a way of downplaying the sublimating power of poetry and questioning the tradition of the *tombeau* in the aftermath of Auschwitz. Cf. Michael Jakob, […] ich spielte zweierlei […]. Nervals *El Desdichado*, in Paul Celan's 'Übertragung', *Comparatio*, Torino, 2/3 (1991), 213–40.

117 Jean-Michel Maulpoix's statement, 'Au commencement serait le deuil' [In the be-ginning there is mourning] is a premise to poetry in general, in *Le poète perplexe* (Paris: Corti, 2001), p. 224.

118 Cf. J. E. Jackson, *Mémoire et subjectivité romantiques*. Rousseau, Hölderlin, Chateaubriand, Nerval, Coleridge, Baudelaire, Wagner (Paris: Corti, 1999).

119 Michel Collot draws upon Ricoeur's expression, '*soi-même comme un autre*' [one-self as another], in Dominique Rabaté, *Figures du sujet lyrique* (Paris: Presses Universitaires de France, 2001), p. 116.

120 As analysed in Rabaté, *Figures du sujet lyrique* and Yves Vadé, Dominique Rabaté and Joëlle de Sermet, *Modernités 8. Le Sujet lyrique en questions* (Bordeaux: Presses universitaires de Bordeaux, 1996).

metaphors in the 'Spleen cycle' in *Les Fleurs du Mal* [*The Flowers of Evil*], where the subject is reduced to an echo chamber of all things lost:[121] it is in the altering force of figurality within subjectivity that Baudelaire's 'critical lyricism'[122] of discordance and dissonance originates. Romanticism certainly gave its impulsion to modernism, but death as a poetic object became consciousness of one's own death in Baudelaire's poetry, an integral part of self-figuration: therein lies the essence of the Baudelairean brand of melancholy – *Baudelairisme*[123] – with its amplified allegorization and displacement into *spleen* – that foreign and strange *mal*, the other within the self. In most nineteenth-century poetry, figuration governs the delineation of the paradoxical status of subjectivity, staging an uncertain source of enunciation, as exemplified by Chateaubriand's coffined utterance and Hugo's altered perspective of a 'je' imagining he is dead, warning his reader that his *Contemplations* must be read '*comme* (*as if* it were) le livre d'un mort'.[124] Mourning and haunting permeate the work of Mallarmé,[125] whose 'elocutory disappearance'[126] equates self-definition with self-omission, to the point of proclaiming a 'mort [...] impersonnel'[127] who will forever mourn the ideal – unrealized and unrealizable – of le Livre. As for Rimbaud, he embraces alterity before withdrawing prematurely. His new agenda for lexical autonomy – his orphaned and exilic word being forever lost in polysemic reverberation – can be construed as both a reminiscence and

---

121   J.-M. Maulpoix reduces him to a mere 'receptacle', a 'receptacle of what is no longer', in *du lyrisme* (Paris: Corti, 2000), p. 103.

122   Cf. J.-M. Maulpoix, *Pour un lyrisme critique* (Paris: Corti, 2009).

123   A pathology that will thrive in fin-de-siècle Decadence. Catherine Coquio provides a brilliant analysis of Baudelaire's legacy in the guise of a spectral model which encompasses *Baudelairisme* and its culmination in *Baudelairianisme*, in 'La Baudelairité décadente: un modèle spectral', *Romantisme* 82 (1993), 91–107 (p. 93). Hence the fetishization or hypostasing of *Spleen* and *Ennui* (p. 96) to the point of disfiguring the Baudelairist model, p. 98.

124   Victor Hugo, 'Préface', *Poésies* t.1 (Paris: Seuil, collection l'Intégrale, 1972), p. 634.

125   Cf. Roseline Hurion, *Mallarmé: une hantise* (preface by M. Deguy, Paris: L'Harmattan, 2003).

126   'Crise de vers', *OC* (Paris: Pléiade, 1945), p. 366.

127   Letter to Cazalis, 14 May 1867, *Correspondance complète, 1862–1871* (Paris: Folio & Classique, 1995), pp. 324–43.

anticipation of mourning. Far from heralding the disappearance of lyricism, this crisis signals the exacerbation of a lyricism of disappearance – reflexive and metapoetic, *critical*. The heightened consciousness that writing is inextricably bound with disappearance and loss – a leitmotiv promoted to structure – permeates the multitudinous figurations of Baudelaire's *spleen*, Mallarmé's *Tombeaux*, Verlaine's *Élégies* and Laforgue's *Complaintes*: all variations on the *chant de deuil*. Caught in the vicious circle of *ennui* and despair, the nineteenth century was the fertile ground for elegy to thrive and vampirize lyricism.

The intertwining of modern and anti-modern tendencies[128] from Joseph de Maistre and Chateaubriand onwards is not so paradoxical; a sense of loss and ensuing melancholy is part of the Revolution's posterity. Modernity is both energized and extenuated by self-critique: an ambivalence best emblematized by Baudelaire, whose treatment of the ironic kernel of what is lost and left – or what is left as loss – finds its most vivid illustration in 'À une passante' ['To a Passerby'],[129] where loss rips through the here and now, filling it with the rich possibilities of impossibility. Baudelaire's theatrical *passante* in deep mourning is, as it were, more than a passing reference here:[130] her evanishment is a peculiar, not to say paradigmatic, form of mourning. Always already lost, captured in the otherworldly otherness of her apparitional presence, she embodies the dialectic of appearance/disappearance poignantly enclosed within a poetics of contingency. The

128 Cf. Antoine Compagnon, *Les antimodernes: de Joseph de Maistre à Roland Barthes* (Paris: Gallimard, 2005).

129 *Les Fleurs du Mal*, p. 99. For a thorough examination of this poem, see Richard Stamelman, 'Under the Sign of Saturn: Allegories of Mourning and Melancholy in Charles Baudelaire', in *Lost Beyond Telling. Representations of Death and Absence in Modern French Poetry*, pp. 49–69.

130 Cf. Michel Deguy's compulsive, litanic musings on the potentialities (unrealized by definition but figuratively explored ad libitum) of the avatars of the Baudelairean passage, with its polyptotonic and polysemic ramifications (*À ce qui n'en finit pas*, unpaginated; *L'Énergie du désespoir*, pp. 44–5), including his own definition of mourning as 'il y a quelque chose qui ne passe pas' ['one cannot get over it or cannot get past the passing'], which folds mourning and *ressassement* into the same phenomenon, in 'Solutions de continuité', in Éric Benoit *et alii*, eds, *Modernités 15. Écritures du ressassement*, p. 91.

dramatization of loss expressed by the past conditional *deuxième forme* –
'Ô toi que j'eusse aimée'– and the excessive aestheticization of that obscure object of desire points to nostalgia in so far as it is nostalgia for an
ideal; a 'nostalgia for possibility'.[131] The grand master of irony, Flaubert
exploited to optimal effect the shrinking of experience to what could or
might have been: all those missed opportunities – not the least an ap-
pointment with History, of which the story of an assignation is a sordid
ersatz – and dashed hopes that reveal the unbridgeable gap between splen-
etic reality and the ideal, which sums up the *Zeitgeist* defined by its loss of
epistemological confidence. *Madame Bovary* is saturated with grief, if not
defined by mourning,[132] which *L'Éducation sentimentale* will complexify.
Formlessness and plotlessness evince melancholy and longing. Entwined
with the law of intermittency[133] – adequately embedding contingency –
the Revolution inaugurated a series of ruptures and fractures, of which
both romanticism – littered with residues and ruins – and realism – with
its growing scepticism towards mimetic procedures – are the receptacles;
dissociating chronology from teleology, it provided a template for innumerable ellipses and elisions, as well as endless interpretative possibilities.
Being at odds with time is not only a symptom of Flaubertian malaise, it
is a sign of the times. Both Emma Bovary and Frédéric Moreau are caught
up in the vicious circle of loss and denial: denying loss leading to yet more
loss. If realism gets the better of romanticism, the latter retains its hold
on the Flaubertian imagination, like all unfulfilled dreams which inevitably transmogrify into alluring fantasies; the more repressed romanticism
is, the more tenacious its appeal: it continues to haunt the Flaubertian

131   Cf. Antonio Tabucchi's title: *La Nostalgie du possible. Sur Pessoa* (Paris: Seuil,
       2003). Equally symptomatic of the pervasiveness of regret is the use 'irréel du passé',
       as analysed by Jean-Luc Steinmetz in 'Chateaubriand et ses possibles', *Annales de
       Bretagne et des pays de l'Ouest* 75/3 (1968), pp. 649–65.
132   Cf. Luke Bouvier for an examination of aspects of Flaubertian mourning: 'Le Bruit
       de l'amer: Time, Loss and Fossilized Romanticism in *Madame Bovary*', *Flaubert*
       [En ligne], 5 | 2011, mis en ligne le 12 juillet 2011, consulté le 05 septembre 2020.
       <http://journals.openedition.org/flaubert/1339>.
133   Cf. Andrew Gibson's *Intermittency: The Concept of Historical Reason in Recent
       French Philosophy* (Edinburgh: Edinburgh University Press, 2012).

unconscious, bubbling up in a series of empty rituals and rites. In the wake of both Balzac and Stendhal, but more dramatically in Flaubert due to the bleaker context, realism and romanticism are two sides of the same coin. Both *Madame Bovary* (1857) and *L'Éducation sentimentale* (1869) manifest Flaubert's impossible mourning, distilled into Emma's and Frédéric's inexorable successions of unacknowledged failures within a temporality of 'disorder'.[134] The unmourned 'disappearance' of Emma's mother[135] is all the more significant as it passes unnoticed, shattering the evenementiality of the event which tips into 'the void that serves as the apparent origin of all future non-events':[136] disappearance as toxic persistence.[137] On the same continuum, a famously (and infamously) failed re-enactment of 1789, the 1848 revolution is the empty centre of Flaubert's nihilistic *L'Éducation sentimentale*, both its structuring and destructuring principle.

In 'Unmourned Histories in Gustave Flaubert's *L'Éducation sentimentale*', Rachel Benoît turns her attention to the Haitian Revolution and its aftermath as one of the many interwoven strands of realized and unrealized democratic possibilities to emanate from the Revolutionary period. Any articulation of the Haitian Revolution remained shrouded in unreality, not only because its history was anathema to the conventions of nineteenth-century historiography, but also because its full political realization was inhibited and hindered by imperialism. Suppressed, 'unthinkable',[138] unwriteable and unmournable, this 'other Revolution', nonetheless

134 Elissa Marder, 'Trauma, Addiction, and Temporal Bulimia in *Madame Bovary*', *Dead Time: Temporal Disorders in the Wake of Modernity (Baudelaire and Flaubert)* (Stanford, CA: Stanford University Press, 2002).

135 Marder, ibid., p. 140.

136 Idem. Emma's symptoms coalesce into the 'malady of modernity', a mix of ennui and melancholia, defined as the impossibility for time to find its way into a meaningful experiential continuum (ibid., p. 131).

137 Idem. Marder reworks Avital Ronell's interpretation in *Crack Wars: Literature Addiction, Mania* (Lincoln: University of Nebraska Press, 1992). What Ronell identifies as 'toxic maternal' (p. 118) contributes to unhinging any sense of meaningful temporality.

138 M.-R. Trouillot draws attention to its status as 'An Unthinkable History', 'unthinkable even as it happened', thus 'a history of the impossible', 'An Unthinkable History: The Haitian Revolution as a Non-Event', in *Silencing the Past*, p. 73.

left traces in literary destabilizations of the hierarchies between the real and the unreal, history and fiction, traces which emerged belatedly, when 'the republican meaning of the Revolution of 1789 seemed to have been obscured and to stand in need of rescuing'.[139] *L'Éducation sentimentale* can be read, not only as an oblique writing of History, but also as an oblique testimony to the desire to mourn the strangled democratic possibilities which haunted nineteenth-century historical consciousness: their being suppressed led to the compulsive revisiting of desired, yet unrealized, events – relayed in the past conditional – anchored in Frédéric's mourning for the child he might have had with Marie Arnoux, who is less figured as an object of desire than pre-figured as an object of mourning. This is a story of obliviousness to History, and an inability to fully engage with real events (most notably the 1848 revolution), which, paradoxically, occur as events that have been missed; the protagonist's failures re-enact the national failure to acknowledge and mourn what the 1789 Revolution could have achieved. A true revolutionary, Dussardier crystallizes the alternative – what might have succeeded … – revolution: he will forever figure the unlikely hero who dies for this impossible ideal and is never mourned. Similarly, what *ought to be* an object of mourning – the child Frédéric fathered with Rosanette – remains unmourned. Hierarchies are topsy-turvy. Her examination of the theme of mourning for unrealized possibilities leads Benoît to argue for the importance of desire, speculation and fantasy in the reception of the Haitian Revolution, and the consequential importance of the literary as a mode of oblique, yet resonant, exploration of the unwriteable history of this 'other Revolution'. Unmourned (unmournable), the 'event' that can hardly sustain itself as event – whether at a personal or collective level – becomes monstrous, taking on the paradoxical tangibility of the elephant in the room. It is as if Flaubert is at his most fiercely ironic in the treatment of mourning. In fact, Flaubert is also mourning the 'alternative novel', departing from the Balzacian brand of realism and Walter Scott's version of the historical novel which haunt his own writing.

---

139   David Scott, *The Tragedy of Colonial Enlightenment* (Durham & London: Duke University Press, 2004), p. 66.

The affinity between literature and disappearance culminates in the unfathomable notion of *'désœuvrement'*:[140] a *temps mort* suffused with *ennui* and *tristesse*, the event stripped of its dramatic potential, the undoing of the work (the so-called *déromanisation*), the Blanchotian worklessness, etc.: some alternative to the œuvre or maybe a shorthand for the counter-factual[141] itself ... We are left with a longing that could never be (or have been) fulfilled, with the dilution and dismantling of evenementiality, with the mere passage of a 'disordered' time extenuated by the onslaught of noth-ingness,[142] and with the aesthetics of mourning enmeshed in melancholia.

Appearance and disappearance, in both Flaubert and Proust, are re-versible: intimations of the latter are already, always already, in the former, as if it were its shadow. Flaubert's conspicuous ellipses – which Proust so admired[143] and will problematize further – in which history is sidetracked and subjects are eclipsed, finally promote intermittency as the law of life. The search for lost time, which peters out in *L'Éducation* and leads to a deferred revelation in *Le Temps retrouvé* [*Time Regained*], accommo-dates a search for the lost self and the lost other. Mourning is a complex, prismatic phenomenon as its object is obscure, elusive and shifting: all those extinct possibilities and tantalizing virtualities will never be unrav-elled, and what might have been is ultimately impossible to pin down, thus reverberating endlessly with the lure of that which has never been

---

140 Flaubert, *L'Éducation sentimentale* (Paris: Garnier Flammarion, 1969), p. 437. The term is symptomatically a leitmotiv.

141 The theory of the counterfactual, which fuses counterfactual history, alternate history, and the alternate-history novel and postulates other possible histor-ical worlds – whereby events are replayed as alternative possibilities – is encap-sulated in Catherine Gallagher's *Telling It Like It Wasn't. The Counterfactual Imagination in History and Fiction* (Chicago: University of Chicago Press, 2018) and Christopher Prendergast's *Counterfactuals: Paths of the Might Have Been* (London: Bloomsbury, 2019) with its heuristic focus on what counterfactual narratives 'permit' rather than what they 'exclude', p. 14.

142 Jeanne Bem, '"Une femme passa": les passantes de *L'Éducation sentimentale*', *Flaubert* [En ligne], 20 | 2018, mis en ligne le 08 décembre 2018, consulté le 05 septembre 2020 <http://journals.openedition.org/flaubert/3226>.

143 Cf. Gérard Genette, 'Flaubert par Proust', *L'Arc*, 79, Paris, Duponchelle (1980), 4–17.

consummated or possessed or fulfilled. The impossible mourning for the
unfathomable Albertine is the impossible mourning for all the multiple
'selves' that make up Albertine herself *and* the narrator – who is intermit-
tently conflated with both the author and the protagonist. 'Disparue' or
'fugitive', Albertine is a metaphor for both the 'inconnu' and the 'nouveau',
and reminiscent of Baudelaire's *passante*[144] who – like all his widows – is
paradigmatic in the fatality she exudes: if her mourning is anticipatory of
the speaker's own death, it also points to a Derridean understanding of the
object of our mourning as a metonymic and iterative entanglement – and
essentially elusive.[145]

II. Inconsolable (Af)filiations

This section on variations on 'impossible mourning'[146] starts with Jennifer
Rushworth's chapter on 'The Rhythm and Mourning in Proust (with

144 The parallel has been established by Marion Schmid, in 'The Disembodied
     Intertext: From Baudelaire's *Passante* to Proust's Albertine', in Julia Prest and
     Hannah Thompson, eds, *Corporeal Practices: (Re)figuring the Body in French
     Studies* (Oxford: Peter Lang, 2000), pp. 107–20.
145 Derrida, *Chaque fois unique, la fin du monde*, p. 37.
146 In contradistinction to Freudian melancholy, J. Derrida underlines the aesthetic
     and ethical value in attending to incomplete and possibly interminable modes of
     mourning, in *Mémoires pour Paul de Man* (Paris: Galilée, 1988), p. 29. Colin Davis
     provides an illuminating description of the Derridean distinction: 'Melancholia,
     here, is ripped away from pathology and transferred to ethics, and in the process
     an abnormal state or character flaw is re-designated as the only proper relation to
     the dead other. In mourning, the other is taken into the self, idealized and there-
     fore effectively forgotten in order to assure the easy conscience of the survivor.
     "Normality" consists in expunging the otherness of the dead other, consigning
     the other to a second death so that life can continue undisturbed. The "abnormal"
     melancholic position, on the other hand, entails a refusal to terminate the process
     of grieving; the dead other-in-the-self cannot be subsumed into the survivor's re-
     found autonomy. The only way of not killing the dead again is, then, to protest
     against the amnesia of mourning and to accept melancholia as an ethical obliga-
     tion to the deceased other', *Haunted Subjects*, p. 148.

Barthes and Derrida)' in the light of Derrida's unstable, unpredictable and paradoxical concept of '*demi-deuil*' [half-mourning].[147] If the death of the grandmother, and the belated mourning of the 'intermittences of the heart', have been celebrated by, most notably, Beckett and Barthes, that of Albertine is now attracting more attention in keeping with a paradigm shift in the treatment of mourning in the *Recherche* [*In Search of Lost Time*] to interminable modes of mourning. In his collection of funeral orations[148] and eulogies *Chaque fois unique, la fin du monde* [*The Work of Mourning*] (2003), Derrida revises the Freudian model – whereby forgetfulness is the natural endpoint of grief – in favour of a more complex, open and ethical alternative, one that maps well onto the complicated rhythm of mourning in *Albertine disparue*, where the beloved is forgotten and remembered in an erratic cycle of repetition. Swinging between mourning and melancholia – which exist on the same continuum – *demi-deuil* generates an intermittent rhythm which is replicated in the open-endedness of the novel.

Barthes, who shared the Proustian intuition of absence as the prerequisite for the production of signification, would have espoused Derrida's theorization of mourning as 'interminable. Inconsolable. Irreconcilable'.[149] Even when reduced to a mere memory, 'the absolute singularity of the other'[150] persists as inalienable and irreducible, in its own voice, alongside the mourner's own personal memories. The quest for an adequate form postulates the rehabilitation of singular experience which may paradoxically be filtered by a literary model – Proust being a source of endless variations.[151]

---

147   Which is at the core of Jennifer Rushworth's *Discourses of Mourning in Dante, Petrarch, and Proust* (Oxford: Oxford University Press, 2016) and Anna Magdalena Elsner's *Mourning and Creativity in Proust* (New York: Palgrave Macmillan, 2017).

148   J. Derrida refers to the paradoxical and aporetic nature of the genre of funeral oration as 'impossible, indecent, unjustifiable' and ultimately 'intolerable' – failure being the condition for successful mourning ('*vrai deuil*'): it is impossible, yet true; true because impossible: Cf. J. Derrida and Elizabeth Roudinesco, *De quoi demain … Dialogue* (Paris: Fayard, 2001), pp. 257–8.

149   Derrida, *Chaque fois unique, la fin du monde*, p. 178.

150   J. Derrida, 'Les Morts de Roland Barthes', *Poétique* 47 (1981), 269–92 (p. 272).

151   Cf. Thomas Baldwin, *Roland Barthes: The Proust Variations* (Liverpool: Liverpool University Press, 2019).

Reverberating with ample citational alterity, Proustian *chagrin* [grief or sorrow][152] conjoins the innermost feelings and a vastness that places it beyond expressibility: a form of vigilance towards the other, towards the mother. *Deuil* is deprecated as a problematic notion in that it is prescriptive and normative, ritualistic and constructed, smacking of recuperation – which operates through ritualized commemoration and the symbolic, all under the aegis of *doxa*. The spasmodic rhythm of the diary proves an ideal form to accommodate Barthes's crises of grief, a grief which is the last vestige of intimacy and which screams for its own utterance.[153] Hence the choice of *chagrin* to convey singularity – in keeping with the Barthesian compulsion to subvert concepts. Writing stakes out a comforting space within which the author-cum-narrator can live with his grief – in keeping with the etymology of *êthos*, which has to do with dwelling – and assume his melancholia: 'J'habite mon chagrin.'[154]

In 'Roland Barthes, Jacques Derrida and the Gift of Tears', Henriette Korthals Altes traces an affective phenomenology of tearfulness – epitomized by Barthes's repeated 'crises de larmes' and Derrida's professed 'goût des larmes' – in Roland Barthes's *La Chambre Claire* [*Camera Lucida*] (1980) and *Journal de deuil* [*Mourning Diary*] (2009) and Jacques Derrida's 'Circonfession' [Circumfession] (1991), all works of mourning dedicated to their respective mothers, in which the confessional is a route into exploring the other (within the self) and the mother.[155] Despite their divergences, these texts share an ethics of mourning that supersedes the Freudian

---

152   Ibidem, p. 83; p. 168. Similarly, 'l'abandonite' (96) is yet another symptom of R. Barthes's attempt to explore the otherness of language in order to name that which remains exclusively and ultimately personal and acutely painful – Cf. Adam Watt, 'Reading Proust in Barthes's *Journal de deuil*', *Nottingham French Studies* 53/1 (2014), Edinburgh University Press. Michel Deguy, too, opts for *chagrin* and *tristesse* in *À ce qui n'en finit pas*.

153   R. Barthes, 'Longtemps je me suis couché de bonne heure', in *Le Bruissement de la langue. Essais critiques* IV (Paris: Seuil, 1984), p. 340.

154   Barthes, *Journal de deuil*, p. 185.

155   Jane Hiddleston examines the fraught nature of this 'confession' with its potential for exploring alterity and alienation and the trauma of the mother's death within an allusive colonial context, in *Poststructuralism and Postcoloniality: The Anxiety of Theory* (Liverpool: Liverpool University Press, 2010), pp. 32–8.

opposition between mourning and melancholy, wavering instead between inconsolable grief and a tentative belief in the consolations of writing. Fleshing out intertextual references – to Proust and Augustine amongst others – Korthals-Altes shows how tears, as the embodied expression of grief, can be read not only as a devotional gesture – the reassertion of the uniqueness of the mother – but also as a transformative practice,[156] which eventuates in an epiphanic 'literary conversion', very reminiscent of Augustine's *Confessions*.

The death of his mother in October 1977 prompted Barthes the semiologist to overcome his suspicion of emotion and downplay his 'theoretical superego'[157] in favour of an aspiration to 'entrer en littérature, en écriture':[158] in the sense of coming to writing *and* coming out as a (fictional) writer. Upon reading about the death of Marcel's grandmother in Proust's *Recherche*, he confesses to being overwhelmed by 'the truth of affect':[159] the death of a beloved is a 'moment of truth' that disrupts the fallacious linearity of time and prompts a reassessment of literary experience, with a new emphasis on the latter. Searching for a form that might preserve the integrity of his grief and the bond with his mother, Barthes ponders over a *tierce forme* [third form] or *Roman* [Novel], in the wake of Proust's *Recherche*: performing the triumph of affect over concept, literature over the science of literature, fiction over metafiction, wisdom over wit, *La Chambre claire* is the nearest to that unfulfilled dream, its obliqueness so

156 In *Fragments d'un discours amoureux* (Paris: Seuil, 1977), R. Barthes hails tears as yielding a 'truer' message than words, p. 215.

157 Alain Finkelkraut, 'Barthes et le roman' (Entretien avec Antoine Compagnon et Eric Marty), *Ce que peut la littérature* (Paris: Stock, 2006), pp. 217–40; p. 222.

158 Barthes, *La préparation du roman*, p. 32. R. Barthes' hommage to Proust, 'Longtemps je me suis couché de bonne heure' already contained the fantasy of writing a novel.

159 Barthes, *La préparation du roman*, p. 155. In 'Longtemps je me suis couché', R. Barthes mentions 'la vérité des affects', p. 345. New appraisals of the role of emotion include Jean-François Vernay's *The Seduction of Fiction: A Plea for Putting Emotions Back into Literary Interpretation* (New York: Palgrave Macmillan, 2016) and Mathilde Bernard, Alexandre Gefen and Carole Talon-Hugon, eds, *Arts et émotions. Dictionnaire* (Paris: Armand Colin, 2015), which examines the ethical stakes of the rehabilitation of affectivity.

apt at rendering the quality of uniqueness achieved through the *punctum* – the neologism is no mere stylistic affectation: it elicits a subjective affective reaction; as the poignancy of *chagrin* exceeds the psychoanalytically circumscribed *deuil*. With its blend of the novelistic, aesthetic, subjectivistic and essayistic registers, *La Chambre claire* approaches the definition of a 'Lazarean novel'[160] with its connotation of resurrection in the sense of re-invention of lyrical self-expression: an attempt to reclaim one's subjectivity, within a form that could contain suffering and transcend it at the same time.[161] The fantasy of the 'Novel' as Barthes envisaged it was truly ethical: a reliquary or mausoleum where the memory of the beloved is being perpetuated and salvaged from oblivion.[162] The rehabilitation of emotion,[163] verging on pathos – which Barthes comes to hail as the essence of the novelistic genre[164] – allowed him to reshape, along the lines of greater humanization, his literary *ethos* by devising a form of egotism untainted by narcissism, one that would subordinate the romantic *topoi* of love and loss to a *poéthique*[165] rooted in compassion.[166]

The Barthesian legacy of the aesthetics of notation reverberates in Abdelkebir Khatibi's poetics of the margin. In 'With Barthes and Derrida in "the Margins of a Funereal Song": The Poetics of Maternal Mourning in the Work of Abdelkébir Khatibi', Khalid Lyamlahy draws out mourning's potential to open channels between the local and the distant, the literary and the theoretical, the personal and the historical, the national and the postcolonial. In *Par-dessus l'épaule* (1988), a composite work made up of

160   Bernard Comment, 'De la pensée comme autofiction', *Le Magazine littéraire*, n° 482 (janvier 2009), p. 60.
161   Barthes, 'Longtemps je me suis couché de bonne heure', p. 335.
162   Barthes, *La Préparation du roman*, p. 34.
163   In his inaugural lecture at the Collège de France, Antoine Compagnon points out that contemporary moral philosophy has given a new legitimacy to emotion and empathy, *La Littérature, pour quoi faire?* Leçons inaugurales du Collège de France (Paris: Fayard, 2007), p. 65.
164   Cf. Barthes, 'Longtemps je me suis couché de bonne heure', pp. 343–5.
165   If M. Deguy's name is synonymous with a form of ethical thinking, so is the later Barthes, whom J.-C. Pinson, in *Poéthique. Une autothéorie* (Seyssel: Champ Vallon, 2013), hails as a 'poèthe' and 'penseur de la poéthique (poéthicien)', p. 205.
166   Barthes, 'Longtemps je me suis couché de bonne heure', pp. 344–5.

notes, maxims and aphorisms, by the Moroccan writer and sociologist Khatibi, the section entitled 'Cendres et reliques' [Ashes and Relics] represents an attempt to come to terms with the loss of the mother through a fragmented and unstable act of writing. The first part of this section consists in a transcription of recorded conversations with his mother preceding her death in 1986; the second part in a series of succinct notes on the question of grief and its relationship to writing. This work of mourning ('travail du deuil'[167]) occurs in a text which incorporates reflections on psychoanalysis, fragments on the poethic concept of *aimance* [lovence][168] and studies of the sacred and of trauma in Muslim culture. Khatibi's hybrid and fragmented text encloses a marginal practice of grief-suffused writing. On the one hand, the transcription of the maternal voice implies selection, translation (from Moroccan Arabic into French) and commentary, which links grief to a twin effort of recuperation and intervention, of rescue and erasure. On the other hand, these notes interrogate the signs and paradoxes of loss, giving form to the so-called 'marges d'un chant funèbre'. Haunted by Barthes's *Journal de deuil* – whose practice of notation is hospitable to traces and relapses – and motivated by an urge to 'manage' or 'control' ('gérer'[169]) his grief, Khatibi's mourning text unfolds as a poetic quest, in the form of a dialogue between the retranscribed maternal speech and episodic personal notes. More than the mere re-staging of trauma or absence, Khatibi's 'Cendres et reliques' ['Ashes and Relics'] displaces the writing of mourning to the margins, thus elaborating a counter-discourse which opposes the *doxa* of mourning in its anticipation of loss, refusal of melancholy and rejection of narrative unity in favour of the dispersal of fragments that always metaphorically recall exile and point to the paradox of communicating the uncommunicable.[170]

---

167 Abdelkebir Khatibi, *par-dessus l'épaule* (Paris: Aubier, 1988), p. 149.

168 This neologism, which stems from an urge to preserve the singularity of a bond, which is neither love nor friendship, but a third term, enriched by notions of affection and affinity, is taken up by J. Derrida in *The Politics of Friendship*, tr. George Collins (London: Verso, 2005), p. 7; p. 25. As a positive and ethical conceptualization of the relation to the other, *aimance* presents some affinities with Glissant's 'poetics of relation' with his concept of 'Tout-monde' (*Traité du Tout-Monde*, Paris: Gallimard, 1997).

169 Khatibi, *par-dessus l'épaule*, p. 148.

170 Ibid., p. 149.

Crises tend to motivate the adoption of fragmentariness,[171] which, paradoxically, figures the immeasurability of loss. What is a fragment if not an allusion pitched against illusion? The metaphor of the orphan remembering that there is something amiss may sound clichéd, but the strategy of the fragment is predicated on lack, an adequate form for uprootedness, vulnerability and precariousness; it figures the frailty of a self alone in his/her insularity; it also operates like the sublime in its figuring a presence of absence. An ethical imperative to otherness, against any totalizing terrorism, underlies fragmentariness. Its destiny is fraught, torn between an anti-totalizing instinct and a hankering after a totality that will never be recaptured. Khatibi's practice of 'fragmentality'[172] is a particular, dramatic, modality of fragmentariness. Challenging certainty, the fragment is the other *of* language or the other *in* language, irreducibly so; no mere posture, rather a gesture, it is ethical – whether it seeks reparation or not – as Khatibi's self-exhortation not to deaden the pain demonstrates: 'ne pas endormir la douleur.'[173]

The postcolonial subjective experience of mourning sketches a kaleidoscopic autobiographical project that involves the tragic fate of the community.[174] Wide in scope and convoluted is Patrick Chamoiseau's treatment

---

171 Cf. Louis-René des Forêts's *Ostinato* (1997). Khatibi's work exemplifies the paradox of this writing strategy. The fragment, which conveys the immeasurability of loss, conjures up Primo Levi and Maurice Blanchot's *L'écriture du désastre* (1980). Leslie Hill has provided a compelling assessment of the imperative or exigency of the fragment, in *Maurice Blanchot and Fragmentary Writing: A Change of Epoch* (London: Continuum, 2012). A more general study is *Poétiques du fragment* by Pierre Garrigues (Paris: Klincksieck, 1995).

172 For Marc Gontard, the category of the 'fragmental' (with its emphasis on the textual unit rather than the incompleteness implied by 'fragmentary') is suited to the interrogation of a multifaceted self, *Le moi étrange: Littérature marocaine de langue française* (Paris: L'Harmattan, 1993), p. 49.

173 Khatibi, *par-dessus l'épaule*, p. 148.

174 In the 1990s postcolonial writing (Giselle Pineau, Maryse Condé, Assia Djebar etc.) took on a more autobiographical orientation with a strong sense of History, a tendency which Chamoiseau appropriated from *Chemin-d'école* (1994) – the second volume of his trilogy – onwards.

of mourning, which weaves connections between his Martinican identity, the traumas of slavery and the Shoah, and, more recently, the migrant crisis. If, following his mother's death in 1999, mourning took on greater prominence in his work, it has been a perennial preoccupation, with *Chronique des sept misères* [*Chronicle of the Seven Sorrows*] (1986) and *Solibo Magnifique* [*Solibo Magnificent*] (1988) lamenting the loss of ethnic culture or 'ethnocide'[175] through the deaths of individual characters. Chamoiseau exploits narrative structure to raise questions about how to relate to the voices of his forebears – literal or literary. In 'Mourning the Mother, Mourning the World: Patrick Chamoiseau's *La Matière de l'absence*', Sara-Louise Cooper scrutinizes the imbrication of the personal, the historical and the literary in the experience of mourning the mother. A much belated meditation on the death of the mother (Man Ninotte) – who was depicted affectionately in his trilogy, *Une enfance créole* [A Creole Childhood] – *La Matière de l'absence* [*The Matter of Absence*] (2016), a transcription of a conversation between the author and his elder sister before their mother's graveside, is a generically fluid text, mixing memories with the tradition of the fable and anthropological or ethnological reflections. Mourning triggers a consciousness of the destructive forces that beset our world – deportation, dehumanization, dispossession, genocide – but are obnubilated by perceptual conventions, forcing the mourner to confront 'l'en-dehors' [the without] – the same annihilation of life which prevailed in the slave ships and the Nazi camps. If this experience of 'l'en-dehors' is universal, it is nonetheless the locus of cultural difference, given each society's idiosyncratic stories to keep 'l'en-dehors' at bay. Cooper shows how Chamoiseau portrays mourning as an all-encompassing, rhizomatic phenomenon and a route into a global, historical, transgenerational and artistic consciousness anxious to retain its attentiveness to the singular.

175 P. Chamoiseau, *Chronique des sept misères* (Paris : Gallimard, 1986), p. 243.

III. *Poéthique*: Between New Elegy and Anti-Elegy

That mourning should sharpen one's perceptive apparatus and that form should thrive in *'incommencement'*[176] [unbeginning openness] takes on particular significance in the elusive and elliptical language of poetry, whose ambiguity is compounded by the uncertain and paradoxical proximity – *irressemblance* (non-resemblance) – between the two regimes of poetry and autobiography,[177] in keeping with poetry's propensity to magnify the heterogeneity of the subject.[178] Variations on non-resemblance or disjunction dramatize loss – in its most universal sense, beyond any personal experience of death – as the condition of the modern poet,[179] who is doomed to perplexity.[180]

Intermittence is the law of poetry; erratic rhythm, which originates in the temporal block triggered by death,[181] is more than ever the defining feature of grief. In ' "The Door Pushed Back the Light": On a Phenomenology of Mourning in Maurice Merleau-Ponty and Jacques Roubaud', Ariane Mildenberg exploits the phenomenological figure of the chiasm, which, mirror-like in its structure, points towards the 'flesh', the intertwining and reversibility of the sensing and the sensed, the self and the other, the sayable and the unsayable, to explore the possibility of 'healing' – a counterpoint

176 Chamoiseau, *La Matière de l'enfance* (p. 69), as analysed by Sara-Louise Cooper.
177 Cf. Michel Braud and Valéry Hugotte, *L'irressemblance. Poésie et autobiographie*. *Modernités 24* (Bordeaux: Presses universitaires, 2007). 'L'irressemblance' is the title of a poem in *Quelque chose noir*, p. 17.
178 In 'La Table ronde I. La part de l'autobiographie dans la poésie contemporaine: un renouvellement', J.-M. Maulpoix argues that poetry's tendency to disperse and disfigure goes against autobiography's inclination to centralize the figuration of the subject, in Éric Audinet and Dominique Rabaté, eds, *Poésie et autobiographie* (Tours: Farrago, 2004), pp. 19–50.
179 Cf. Richard Stamelman, 'Landscape and Loss in Yves Bonnefoy and Philippe Jaccottet', *French Forum*, University of Pennsylvania Press, 5/1 (January 1980), 30–47, 31.
180 Cf. Jean-Michel Maulpoix's *Le poète perplexe*.
181 Dominique Rabaté calls it 'blocage du temps', in 'Maintenant sans ressemblance', in Glaudes and Rabaté, eds, *Deuil et Littérature*, p. 320.

to the Derridean emphasis on impossibility.[182] In Roubaud's composite
and artfully shaped[183] *Quelque chose noir* (1986), written in response to
his wife's death, language's failure reflects an altered embodied engagement with the world. Against a background of absence and loss there is
the poet's persistence in composing lines from 'débris':[184] no remedy; just
residue, with the disfiguration of the body-corpse as the ultimate image
of dereliction, and remainders being transfigured as reminders – wounds
being left open. Despite its stumbling nature, Roubaud's syntax highlights
a chiasmic intertwining of mourning and healing, thus promoting the possibility of writing as a reparatory, albeit hesitant, power.

Imprinted with scepticism, the address to the beloved peters out in
the void of a keenly felt absence, exacerbated by the painful persistence of a
non-cathartic present participle which could be defined as anti-elegiac presence.[185] Blanks and aposiopesis are given pre-eminence, flaunting their noth-
ingness, stifling pathos, resisting consolation through the antiredemptive
obstinacy of the privative prefix and negative constructions, yet these palpable disjunctions in the flow of time – 'time lived, without its flow'[186] – restore some unexpected signifying force within the reverberant spacious-
ness of a 'maintenant sans ressemblance'.[187] If the grief-stricken speaker
clings on to the rich concept of 'maintenance',[188] it is surely because he is
anxious to 'maintain' (both in the sense of perpetuating and taking care
of) grief as grief. Roubaud's quest for some kind of coincidence consists
in superimposing poetic invention upon the archival truth of Alix Cléo's
own diary, which accommodates inevitable variations to convey this non-
resemblance – here the Merleau-Pontyan notion of *écart* [gap] proves

---

182   Cf. Jack Reynolds, *Merleau-Ponty and Derrida: Intertwining, Embodiment and
      Alterity* (Athens: Ohio University Press, 2004).
183   Richard Stamelman, Roubaud's elegy reveals 'a logarhythm of mourning', in 'Le
      poétique et l'expérience de la perte', *Poétique du texte offert*, p. 44.
184   Roubaud, *Quelque chose noir*, p. 23; p. 127.
185   Roubaud, ibid., p. 61.
186   Denise Riley, *Time Lived, Without Its Flow*, intr. Max Porter (London: Picador,
      2012). Cf. Ariane Mildenberg's contribution which looks at Riley's engagement
      with Roubaud.
187   The title of a poem in *Quelque chose noir*, p. 107.
188   Rabaté, 'Maintenant sans ressemblance', in *Deuil et Littérature*, p. 332.

fruitful. Necessarily lacunary, just like memory, poetic language promotes a principle of non-coincidence between what is lost and what is left, exploring the hinterland between what is left to say, what is left unsaid and what will remain unsayable; it invests that present which is like no other, left to a sense of loss: the so-called 'maintenant sans ressemblance'.[189] This *maintenant* conjures *maintenance* – and its coextensive notions of *souvenance*,[190] for which Chamoiseau has a particular fondness, and *revenance*, not to mention vigilance.

If Roubaud confesses to having lost any taste for poetry, it was because the rhythmic register that is an integral part of the genre[191] seemed incongruous and incompatible with grief. Mimicking the turmoil felt by the poet, fragmentation – as epitomized by the syntactic disorganization in the section entitled 'Nonvie'– and repetition join forces in a 'rumination'[192] through which poetic power, in its rhythmic modality, will eventually burst forth.

The relentless search for authenticity calls for a suitably syncopated staccato form, such as the stuttering rhythm[193] of Valérie Rouzeau's idiolectical performance of mourning. The incipient present participle in *Pas revoir* (1999), 'Toi mourant'[194] gathers momentum in a trembling rhythm of punning neologisms: 'Pas mouranrir désespérir père infinir/ lever courir –' ['Not deadying oh not desperish father everlast get up run fast –'],[195] which resonates with a sense of irretrievable complicity. In 'The Ends and Beginnings of Language in Valérie Rouzeau's *Pas Revoir*', Daisy Sainsbury examines the idiolect of mourning forged by the poet to address the inevitable deficiency of language – whether literary, medical or

---

189   Cf. The poem thus entitled in *Quelque chose noir*, p. 107.
190   P. Chamoiseau, *Antan d'enfance* (Paris: Gallimard, 1996), p. 51.
191   Roubaud, *Quelque chose noir*, p. 33.
192   Ibid., p. 128.
193   A feature of much testimonial writing. Cf. Ross Chambers on 'time's out-of-jointedness' in Charlotte Delbo's *Aucun de nous ne reviendra* in *Untimely Interventions. Aids Writing, Testimonial, & the Rhetoric of Haunting* (Ann Arbor: University of Michigan Press, 2004), p. 213; and Colin Davis, *Elie Wiesel's Secretive Texts* (Gainesville: University Press of Florida, 1994), p. 27.
194   Rouzeau, *Pas revoir*, p. 7.
195   *Cold Spring in Winter*, tr. Susan Wicks (Todmorden: Arc Publications, 2009), p. 21.

everyday. Written shortly after the death of her father, Rouzeau's collection is peppered with disordered phrases, stuttered lines and agrammatical clauses which conjure up the aphasic speech of grief, inflecting language with a strange or foreign quality.[196] Intent on fending off the impending threat of 'definitive aphasia', she undertakes to emulate her father's role as 'récupérateur' – he was a scrap metal merchant by trade – by assembling fragments of conversation between her younger self and her father to coin 'something like a father tongue/paternal language'. Language is poised between its construction – in a child-like idiolect, made up of the lexical, syntactic and phonetic forms – and disintegration.

That aphasia, which also beset Roubaud for nearly three years,[197] is defeated and poetic language reconquered testifies to the sheer power of a rhythm[198] that amplifies the potential of resonance of the voice of the aftermath. It may be in its rhythmic arrangement that the true ethical value of poetry is concentrated, 'at the cryptologic level where it [language] exists as forms before existing as signs'.[199] Exceeding semantics and semiotics, rhythmical and phonetic intensity fosters a sense of immediacy. Transferring existence into form, rhythm retains something of the jerkiness of life, a life haunted, hampered and hindered by loss.

The ethical demand to bear witness to the life of the other can spur articulations of physicality, whether it is the difficulty of apprehending the unanswering body of the deceased[200] or the perpetuation of grief in sighs and tears – as in Barthes' *Journal de deuil*. This embodied memory – which is also vividly illustrated in Chamoiseau's *La Matière de l'absence* – is a wounded memory that thrives in fragmentary writing, deploying varying degrees of affectivity in the attempt to conflate testimony and homage. The polysemic *lambeau*[201] is screaming for ethical recognition in Roubaud's

196 Cf. Julia Kristeva, *Soleil noir: dépression et mélancolie* (Paris: Gallimard, 1982), p. 64.
197 Roubaud, *Quelque chose noir*, p. 131.
198 For Henri Meschonnic Being is 'irreducible to sign', *Critique du rythme: anthropologie historique du langage* (Lagrasse: Verdier, 1981), p. 705.
199 Henri Maldiney, *Regard, Parole, Espace* (Lausanne: L'Âge d'homme), p. 34.
200 Cf. Emmanuel Levinas, *La Mort et le temps* (Paris: L'Herne, 1992).
201 Shreds of flesh, scraps of conversation, fragments or remnants of the past; surgical flap of skin; anything that is in tatters or torn to shreds. Amongst the variations on the richly polysemic motif of the 'lambeau' – which fuses form and substance,

Quelque chose noir and throughout Emmanuel Merle's œuvre. Scattered across our corpus are innumerable eclectic signifiers of grief – tears, vile instant coffee, ashes, volcanic eruptions, rusty metal, trees, shattered tiles, etc. – multiple marks of a mournful memory of loss, traces of the dead other, all relentlessly resisting the seductiveness of idealization, rejecting false consolations and thus fulfilling their ethical vocation as signifiers of a precious singularity. The apparent insignificance of concrete or mundane details paradoxically lends them an aura of significance through the empathy that they may evince, poised as they are between a past that is irretrievable and a future that has been obliterated;[202] their ghostly existentiality acting as a catalyst for the imagination.

The Baudelaire-inspired *poethics* of Bonnefoy and Merle epitomizes the promotion of the experiential to the detriment of the conceptual. In Carole Bourne-Taylor's '*Poethic* Justice: *Re-incarnations* in Emmanuel Merle's Poetry', Merle's poetic universe composes an intricate network of echoes and traces, in which evocation, invocation and incarnation – in a secular Bonnefoyan sense – are entwined. Merle's raucous poetry seeks to emulate Bonnefoy's 'vérité de parole' [truth of speech] – a prime example of Baudelaire's lasting legacy – which derives its efficacy from the thought of mortality. From *Un Homme à la mer* [*Man Overboard*] (2007) to the denser and starker *Olan* (2014), the incessant process of revisiting the

---

sensory memory and textual texture – it is worth singling out Charles Juliet's *Lambeaux* (1995) – with its telescoping of biography and autobiography – an address to the unknown mother in an attempt to rehabilitate her memory. Philippe Lançon's mourning diary, half-chronicle, half-fiction, *Le Lambeau* (2018) – a title resonating with the memory of Racine's *Athalie* – in which the author reconstructs not so much his frail memories, as his own *revenance* in the aftermath of the 2015 terrorist attack on Charlie Hebdo. In this account of mutilated memory haunted by Proust, Kafka and Mann – amongst others – which has found its place in the *littérature de l'extrême*, the shunning of stylization and pathos lays bare an emotional substratum. Assia Djebar's autofiction *L'Amour, la fantasia* is made up of 'lambeaux du parler d'enfance' ['shreds of the language of a childhood which cannot or can no longer be written'] (Paris: Albin Michel, 1995, p. 224), an exile and an open wound, not only oozing her own blood, but that of her people.

202 Michel Deguy calls it 'le défoncement du futur', in *À ce qui n'en finit pas*, unpaginated.

moment of the father's death has been one of fine-tuning: Merle has been seeking minimal pathos in an attempt to grasp the violence of death and its aftermath. Shunning the seductiveness of rhetoric and smoothness of musicality – or any kind of harmony – Merle is constantly striving for a grieving sincerity characterized by intensity and lucidity. A symptom of absence, the phobia of dismembering which culminates in *Démembrements* [*Dismemberments*] (2018) with its syntactic and phonetic discordance and poetics of disintegration is subsumed into the imperative to remember. Merle's ethical agenda transcends personal loss, most notably in *Amère Indienne* [*Elsewhere on Earth*] (2006) and his post-Holocaust *Pierres de folie* [*Stones of Madness*] (2010) which both honour the memory of victims of genocides. Filiations and *re-incarnations* inform Merle's humanistic stance, which whilst being all too aware of the precariousness of the poetic endeavour, promotes compassion and hope in the wake of Bonnefoy.

The tropology of restitution, which incorporates figuration within a logic of interlocution and homage, nurtures poetry's vocation as a 'prosopopoeic art'[203] – speaking for, on behalf of *and* with, lending one's voice to the other *and* hosting the other's voice. Harking back to Hugo's *Contemplations*, texts of mourning assert their interlocutory value, thus honouring its principle of hospitality, not only to the beloved, but to the community. Eschewing any kind of idealizing or elevated rhetoric, Roubaud, Rouzeau and Merle claim conflicting aesthetic regimes and styles – prosaic, quirky, ascetic – to perform their lamentation.

If there is emotion, it is more often than not displaced onto sublime mountainscapes or everyday objects through metonymic transfer: standing at opposite ends on the spectrum of figuration they all inscribe loss, while yielding no closure. Myriad concrete details are imported into the poems, uncompromising reminders of one's humanity and contingency, stubbornly resisting any process of working through grief. Rather than some aesthetic smoothing-over of the loss, we see

---

203 M. Deguy construes prosopopoeia (i.e. personification, apostrophe) as the trope of emotion, in *L'Énergie du désespoir*, p. 7; and Nouri Gana as 'the master trope of mourning', in *Signifying Loss. Towards a Poetics of Narrative Mourning* (Lewisburg: Bucknell University Press, 2011), p. 13.

bluntness and violence, fatality and poignancy. This *poéthique* is re-
plete with figurative substitutes, vestigial signs, signifiers of *revenance*,
of some shared inheritance; signs, which, for all their arbitrariness, are
also gestures towards the other – in the sense of *faire signe*,[204] for designation postulates a destination, albeit a vacant one.[205] Bordering on
aporia,[206] the quest for enunciative proximity in the apostrophe peters
out in the abrupt apophatic oxymoronic renaming 'rien-toi'[207] which
reverberates in the 'Nonvie':[208] a void which is visited by neither nostalgia nor hope, just raw emotion without pathos – an irrefutable, yet
ambiguous presence against a background of insubstantiality. Gaping
holes or stylistic gaps host a new relationship with the diffuse alterity
of an addressee who has become a vacant interlocutor, a lost object,
an irrecoverable absence, the second person pronoun. Yet, the vocative
preserves, amidst deprivation, its potency[209] in the allocutory vocation of poetry. The common denominator between these testimonial
threnodies is a 'dialogue' – to take up the title of a poem from *Quelque
chose noir*.[210] The apostrophic enunciative structure generates gesture.
The *tombeau* – less a monument than a secluded space within which

204   J.-C. Pinson's equation between poetics and po-ethics lies in this gesturing: '[u]ne
      poétique fait toujours signe vers une *poéthique*', in *Habiter en poète. Essai sur la
      poésie contemporaine* (Seyssel: Champ Vallon, 1995), p. 135.
205   What D. Rabaté calls 'vacance de la destination', in *Deuil et Littérature*, p. 324.
206   'inaccessible to his appellation', as J. Derrida would say in *Chaque fois unique, la fin
      du monde*, p. 285.
207   Roubaud, *Quelque chose noir*, p. 49.
208   'Nonvie' is the title of several poems in *Quelque chose noir*, pp. 140–3.
209   For D. Rabaté, it is less in terms of reconquest than accompaniment that one
      should view such endeavours which exceed the *tombeau*, *Deuil et Littérature*,
      p. 332. A vivid example is Jean-Michel Espitallier's *La première année*, in which
      the ubiquitous second-person pronoun, despite being grammatically incongruous,
      takes on ontological and literary value beyond any noble notion of a monument
      that would ceremoniously enshrine absence. Literature can thus achieve some kind
      of 'hyper-presence of your absence'.
210   The title of a poem in *Quelque chose noir*, p. 124. The default position for the poem
      is a virtual dialogue.

to preserve a vivid or shadowy memory – promotes poetry as a 'pensée critique de l'hospitalité'[211] and asserts its *trans*formative power.[212]

****

This tour d'horizon presents variations on *poéthique*, brought about by the rehabilitation of experience (a key-notion in phenomenological hermeneutics) as being as inexhaustible as loss is unrepresentable, and opens up possibilities for enduring connections with the deceased, for productive (af)filiations and *reincarnations* and for the promotion of a 'memory across borders'.[213] *Poéthique* is involvement ('implication'[214]) and commitment, best emblematized by Chamoiseau's espousal of Glissant's *relationalité [relationality]*[215] and his equation with *mondialité [worldmentality/worldliness/worlding]* as an antidote to *mondialisation [globalization]* and, in the same vein, Khatibi's *aimance*; on the same continuum, Emmanuel Merle's incessant invoking of the Celanian analogy between a handshake and a poem and his embracing Bonnefoy's agenda of *ensemble encore*.[216] The ethical value of literature, insofar as it welcomes life (each life) into its fold, lies in 'rapprochement' as the operation of *revenance*,[217] in *attachement*:[218] a relationality – all the more

---

211   Cf. Évelyne Lloze, *Poésie et Question: de la poésie comme pensée critique* (Brussels: La Lettre volée, 2013). For M. Deguy, 'The Principle of Poetry Is the Principle of Hospitality', *L'Énergie du désespoir*, p. 116.

212   Cf. M. Deguy, *Un homme de peu de foi*, p. 29g.

213   Cf. Sara-Louise Cooper, *Memory Across Borders* (London: Legenda, 2016).

214   Cf. Bruno Blanckeman, 'L'écrivain *impliqué*: écrire (dans) la cité', pp. 71–81, in Bruno Blanckeman and Barbara Havercroft, eds, *Narrations d'un nouveau siècle: Romans et récits français. 2001–10* (Paris: Sorbonne Nouvelle, 2013).

215   *Frères migrants*, which is a poetic intervention with its plea for a politics of open borders, hosts innumerable artists and writers, including Emmanuel Merle who contributed an unpublished poem on migrancy (p. 58).

216   As encapsulated in Yves Bonnefoy's testamentary collection, *Ensemble encore suivi de Perambulans in noctem* (Paris: Mercure de France, 2016).

217   Deguy, *L'Énergie du désespoir*, p. 42.

218   Jean-Michel Maulpoix invokes this paradigm of attachment (to those we love and lose, to our world and life) as writing's main value in *L'hirondelle rouge* (2017) and *Le jour venu* (2020).

acute as it is non-reciprocal – that is the mainspring of a deconstructive or anticonsolatory practice of mourning.[219] Located in the indeterminate spatio-temporality of affliction and caught in the paradox of duration and discontinuity, mourning stretches to a never-ending quest, performing its (haunting and haunted) enigma variations (in its musical sense, with the emphasis on *alteration*), charting its Sisyphean endeavour of 'encore et jamais'.[220] Endless reconfigurations of the paradigm of *To that which is never-ending* (never, ever ending) – channelled and performed by the so-called 'energy of despair' – perpetuate the other and the loss of the other against their reification in commemorative practices or the complacent nostalgia of reminiscence. The phenomenological logic of incompleteness and inchoateness and the Proustian law of intermittence govern the ambiguous and porous duration of mourning, which, more often than not, comes across as a form of endurance, modulated as '*survivance*':[221] *deuil* extends to a boundless *endeuillement*, which endlessly defers any apprehension of its workings. *Endeuillement* may be the definition of the mimetic hurdle faced by *deuil*, the very impossibility of *deuil*. The enduring Nervalian trope of the disconsolate widower (*inconsolé*) thus stretches to its indefinite corollary, *inconsolable*. The so-called work of mourning is a work of grieving. So, mourning not as teleologically moving on, but moving on and on – forever ongoing or never-ending, haunting and taunting;[222]

219   Of which Claude Lanzmann's film, *Shoah* (1985) is one of the most compelling examples, precisely because of its insistence on the Holocaust being more present than past. Michel Deguy, ed., *Au sujet de Shoah: le film de Claude Lanzmann* (Paris: Belin, 1990). Cynthia Fleury describes mourning as 'a constant resurrection of death' (my translation), in *Les Irremplaçables* (Paris: Gallimard, 2015), p. 83. Which is poignantly exemplified by the pivotal role of *ressassement* in Philippe Forest's poetics of pathos from *L'enfant éternel* (1997) onwards.

220   Cf. Camille Laurens, *Encore et jamais. variations* (Paris: Gallimard, 2013), which is essentially a text of mourning.

221   A major category in contemporary literature. J. Derrida plays on the terms 'survie' and 'survivance' as both survival/survivorhood and excess or intensity of life, 'la vie au-delà de la vie, la vie plus que la vie [...] la vie la plus intense possible', in *Apprendre à vivre enfin* (Paris : Galilée, 2005), pp. 54–5.

222   'deuil lancinant', in *À ce qui n'en finit pas*, unpaginated. Similarly, E. Glissant's vision of a traumatic past is encapsulated by the notion of 'lancinement' [taunting pain], in *Le Discours antillais* (Paris: Gallimard, 1997), p. 226.

and language moving from one level of meaning to the next, multiplying its power of resonance: could music alone – which helped to alleviate Proust and Barthes's sorrow – incarnate this mystery?[223]

It is because it is faced with a Beckettian dilemma – the rift between the necessity of responding, but the impossibility to do so, encapsulated in the 'you must go on' mantra – and torn between iteration and invention, that literature, filtering the referential through the literary, fluctuating between sadness and beauty,[224] can express both 'the brilliance and suffering of the world'[225] and assert its irreplaceable quality as the receptacle of the irreplaceable.[226] Its double postulation – the reiterating pain vs. the repairing instinct[227] – is but an ambiguous reconciliation – just like the contrapuntal oscillation between unwriteability and *writerliness* – best summed up, perhaps, by the tentative 'ineffacer'[228] [to un-erase, to un-efface]. The 'singularity of literature' lies precisely in the ability of each

---

223   Cf. H. Korthals Altes, 'Barthes's Orphic Quest: Music and Mourning in Camera Lucinda', in Helen Dell and Helen M. Hickey, eds, *Singing Death: Reflections on Music and Mortality* (London: Routledge, 2017).

224   In *Le jour venu*, J.-M. Maulpoix, the urge to write about beauty in order not to let suffering have the last word (Paris: Mercure de France, 2020), p. 115.

225   This is the prerogative of the Novel as envisaged by R. Barthes: 'exprimer à la fois la brillance et la souffrance du monde', 'Longtemps je me suis couché de bonne heure', p. 346.

226   In the wake of Vladimir Jankélévitch, Cynthia Fleury conceptualizes the 'irreplaceability' of the poetic *tombeau* as a substitute for the 'irreplaceability' of the deceased, underlining that it is less substitution than continuity, hence we end up with 'a continuity of irreplaceabilities', *Les Irremplaçables*, p. 88. Commenting upon R. Barthes' belief in the conception of literature as 'savoir des singularités', Antoine Compagnon invokes the same notion of irrepleaceability when considering the merits of literature. Cf. *La Littérature, pour quoi faire?* Leçons inaugurale du Collège de France (Paris: Fayard, 2007), p. 60.

227   As M. Deguy encapsulates this dilemma or conundrum through the preposition: 'la réparation lutte *avec* l'irréparable', 'Solutions de continuité', *Écritures du ressassement*, p. 294.

228   This Deguyan neologism has been thoroughly explored in Michael Brophy, ed., *Ineffacer: l'œuvre et ses fins: Esthétiques et poéthiques des XXe et XXIe siècles* (Paris: Hermann, 2015), which includes a contribution by S.-L. Cooper: 'Des cicatrices qui (s')ineffacent: *W ou le souvenir d'enfance* de George Perec' (pp. 239–53).

text to take care of singularity and invent its alterity,[229] making it an event through the reader's experience and their bringing their own alterity into the equation. Rooted in singularity, enmeshed in existential and historical contingency, the literary work aspires to a universality of flesh and blood.

If the 'ethical turn' has forced literature to take a fresh look at itself and mobilize its own resources[230] to express a vision that is irreducible, so has mourning with its power of reassessment and low-key reconceptualization of language and subjectivity through the philosophically charged concepts of alterity, community and humanity – with its fusing of the values of humility and luminosity.[231] Responsibility is embryonically located in each response articulated by an author. The convergence of invocation and evocation confirms the ethical vocation of literature as transfiguration of *deuil* into *endeuillement* and loss into love.[232]

Compelled by compassion and celebrated as sublimation, sometimes promoted as reparation,[233] literature, in this 'age of scrupulousness',[234] fulfils its duty to attend to that which is never ending, fostering the concomitant ideals of continuation[235] and consideration,[236] *justice* and

---

229   Cf. Derek Attridge's Derridean and Levinasian inspired *The Singularity of Literature* (London & New York: Routledge, 2004), p. 51.

230   Amongst studies on the power of literature, one can single out Tzvetan Todorov's *La littérature en péril* (Paris: Flammarion, 2007) and Yves Citton's *Gestes d'humanités. Anthropologie sauvage de nos expériences esthétiques* (Paris: Armand Colin, 2012), as well as Jacques Bouveresse's *La Connaissance de l'écrivain. Sur la littérature, la vérité et la vie* (Marseille: Agone, 2008), which argues for literature providing an irreplaceable form of moral knowledge.

231   Chamoiseau, *Frères migrants*, p. 123.

232   So vividly illustrated by Daniel Pennac's *Mon frère* (Paris: Gallimard, 2018).

233   Cf. Alexandre Gefen, *Réparer le monde; la littérature française face au XXIème siècle* (Paris: Corti, 2017) and Patrick Colm Hogan, *What Literature Teaches Us about Emotion* (Cambridge: Cambridge University Press, 2011), especially its notion of 'mood-repair' (p. 112 sq.).

234   D. Viart, 'Le scrupule esthétique: que devient la réfléxivité dans les fictions contemporaines?', *Studi Francesi* 177 (LIX | III) | 2015, p. 489–99.

235   Which is the underlying tenet of J. Derrida's theorization of mourning, *Mémoires pour Paul de Man*.

236   As advocated by M. Macé in *Sidérer, considérer*.

justesse[237] to ensure that mourning persists as an ethical gesture[238] rather than indulging in being a mere aesthetic object: therein lies the value of *poéthique*.

237   R. Barthes aspires to this equation in *La Chambre claire*. The term 'justesse' is crucial in Philippe Jaccottet's *Observations et autres notes anciennes* 1947–62 (Paris: Gallimard, 1998), p. 37; p. 75.
238   In *Gestes lyriques* (Paris: Corti, 2013), D. Rabaté frames modern poetry in terms of a gesturality that configures a performativity of form-meaning from Hugo and Baudelaire to Roubaud, Bonnefoy and Deguy. Gesture also, and perhaps more importantly, in the sense of gift as the essence of lyricism is the address, which is the thrust of J.-M. Maulpoix's *Poétique du texte offert* (Fontenay & St Cloud, MN: ENS, 2002).

PART I

Unmournable Revolutions

BENJAMIN THURSTON

Impossible Mourning: Funeral Orations for Louis XVI (1814–1815)

ABSTRACT

Before it was expunged from the list of national festivals by Napoleon, 21 January (*2nd pluviôse* of the Republican Calendar) was dedicated to the 'just punishment' of the king and to an oath of hatred of royalty. To mourn the death of Louis XVI during the Restoration was to experience a long-repressed mourning and at the same time to attempt to erase the memory of a sacrilegious festival. This chapter highlights the stakes involved in the representation of the regicide in the royalist imagination from 1815 onwards by means of an original analysis of the funeral orations of the French clergy. Not only do the vocabulary of repentance and the gestures of traditional mourning appear inadequate and outdated to express the trauma of 21 January, but the language of commemoration and reflection is itself disrupted by the undecidable status of death, of this particular death. In their grief, the French struggle to understand the meaning of sacrifice, atonement and forgiveness, while seeking to orientate themselves by the deceased figures of ancient or recent history. Perhaps we should see this as a desperate and repeatedly renewed attempt on the part of the French to exorcize themselves, to bury once and for all this king who is never done with dying?

Le Roi, dans un char funèbre, est trainé à pas lents pendant deux longues heures à son dernier moment. Tout entier au sein de Dieu, il est déjà détaché de la terre. Il arrive: quel spectacle, grand Dieu! mon cœur se glace et je frissonne d'horreur. FILS DE SAINT LOUIS, MONTEZ AU CIEL, lui dit le Saint Prêtre qui l'accompagnoit. Le Roi monte: sa grandeur est sans effort, sa fermeté sans ostentation; il ne s'apperçoit pas que le monde entier a les yeux fixés sur lui. Le monstre exécuteur de l'odieux décret s'avance … Arrête barbare! l'Huile sainte a coulé sur sa tête, c'est le fils de nos Rois, c'est ton Roi, c'est ton Maître que ton bras va immoler. Louis XVI veut parler; il n'a que le tems de dire QU'IL EST INNOCENT ET QU'IL PARDONNE. Le peuple S'attendrit: Santerrre, le farouche Santerre qui n'est sans doute ni fils, ni père, ni époux … ni homme, précipite l'infernale exécution, de crainte que le remords ne sauve une fois l'innocence. Le signal est donné; l'Enfer fait mouvoir l'horrible machine; on diroit qu'elle se refuse à un aussi grand crime, elle hésite … mais, grand Dieu! c'est pour augmenter le supplice de sa victime. Un cri douloureux se fait entendre: il déchire mon cœur, il retentit dans le Ciel, il afflige toute la terre; l'éternité va commencer pour lui, le Roi n'est plus, et la France est descendue au tombeau. Plus grand sur l'échafaud qu'il n'est possible de l'être sur le Trône, Louis XVI vécut comme un sage, et meurt comme un Dieu: son supplice finit et le nôtre commence.[1]

[For two long hours the king is dragged slowly in a funeral carriage to his doom. Having submitted himself entirely to God's will, he has already slipped the bonds of earth. He arrives: O Lord! what a sight! My heart is frozen, and I tremble with horror. SON OF SAINT LOUIS, RISE UP TO HEAVEN, says the priest accompanying him. The king climbs the steps: his greatness is natural, his resolution unassuming; he does not see that all eyes are on him. The monster who will carry out the hateful sentence approaches … Stop, o barbarian! Holy oil has anointed this man's head: the son of our kings, your king, your lord whom you are about to slaughter. Louis XVI wishes to speak: he has only the time to say THAT HE IS INNOCENT AND THAT HE FORGIVES. The people are moved: Santerre, surely no son, nor father, nor husband he … no, not even a man, the fierce Santerre hastens the fiendish execution, lest re- morse come to the rescue of innocence. The signal is given; the legions of horrid hell set the machine in motion; it seems to balk at such a heinous crime, it hesitates … but good heavens! it only draws out the torture of the victim. A painful cry is heard; it pierces my heart, it shakes the heavens, it harrows the whole earth; eternity begins here for him, the king is dead, and France has gone down to its grave. Greater on the scaffold than it is possible to be on the throne, Louis XVI lived a life of virtue and dies like a God: his torment is over and ours begins.]

The story of Louis XVI's execution on 21 January 1793, as told here with characteristic hyperbole and pathos by Geoffroy de Limon (1746–99) in his seminal *La Vie et le martyre de Louis XVI* (1793), is well known. A ma- jority of deputies in the National Convention voted in favour of the death penalty for the king in an all-night session on 16–17 January. Louis and his family, who had been held as prisoners in the Temple since August 1792, were informed of the sentence on 20 January in the evening. Early the next day, Louis was driven in a carriage under armed guard to the place de la Révolution, the site of the guillotine. There, in accordance with the

---

1   Geoffroy de Limon, *La Vie et le martyre de Louis Seize, Roi de France et de Navare, immolé le 21 janvier 1793* (Brussels: Imprimerie Royale, 1793), pp. 94–5 (hereafter referenced in main text). Limon's biography of the king proved immensely popular and established many of the themes and rhetorical conventions of the commemora- tive literature dedicated to Louis XVI from 1793 onwards.

usual practice, his hair was cut and his hands were tied. He mounted the steps of the scaffold and attempted to address the crowd, but his words were deliberately drowned out by a drum roll ordered by Antoine Joseph Santerre (1752–1809). Louis was then strapped to a board and pushed forward until his head was held in place by the hinged brace of the guillotine. After his execution, his corpse was taken to the Madeleine cemetery, placed in a wooden coffin and buried in a common grave.

For the next twenty-two years, including most of the First Restoration (April 1814–March 1815), the remains of the king's body lay unidentified and unrecovered in the ground. It was not until 19 January 1815 that a fragile and degraded skeleton was finally exhumed from the mess of soil and quicklime in the Madeleine cemetery.[2] Two days later, on the anniversary of the regicide, it was transferred in a lead-lined coffin to the Basilica of Saint-Denis. The *Ami de la Religion et du Roi* judged that the Revolution had committed the twin crimes of sundering the king from the living (his people) and the dead (his ancestors in the royal crypt) (*L'Ami*, IV, 17). This 'double désacralisation' – the indignity of the execution being compounded by a deliberate disregard for royal funeral rites – accounts in part for the uncertainty that complicated the articulation of grief.[3] What sort of mourning was possible in the absence of an identifiable body and tomb? On 21 June 1814 in the Church of Sainte-Croix in Nantes, Père Majeune takes the words of Hosea 13:10 ('Ubi est Rex tuus?') as the starting point for his meditation on the 'missing king', and points out the hollowness of all funerary ceremony:

> Où est-il ce bon Roi, ce Roi bienfaisant, qui ne vouloit que le bonheur de son Peuple?
> [...] Tout l'éclat du trône est donc réduit à la célébration d'une pompe funèbre! De tout ce qu'il était, il ne nous reste plus que cette funeste pensée ... il n'est plus!'[4]

2   *L'Ami de la religion et du roi*, 5 vols (Paris: Le Clère, 1814–15), IV, 29 (hereafter referenced in main text as *L'Ami*).

3   Emmanuel Fureix, 'Le Deuil de la Révolution dans le Paris de la Restauration (1814–1816)', in Jean-Yves Mollier, Martine Reid and Jean-Claude Yon, eds, *Repenser la Révolution* (Paris: Nouveau Monde 2005), p. 21.

4   F. Majeune, *Oraison funèbre de Louis XVI, prononcée le 21 juin 1814, dans l'église paroissiale de Sainte-Croix de Nantes, par le Père Majeune, Cordelier, Docteur en Théologie* (Nantes: Busseuil aîné [1814(?)]), p. 1 (hereafter referenced in main text).

[Where is he, this goodly king, this benevolent king, who wanted only the happiness of his people? All the splendour of the throne is reduced to a funerary rite! Of all that he was, we are left only with the sombre thought that ... he is no more!]

The idea of Louis's absence, his anonymity in the grave, haunted the royalist imagination, since it nullified traditional codes of public mourning.[5] How was one to remember a king who had died as a criminal and whose corpse had been left to dissolve in quicklime in a common grave?[6]

Public mourning of the king's death during the First Restoration was complicated by the sheer length of time that had elapsed since 1793. Not only had a generation grown up with no memory of Louis XVI's reign, but sensibilities and social practices had also evolved in ways that precluded a simple revival of *ancien régime* funerary rites and commemorative practices. Chateaubriand, for example, recognized that the transformation of the place Louis XV from revolutionary killing field to fashionable thoroughfare effectively ruled out the site as an appropriate location for a funerary monument.[7] The dereliction of churches, the vandalism of graves, the practice of mass burial and the persecution of the clergy were some of the factors that had contributed to the disruption of traditional funeral observances and codes of public mourning in France at the end of the eighteenth century.[8]

5   Pierre-Étienne de Bonnevie, *Oraison funèbre de très-haut, très-puissant et très-excellent Prince Louis XVI, Roi de France et de Navarre; de très-haute, très-puissante et très-excellente Princesse, Marie-Antoinette, Archiduchesse d'Autriche, Reine de France et de Navarre; de très-haut, très-puissant, très-excellent Prince, Louis XVII, Roi de France et de Navarre; de très-haute, très-puissante et très-excellente Princesse, Madame Élisabeth de France, sœur de Louis XVIII le Désiré; prononcée le 13 juillet 1814, dans l'église paroissiale de St. Polycarpe, par M. Bonnevie, chanoine de l'Église primatiale de St. Jean* (Lyon: Ballanche, 1814), p. 6 (hereafter referenced in main text).

6   On the taboo concerning the neglect or violation of burial rites in western Europe, see Thomas Laqueur, *The Work of the Dead: A Cultural History of Mortal Remains* (Princeton, NJ: Princeton University Press, 2015).

7   François-René de Chateaubriand, *Journal des débats politiques et littéraires*, 19 January 1815, pp. 1–2 (p. 2) (hereafter referenced in main text).

8   For surveys of the evolution of funerary practices and attitudes towards death in France, see John McManners, *Death and the Enlightenment: Changing Attitudes to Death in Eighteenth-Century France* (Oxford: Oxford University Press, 1981),

Mourning the king was also overshadowed by the memory of the 'black festival' of *2 pluviôse*, when citizens were enjoined to make an oath of hatred for royalty and anarchy and to swear their loyalty to the Republic and the constitution of An III.[9] This festival was observed sporadically and in different degrees throughout France from its institution in 1795 until its abolition in 1799. Although these festivals were subject to local variations, instructions from the Minister of the Interior to regional administrators prescribed a certain coherence and uniformity in the proceedings.[10] A typical *fête du 2 pluviôse* might involve government officials and members of the National Guard marching in file to a Temple of the Supreme Being, where there would be a military parade, a patriotic speech invoking the example of illustrious republicans such as Brutus, Algernon Sidney and Jean-Jacques Rousseau, and then the oath-taking (the centre-piece of the ceremony) followed by the planting of a liberty tree and singing of the *Chant du départ*. In the evening, there might be a banquet and perhaps a performance of Grétry's *Guillaume Tell* or dancing and festivity on the public square. The vices attributed to monarchy are catalogued endlessly in the speeches made on these occasions: hereditary rule is inherently venal and unstable; its deficiencies are compounded when power is exercised by misfits;[11] all the discord, enmity and bloodshed of the past (the Crusades, the Hundred Years' War, the Saint Bartholomew's Day Massacre,

---

and Thomas Kselman, *Death and the Afterlife in Modern France* (Princeton, NJ: Princeton University Press, 1993). Avner Ben-Amos has explored the history of ritual and memory in France via state funerals, particularly the contestation of memory on these occasions, in *Funerals, Politics, and Memory in Modern France, 1789–1996* (Oxford: Oxford University Press, 2000).

9   Mona Ozouf, 'The Festival in the French Revolution', in Jacques Le Goff and Pierre Nora, eds, *Constructing the Past: Essays in Historical Methodology* (Cambridge: Cambridge University Press, 1985), pp. 181–97 (p. 194).

10 Nicolas François de Neufchâteau, Nicolas François de, *Solemnité du 2 pluviôse: le ministre de l'Intérieur aux administrations centrales et municipales* (Paris: Bureau des Beaux Arts et Fêtes Nationales, 1798), p. 5.

11 Étienne Barry, *Discours prononcé à la fête du deux pluviôse, an cinquième de la République, avant la prestation du serment de haine à la royauté et à l'anarchie, et de fidélité à la Constitution de l'an 3me* (Toulon: Aurel [1797]), p. 3.

the Fronde, the Dragonnades) are the fault of kings.[12] The language of such speeches frequently betrays the fear of royalist or foreign threats to the Republic: the Bourbons and their acolytes are bogeymen, ogres, malevolent, ubiquitous, unkillable (Grimmer 11). Louis himself is variously portrayed as 'un grand scélérat' [a great villain] (Grimmer 6), a 'perfide monarque' [treacherous monarch],[13] a tyrant, unscrupulous and deceitful, the author of arbitrary and oppressive laws, contemptuous of his people, an ambitious and Machiavellian villain.[14] There was, however, a curious gap in these festivals. Ozouf notes that a 'Puritan hostility to the theatre', together with a fear of stoking royalist sympathies, accounts for the rarity of representations of the regicide itself.[15] The killing of the king, 'the historical kernel at the centre of the whole ceremonial', was thus abstracted to the point of invisibility.[16]

Ironically, critics of the *fête du 2 pluviôse* focused on the (missing) violence at the heart of the festival, portraying it as a callous celebration of barbarity. Bernard Lambert (1738–1813), a priest from Angers, described the day as 'une école publique de cruauté' [a public lesson in cruelty], a perverse post-mortem repetition of regicide, a perpetual bloodletting, a harrying of the king beyond the grave. He accuses the revolutionaries of setting up scaffolds in men's minds in the warped belief that 'un corps mutilé et une tête sanglante' [a mutilated body and a bloody head] could

---

12   Johann Gotthard Grimmer, *Discours prononcé à Strasbourg, le 2 pluviôse an VII, jour de la célébration de la fête anniversaire de la juste punition du dernier roi des Français, par le citoyen Grimmer, président de l'administration centrale du département du Bas-Rhin; suivi des imprécations contre les parjures prononcées à la même fête par le citoyen Bottin* (Strasbourg: Levrault, 1799), pp. 7–8 (hereafter referred to in main text).

13   Gustave Langlois, *Discours prononcé par le citoyen Langlois, président de l'administration centrale du département de l'Eure, à la fête du 2 pluviôse an 7, jour anniversaire de la juste punition du dernier Roi des Français* (Evreux: Ancelle, [1799]), p. 10.

14   Lengrand, *Discours prononcé à Mons le 2 pluviôse 3e année républicaine, au Temple de la Raison; tant pour son inauguration que pour célébrer l'anniversaire de la mort du dernier tyran de France* (Mons: [n. pub.] [1795]), pp. 5–7.

15   Ozouf, 'The Festival in the French Revolution', p. 191.

16   Ibid., p. 193.

be the source of joyful celebrations.[17] The abbé Arnaud saw the *fête du 2 pluviôse* – 'ces sanglantes saturnales' [these blood-drenched orgies] – as a cynical ruse, the aim of which was to make the French people complicit in the murder of their king (*L'Ami*, 1, 114).[18]

For the Catholic and royalist media, the Restoration was a time for a different sort of commemoration: 'Le temps est venu de célébrer d'une autre manière cette triste époque. Le temps est venu de rendre à la mémoire d'un prince malheureux le tribut d'hommages et de regrets que sa cendre attendoit depuis vingt ans' [The time has come for us to mark this unhappy period in a different way. The time has come for us to pay tribute in praise and sorrow to the memory of an unhappy prince, a tribute for which his ashes have waited twenty years] (*L'Ami*, 1, 114). What, then, were the appropriate ceremonies of Restoration mourning? By what resources or customs could the French mourn their king? This aporia was the starting point for Chateaubriand's reflections on the commemoration of 21 January in the *Journal des débats* (19 January 1815): 'Que ferons-nous? Que fera la France?' [What shall we do? What will France do?] (Chateaubriand 1). Citing but discarding examples of public reparation and atonement from Sparta (Agis IV) and England (Charles I), Chateaubriand claims that there are expiatory rituals native to France, in particular the sumptuary laws introduced after the capture of John II at the Battle of Poitiers in 1356, but this point is so weakly developed that it is unlikely that Chateaubriand took it seriously himself (Chateaubriand 1).[19]

Desolation and grief were publicly disciplined and articulated by the liturgy and ritual of the services conducted in Notre-Dame on 14 May 1814 and in Saint-Denis on 21 January 1815. At the requiem mass for Louis XVI

---

17   Bernard Lambert, *Réflexions sur la fête du 21 janvier* ([n.p.] [n. pub.] [1795/96 (?)]), pp. 12, 22, 16.

18   Arnaud, *Éloge funèbre de Sa Majesté Louis XVI, Roi de France et de Navarre, prononcé le jour de l'anniversaire de sa mort, 21 janvier 1815, dans l'Église paroissiale de Leudeville, diocèse de Versailles*, 2nd edn (Paris: Blaise, 1816), p. 6 (hereafter referenced in main text); Pierre-Simon Ballanche, *L'Homme sans nom* (Paris: Didot, 1820), p. 85.

19   Much of Chateaubriand's work was written in the shadow of the scaffold, from the *Essai sur les révolutions* (1797) to the *Mémoires d'outre-tombe* (1849–50).

and 'other royal victims of the Revolution' in Notre-Dame, the nave and vault of the cathedral were draped in black to create an enclosed *chapelle ardente* and the catafalque was surrounded by allegorical figures representing the cardinal virtues of prudence, justice, temperance and fortitude. After the sermon by the abbé Legris Duval and the concluding ceremonies of the mass, prayers were said for the pardon and remission of the sins of the deceased. Eight months later, the encoffined remains of Louis XVI and Marie-Antoinette were transferred in funerary pomp from an improvised chapel of rest in the rue d'Anjou through the silent streets of the capital to Saint-Denis. The Bishop of Aire, Sébastien-Charles-Philibert de Roger de Cahuzac de Caux (1745–1817) celebrated the mass, while the funeral oration was read by Étienne Antoine Boulogne, Bishop of Troyes (1747–1825). After the absolution, the coffins were taken into the crypt, followed by the princes of the blood, each bearing a candle.

For all the manifold differences in their approach to mourning the king, the funeral orations of the First Restoration had certain features in common. A typical funeral oration lasted about forty-five minutes and began with an exordium, a brief clarification of the preacher's argument in relation to the chosen biblical text. Scriptural quotations were typically taken from the Old Testament on themes such as kingship and mourning (II Samuel 1:24), lament and deliverance (Psalm 85:14–17), martyrdom (II Maccabees 6:31), or the violation of holy days (Leviticus 23:29). Quotations from the New Testament were less common but included themes such as the propitiatory sacrifice of Christ (John 11:50) and the suffering of Jerusalem (Luke 23:28). The body of the funeral oration was composed of two parts or divisions; the first part was the eulogy, an edificatory sketch of the life of the king as a paradigm of virtue; the second part was an account of Louis's trial and execution. The funeral oration typically concluded with an exhortation to give thanks to God for the return of Louis XVIII – a new Hezekiah – and the blessings of justice and harmony in civil society.[20]

---

20   Pierre-Hubert-Christophe Siret, *Éloge funèbre de Louis XVI, Roi de France et de Navarre, prononcé par Monsieur l'Abbé Siret, licencié en théologie, ancien chanoine régulier, prieur de la congrégation de France, et vicaire de Saint Merry, dans l'Église Royale et Paroissiale de Saint Germain-l'Auxerrois, le 23 mai 1814* (Paris: Méquignon l'aîné, 1814), p. 5 (hereafter referenced in main text).

The clergy frequently preface their funeral orations with complaints about the inability of language to articulate the full extent of the trauma of 21 January 1793, deploring the poverty of their own eloquence when measured against the depth and vigour of preachers such as Bossuet, Fléchier and Massillon (Bonnevie 22).[21] In practice, however, the golden age of pulpit oratory was perhaps not an obvious source of inspiration for a clergy struggling to express the singular horror of the regicide.[22] The abbé Siret, for example, claims to dispense with all rhetorical artifice in his effort to speak to the hearts of his congregation (Siret 26), and Boulogne wonders whether an entirely new vocabulary is needed in order to speak of the Revolution: 'ne semble-t-il pas que pour vous raconter des événemens si étranges, il nous faille créer des expressions nouvelles?' [in order to tell you about such unusual events, does it not seem that we have need of new expressions?].[23] Jaunet regards the conventions of ceremonial oratory as

21 Jacques-Michel-Benjamin Baudard, *Oraison funèbre de Louis XVI, prononcée dans l'église paroissiale de Sainte Foi de la ville de Conches et dans l'église de Séez-Mesnil* (Evreux: Ancelle fils, 1814), p. 10; Jacques Jaunet, *Oraison funèbre de Louis XVI, son testament en vers, et quelques autres écrits, soit en prose, soit en vers, analogues à l'heureux retour des Bourbons* (Nantes: Forest, 1814) (both hereafter referenced in main text). Boulogne argues that eighteenth-century French pulpit oratory was corrupted by a number of influences, including the fashion for philosophical and scientific terminology, the cultivation of an obsequious and timid *esprit académique*, and the worldly tone of Massillon's *Petit Carême*. See: *Discours sur la décadence de l'éloquence en France et en particulier de l'éloquence de la chaire*, in *Œuvres de Monseigneur de Boulogne Évêque de Troyes*, 8 vols (Paris: Le Clère, 1826–28), I, 5–137. For a summary of the development and theory of pulpit oratory during this period, see: Frank Paul Bowman, *Le Discours sur l'éloquence sacrée à l'époque romantique: rhétorique, apologétique, herméneutique (1777–1851)* (Geneva: Droz, 1980).

22 The main character in Ballanche's *L'Homme sans nom* similarly emphasizes the redundancy of classical pulpit oratory when he claims that Bossuet's eloquence would be powerless to articulate the suffering of the royal family in their captivity: 'Toute expression humaine devient froide, et Bossuet lui-même ne saurait où prendre des paroles pour les égaler à la douleur' [All human expressions seem cold, and Bossuet himself would struggle to find the words to articulate this pain]: *L'Homme sans nom*, p. 78.

23 Étienne-Antoine de Boulogne, *Oraison funèbre de Louis XVI, prononcée dans l'Église Royale de Saint-Denis, le 21 janvier 1814* [sic 1815], *jour de l'anniversaire de la mort*

obsolete because of the 'unnatural' violence of Louis's death (Jaunet 5), whereas Ferrère is concerned that his words will simply fail to move a divided and sceptical public.[24]

We find a strong performative aspect in the funeral orations, a sense of the pulpit as theatre, a space for dramatic experiment, what Fureix calls 'un laboratoire rhétorique' [a laboratory of rhetoric].[25] Majeune not only confesses that he lacks the words to express the pathos of Louis's plight (Majeune 12), but in a metaleptical 'short-circuit' of his own sermon he also re-enacts the speechlessness of the crowd at the moment of the execution:[26]

> Le voilà, couvert d'un simple gilet, les cheveux coupés, les mains liées, comme un vil criminel, la tête! … France, couvre toi d'un voile funèbre … LOUIS n'est plus … A ce mot déplorable, le coeur se serre, l'ame est comme brisée, et ma voix succombe à la douleur. (Majeune 5)

> [Behold him, dressed in a simple waistcoat, his hair cut, his hands bound, like a common criminal, his head! … France, veil yourself in mourning … LOUIS is no more … At this distressing news, our hearts contract, our souls are inconsolable, and my voice expires with the pain.]

---

du Roi, et du transport solennel de ses cendres, ainsi que celles de la Reine; en présence de Leurs Altesses Royales Monsieur, frère du Roi, Monseigneur le Duc d'Angoulême, Monseigneur le Duc de Berry, de tous les Princes et Princesses du sang royal (Paris: Le Clère, 1817), p. 8. Cf. M. Normand, Oraison funèbre de Sa Majesté Louis XVI, Roi de France et de Navarre, prononcée dans la cérémonie du service expiatoire, célébré à Tours, dans l'église de Saint-François-de-Paule, le 28 juillet 1814, en mémoire de leurs Majestés Louis XVI, Roi de France et de Navarre; Marie-Antoinette-Joséphine-Jeanne de Lorraine, Archiduchesse d'Autriche, Reine de France et de Navarre; Louis XVII, Roi de France et de Navarre; et de Son Altesse Royale Madame Élisabeth de France (Tours: Letourmy, [1814(?)]), p. 27 (both hereafter referenced in main text).

24   M. J. Ferrère, Oraison funèbre de Louis XVI, roi de France et de Navarre, prononcée à Tarbes, dans l'Église de Saint-Jean, le 21 janvier 1815, en présence de M. le Marquis de Villeneuve, préfet du département, et des autorités constituées (Bordeaux: Pinard, [1815(?)]), pp. 7–8 (hereafter referenced in main text).

25   Emmanuel Fureix, La France des larmes: deuils politiques à l'âge romantique (1814–1840) (Seyssel: Champ Vallon, 2009), p. 171.

26   Brian McHale, Postmodernist Fiction (London: Routledge, 2004), p. 213.

There is a similar disruptive convergence of narrative and ontological time frames in Paradis's account of Louis's final moments on the guillotine, where an apparent digression on Providence is interrupted by the fall of the blade: 'Mais pendant que je parle, LOUIS n'est déjà plus' [But while I am speaking, LOUIS has already died].[27] In the abbé Cazaintre's *Oraison funèbre du roi martyr*, the pathos and horror of the narrative repeatedly impinge upon the narration: 'mon esprit confondu se trouble, mon coeur désolé se déchire, ma langue, presque muette d'effroi, se glace dans ma bouche, lorsqu'il s'agit de retracer, par la parole, un si lamentable et si funeste souvenir' [my bewildered mind reels, my sorrowful heart breaks, my tongue, almost speechless with terror, freezes in my mouth, when I attempt to turn such an unfortunate and dire event into words] (cf. Baudard 41; Majeune 11; Siret 43; Arnaud 15).[28] The difficulty of finding words to express the horror of king's plight is also enacted in the oratorical devices of ecphonesis (emotional exclamation) and aposiopesis (breaking off suddenly in the middle of speaking). Here is Baudard's account of Louis's final moments:

> O cruel souvenir, tu déchires mon coeur! Mes yeux se remplissent de larmes! Ma voix s'éteint!… O victime pure, innocente, sans tache!… O mon Roi!… te voilà dans la salle du Prétoire! bientôt sur le Calvaire!… Laissons un instant se passer ce mouvement de la douleur … O mon Dieu! serais-je moins fort que le généreux Martyr dont j'ai à peindre les souffrances!… LOUIS dans la salle du Prétoire! LOUIS sur le Calvaire!… O mon divin Jesus, armez-moi de cette même force qui me soutient, chaque année, lors du récit de votre Passion! J'ai à présenter un Roi, homme de

---

27 Paradis, Léonard Paradis, *Oraison funèbre de très-haut, très-puissant et très-excellent Prince Louis XVI, Roi très-chétien de France et de Navarre; prononcée en l'Église de Saint-Roch, le 21 janvier 1815* (Paris: Le Clère, 1819), p. 38 (hereafter referenced in main text).

28 Cazaintre, *Oraison funèbre du Roi martyr Louis XVI, roi de France et de Navarre*, 2nd edn (Castelnaudary: Labadie, 1815), p. 3 (hereafter referenced in main text). Cf. Charles-Auguste Parfait de Villefort, *Oraison funèbre de Louis XVI, Roi de France et de Navarre, mis à mort sur la place de la Révolution, le 21 janvier 1793; prononcée à Paris le 21 janvier 1815, en l'Église paroissiale de Saint-Vincent-de-Paule [sic], après la restauration de Louis XVIII* (Paris: Marchands de Nouveautés, 1816), p. 41 (hereafter referenced in main text).

douleur; comment découvrir ses traits s'ils sont couverts de larmes?… Pardondonnez [*sic*], M. F., cet excès de sensibilité; ce sentiment ne se maîtrise pas; vous-mêmes, je vous vois déjà émus: le souvenir vous trouble; que sera-ce donc du tableau? Encore une fois, un instant de repos, et je continue. (Baudard 29)

[O cruel recollection, how my heart is torn! My eyes fill with tears! My voice dies!… O pure, innocent, and immaculate victim!… O my King!… here you are in the Praetorium! Soon to be on Calvary!… Let us allow this moment of pain to pass … O Lord! Shall I prove less resolute than the goodly Martyr whose suffering I have to describe!… LOUIS in the Praetorium! LOUIS on Calvary!… O Lord Jesus, grant me the same strength with which I bear the story of your Passion every year! I must show you a King, a man of sorrows; how should I speak of his features if they are covered by tears?… O friends, forgive my overwrought emotions; this feeling will not be checked; I see that you yourselves are moved; the memory is upsetting; how then will you respond to the rest of my tale? Grant me another moment to recover and I shall go on.]

Although Louis alone has the authority and authenticity – as both king and victim – to speak of the regicide, he is doubly dispossesed of speech: initially by the drum roll commanded by Santerre and secondly by his own death on the scaffold (Villefort 49; Siret 43). The literal and metaphorical ineffability of the regicide is most powerfully illustrated in Cazaintre's macabre image of the king's severed head held aloft before the crowd while post-mortem muscular spasms jerk his mouth silently open and closed:

Peuple, ton bon Roi n'est plus. On élève, on expose à tes regards sa tête sanglante, afin que tu ne puisses douter ni de tes malheurs, ni des crimes de la faction. Contemple un moment […] cette bouche entr'ouverte et décolorée, qui semble articuler encore des vœux pour ton bonheur. (Cazaintre 42–3)

[O people, your good king is no more. His bloody head is lifted aloft for you to see, so that you should be in no doubt about your misfortune or the crimes of the faction. Consider […] this pale and half-open mouth, which seems still to pronounce wishes for your happiness.]

In his sermon before the royal family in Saint-Denis, Boulogne 'resurrects' the dead king and, in an unsettling example of post-mortem ventriloquism, puts the Lord's rebuke of Israel from Micah 6:3 into his mouth:

Ah! il me semble le voir ici, ce royal cœur, se ranimer et palpiter encore au nom de ce peuple qui lui fut si cher, et dont il s'étoit proclamé solennellement *le premier ami*. Il me semble voir sa poussière se réveiller sous ce drap mortuaire, et nous adresser, du fond de son tombeau, ces tendres et touchans reproches: *O mon peuple, que vous ai-je fait, et en quoi vous ai-je donc été contraire?* Répondez-moi: *responde mihi*. (Boulogne 34; cf. Arnaud 12–14)[29]

[Oh! I seem to see this royal heart take life and beat again before me in the name of this people who were so dear to him and whose first friend he had solemnly proclaimed himself to be. I seem to see his dust stir beneath this funeral pall and to reproach us from the grave with these tender and touching words: *O my people, what have I done unto thee? and wherein have I wearied thee?* Answer me: responde mihi.]

If pulpit oratory struggled to express the revulsion or to articulate the sorrow of Restoration France, other forms of grief obviated the need for language altogether. Weeping is an integral part of the economy of mourning, a visible sign of contrition, a token of personal repentance for the 'crime presqu'irrémisible' [almost unforgivable crime] (Arnaud 17) of regicide. Shedding tears is legitimated as a natural expression of loss by the examples of Louis's grief after the death of his 7-year-old son in 1789 and of Christ's weeping before the tomb of Lazarus (John 11:35) and his compassion for the widow of Nain (Luke 7:11–17; Siret 32). Normand enjoins his congregation to weep with confidence (Normand 38) and Cazaintre exhorts his listeners to prodigious displays of lamentation: 'Cache ton front déshonoré dans la poussière; laisse tomber de tes yeux d'intarissables torrens de larmes; et fais retentir tout l'univers, de l'éclat de tes inconsolables douleurs' [Bow your chastened forehead to the dust; let streams of tears flow unceasing from your eyes; and let the whole world reverberate with the sound of your inconsolable sorrow] (Cazaintre 35). In his evocation of the 'betrayal' of Louis by the deputies of the Convention, Majeune imagines himself weeping tears of blood (Majeune 14). In part, this explosion of lachrymose grief was a reaction against the suppression of mourning,

29 The king's voice was paradoxically amplified in death following the prohibition of sermons from commemorative services in 1816; thereafter, the public reading of Louis's testament by the clergy became the focal point of all such ceremonies.

against the deliberate amnesia of revolutionary and imperial regimes.[30] At the same time, the cult of sensibility, the premium placed on the shedding of tears and effusive demonstrations of grief, function as a means of cohesion in the severely fragmented society of Restoration France. According to Fureix, 'seul le *sentiment*, entendu comme un transport affectif inscrit dans la durée et spiritualisé, à la différence du sensualisme des Lumières, peut rétablir une communauté politique brisée par l'expérience de la Révolution et de l'Empire' [sentiment alone, understood as a spiritualized and enduring emotion, unlike the sensualism of the Enlightenment, can restore a political order fragmented by the experience of the Revolution and the Empire].[31]

For all their protestations about the inadequacy of inherited rhetorical conventions and the ineffability of the regicide, the French clergy use language in powerful and inventive ways to recreate the events of 21 January 1793 in vivid colours, to compel their congregations to relive the horror of the king's final moments on the scaffold. For Boulogne, the purpose of the ceremony is precisely to excite dread and anguish in order to awaken a spirit of active repentance: 'Il faut qu'en cette grande commémoration se renouvelle cette vive horreur, cette consternation profonde où fut plongée la nation le jour de la fatale catastrophe' [On this day of remembering we must relive that lively horror, that deep dread, into which the nation was

---

30   An article in *L'Ami de la religion et du roi* of 1814 urges understanding for this period of expedient self-censorship and emotional dissimulation: 'Lorsqu'arriva l'affreux attentat qui nous arrache encore des larmes, la France, courbée sous le joug, ne put ni faire éclater son deuil, ni laisser entendre ses plaintes douloureuses. Muets de terreur, nous fûmes contraints de soupirer en secret, et on ne pouvoit parler tout haut d'un crime atroce que pour y applaudir' [When the dreadful event took place that still makes us weep today, France, oppressed beneath the yoke, was able neither to give vent to its grief nor voice to its sorrowful lamentations. Mute with fear, we were obliged to sigh in secret, and we could only talk publicly of a despicable crime if we praised it] (*L'Ami*, I, 259). Cf. Julia Douthwaite's comments on the codified mourning for the royal family at the end of the eighteenth century, exemplified by ambiguous engravings on artefacts such as plates and bowls: *The Frankenstein of 1790 and Other Lost Chapters from Revolutionary France* (Chicago: University of Chicago Press, 2012), p. 122.

31   Emmanuel Fureix, 'Du culte des morts au combat politique: Paris, 1814–1840', *Frontières* 19/1 (2006), 15–20 (p. 16).

dragged on the day of the fatal catastrophe] (Boulogne 72). And we do not have to look very far to find examples of funeral orations that dwell graphically on the blood and gore of the regicide. Cazaintre asks:

> Sont-ce des hommes, mes chers Auditeurs, ou des bêtes féroces, ces monstres […] qui plongent leurs sacriléges mains dans le sang de la victime; qui rougissent de ce beau sang leur hideux visage; et qui osent en faire couler sur leurs lèvres cruelles, pour en savourer le goût? (Cazaintre 43; cf. Majeune 2; Siret 36)

> [Dearly beloved brethren, are these men or wild beasts, these monsters […] who plunge their profane hands in the victim's blood; who smear this precious blood across their foul features; and who dare to let it run down their sneering lips so as to savour its taste?]

Fureix describes the use of this sort of language as 'une rhétorique de type terroriste' [a rhetoric of terror], an inversion of earlier Jacobin caricature and calumny.[32] While representations of revolutionary cannibalism supposedly illustrate a reversion to an unthinkable state of savagery, they also betray a morbid fascination with transgressive violence that is the shadow side of Restoration mourning.[33]

There is a palpable tension in many sermons of the First Restoration, an ambivalence towards the central drama of the execution, a play between attraction and repulsion, that makes them curiously hybrid expressions of mourning. According to Fureix, contemporary attitudes towards physical death were essentially ambivalent:

> Le regard médusé porté sur la mort violente, les corps en morceaux et le sang jaillissant, s'accompagne simultanément d'une extrême sensibilité au cadavre, d'une hantise de la putréfaction, d'un respect religieux des ossements, et d'un désir exacerbé de conservation du corps trépassé.[34]

---

32 Emmanuel Fureix, 'Regards sur le(s) régicide(s), 1814–1830', *Siècles* 23 (2006), 31–45 (p. 44).

33 For a discussion of the 'expiatory rhetoric' in contemporary funeral orations, see Martin Pappenheim, 'Les Oraisons funèbres de Louis XVI et Marie-Antoinette des années 1814–16: la rhétorique expiatoire', in Roger Bourderon, ed., *Saint-Denis ou le jugement dernier des rois* (Saint-Denis: PSD Saint-Denis, 1993), pp. 315–23.

34 Fureix, *La France des larmes*, p. 48.

[The stunned gaze that takes in violent death, dismembered bodies and jets of blood, co-exists with an extreme sensitivity to corpses, a dread of rotting flesh, a religious reverence for the bones of the dead, and a compulsion to conserve the bodies of those who have passed away.]

This interweaving of prurience and propriety inevitably complicates our understanding of what was involved in mourning the king.[35] In his narration of Louis's final days, Dessain, for example, makes his readers almost an accessory to the misery and torment: 'si votre ame est avide de ces douloureuses narrations, écoutez encore' [if you have not yet had your fill of these painful tales, listen to me].[36] And Villefort's gruesome account of the execution ironically blurs the distinction between the bloodthirsty Jacobins huddled around the scaffold in 1793 and the impeccably royalist congregation in the church of Saint-Vincent-de-Paul in 1815:

> Saisi, lié, étendu sur cet instrument de son supplice, la hache meurtrière déjà élevée glisse, tombe, frappe, et sépare à jamais cette tête ensanglantée … Par la main d'un vil bourreau elle est offerte à des monstres avides de voir couler le sang de leur Roi. – Il vous falloit du sang, barbares; eh bien! rassasiez-vous-en, le crime est consommé: *consummatum est*. (Villefort 49)

> [Seized, bound, laid on this instrument of his torment, the murderous blade winched aloft slips, falls, strikes, and severs for all time this bloody head … The vile executioner's hand holds the head aloft before monsters desperate to see the blood of their king flow. – You demanded blood, you savages; well then: feast your eyes, the crime is finished: *consummatum est*.]

Such rhetorical *dérapages* were unwelcome in the febrile political atmosphere of the First Restoration. Louis XVIII had no wish to see

---

35   Andrew Counter similarly demonstrates how interest in a scene of sexual violence is both stimulated and accommodated 'within a frame of indignation and moral censure' in his examination of the discursive afterlife of the murder of a young woman by a parish priest in Restoration France. Andrew Counter, *The Amorous Restoration: Love, Sex, and Politics in Early Nineteenth-Century France* (Oxford: Oxford University Press, 2016), p. 194.

36   Louis Dessain, *Réflexions sur la mort de Louis XVI* (Paris: Demonville, 1815), p. 10 (hereafter referenced in main text).

old animosities rekindled by an insensitive militancy in the language and gesture of public ceremonies and the law of 19 January 1816 was an attempt to reset the parameters of public mourning, in particular by excluding sermons – with their unpredictable and potentially inflammatory content – from memorial services. Henceforth there were to be no references to the 'lurid details' of the regicide and Louis's testament, with its emphasis on forgiveness, was to be the focus of the ceremony.[37]

The re-sacralization of the Bourbon monarchy by the clergy involved remembering the enormity of the crime committed on 21 January 1793 against God's representative on earth and at the same time celebrating the 'miracle' of the Bourbon restoration in 1814. The violent and morbid narratives of the regicide frequently spill over into sentimental appeals for amnesty and reconciliation: 'que toutes les passions se taisent devant l'intérêt public, que toutes les haines s'éteignent, que tous les ressentimens s'effacent' [let the hubbub of passions fall silent before public interest, let all hatreds be extinguished, and let all grudges be put away] (Ferrère 52; cf. Arnaud 22). Thus we find jarring contrasts of melancholy and euphoria, exhortations to weep without restraint and to dry one's tears. The incongruity of such transitions is captured in Bruchet's words to his congregation: 'Chrétiens, il est temps de faire succéder à l'hymne funéraire les cantiques de joie et les chants de triomphe' [Christians, the time has come for funeral hymns to give way to canticles of joy and songs of triumph] (cf. Baudard 47; Villefort 53–4; Majeune 17–18; Bonnevie 7).[38]

In Restoration funeral orations, Louis XVI is portrayed as an enlightened and socially progressive monarch, a good steward of the French economy, a charitable patron of the arts, industry and agriculture, a humanitarian advocate of religious and judicial reform, a friend of the poor, and a reluctant but successful military strategist (Ferrère 12–15; Boulogne

---

37 Sheryl Kroen, *Politics and Theater: The Crisis of Legitimacy in Restoration France, 1815–1830* (Berkeley: University of California Press, 2000), p. 65.

38 Edmé-François-Charles Bruchet, *Oraison funèbre prononcée au service expiatoire, célébré en l'Église de Saint-Étienne d'Auxerre, le 21 juillet 1814, pour Louis XVI, et les quatre autres victimes royales* (Auxerre: Fournier, 1814), p. 41. Cf. Baudard 47, Villefort 53–4, Majeune 17–18, Bonnevie 7.

26–7; Baudard 18; Bonnevie 14; Normand 14; Villefort 22; Majeune 6–7; Arnaud 8–9).[39] He is a new Saint Louis (Ferrère 51; Siret 7), a father among his children (Bonnevie 13), a man with a naturally Christian soul (Bonnevie 10; cf. Arnaud 7). Such pangeyrics were standard fare of funerary rhetoric, but were also deliberate correctives to earlier, revolutionary representations of Louis as a perfidious and blood-slaked monster. An article in *L'Ami de la religion et du roi* of 1814 makes clear how tenacious was the afterlife of these slanders:

> Il ne suffit pas d'effacer de notre histoire ces odieuses et absurdes dénominations de despote, de tyran, si ridiculement prodiguées au plus modéré des rois, et si cruellement démenties par les faits. Il faut encore montrer que ce Prince, qu'on a peint sous de si fausses couleurs, avoit une ame droite, un jugement sain, des connoissances étendues, un vif amour pour ses peuples, un grand désir de les rendre heureux. (*L'Ami*, I, 225)
>
> [It is not enough to erase from our history this hateful and ridiculous nomenclature of despot and tyrant – terms which have been so absurdly applied to the most moderate of kings and which were so cruelly contradicted by the facts. We have furthermore to demonstrate that this prince, who has been portrayed in such a false light, had an honest character, a balanced judgement, a broad culture, a spirited love for his people, and a strong wish to make them happy.]

The emphasis on Louis's devoutness and piety brought the sorrows and afflictions of his final years into sharp relief but risked making his death on the scaffold appear all the more incomprehensible, to a point which seemed almost irreconcilable with any meaningful notion of divine providence (Cazaintre 6).

And yet in the suffering and destruction of this perfect and upright man, many royalist commentators heard not meaningless sound and fury, but the confirmation of a holy mystery, founded on the sacrifice of the king. The veneration of Louis as a martyr was based on the belief that he had died for the faith, that his testimony had been sealed with his blood on the Place de la Révolution. Louis appears again and again in sermons of the First Restoration as the 'Roi-Martyr' (Normand 2; Ferrère 21; Cazaintre

---

39   Pierre-Nicolas Anot, *Oraison funèbre de Sa Majesté Louis XVI, prononcée dans la Chapelle de Saint-Nicolas de l'Hôtel-Dieu de Reims, le mardi 26 juillet 1814* (Reims: Brigot, [1814 (?)]), p. 6 (hereafter referenced in main text).

48; Villefort 50; Arnaud 17),[40] although the authority to grant him this title was acknowledged by his more cautious eulogists to reside with the Vatican (Paradis 41).[41] The narrative of martyrdom paradoxically turned the triumph of Jacobin desacralization – the immolation of the citizen Capet and the disposal of his corpse in a common grave – into the most powerful illustration of the king's right to the title of *rex christianissimus*.[42]

The cult of royal martyrdom was reinforced, but also complicated, by analogies between the trial and execution of Louis XVI and the Passion of Christ. Jaunet claimed that 'la ressemblance qui se trouve entre la fin de Louis et la mort de Jésus-CHRIST, est si frappante, qu'elle doit se présenter d'elle-même aux yeux les moins apercevans' [the similarities between the final moments of Louis and the death of Jesus CHRIST are so striking that they are self-evident to even the most short-sighted] (Jaunet 35), while Christine saw in Louis 'la fidelle image d'un Dieu crucifié' [the true image of a crucified God].[43] The Gospels provided a narrative of redemptive suffering that was immediately comprehensible to French men and women at the end of the eighteenth century and helped to structure their understanding

---

40   *Mandement de messieurs les vicaires généraux du chapitre métropolitain de Paris, le siége vacant, qui ordonne que le 21 janvier, jour anniversaire de la mort du Roi Louis XVI, il soit célébré dans toutes les églises du diocèse un service solennel, qui sera précédé d'une cérémonie expiatoire* (Paris: Le Clère, 1815), p. 13 (hereafter referenced in main text).

41   On the aborted beatification of Louis XVI, see Philippe Boutry, 'Le Roi martyr: la cause de Louis XVI devant la Cour de Rome (1820)', *Revue d'histoire de l'Église de France* 76/196 (1990), 57–71.

42   Geoffroy Cubbit argues that the idea of Louis's martyrdom salvages a moment of historical failure: 'The judicial murder of the monarch – the very action which, on a historical plane, revealed the insecurity of the relationship between monarchy and nation, and thus called in question the central premise of the dynastic discourse – became, through a shift in perspective, the moment of the monarchy's greatest service, and its finest title to the gratitude of the nation': 'Legitimism and the Cult of Bourbon Royalty', in Nicholas Atkin and Frank Tallett, eds, *The Right in France: From Revolution to Le Pen* (London: I.B. Tauris, 2003), pp. 51–70 (p. 58).

43   M. Christine, *Oraison funèbre de Louis XVI, Roi de France et de Navarre, prononcée dans l'Église métropolitaine d'Aix, le 10 juin 1814, après le retour de S. M. Louis XVIII* (Aix: Mouret, 1814), p. 4 (hereafter referenced in main text).

of the regicide. Thus, the 'bonnet rouge' worn by Louis on 20 June 1792 is likened to a crown of thorns (Jaunet 26; Baudard 34) and the place de la Révolution to a new Calvary (Jaunet 39; Boulogne 63; Arnaud 15). From this 'higher' perspective, the regicide, the nadir in the process of desacralization, is in reality a providential mechanism to obtain remission of the nation's sins. In death, Louis becomes a heavenly intercessor whose tears and blood plead the cause of his people (Boulogne 78).[44] While it might have been rhetorically persuasive, the association of Louis XVI with Christ gave rise to what Jean-Christian Petitfils calls 'ambiguïtés théologiques'.[45] If Christ's death was the unique and definitive sacrifice for all humankind (Romans 5:9; Ephesians 1:7), what was the purpose of Louis's execution? Did it make sense to talk of his dying 'for' his people or to 'atone for' their sins? Or, in words attributed to the king himself, to claim that his blood might appease the wrath of God?[46] In his *Lettre à Monseigneur l'Évêque de Troyes* (1817), the abbé Pierre François Théophile Jarry (1764–1820) pours scorn on what he sees as the half-baked theology of Boulogne's funeral oration and in particular his conflation of the human and the divine. To call the French king the 'saviour' of his people betrays a profound misunderstanding of the sacrificial death of Christ, while to speak of Louis's execution as an act of voluntary sacrifice is both historically false and psychologically implausible.[47] Jarry's sober and meticulous objections to the theological laxity of Boulogne's sermon, to the misplaced hyperbole of his 'enthousiasme oratoire', may appear abstruse or merely trivial today, but their fundamental purpose is to reassert the integrity of Trinitarian

---

44   René-Michel Legris Duval, *Sermons de Monsieur l'Abbé Legris Duval, Prédicateur Ordinaire du Roi* (Louvain: Vanlinthout et Vandenzande, 1822), p. 149; Thévenard, *Oraison funèbre de Louis XVI* (Dijon: Frantin, 1814), pp. 7–8 (both hereafter referenced in main text).

45   Jean-Christian Petitfils, *Louis XVI* (Paris: Perrin, 2005), p. 969.

46   *Revolutions de Paris*, no. 185 (Paris: 19–26 January 1793), p. 202 (hereafter referenced in main text).

47   Pierre-François-Théophile Jarry, *Lettre à Monseigneur l'Évêque de Troyes, au sujet de l'oraison funèbre de Louis XVI* (Paris: Gueffier, 1817), pp. 5, 6 (hereafter referenced in main text).

orthodoxy (Jarry 1). The crux of Jarry's argument is that the apotheosis of the king by the French clergy in their funeral orations risks undermining belief in the full divinity of Christ, thereby opening the door to Socinian or Unitarian heresies:

> L'idée de la divinité de Jésus-Christ s'affaiblit et s'efface de plus en plus; et à force de lui voir comparer un simple mortel, on finit peut-être par ne regarder le Sauveur que comme un homme plus parfait, et à ne voir rien que de naturel et d'humain dans ses souffrances et dans sa mort. (Jarry 13)

> [The idea of Christ's divine nature increasingly weakens and diminishes; and by repeatedly seeing him compared to an ordinary mortal, we perhaps imagine that the Saviour is only a more perfect human being, whose suffering and death can be explained in purely natural and human terms.]

Jarry further claims – although this is a point of secondary importance from his theological perspective – that the trope of the Passion narrative is itself at odds with the aims of royalist hagiography in so far as empathy with the suffering of Christ inevitably inhibits, or at least relativizes, empathy with the suffering of the French king: 'Reste-t-il des larmes à donner au sort d'un homme, quelque juste et quelque malheureux qu'il soit, quand on a l'âme préoccupée de l'image accablante d'un Dieu expirant sur une croix?' [Do we have any tears left to shed for the fate of a man, however just and however unfortunate he may be, when our mind is preoccupied by the distressing image of a God dying on a cross?] (Jarry 13). Jarry thus draws attention to the way in which the militant agenda of royal funeral orations – their obsession with suffering and their insistence on the need for expiation on a grand scale – can inflect the theology and ethics of mourning. Deriving from severely truncated and selective readings of the Gospel narratives, the analogies between Louis XVI and Christ are focused almost entirely on the themes of betrayal, degradation and torture. Of Christ's ministry and Resurrection, they have almost nothing to say.

The question of how to mourn the king involved a reckoning, a processing of collective and individual guilt. Who was to blame for the regicide? Borrowing from the catalogue of eschatological signs in Matthew's account of the Crucifixion, Normand shows Nature in tumult, reeling in horror at the scandal of the king's murder: 'Ici, comme au Calvaire,

astre brillant du jour, couvre-toi de ténèbres profondes! Terre, tremble et
frémis! Pierres et rochers, fendez-vous d'horreur!' [Here, as on Calvary,
refulgent day-star, cover yourself in darkness! Shake, earth and shudder!
Stones and rocks, crack in horror!] (Normand 37). Anot, echoing Limon,
imagines the guillotine itself defying human agency, willing its own immobility: 'l'horrible machine semble se refuser au crime' [the horrible
machine seems to resist the crime] (Anot 14). Christine reassures his congregation that the offence cannot be imputed to the nation as a whole: 'ce
n'est pas la France qui est coupable du parricide' [it is not France that
is guilty of parricide] (Christine 18). And citing Deuternonomy 21:7
('Manus nostrae non effuderunt sanguinem hunc'), Bonnevie also rejects the notion of universal guilt for the death of the king, pinning the
blame instead on an ungodly and unprincipled minority (Bonnevie 28;
cf. Anot 12; Paradis 36).

Not all congregations were permitted to wash their hands so easily of
the blood of their former king, however. Cazaintre denies that there can be
any shuffling: all of the French have to atone for their vicarious complicity
in the death of Louis XVI: 'Hélas! si nous remontons à l'origine, si nous
examinons attentivement les premières causes de tout cet amas d'horreurs,
qui ont fondu sur nos têtes, nous nous trouverons tous coupables, et Louis
seul innocent' [Alas! If we go back to the beginning, if we examine care-
fully the first cause of all these horrific events, which have befallen us, we
shall find ourselves all guilty and Louis alone innocent] (Cazaintre 50).
Boulogne hammers home a similarly rigorous message. As a result of their
permissiveness and irreverence, the French had become Louis's execu-
tioners by proxy:

> Quel que soit le deuil que nous en portons, et quelque détestation que nous en
> fassions, il n'en est pas moins vrai de dire qu'elle est notre péché; parce que si nous ne
> l'avons pas consommé, nous l'avons préparée par nos désordres et nos scandales, par le
> mépris de Dieu et de ses lois, […] notre péché, parce qu'elle s'est commise au milieu
> de nous, et que notre gloire en sera éternellement souillée: enfin, notre péché, parce
> que si nous ne l'avons pas commise, nous l'avons laissé commettre. (Boulogne 73–4)

> [However much we may grieve and curse this event, it remains true that it is our sin;
> because, if we did not ourselves finish it, we set it in motion by our faults and scan-
> dals, by our scorn for God and his laws, […] our sin, because it came to pass among

us, and our glory will be forever besmirched by it: our sin, finally, because if we did not do it ourselves, we allowed it to be done.]

Whereas the revolutionary festivals of *2 pluviôse* had sought to encourage complicity in, or at least assent to, the regicide by means of the oath of hatred for royalty, the Church offered to reverse this process and to absolve the French of their guilt by association. The expiatory and memorial services held on 21 January thus appear as collective rituals of decontamination, 'une *sorte d'aspersion qui efface la tache* contractée par la Nation entière' [a sort of sprinkling which removes the stain incurred by the whole nation] (*Mandement* 8).

Questions of personal and collective guilt translated into a fascination with the blood shed on 21 January 1793. Addressing an eminently royal and aristocratic congregation in Notre-Dame on 14 May 1814, Legris Duval holds a mirror up to the blood-boltered company: 'Jetons les yeux sur nous-mêmes. Grand Dieu! De quels crimes nous sommes souillés! de quel sang nous sommes couverts!' [Let us take a look at ourselves. Heavens above! With what crimes are we besmirched! with what blood are we covered!] (Legris Duval 156). Was Louis's blood a stain to be washed away through repentance and prayer or was it the means by which expiation and forgiveness could be purchased? There was no consensus on this point. Some declared that only tears of sincere penitence could dissolve the blood of the king, but made this appear a vanishingly remote prospect: 'Ah! Il te faudroit plus de pleurs pour te laver, que les mers qui t'environnent ne contiennent de gouttes d'eau dans leurs vastes enceintes!' [Ah! You would need more tears to clear yourself of this deed than there are drops of water in the vast chambers of the encompassing oceans!] (Normand 37; cf. Legris Duval 156–7). Others argued that the bloody deed of 21 January was forever irreparable and the whole vocabulary of belated grief mere mouth honour: 'il n'est point de soupirs ni de torrens de larmes, capables de laver la tache de sang qui demeure empreinte au sein de la France' [there are no sighs or rivers of tears capable of washing away this blood that has stained France] (Dessain 2; cf. Baudard 43). One commentator argued that the blood spilled on the place Louis XV could only be purified by fire: 'qu'on y dresse un large bûcher, et que l'ardeur de

sa flamme dessèche à jamais cette terre encore imbibée d'un sang pur et
royal' [let us prepare a large pyre whose fierce flame will scorch the earth
that is still soaked with a pure and royal blood].[48] According to Boulogne,
Louis's blood had cried out from the ground for vengeance and France had
paid the price in the lives of her children sacrificed in the Revolutionary
and Napoleonic Wars:

> N'en doutons pas, Messieurs, c'est pour venger la mort de l'innocent que tant
> d'innocens ont péri. C'est pour venger le sang le plus pur et le plus auguste de la
> France qu'a été versé par torrens le sang de nos enfans. (Boulogne 70; cf. Bonnevie
> 32, Arnaud 3)

> [Dearly beloved, it is without doubt to avenge the death of an innocent man that so
> many innocents have perished. It is to avenge the purest and most illustrious blood
> of France that the blood of our children has run in rivers.]

This forbiddingly austere notion of a jealous God visiting the iniquity
of the fathers upon the children ascribed a primordial importance to
the execution of Louis XVI as the catalyst of a macabre economy of
blood, a hecatomb of human sacrifice. This idea appeared in Joseph de
Maistre's *Considérations sur la France* (1797), the vade mecum of counter-
revolutionary orthodoxy during the First Restoration: 'Chaque goutte du
sang de Louis XVI en coûtera des torrents à la France; quatre millions de
Français, peut-être, payeront de leurs têtes le grand crime national d'une insurrection anti-religieuse et anti-sociale, couronnée par un régicide' [Each
drop of Louis XVI's blood will be paid for in rivers of blood by France; this
great national crime of an anti-religious and anti-social revolt, crowned by
a regicide, will cost the lives of perhaps four million Frenchmen].[49]

This harsh theodicy did not convince everyone, however. For one thing,
it seemed to sanction an interminable blood feud, an infinite regression of
sacrificial violence in the name of an inscrutable and savage god. Against this
idea, Thévenard represents Louis as a sacrificial victim whose blood washes
away the sin of his own murder, thereby forestalling any need for a renewal
of the original violence (Thévenard 2). And Arnaud celebrates the 'miracle'

48   *Pompe expiatoire: 21 janvier 1815* (Paris: Le Normant, 1815), p. 2.
49   Joseph de Maistre, *Œuvres*, ed. Pierre Glaudes (Paris: Robert Laffont, 2007), p. 205.

of the Restoration, 'qui s'est opéré sans qu'il en ait coûté ni une larme ni une goutte de sang' [which took place without requiring the shedding of a single tear or drop of blood] as a New Creation (Arnaud 23), a special covenant between God and his holy nation that was inaugurated precisely by means of the violent immolation of the king: 'Le sang innocent de ce Prince va devenir, en quelque sorte, un nouvel holocauste, une nouvelle victime de Propitiation entre le ciel et la France' [The innocent blood of this Prince will become as it were a new holocaust, a new victim of Propitiation between Heaven and France] (Arnaud 24). Jaunet likewise sees in Louis's death the corroboration of an emphatically Christian imperative of forgiveness: 'le sang de votre roi n'appelle point la vengeance; c'est le cri du pardon, le cri seul de la clémence qu'il fait entendre' [the blood of your king does not cry for revenge; it is the cry of forgiveness, the cry of mercy that we hear] (Jaunet 42).

The Revolution bequeathed a complex legacy of suppressed and be-lated mourning to subsequent generations. One of Louis XVIII's priorities after his return from exile was to reclaim the body of the king his brother, to salvage a token of corporeal identity from death and decomposition. In the event, the gravediggers recovered not a corpse, but unnameable scraps of mortality ('ces ossemens mêlés à un peu de terre abreuvée du sang et chargée des dépouilles mortelles de ce martyr' [these bones mixed with a little earth soaked in the blood and clotted with the mortal remains of this martyr]) which the alchemy of mourning would attempt to transform into objects of veneration ('des précieuses reliques' [precious relics]) (Villefort 6–7; cf. Boulogne 3). Prior to the exhumation of Louis's remains in 1815, royalist mourning lacked even the material culture (a body, funerary rites, a tomb, commemorative monuments) by which the living might collect-ively orientate and structure their shows of grief.

Restoration mourning was further complicated by Jacobin caricatures of Louis XVI as a monster, a pariah and ultimately a sacrificial victim whose blood had purged the stain of tyranny from France and whose death was the necessary precondition for the survival of the Republic (*Révolutions de Paris* 194). The festival of *2 pluviôse* ratified the idea that the regicide was a cause for public celebration and that mourning the king was an act of pol-itical treason. Royalist commemorations of Louis XVI can be understood as an attempt to overwrite this earlier draft of history, a palimpsest rather than a blank slate. The royalist commemoration of 21 January is a calculated reappropriation of this day from the republican calendar:

> On avoit voulu, il y a quelques années, ériger en fête la journée désastreuse qui éclaira le supplice du Roi. N'est-il pas juste d'expier par une fête contraire cette sanglante époque ? Les auteurs de la mort de Louis avoient cherché à rendre la nation complice de leur arrêt. Ne convient-il pas de donner le même éclat à la réparation, et de fléchir la Providence par une réunion de vœux, de regrets et de prière ? (*L'Ami*, III, 408)

> [Several years ago, some people had wanted to turn this fateful day on which our king was killed into a festival. Those responsible for Louis's death had attempted to make the nation party to their sentence. Should we not give a similar publicity to the reparations we are making and implore Providence by our common vows, regrets, and prayers?]

The Restoration had simultaneously to exorcize the ghost of Jacobin obituaries and to reassert Louis's 'true' identity as *rex christianissimus* within a nominally Christian economy of salvation. By calling the king a martyr and by identifying the regicide with the Crucifixion, however, the French clergy made an ultimately mistaken assumption about the Vatican's approval of Louis's beatification and arguably allowed their 'enthousiasme oratoire' to override their observance of doctrinal orthodoxy.

Mourning the king was made immeasurably more difficult by contradictory political agendas. On the one hand, the clergy preached reconciliation and forgiveness as a Christian imperative (*Mandement* 5). This deliberate forgetting of the past ('oublions tout, pardonnons tout' [let us forget all, let us forgive all]) was also consonant with Article 11 of the Charter, which prohibited the investigation of opinions and votes before the Restoration (Arnaud 24; cf. *L'Ami*, II, 41).[50] On the other hand, the clergy revisited the violence and horror of the regicide with a sometimes morbid avidity, confusing the lines of demarcation between their congregations and the blood-spattered revolutionary mob. Remembering, often

---

50   'Toutes recherches des opinions et votes émis jusqu'à la restauration sont interdites. Le même oubli est commandé aux tribunaux et aux citoyens' [All investigation of opinions and votes prior to the Restoration are forbidden. This forgetting is the duty of both courts and citizens].

in painful detail, was critical for this militant strain of mourning with its emphasis on trauma, guilt and expiation, and its belief that these were properly the engines of spiritual renewal. The practice of mourning the king was thus suspended between contradictory impulses and incompatible aims, what Fureix calls 'le désir d'effacement de la Révolution, et le ressassement constant des souvenirs douloureux qui lui étaient associés' [the wish to erase the Revolution and the permanent revisiting of painful memories associated with it].[51]

For royalists of the First Restoration, mourning the king was an attempt to make sense of both mortality and history, to situate the death of the sovereign within a longer narrative that would encompass and explain both the Revolution and the Empire. The funeral orations of the First Restoration bring into focus some of the complex issues that inflected public expressions of grief for Louis XVI at the beginning of the nineteenth century.[52] They also provide the matrix for subsequent reflections on martyrdom, violence and sacrifice, from the July Days and the Commune to the traumatic events of the twentieth century. The legacy of 21 January 1793, the scandal and stumbling block of the regicide, the question of how to fill the void (of authority, of meaning, of death …), has engaged thinkers from Tocqueville and Sorel to Camus and Bataille, and arguably retains its disturbing and divisive potency today.[53]

51 Emmanuel Fureix, 'La Ville coupable: l'effacement des traces de la capitale révolutionnaire dans le Paris de la Restauration, 1814–1830', in Christophe Charle and Daniel Roche, eds, *Capitales culturelles, capitales symboliques: Paris et les expériences européennes* (Paris: Publications de la Sorbonne, 2002), pp. 25–43 (p. 39).

52 Both during and after the Restoration, many writers continued to explore the significance of the regicide, often within a Christological or sacrificial paradigm, and to raise questions of national guilt and redemption in a range of different genres, including Ballanche's *L'Homme sans nom* (1820), Lamennais's *Essai sur l'indifférence en matière de religion* (1817–24), Balzac's *Un épisode sous la Terreur* (1829), and Hugo's *En passant dans la place Louis XV un jour de fête publique* (1840).

53 The various 'afterlives' of Louis XVI are described in: Richard Burton, *Blood in the City: Violence and Revelation in Paris, 1789–1945* (New York: Cornell University Press, 2001); Susan Dunn, *The Deaths of Louis XVI: Regicide and the French Political Imagination* (Princeton, NJ: Princeton University Press, 1994); Jesse Goldhammer, *The Headless Republic: Sacrificial Violence in Modern French Thought* (New York: Cornell University Press, 2005).

RACHEL BENOÎT

Unmourned Histories in Gustave Flaubert's *L'Éducation sentimentale*

ABSTRACT
Unwriteable within the conventions of nineteenth-century history, the Haitian Revolution (1791–1804) remained tethered to the sphere of the unreal. Suppressed in French historical consciousness, this unmournable event nonetheless leaves traces in literary destabilizations of the hierarchies regulating divisions between the real and the unreal, history and fiction. Such literary destabilizations occur in Gustave Flaubert's *L'Éducation sentimentale* (1869). In this text, set during the disappointments of the revolution of 1848 in Paris, the protagonist and the narrative compulsively revisit desired but unrealized events. The protagonist can never fully engage with events as they occur in the sphere of the real; reality occurs as a set of events he has always already missed. Through an examination of the novel's theme of mourning for unrealized possibilities and its portrayal of missing histories, this essay argues for the importance of the literary as a mode where the unwriteable history of the Haitian Revolution is obliquely but resonantly explored.

Circumventing History

L'Éducation sentimentale, a story as uneventful as its protagonist is insipid, is a discomfiting read. Frédéric Moreau, a young bourgeois living in Paris during the politically tumultuous years of 1830 to 1851, is numb to realities beyond those he creates for himself.[1] The protagonist and narrative

---

1   The novel spans across a period of revolution and reform in France that abolished the monarchy and slavery, and in 1848 established the Second Republic. Initial unity quickly gave way to division amongst revolutionaries and the regime ended in failure when President Louis-Napoleon Bonaparte carried out a *coup d'état* in 1851 to crown himself emperor.

compulsively revisit desired but unrealized events, so that each narrative step forward is undermined by a countercurrent that looks backwards to what might have been. The novel misleadingly opens with the sanguine thoughts of its protagonist:

> Frédéric pensait à la chambre qu'il occuperait là-bas, au plan d'un drame, à des sujets de tableaux, à des passions futures. Il trouvait que le bonheur mérité par l'excellence de son âme tardait à venir. Il se déclama des vers mélancoliques.[2]

> [Frédéric thought of his room at home, the kind of play he might write, the pictures he might paint, and of future passions. The happiness his noble soul deserved seemed a long time coming. He recited melancholy verses to himself].[3]

He spends most of the novel fashioning his life into 'vers mélancoliques' [melancholy lines] and very little time achieving any of his fickle ambitions. His writerly aspirations ('il ambitionnait d'être un jour le Walter Scott de la France' [his ambition was to be one day the Walter Scott of France], *ES* 36; *SE* 13), law studies and dalliance with painting are all subordinated to his fevered chase of Mme Arnoux, a married woman he meets aboard a ship in the opening scene.

For Frédéric, mourning is an aesthetic ideal. Consumed by his fantasy of a relationship he might have had with Mme Arnoux, Frédéric uses his devotion to their potential union as an excuse to dodge reality. Rather than mourn the loss of the child he fathers with a *courtisane* named Rosanette, or the death of his friend Dussardier during political upheaval, Frédéric wallows in the imaginary loss of a counterfactual life he might have had with Mme Arnoux. In their last encounter, after twenty-seven years of longing, it is Mme Arnoux who comes to find Frédéric, he suspects, 'pour s'offrir' [coming to give herself to him] (*ES* 552; *SE* 389). Repulsed by her now whitened hairs and faced with the reality of her desire for him, he casts their romance back to the less threatening realm of the unreal with a

---

2   Gustave Flaubert, *L'Éducation sentimentale* (Paris: Gallimard, 1978), p. 23 (further references to this edition will appear in main text as *ES*).

3   Gustave Flaubert, *Sentimental Education*, ed. Patrick Coleman, trans. Helen Constantine (Oxford: Oxford University Press, 2016), p. 4 (further references to this edition will appear in main text as *SE*).

lamentation in the past conditional, the tense of impossible futures: 'quel bonheur nous aurions eu' [What happiness we should have had!] (*ES* 551; *SE* 388). The use of this tense confirms what the reader has long sus-pected: Frédéric is far less interested in the reality of an ageing woman than he is in the melancholic retrieval of the memory of his desires. In one of literature's more underwhelming scenes, Flaubert curtly concludes both the chapter and their romance with: 'Et ce fut tout' [And that was all] (*ES* 553; *SE* 390).

These professional, artistic and romantic failures are shrewdly set amid the political disappointments of France's 1848 uprisings.[4] Remembered as an awkward false-start in French historical consciousness, the revolution of 1848, haunted by its own potentiality, was defined by the promises it failed to keep.[5] In the novel, like the loss of Frédéric's child and the death of his friend Dussardier, the failure of the Second Republic and the cas-ualties of 1848 are never properly mourned. Instead, the memory of the revolution that might have been dissipates into a haunting absence. The last pages show Frédéric wistfully recalling to his childhood friend Deslauriers their adolescent failure to enter their local brothel, neatly tying the end of the novel to its beginning in a closed circuit of aborted intentions: 'Et ils résumèrent leur vie. Ils l'avaient manqué tous les deux' [They looked

4   Deslauriers exemplifies the false hopes of 1848 when he confidently declares at
      the novel's outset: 'Patience! un nouveau 89 se prépare!' [Just you wait! There's
      a new '89 brewing!] (*ES* 39; *SE* 16). Robert Tombs notes, 'France's special extra
      problems were the fears and also the expectations that it inherited from the [1789]
      Revolution [...]. France was caught in the trap of its own spectres'. Robert Tombs,
      France, 1818–1914 (London: Longman, 1996), p. 394.
5   Writing just after the *coup d'état* of Louis-Napoleon, Karl Marx is vehement about
      the ineptitude of the 1848 Revolution to bring tangible change to the lives of
      France's working class. He highlights the disparity between what was imagined and
      the disappointing reality: 'What [the republican faction of the bourgeoisie] had
      imagined as the *most revolutionary* event occurred in reality as the *most counter-
      revolutionary*'. Karl Marx, 'The Eighteenth Brumaire of Louis Bonaparte', in Terrell
      Carver, ed., *Marx: Later Political Writings*, Cambridge Texts in the History of
      Political Thought (Cambridge: Cambridge University Press, 1996), pp. 31–127
      (p. 42).

back over their lives. They had both failed] (*ES* 555; *SE* 302). These contexts of historical frustration and disillusion underpin the dominance of the counterfactual mode in the novel and dictate the currents of its melancholic progression.[6]

Flaubert disrupts traditional modes of historical fiction by presenting an amputated rendition of the events of 1848.[7] By removing the explicitly historical and focusing instead on private melancholic yearnings, Flaubert's narrative lingers on the moments that fall just beyond the reach of recognizable dates or political figures: familiar scenes such as Alphonse de Lamartine addressing an unruly crowd in front of the *hôtel de ville* appear on the periphery of the plot.[8] Flaubert repeatedly shifts the novel's attention away from the public historical stage to the flippancy of private concerns. On the day of Louis-Napoleon's *coup d'état* which exchanged the Second Republic for a

6   According to Catherine Gallagher's work on counterfactual history narratives, the appearance of the alternate-history genre coincided with Flaubert's literary career: 'the first alternate histories were French, and they candidly expressed their authors' disappointment about the nation's early nineteenth-century reversals of military and political fortunes'. These publications include Charles Renouvier's 1857 *Uchronie* (*l'Utopie dans l'histoire*), which reimagined the defeat of the 1848 revolutions, and Auguste Blanqui's 1872 *L'Éternité par les astres* about the 1870 Paris Commune. Catherine Gallagher, *Telling It Like It Wasn't: The Counterfactual Imagination in History and Fiction* (Chicago: University of Chicago Press, 2018), pp. 49–50. For a discussion of the role of counterfactuals in literature, see Christopher Prendergast, *Counterfactuals: Paths of the Might Have Been* (London: Bloomsbury Academic, 2019).

7   For a discussion of Flaubert's fraught relationship with History and the wider alterations in the genre of the historical novel, see Anne Green, *Flaubert and the Historical Novel* (Cambridge: Cambridge University Press, 1982).

8   On 24–26 February, Alphonse de Lamartine addressed the mob surrounding the *hôtel de ville* as the newly formed Provisional Government met inside. As Richard Sennett, explains, in 1848 'Lamartine becomes the emissary of the government to quell the mob'. Richard Sennett, *The Fall of Public Man* (Cambridge: Cambridge University Press, 1977), p. 229. The scene has frequently been visually rendered as a focal point of the revolution, such as in Henri Félix Philippoteaux, *Lamartine refusant le drapeau rouge devant l'Hôtel de Ville* (Paris: Petit Palais, Musée des Beaux-Arts de la Ville de Paris, 1848).

Second Empire, he writes, 'L'état de siège était décrété, l'Assemblée dissoute [...]. Les affaires publiques le laissèrent indifèrent, tant il était préoccupé des siennes' [A state of siege was declared, the Assembly was dissolved [...]. Public affairs left him indifferent, he was so preoccupied with his own private ones] (*ES* 544; *SE* 383).[9] During one of the most violent nights of 1848, Frédéric's thoughts are pointed inward. Having devotedly prepared a room for a failed rendezvous with Mme Arnoux, he spitefully brings Rosanette to 'le logement préparé pour l'autre' [the lodgings he had prepared for the other woman] as an act of private revenge (*ES* 378; *SE* 263).[10] Distraught that he has spent the night with the wrong woman, he sobs for himself in his pillow as the text alludes to the sound of carts carrying the bodies of dead insurgents through the streets below.[11] By confining his reader within Frédéric's disinterested perspective, Flaubert frustrates attempts to isolate the important events of 1848 or follow a coherent chronology.

Discussions about the influence of nineteenth-century events on Flaubert's fragmented version of 1848 presume a genealogy of revolutions that elides one of the century's defining moments. The Haitian Revolution remained tethered to the sphere of the unreal in written history, both because it could not be articulated within the conventions of nineteenth-century historiography and because its full political realization was stifled as far as possible by contemporary imperial powers.[12] Despite no explicit mention of Haiti in *L'Éducation sentimentale*, it is valuable to do our own counterfactual exercise and imagine ways in which the events in Haiti

9   Louis-Napoleon staged a *coup d'état* on 2 December 1851, marking the end of the French Second Republic.

10   After days of unrest, King Louis Philippe abdicated and a Provisional Government was established between February and May 1848. This crucial date appears euphemistically in a parenthetical mention: '(vers le milieu de février)' [(towards the middle of February)] (*ES* 366; *SE* 254).

11   This scene is one of several instances where the use of free indirect discourse allows Flaubert to let the reader in on the historical events that Frédéric ignores.

12   For example, in 1806 the United States punitively signed into law a ban on all trade with Haiti, and did not lift the embargo until 1810.

might have penetrated Flaubert's work.[13] The literary tropes spawned by the Haitian Revolution in early nineteenth-century France, even if silenced, leave unwritten traces in Flaubert's prose. Whether or not he took direct interest in the events on the former colony of Saint-Domingue, the French elision of this event could not have escaped the notice of an author so invested in circuitous modes of writing history.[14]

Frédéric's circumvention of history mimics a distinguishing characteristic of the historiography of the Haitian Revolution; just as Frédéric conveniently finds himself away on holiday during the most eventful days of 1848, so did many French historians and newspapers deny the legitimacy of Haitian independence.[15] As Michel-Rolph Trouillot writes in *Silencing the Past: Power and the Production of History*, the scale and success of the slave insurrection on Saint-Domingue was unprecedented, and therefore:

> Entered history with the peculiar characteristic of being unthinkable even as it happened. Official debates and publications of the times, including the long list of pamphlets on Saint-Domingue published in France from 1790 to 1804, reveal the incapacity of most contemporaries to understand the ongoing revolution on its own terms.[16]

13   While beyond the scope of this essay, Flaubert's early work 'Quidquid volueris' (1837) tells the story of Djialioh, the offspring of a Brazilian slave and an orang-utan, who is brought to France by the scientist who orchestrated his experimental conception. The text explores the collision between anxieties of miscegenation, the grotesque and the imaginary, offering insight into the colonial themes that preoccupied even Flaubert's early writing. Gustave Flaubert, 'Quidquid volueris', in *Bibliomanie et autres textes, 1836–1839* (Paris: Godefroy, 1982), pp. 118–51.

14   Susan Buck-Morss writes that the 'Haitian Revolution was the crucible, the trail by fire for the ideals of the French Enlightenment. And every European who was part of the Bourgeois reading public knew it': *Hegel, Haiti, and Universal History* (Pittsburgh, PA: University of Pittsburgh Press, 2009), p. 42. Further proof of this interest was the commercial success of Haitian historian and politician Beaubrun Ardouin's *Études sur l'histoire d'Haïti* in France in 1859. See Joan Dayan, *Haiti, History and the Gods* (Berkeley: University of California Press, 1998), p. 13.

15   See Dayan, *Haiti, History and the Gods*, p. 6.

16   Michel-Rolph Trouillot, *Silencing the Past: Power and the Production of History* (Boston: Beacon Press, 2015), p. 73.

Trouillot thus asks, 'Can historical narratives convey plots that are un-thinkable in the world within which these narratives take place? How does one write a history of the impossible?'.[17]

This is a question that would likely have interested Flaubert, who sought to write in the sort of anti-historical zone that Haitian histori-ography was forced into. Kaiama L. Glover points out that 'the Haitian aesthetic tradition has been marked by a fearless capacity to imagine alter-natives'.[18] This occurred largely by necessity; the lack of surviving contem-porary manuscript sources from the insurrection placed greater importance on unconventional historical methods. For instance, the Vodou ceremony in the forest of Bois Caïman has been largely accepted as the germination of the slave insurrection of 1791, mythologized through song, paintings and oral traditions.[19] Yet one of the most intriguing traits of this event is its contested plausibility, and the restless debates around its details.[20] Hoping to offer a counter-history to the often denigrating French renditions of this ceremony and the Revolution at large, Haitian historian Hérard Dumesle opted for an account that moves between verse and prose to reconstruct the event through memories, both collected and imagined. Dumesle travelled the region surrounding Bois Caïman thirty years after the event, piecing

17   Ibid. For a discussion of contemporary scholarship since Trouillot, see Alyssa Goldstein Sepinwall, 'Still Unthinkable?: The Haitian Revolution and the Reception of Michel-Rolph Trouillot's *Silencing the Past*', *Journal of Haitian Studies*, 19/2 (2013), 75–103.

18   Kaiama L. Glover, *Haiti Unbound* (Liverpool: Liverpool University Press, 2010), p. vii.

19   Marc A. Christophe contends that the 'Bois Caïman blood pact is considered by Haitian historians and researchers to be the most decisive and significant moment in the fight for Haiti's independence'. Marc A. Christophe, 'Legacies of Vodou', in Cécile Accilien, Jessica Adams and Elmide Méléance, eds, *Revolutionary Freedoms: A History of Survival, Strength and Imagination in Haiti*, (Coconut Creek, FL: Educa Vision, 2006), p. 99. On the integral role of the *Petro* branch of Vodou in the history of the revolution, see Maya Deren, *Divine Horsemen: The Living Gods of Haiti* (Kingston, NY: McPherson, 2004), pp. 62–7.

20   For a discussion of debates around the historiography of the Bois Caïman cere-mony, see David Geggus, 'The Bois Caïman Ceremony', *The Journal of Caribbean History* 25/1 (1991), 41–57.

together details from oral traditions with his own imagined testimonies of deceased generals, monuments and the natural landscape, making it an unpalatable source for many historians.[21] Written in 1824, Dumesle's *Voyage dans le nord d'Hayti* disrupts conventional historiography by demonstrating the importance of desire, speculation and fantasy in the historical memory of the Haitian Revolution. Understanding Flaubert's literary strategies in light of a revised genealogy of revolutions that moves from the French Revolution and *through* the Haitian Revolution allows for a deepened understanding of why and how imagined alternatives consume the aesthetic focus of his novels.

Writing the Unthinkable Revolution

In her pioneering work on the exclusion of emancipatory histories that were incompatible with the interests of Western powers, Sibylle Fischer notes that this friction, compounded with ideological differences between slave uprisings across the Caribbean, might account for why 'the historical imaginary that develops in the course of the nineteenth century has a peculiarly warped and melancholy quality'.[22] These unspoken histories of the nineteenth century, which had to exist almost entirely in the realm of fantasy, appear in French literature the way Frédéric's counterfactual desires operate in the novel: their ubiquitous presence functions to place pressure upon accepted realities.

Chris Bongie describes the 'outpouring in France of books, pamphlets, and newspaper articles dealing with Saint-Domingue/Haiti' in the decades following the Haitian Declaration of Independence as 'essentially

---

21   On Dumesle and the politics of historical analyses in nineteenth-century Haiti, see Marlene L. Daut, '"Nothing in Nature Is Mute": Reading Revolutionary Romanticism in *L'Haïtiade* and Hérard Dumesle's *Voyage dans le nord d'Hayti* (1924)', *New Literary History*, 49/4 (2018), 493–520.

22   Sibylle Fischer, *Modernity Disavowed: Haiti and the Cultures of Slavery in the Age of Revolution* (Durham, NC: Duke University Press, 2005), p. 133.

melancholic attempts at reincorporating the forever lost imperial object'.[23] The appearance of the former colony in romantic-era literature 'returned, with obsessive frequency, to the topic of Saint-Domingue/Haiti in an attempt to grapple with the effects of this loss through discursive revisitings'.[24] Frédéric is a convolution of the melancholic hero of romantic novels; he performs the rituals of loss, but only for imagined sadness as he is unable to engage with the real losses that surround him. Frédéric's performance of melancholia can be read as Flaubert's oblique testimony to the 'postimperial melancholia' (to borrow, as Bongie does, from Paul Gilroy) in nineteenth-century France.[25] France's refusal to fully accept Haitian independence interrupted the process of mourning its colonial loss, which remains at once unspoken, and omnipresent in the novel. Mme Arnoux, the revolution of 1848, and Haiti, all intersect as lost possibilities, articulated through ellipses and fantasy.[26]

As the world's first Black republic, Haiti, as Dayan puts it, 'forced imagination high and low: expression moved un-easily between the extremes of idealization and debasement'.[27] Haiti appeared in both extremes, sometimes simultaneously, such as in Victor Hugo's *Bug-Jargal* published in 1826.[28] Despite attempts to write Haiti and its revolution out of history, the

---

23   Chris Bongie, 'Victor Hugo and the Melancholy Novel: Reading the Haitian Revolution in *Bug-Jargal*', *French Studies* 72/2 (2018), 176–93 (p. 176).

24   Ibid., p. 177.

25   Paul Gilroy, *Postcolonial Melancholia* (New York: Columbia University Press, 2005), p. 90.

26   Jennifer Yee notes that indirect evocations of French imperialism in North Africa, which began in the 1830s, also appear in the novel: 'Just as Flaubert gives us deliberately fragmentary glimpses of events leading up to the revolution of 1848, so too he introduces elliptical links between the metropolis and the broader context of France's new colonial expansion'. Jennifer Yee, *The Colonial Comedy: Imperialism in the French Realist Novel* (Oxford: Oxford University Press, 2016), p. 43.

27   Dayan, *Haiti, History and the Gods*, p. 66.

28   Hugo claimed that he wrote this early work in 1818 and published a revised version in 1826. For a discussion of the novel in relation to the Haitian Revolution, see Jennifer Yee, *Exotic Subversions in Nineteenth-Century French Fiction* (Oxford: Legenda, 2008), pp. 45–60 and Victor Hugo, *Bug-Jargal*, ed. and trans. Chris Bongie (Ontario: Broadview, 2004), pp. 275–90.

years leading up to the events of 1848 saw an uptick in publications about the slave insurrection of 1791. This was partly due to France's new financial interest in the former colony from 1825, when Haiti began to pay France an indemnity that left the new nation in debilitating debt. As Philip Kaisary describes, during the time Flaubert was drafting *L'Éducation sentimentale* 'a vast range of literary and historical works, travelogues, memoirs, and artworks were produced by notable nineteenth-century writers seeking to celebrate, appropriate, or dramatize the event for their own social and political milieu'.[29] These appearances had confused and conflicting motivations, and reveal more about the state of events in France than Haitian interests. For example, to deflect attention away from political violence during the June Days of 1848, Louis-Napoleon criticized Haitian president Faustin Soulouque for violent events on the island, and is quoted as saying 'Haïti, Haïti, pays de barbares!'[30] In his scathing 'The Eighteenth Brumaire of Louis Bonaparte', Karl Marx used Soulouque as a demeaning comparison for Louis-Napoleon's henchmen, writing that they had 'the same grotesque dignity as Soulouque's stuffed shirts'.[31]

In April of 1848, the Second Republic permanently abolished slavery. The decree allowed longstanding abolitionists (including Lamartine) to bolster their own political agendas.[32] In *L'Éducation sentimentale*, Flaubert plays with the Second Republic's abolition of slavery to highlight the tensions between the vapid nature of their rhetoric and their claims to humanistic principles. He ridicules conservative attempts to compare the Second Republic to the Terror of 1793 when he writes:

29   Philip Kaisary, *The Haitian Revolution in the Literary Imagination* (Charlottesville: University of Virginia Press, 2014), p. 5.

30   Dayan, *Haiti, History and the Gods*, p. 10.

31   Marx, 'The Eighteenth Brumaire of Louis Bonaparte', p. 126. In response to such attempts to undermine Haitian sovereignty, Haitian writer Louis-Joseph Janvier cited the bloodshed in Paris in 1848 and 1851 as examples of Europe's own barbarism. See Louis-Joseph Janvier, *La République d'Haïti et ses visiteurs (1840–1882)* (Paris: Marpon & Flammarion, 1883).

32   As Minister of Foreign Affairs, Lamartine signed the official emancipation document. Alsatian parliamentarian Victor Schœlcher also fought adamantly for abolition, visited Haiti in 1841 and published a biography of Toussaint Louverture in 1879.

> Malgré la législation la plus humaine qui fut jamais, le spectre de 93 reparut, et le couperet de la guillotine vibra dans toutes les syllabes du mot République; – ce qui n'empêchait pas qu'on la méprisait pour sa faiblesse. La France, ne sentant plus de maître, se mit à crier d'effarement. (*ES* 392)

> [In spite of the most humane legislation there had ever been, the spectre of '93 reappeared, and the sound of the guillotine echoed through all the syllables of the word 'Republic' – which did not stop them pouring scorn on it for its weakness. France, feeling she no longer had a master, began to shout with fear.] (*SE* 275)

Patrick Coleman notes that the 'narrator does not specify what that legislation was, but given what we know of Flaubert's convictions such measures would surely include the ending of slavery in the French colonies'.[33] The evocation of slave imagery with 'master' helps to solidify the connection with the colonies, and the 'guillotine' and '93' link the Second Republic's legislation with Maximilien Robespierre's own abolitionist decree of 1794.[34] When more explicit reference to the abolition of slavery does appear in the novel, it is shrouded in irony. Frédéric's friend Hussonnet, resentful of hypocritical bourgeois students supporting the uprisings of 1848, is seen mocking 'les principes de 89, l'affranchissement des nègres, les orateurs de la gauche' [the principles of '89, the emancipation of the Negroes, the orators of the Left] (*ES* 456; *SE* 320). Flaubert repeatedly belittles the politicians of the Second Republic and mocks their ineffective use of the language of sentiment.[35] Marx wrote: 'In no period do we find a more confused mixture of superfluous phrases and practical

---

33   Patrick Coleman, 'Introduction', in Flaubert, *Sentimental Education*, ed. Coleman and trans. Constantine, p. xxiii.

34   For Robespierre's views on Haiti and slavery, see Peter McPhee, *Robespierre: A Revolutionary Life* (New Haven, CT: Yale University Press, 2012), p. 184. This initial decree of 1794 was revoked in 1802.

35   James Livesey explains: 'In their use of the language of sentiment as an integrating language for the French nation, the radicals were in the great tradition of the eighteenth century. Like 1789, 1848 was inspired by a dream of the collective regeneration of the nation. The very failure of the language of sentiment to provide a base for a political culture transformed the nature of politics in France'. James Livesey, 'Speaking the Nation: Radical Republicans and the Failure of Political Communication in 1848', *French Historical Studies* 20 (1997), 459–80 (p. 460).

uncertainty and helplessness.'[36] Frédéric echoes these words of frustration to Deslauriers: 'Quant aux ouvriers, ils peuvent se plaindre [...] vous n'avez rien fait pour eux que des phrases!' [As for the workers, they have a reason to complain; [...] you have given them nothing but fine phrases!] (*ES* 485; *SE* 341).

An example of such language appears in Lamartine's dramatic poem, *Toussaint Louverture*, based on the life of the Haitian revolutionary leader.[37] According to Marlene L. Daut, Lamartine's pseudo-historical imagining uses the trope of the tragic mulatto to dramatize Toussaint's life as a family romance, in which his mixed-race children are torn between allegiances to their father, and to France.[38] In Flaubert, such themes allow traces of Haiti to permeate the novel beyond explicit political references. The novel's centripetal force, Mme Arnoux, is herself a prompt for the trope of the tragic mulatta. While the doomed mulatta is most often said to have originated in American nineteenth-century fiction, Daut argues that the 'image can be traced to early nineteenth-century French colonial literature, where the trope surfaced in conjunction with the image of the Haitian Revolution as a family conflict'.[39] Upon meeting her, Frédéric fantasizes about her

36   Marx, 'The Eighteenth Brumaire of Louis Bonaparte', p. 37.
37   Arnold notes that the 1850 audience of Lamartine's *Toussaint Louverture* included 'Louis-Napoléon Bonaparte, then president of the republic'. A. James Arnold, 'Recuperating the Haitian Revolution in Literature: From Victor Hugo to Derek Walcott', in Doris Garraway, ed., *Tree of Liberty: Cultural Legacies of the Haitian Revolution in the Atlantic World* (Charlottesville: University of Virginia Press, 2008), pp. 179–99 (p. 184).
38   On Lamartine's use of the trope of the tragic mulatto/a in *Toussaint Louverture* see Marlene L. Daut, *Tropics of Haiti: Race and the Literary History of the Haitian Revolution in the Atlantic World, 1789–1856* (Liverpool: Liverpool University Press, 2015), pp. 374–411.
39   Marlene L. Daut, '"Sons of White Fathers": Mulatto Vengeance and the Haitian Revolution in Victor Séjour's "The Mulatto"', *Nineteenth-Century Literature*, 65/1 (2010), pp. 1–37 (p. 2). See also Léon-François Hoffmann, *Le Nègre romantique: personnage littéraire et obsession collective* (Paris: Payot, 1873). Jennifer DeVere Brody argues that the first literary appearance of this figure was in Thackeray's *Vanity Fair* from 1848. See Jennifer DeVere, *Impossible Purities: Blackness, Femininity, and Victorian Culture* (Durham, NC: Duke University Press, 1998), p. 27.

ambiguous racial origins: 'Il la supposait d'origine andalouse, créole peut-être; elle avait ramené des îles cette négresse avec elle?' [He supposed her to be of Andalusian extraction, possibly Creole; had she brought this Negro woman back with her from the islands?] (*ES* 26; *SE* 7). These unanswered questions, paired with explicit reference to her dark complexion, evoke the trope of the racially ambiguous woman familiar to the French literature of the nineteenth century, and gesture towards France's colonial ghosts (*ES* 16; *SE* 26). When Frédéric indulges in a nostalgic summary of their romance as he says goodbye to Mme Arnoux forever, the Black maid features pointedly as the last lost memory, and the only one given a possessive pronoun: 'Il lui rappela le petit jardin d'Auteuil, des soirs au théâtre, une rencontre sur le boulevard, d'anciens domestiques, sa négresse. Elle s'étonnait de sa mémoire' [He reminded her of the small garden at Auteuil, the evenings in the theatre, the time they met on the boulevard, old servants, her Negro woman. She was amazed at his memory] (*ES* 549; *SE* 387). These colonial or exotic allusions exist almost exclusively in counterfactual scenarios that are mourned as soon as they are created.[40]

Similarly, when Frédéric imagines a preferable life for himself, the imagery cues to an abstract exoticism:

> Frédéric se meublait un palais à la moresque, pour vivre couché sur des divans de cachemire, au murmure d'un jet d'eau, servi par des pages nègres; – et ces choses rêvées devenaient à la fin tellement précises, qu'elles le désolaient comme s'il les avait perdues. (*ES* 87)[41]
>
> [Frédéric would have a palace furnished in the Moorish fashion, to spend his life reclining on cashmere divans, to the murmur of a fountain, attended by negro

---

40 Lisa Lowe and Jennifer Yee have studied the 'oriental' and the 'exotic' in Flaubert's fictions as sites that reveal the wider cultural anxieties of nineteenth-century France as it grappled to find its post-Revolutionary identity. See Lisa Lowe, *Critical Terrains: French and British Orientalisms* (Ithaca, NY: Cornell University Press, 2018), pp. 75–101.

41 Yee argues that materialistic and fetishistic references to exotic objects show how 'Frédéric Moreau remains in thrall to the Romantic ideal of the exotic as transcendence, but this allegiance is repeatedly satirized, specifically through the linkage of the exotic with capitalism and colonialism'. Yee, *The Colonial Comedy*, p. 37.

pages – and these things, of which he had only dreamed, became in the end so definite that they made him feel as dejected as if he had lost them.] (*SE* 59)

The narrative buys into the reality of these desires while simultaneously accepting their impossibility. Inclusions of 'pages nègres' or 'divans de cachemire' serve as points of entry where unspoken histories of the nineteenth century can roam freely within descriptions of fantasy. While the novel retracts Mme Arnoux's colonial origins by the revelation that she is from Chartres, its utterance leaves residue.[42] As Richard Terdiman notes: 'Once imagined, even so that it might be proscribed, difference acquires a phantom but fundamental existence. If it is countenanced at all, its legitimation, its inclusion […] has to that extent begun.'[43] This delineation of the unreal allows Frédéric to invest in the fantasy. By mourning its loss, the imagined lost object subsists despite its unreality.[44]

Mourning the Counterfactual

Rather than a linear movement towards an ideal of human progress, like those that motivate his friends to join the uprisings of 1848, Frédéric is

42   Yee notes: 'Madame Arnoux's darkness – both her own "peau brune" and the darkness conferred on her metonymically by her maidservant – is in fact misleading, since she is from prosaic Chartres. […] the sexual fantasy of Andalusian or creole exoticism is Frédéric's own'. Yee, *The Colonial Comedy*, p. 159.

43   Richard Terdiman, *Discourse/Counter-Discourse: The Theory and Practice of Symbolic Resistance in Nineteenth-Century France* (Ithaca, NY: Cornell University Press, 1985), p. 14.

44   Giorgio Agamben rereads Freud, positioning his work within a broader philosophical context to emphasize the role of the imaginary in melancholia: 'insofar as such mourning is for an unobtainable object, the strategy of melancholy opens a space for the existence of the unreal and marks out a scene in which the ego may enter into relation with it and attempt an appropriation such as no other possession could rival and loss possibly threaten'. Giorgio Agamben, *Stanzas: Word and Phantasm in Western Culture*, trans. Ronald L. Martinez (Minneapolis: University of Minnesota Press, 1992), p. 20.

locked into a melancholic orbit around the idea of Mme Arnoux. She provides an organizing principle to his time, financial expenses and thoughts:

> Il se demanda, sérieusement, s'il serait un grand peintre ou un grand poète; – et
> il se décida pour la peinture, car les exigences de ce métier le rapprocheraient de
> Mme Arnoux. Il avait donc trouvé sa vocation! Le but de son existence était clair
> maintenant, et l'avenir infaillible. (*ES* 83)

> [He seriously wondered whether to become a great painter or a great poet. And
> made up his mind to be a painter, for the demands of that profession would bring
> him closer to Madame Arnoux. He had found his vocation then! The aim of his life
> was now clear to him and his future was assured.] (*SE* 47)

When Deslauriers writes '*nous comptons sur toi*' [we are counting on
you, as you promised], imploring him to join the protests, Frédéric uses
Mme Arnoux as an escape: 'Oh! Je les connais, leurs manifestations.
Mille grâces! J'ai un rendez-vous plus agréable' [Oh, I know all about
their demonstrations. Spare me! I have a more pleasant rendezvous] (*ES*
368, 369; *SE* 256). Frédéric is persistently missing History as he pursues
Mme Arnoux, who is cast as the alternative route to the novel's historical
storyline. When Frédéric witnesses the violent arrest of young protesters,
he is distressed only by an alternative reality in which his involvement
might have kept him from her: 'on aurait pu le prendre avec les autres,
et il aurait manqué Mme Arnoux' [he might have been arrested along
with the others, and then would have missed Mme Arnoux] (*ES* 370; *SE*
293). When Bongie speaks of France's perpetual return to the lost colonial object, we here see it mirrored in Frédéric's obsessions. Like France,
Flaubert's characters are haunted by the spectres of their own counterfactual existences.[45]

Flaubert capitalizes upon the aesthetic potential of mourning to
fuel the imaginary and supplant the real. Sigmund Freud's definition in
Mourning and Melancholia is useful to give language to this pivot from a
real to an imaginary lost object.[46] It is melancholia, the pathological failure

---

45   Marx writes: 'the period 1848 to 1851 saw only the spectre of the old revolution on
     the move': 'The Eighteenth Brumaire of Louis Bonaparte', p. 33.
46   In Freudian terms, decathexis is a sign of a successful mourning process, while mel-
     ancholia sits as its pathological failure.

of mourning, that allows for an imaginative process that enables an unreal past to continue to exist in the present. Through failed mourning, the unreal aerates and expands definitions of the real. Subsequent thinking around mourning has complicated Freud's neat distinction.[47] Jacques Derrida posits that the work of mourning is in itself a creative force, and one might speak of 'working *at mourning* as one would speak of a painter working *at a painting*'.[48] Flaubert writes about mourning for its own sake; rather than a ritualistic means to a redemptive end, a coping mechanism for releasing a real lost object, mourning here becomes a mechanism to prolong obsessively the imagined loss of a non-existent yet desired object, dragging an always already lost past into the present. This construal of mourning reveals its generative and creative potential.[49]

The past conditional tense is the conjugational mode of mourning, allowing the possible and the impossible to coexist. For example: 'il raconta comment il serait mort le 15 mai, sans le dévouement d'un garde national' [he told them how he would have been killed on the fifteenth of May had it not been for the devotion of a National Guard] (*ES* 423).[50] The tense creates two realms: that of the lost possibility and that of the realized event, placing them in opposition to one another. The result is that the

47   For instance, Jacques Derrida sees Freud's 'successful' mourning as a betrayal to the deceased. He offers instead a 'demi-deuil' which succeeds (i.e. preserving a connection to the deceased), through its failure to fully release the lost object. For Derrida, to release and forget would be a betrayal. See 'Circonfession', in Geoffrey Bennington and Jacques Derrida, *Jacques Derrida* (Paris: Seuil, 1991), pp. 5–291; in English as 'Circumfession', in Geoffrey Bennington and Jacques Derrida, *Jacques Derrida*, trans. Geoffrey Bennington (Chicago: University of Chicago Press, 1993), pp. 3–315.

48   Jacques Derrida, 'By Force of Mourning', trans. Pascale-Anne Brault and Michael Nas, *Critical Inquiry* 22/2 (1996), 171–92 (p. 172).

49   In Patrick Coleman's discussion of mourning in French Realism, he argues that 'realist perspectives originate in melancholy experiences of powerlessness and loss' and that these produce 'art through the writer's work of mourning'. Patrick Coleman, *Reparative Realism: Mourning and Modernity in the French Novel* (Geneva: Droz, 1998), p. 12.

50   Gustave Flaubert, *Sentimental Education*, ed. and trans. Adrianne Tooke (Ware: Wordsworth Editions, 2003), p. 337.

realized event is understood in terms of the non-event it prevented. Thus, the 'dévouement d'un garde national' is made subordinate to his death, which did not occur. The counterfactual mode is intensified in such acts of doubling: both revolutionary action and ordinary events occur more in the imaginary than in the real. With the past conditional mode, Flaubert wrote against the neat notion of progress found in the nineteenth-century utopian reflections by writers such as Fourier and Saint-Simon. Instead he created an aesthetics of stagnation with a cyclical narrative structure, and the verb tense of lost possibilities.

Frédéric creates instances of loss to justify the act of mourning and evade the real. Rather than engage with Rosanette's unwanted announcement that she is pregnant with their child, Frédéric fabricates an imaginary child to mourn:

> L'idée d'être père, d'ailleurs, lui paraissait grotesque, inadmissible. Mais pourquoi? Si, au lieu de la Maréchale …? Et sa rêverie devint tellement profonde, qu'il eut une sorte d'hallucination. Il voyait là, sur le tapis, devant la cheminée, une petite fille. Elle ressemblait à Mme Arnoux et à lui-même, un peu; – brune et blanche, avec des yeux noirs, de très grands sourcils, un ruban rose dans ses cheveux bouclants! (Oh! comme il l'aurait aimée!) Et il lui semblait entendre sa voix: 'Papa! Papa!' (*ES* 473)

> [Besides, the idea of becoming a father seemed grotesque, unthinkable. But why? If, instead of the Maréchale …? And he became so lost in his reverie that he had a kind of hallucination. On the rug in front of the fireplace he saw a little girl. She looked like Madame Arnoux, and a little like him; dark, with a pale face, black eyes, dark eyebrows, a pink ribbon in her curly hair. (Oh, how he would have loved her!) And he thought he heard her voice: 'Papa! Papa!'] (*SE* 333)

The past conditional tense here insists that the imaginary should be mourned, and reality silenced. Before this imagined child has ever been conceived, the verb tense ('il l'aurait aimée!') convinces Frédéric of her loss, as though she has been killed by the news of Rosanette's pregnancy. Whereas the imagined child lives and breathes, with bouncing curls and a skin tone that conjoins Mme Arnoux's racial otherness with his own corporeality ('brune et blanche'), Frédéric's real child is a grotesque corpse from its birth: 'quelque chose d'un rouge jaunâtre, extrêmement ridé qui sentait mauvais et vagissait' [a yellowish-red object, exceedingly wrinkled, which had a bad smell and was wailing] (*ES* 506; *SE* 406). Even the novel undermines the plausibility of Rosanette's pregnancy by carelessly extending it over two years. Frédéric's child dies soon after its birth, yet he is unable to engage with this loss. While Rosanette becomes a weeping Niobe ('elle restait la bouche ouverte, avec un flot de larmes tombant de ses yeux fixes' [she remained open-mouthed, with a flood of tears streaming from her frozen eyes]) Frédéric 'croyait presque rêver' [thought he might be dreaming] (*ES* 525; my translation).

In the absence of a living child, Rosanette fashions an imaginary version of her son in the counterfactual mode. She is able to keep him alive by repeatedly moving through the patterns of grief:

> Tous les quarts d'heure, à peu près, Rosanette ouvrait les rideaux pour contempler son enfant. Elle l'apercevait, dans quelques mois d'ici, commençant à marcher, puis au collège, au milieu de la cour, jouant aux barres; puis à vingt ans, jeune homme; et toutes ces images, qu'elle se créait, lui faisaient comme autant de fils qu'elle aurait perdus, – l'excès de la douleur multipliant sa maternité. (*ES* 533)

> [Every quarter of an hour or so, Rosanette opened the curtains to look at her baby. She could imagine him beginning to walk in a few months' time, then at school, in the middle of the schoolyard playing prisoner's base, then as a young man of twenty; and all these images she conjured up seemed to her like all the sons she had lost – the extremes of grief multiplying her motherhood.] (*SE* 376)

As Rosanette moves through this sequence, the free indirect discourse pans to reveal Frédéric, across the room, deep in counterfactual thoughts:

> Frédéric, immobile dans l'autre fauteuil, pensait à Mme Arnoux. [...] Que deviendrait-elle? Institutrice, dame de compagnie, femme de chambre, peut-être? [...] Il aurait dû s'opposer à sa fuite ou partir derrière elle. N'était-il pas son véritable époux? Et en songeant qu'il se la retrouverait jamais, que c'était bien fini, qu'elle était irrévocablement perdue, il sentait comme un déchirement de tout son être; ses larmes accumulées depuis le matin débordèrent. (*ES* 533)

> [Frédéric, inert in the other armchair, was thinking of Madame Arnoux. [...] What would become of her? A teacher, a paid companion, or perhaps even a chambermaid? [...] He ought to have prevented her from fleeing or followed after her. Was he not her real husband? Then, thinking he would never see her again, that it was truly over, that she was irrevocably lost, he felt something like a wrenching of his entire being; his tears that had been accumulating since the morning overflowed.] (my translation)

Frédéric inserts himself into her life by mourning her hypothetical loss and positioning himself as her 'real' husband. With irony, Flaubert finally lets Rosanette and Frédéric find common ground in the act of grieving: 'tous deux sanglotaient en se tenant embrassés' [they both sobbed in each other's arms] (*ES* 533; my translation).

Thinking he has lost Mme Arnoux forever, Frédéric leaves Paris on the day of Louis-Napoleon's *coup d'état*, returning just in time to witness the brutal murder of his friend Dussardier. Flaubert counts a beat by ending the chapter with Frédéric standing 'béant' [open-mouthed] (*ES* 546; *SE* 385). Opening the following chapter with a brief paragraph that nimbly spans a decade, the novel nonchalantly skips from 1851 to 1867, with no mention of Dussardier:

> [Frédéric] voyagea. Il connut la mélancolie des paquebots [...]. Il revint. Il fréquenta le monde, et il eut d'autres amours encore. Mais le souvenir continuel du premier les lui rendait insipides [...]. Des années passèrent; et il supportait le désœuvrement de son intelligence et l'inertie de son cœur. (*ES* 547)

> [He travelled. He learned about the melancholy of steamships [...]. He came back. He mingled in society, and he had other loves. But the constant recollection of the first love made these insipid to him [...]. Years passed, and he had grown to accept his mental stagnation and the inertia of his heart.] (*SE* 440)

The languid imperfect tense mimics Frédéric's obsessive and melancholic rhythms. Time passes without mention, he leaves and returns and loses all motivation other than the obstructionist 'constant recollection of the first', which resists expulsion, preventing him from finding a new love object. The novel obscures the real loss of Dussardier with an immediate transition to Frédéric's melancholic yearning for Mme Arnoux. Even as Frédéric and Deslauriers take stock of their lives and think back to their friends and what has become of them, Dussardier is never mentioned (*ES* 555).

It is worth lingering on Dussardier's death – even if the novel does not – because he exists as a figuration of the alternative revolution 1848 might have been. Regarded as perhaps the only earnest symbol of the efforts of 1848, Dussardier, like the revolution, is repeatedly patronized by the text.[51] Neither he nor his revolutionary ideals are allowed to survive,

---

51 Albert Thibaudet names Dussardier the novel's only 'vrai révolutionnaire de 1848' [the only true revolutionary of 1848]: 'Préface' (*ES* 13; my translation).

or even to be mourned. The novel's omission of this act of mourning confirms that his belief in progress and revolutionary idealism stands neatly against the circular current of the novel. Dussardier himself participates in the novel's cycles of mourning, bemoaning the impending failure of the revolutionary effort to Frédéric: 'Je suis tellement désespéré! Est-ce que tout n'est pas fini, d'ailleurs? – J'avais cru, quand la Révolution est arrivée, qu'on serait heureux. Vous rappelez-vous comme c'était beau! comme on respirait bien! Mais nous voilà retombés pire que jamais' [I am so desperate! Isn't it the end of everything anyway? – I thought when the Revolution came we should be happy. Do you remember how good it was? How we breathed again? But now we are worse off than before] (*ES* 521–2; *SE* 367).

It is only with a sardonic stroke that Flaubert will paint the hero of 1848 as an earnest figure. Take, for instance, the description of Dussardier's posture as he speaks of his despair: 'écartant les bras comme dans une grande détresse' [flinging his arms up as if in great distress]. 'Comme' tinges the fatalistic words that follow with the narrator's scepticism: 'Et il n'y a pas de moyen! pas de remède! Tout le monde est contre nous! […] J'ai envie de me faire tuer' [There nothing to be done about it! No remedy. Everyone is against us. […] I want to kill myself] (*ES* 522; *SE* 368). Dussardier's lamentations and political sincerity are continuously dipped in Flaubertian irony, pathetic in their passive self-victimization and yet simultaneously achieving rare moments of political poignancy. The narrative weight of Dussardier's death, in both its placement near the novel's end and the rare drama of an event that Frédéric witnesses in real time, is such that it cannot be dismissed as yet another instance of Flaubert's defeatist portrayal of the aspirations of 1848.[52] Instead, the opportunity to weave irony into sincerity suggests the character is designed to point beyond his own political beliefs towards a wider aesthetic of doom. The novel's refusal to mourn Dussardier's death suggests that such a frank and political figure must remain in the realm of the unsaid, and the unmourned.

---

52 Marion Schmid notes that setting this scene during the *coup d'état* allows Dussardier's assassination to signify 'the final liquidation of the Second Republic. His end is the end of an era; Frédéric's disillusionment is that of his whole generation': *Processes of Literary Creation: Flaubert and Proust* (Oxford: Legenda, 1998), p. 85.

The figure of Dussardier straddles sincerity and the ridiculous, and this coexistence might suggest that Flaubert views political sincerity *as* ridiculous. The first account of Dussardier demonstrates this contradiction. An initially Herculean description, 'Alors parut le robuste visage de Dussardier' [Then appeared the sturdy face of Dussardier] is immediately undermined by a belittling docility: 'avec ses petits yeux francs et son nez carré du bout, rappelait confusément la physionomie d'un bon chien' [his honest little eyes, and his square-tipped nose, suggested to one's mind in a confused sort of way the physiognomy of a good dog] (*ES* 23; *SE* 34). Though Flaubert portrays Dussardier's dedication to the republican cause with pathos, it is inflected with a farcical martyrdom. When Dussardier is deemed a hero during the uprisings for his bravado atop a barricade, it is retold to Frédéric with all the pomp of a Hugo novel, but only retrospectively: 'Dussardier avait jeté bas son fusil, écarté les autres, bondi sur la barricade, et, d'un coup de savate, abattu l'insurgé en lui arrachant le drapeau' [Dussardier had thrown his gun on the ground, got the others out of the way, jumped on to the barricade, and with one kick had brought down the insurgent, tearing the flag off him] (*ES* 444; *SE* 311). In contrast to Dussardier's death, this scene of heroism, like most of the action of this novel, is told and retold before it reaches Frédéric or the reader.

Dussardier is unable to relish his heroic revolutionary moment: 'on exaltait sa belle action. Ces hommages paraissaient l'importuner. Il avoua même à Frédéric l'embarras de sa conscience' [his brave conduct was commended. This praise seemed to embarrass him. He even admitted to Frédéric that his conscience was not clear] (*ES* 444; *SE* 311). Instead, he becomes consumed by alternative renditions of what he might have done:

> Peut-être qu'il aurait dû se mettre de l'autre bord, avec les blouses; car enfin on leur avait promis un tas de choses qu'on n'avait pas tenues. […] et le brave garçon était torturé par cette idée qu'il pouvait avoir combattu la justice. (*ES* 444)

> [Perhaps he ought to have gone over to the other side and joined the working people; for it must be said they had been promised a whole lot of things which had not been delivered. […] And the young man was tormented by the idea that he might have been fighting against justice.] (*SE* 312)

'Brave garçon' reads with a patronizing glint, his earnest motivations launching him backwards rather than forwards with the past conditional tense ('peut-être qu'il aurait dû') to relive an alternative, perhaps equivalent, act of heroism. Rather than lauding the action he did achieve, he mourns the alternative course he might have taken.

Ultimately, counterfactuals overtake the factual, in both the narrative and the literary meta-narrative constructed by the author. Repeated gestures towards the Balzacian character Frédéric fails to become and allusions to Walter Scott remind us of the historical novel Flaubert might have written.[53] Flaubert sought to write about history while problematizing the genre of historical fiction. He wrote to his friend Jules Duplan: 'j'ai bien du mal à emboiter mes personnages dans les évènements politiques de 48! J'ai peur que les fonds ne dévorent les premiers plans. C'est là le défaut du genre historique' [I'm struggling to place my characters within the political events of 1848. I'm worried the background will devour the foreground. That's the trouble with the historic genre].[54] His solution was to push the recognizable figures and events to the periphery of his protagonist's consciousness. With the wandering perspective of his free indirect discourse, he shifts his reader's focus away from Victor Hugo's barricades, and plunges it into Frédéric's fantasies. Within this counterfactual zone, the historical contexts of the novel widen beyond those explicitly mentioned and reveal the tacit influence of the Haitian Revolution on the ways in which history was digested and represented in nineteenth-century France. If we are to disrupt a legacy of silencing, Flaubert's historical scepticism offers a good place to start writing such histories back into the literature they undoubtedly influenced.

53   Frédéric says, 'Mais je te dis là des choses classiques, il me semble? Rappelle-toi Rastignac dans *La Comédie humaine*! Tu réussiras, j'en suis sûr!' [But I'm not saying anything new, I think? Remember Rastignac in the *Comédie Humaine*. You will succeed, I have no doubt!] (*ES* 41; SE 19). For a discussion of Flaubert's reversal of Balzacian tropes, see Peter Brooks, *Reading for the Plot: Design and Intention in Narrative* (New York: Vintage, 1985), pp. 171–215.

54   Gustave Flaubert, letter to Jules Duplan, 1868, in Gustave Flaubert, *Correspondance* (Paris: Gallimard, 1998), p. 530 (my translation).

PART II

Inconsolable (Af)filiations

JENNIFER RUSHWORTH

The Rhythm of Mourning in Proust (with Barthes and Derrida)

ABSTRACT

This essay considers a selection of the writings on grief by Marcel Proust, Roland Barthes and Jacques Derrida. It argues both for the inevitable imbrication of the theoretical and the particular in narratives of mourning and, especially, for the importance of rhythm in such narratives. I show first of all how Derrida offers an alternative to the Freudian binary of finite mourning and endless melancholia. Derrida's unstable, intermediary, alternating position is further analysed for its rhythmical qualities, inspired by connections made by Barthes between rhythm and mourning. I approach rhythm as a multifaceted phenomenon that crosses literary, medical and musical boundaries, and consider in particular its inherent tension between regularity and irregularity. These theoretical insights are brought into dialogue with mournful episodes from Proust's novel relating to the deaths of the grandmother and Albertine. From these examples, I ultimately suggest the mutual dependency of rhythm, mourning and narrative.

There has been much recent critical interest in mourning in Proust, with, in particular, a ground-breaking book published by Anna Magdalena Elsner in 2017.[1] The subject has been invigorated by two fundamental insights. On the one hand, there has been a very welcome shift in perception from a notion that mourning in Proust is finite to a recognition that mourning in Proust is endless though intermittent.[2] In other words,

---

1   Anna Magdalena Elsner, *Mourning and Creativity in Proust* (New York: Palgrave Macmillan, 2017). See also Jennifer Rushworth, *Discourses of Mourning in Dante, Petrarch, and Proust* (Oxford: Oxford University Press, 2016) and, most recently, Maria Maruggi, 'Le Deuil dans *Le Temps retrouvé* de Marcel Proust', *Études francophones* 30 (Spring 2019), 28–43.

2   The former view is represented, for instance, by Alessia Ricciardi, *The Ends of Mourning: Psychoanalysis, Literature, Film* (Stanford: California University Press, 2003), esp. 'Cool Memories', pp. 69–119.

Proustian mourning may appear to come to an end – witness statements by the narrator such as 'j'avais bien oublié ma grand-mère' [I had after all forgotten [...] even my grandmother] – but, thanks to the mechanism of involuntary memory, a return to grief is always possible and always imminent.[3] The role of memory in reviving grief is clear from the narrator's sudden mourning for his grandmother, a year after her death, when he rediscovers his 'grand-mère véritable' [true grandmother] and his loss of her at one and the same time (*ALR* III, 153; *SG* 158). This episode acts as the blueprint for other experiences of mourning in the novel, including the narrator's mourning for Albertine in the penultimate volume of *À la recherche du temps perdu* [*In Search of Lost Time*], *Albertine disparue* [*The Fugitive*]. Reading mourning in Proust as intermittent means granting Proust's protagonist a more ethical relationship with the lost love object. Instead of faithless forgetting, we witness a more complicated, enduring relationship.

On the other hand, our understanding of mourning in Proust has been illuminated by the instigation of a productive critical dialogue between *À la recherche* and particular theories of mourning. The theories chosen have been primarily psychoanalytical, drawing on the work of Sigmund Freud and Melanie Klein.[4] Yet two thinkers outside the purview of psychoanalysis have also proven helpful for thinking about mourning in Proust: Roland Barthes and Jacques Derrida. It is the reflections of these two writers on grief which this essay will triangulate with a reading of the rhythm of mourning in Proust.

What is especially attractive about the writings of Barthes and Derrida on mourning is their explicit rootedness in personal experience. Derrida

3   All quotations from Proust are taken from *À la recherche du temps perdu*, ed. Jean-Yves Tadié, 4 vols (Paris: Gallimard, 1987–9) (hereafter referenced in main text as *ALR*). English translations are from Marcel Proust, *In Search of Lost Time*, ed. Christopher Prendergast, 6 vols (London: Penguin Classics, 2003), more particularly: *The Way by Swann's*, trans. Lydia Davis (*WS*); *In the Shadow of Young Girls in Flower*, trans. James Grieve (*SYG*); *The Guermantes Way*, trans. Mark Treharne (*GW*); *Sodom and Gomorrah*, trans. John Sturrock (*SG*); *The Prisoner and the Fugitive*, trans. Carol Clark and Peter Collier (*PF*); *Finding Time Again*, trans. Ian Patterson (*FTA*). For this quotation see *ALR* IV, 64; *PF* 449.

4   See especially Elsner, *Mourning and Creativity in Proust*.

argues that there cannot be a metalanguage of grief, and his thoughts on grief are, accordingly, inseparable from his own, personal experiences of loss.[5] *Chaque fois unique, la fin du monde* (published first in English under the title *The Work of Mourning*) gathers together sixteen different texts written by Derrida after the death of friends, many of whom are also famous French intellectuals. One such figure is, in fact, Barthes himself, to whom the first text is devoted.[6] These texts span a range of genres including funeral eulogies and obituaries; they contain theoretical observations, but these observations are always rooted in and mediated by very specific losses. As a consequence, Derrida's reflections on grief are particularly revealing when brought to bear on literary examples, since they share with literature such as Proust's novel a predilection for specificity (specific situations, specific characters), embedded, nonetheless, within a broader urge towards the more general and theoretical.[7] As Proust writes, 'c'est à la cime

5   In his text on the death of Louis Marin, Derrida writes, 'On ne peut pas tenir un discours *sur* le "travail du deuil" sans y prendre part […]. Il n'y a donc pas de métalangage quant au langage où s'engage un travail du deuil' [One cannot hold a discourse *on* the 'work of mourning' without taking part in it […]. There is thus no metalanguage for the language in which a work of mourning is at work]: 'Louis Marin (1931–1992): à force de deuil', in *Chaque fois unique, la fin du monde* (Paris: Galilée, 2003), pp. 175–204 (pp. 177–8); 'By Force of Mourning: Louis Marin', in Derrida, *The Work of Mourning*, ed. and trans. Pascale-Anne Brault and Michael Naas (Chicago: University of Chicago Press, 2001), pp. 142–64 (pp. 142–3). The other deaths on which Derrida meditates are those of the following: Roland Barthes, Paul de Man, Michel Foucault, Max Loreau, Jean-Marie Benoist, Louis Althusser, Edmond Jabès, Joseph N. Riddel, Michel Servière, Sarah Kofman, Gilles Deleuze, Emmanuel Lévinas, Jean-François Lyotard, Gérard Granel and Maurice Blanchot. Elsner points to the productiveness of this volume for thinking about Proust in *Mourning and Creativity in Proust*, p. 21.

6   Jacques Derrida, 'Roland Barthes (1915–1980): les morts de Roland Barthes', in *Chaque fois unique, la fin du monde*, pp. 59–97; 'The Deaths of Roland Barthes', in *The Work of Mourning*, pp. 34–67.

7   On the place of theory in Proust see Malcolm Bowie, *Freud, Proust and Lacan: Theory as Fiction* (Cambridge: Cambridge University Press, 1987), and most recently Patrick Bray, *The Price of Literature: The French Novel's Theoretical Turn* (Evanston, IL: Northwestern University Press, 2019).

même du particulier qu'éclot le général' [the general flourishes when the particular is at its height].[8] This last quotation is also one of Barthes's favourite Proustian maxims.[9] Barthes's writings on grief are both personal, like Derrida's, and yet, unlike Derrida's, explicitly and consistently mediated through Proust.[10] Barthes writes most intimately of his experience of the death of his mother on 25 October 1977 in his posthumously published *Journal de deuil* [*Mourning Diary*].[11] Once more, mourning is inseparable from the specific and the personal.

These two insights – that mourning in Proust is not finite and that *À la recherche* can benefit from a theoretical approach – are, of course, connected, since the question of whether mourning can or cannot end is at the heart of Freud's seminal essay 'Mourning and Melancholia' (1917).[12] This

8   Marcel Proust, *Correspondance*, ed. Philip Kolb, 21 vols (Paris: Plon, 1970–93), XVIII (1990), 334; Marcel Proust, *Selected Letters*, ed. Philip Kolb and trans. Ralph Manheim, Terence Kilmartin and Joanna Kilmartin, 4 vols (London: Harper Collins, 1983–2000), IV, 86. This quotation comes from a letter to Daniel Halévy dated by Kolb 19 July 1919.

9   See Lucy O'Meara, *Roland Barthes at the Collège de France* (Liverpool: Liverpool University Press, 2012), pp. 77–8.

10   Of the extensive bibliography on Barthes and Proust, see, with a particular focus on mourning: Adam Watt, 'Reading Proust in Barthes's *Journal de deuil*', *Nottingham French Studies* 53/1 (2014), 102–12; Éric Marty, 'Marcel Proust dans "la chambre claire"', *L'Esprit créateur* 46 (2006), 125–33; Jennifer Rushworth, 'Mourning and Intermittence between Proust and Barthes', *Paragraph* 39/3 (2016), 269–86.

11   Roland Barthes, *Journal de deuil: 26 octobre 1977–15 septembre 1979*, ed. Nathalie Léger (Paris: Seuil/IMEC, 2009); *Mourning Diary: October 26, 1977–September 15, 1979*, ed. Nathalie Léger and trans. Richard Howard (London: Notting Hill Editions, 2011). On the mournful Barthes see also, with reference to *La Chambre claire* [*Camera Lucida*], Neil Badmington, '*Punctum saliens*: Barthes, Mourning, Film, Photography', *Paragraph* 35/3 (2012), 303–19.

12   Sigmund Freud, 'Mourning and Melancholia', in *The Standard Edition to the Complete Psychological Works of Sigmund Freud*, ed. and trans. James Strachey, 24 vols (London: Hogarth Press, 1953–74), XIV, 243–58. Despite the importance of this essay, critics have also warned against reducing Freud's views to this one, early text. See Richard Goodkin, 'Mourning a Melancholic: Proust and Freud on the Death of a Loved One', in his *Around Proust* (Princeton, NJ: Princeton University Press, 1991), pp. 127–45; L. Scott Lerner, 'Mourning and Subjectivity from Bersani to Proust, Klein, and Freud', *Diacritics* 37/1 (Spring 2007), 41–53; Elsner, *Mourning*

text famously and controversially defines melancholia as endless grief in contrast to the finite process of the work of mourning. Notwithstanding, what is especially useful about Derrida's writings on mourning is that they encourage us to move beyond Freudian binaries (the work of mourning vs melancholia; finitude vs endlessness; what is considered normal vs what is deemed pathological; infidelity vs fidelity, etc.). Derrida's analysis of mourning is markedly tentative and uncertain (relying on questions and hypotheses), personal (couched in the first person singular), and paradoxical (embracing contraries and opposites):

> Est-ce que la fidélité c'est le deuil? C'est aussi le contraire: le fidèle ou la fidèle, c'est quelqu'un qui est endeuillé. Le deuil c'est une intériorisation de l'autre mort en soi; faire le deuil, c'est garder, c'est une expérience de fidélité, mais c'est aussi le contraire. Donc l'impossibilité de faire son deuil, et même la volonté de ne pas faire son deuil, c'est aussi une forme de fidélité. Si faire son deuil et ne pas faire son deuil sont deux formes de fidélité et deux formes d'infidélité, la seule chose qui reste – c'est là que je parle de demi-deuil – c'est une expérience entre les deux; je n'arrive pas à faire mon deuil de tout ce que je perds, parce que je veux le garder, et en même temps, ce que je fais de mieux, c'est le deuil, c'est le perdre, parce qu'en faisant le deuil, je le garde au-dedans de moi.

> [Is fidelity mourning? It is also the contrary: the faithful one is someone who is in mourning. Mourning is an interiorization of the dead other, but it is also the contrary. Hence the impossibility of completing one's mourning and even the will not to mourn are also forms of fidelity. If to mourn and not to mourn are two forms of fidelity and two forms of infidelity, the only thing remaining – and this is where I speak of semi-mourning – is an experience between the two. I cannot complete my mourning for everything I lose, because I want to keep it, because by mourning, I keep it inside me.][13]

Ultimately, in my own work on Proust and mourning I have found Derrida's concept of 'demi-deuil' (typically translated as 'mid-mourning')

---

and Creativity in Proust, pp. 12–14; Madelon Sprengnether, *Mourning Freud* (New York: Bloomsbury, 2018).

13　Jacques Derrida, 'Dialangues', in Elisabeth Weber, ed., *Points de suspension: entretiens* (Paris: Galilée, 1992), pp. 141–65 (p. 161); 'Dialanguages', in *Points: Interviews, 1974–1994*, ed. Elisabeth Weber and trans. Peggy Kamuf and others (Stanford, CA: Stanford University Press, 1995), pp. 132–55 (pp. 151–2).

or 'semi-mourning') to be particularly resonant with Proust's novel.[14] Kathleen Woodward is not alone in calling for 'something *in between* mourning and melancholia', and Derridean *demi-deuil* – which Derrida himself calls 'une expérience entre les deux' [an experience between the two] – is, I argue, one attractive answer to this call.[15] In this essay, I do not want to repeat my earlier analysis; rather, I want to revisit Proustian mourning, Derridean *demi-deuil*, and Barthesian grief from a new point of view: that of rhythm. My analysis is in two parts: firstly, a more general consideration of rhythm and its relevance to narrative such as Proust's; secondly, an explanation of the particular rhythm of mourning in Proust, with Barthes and Derrida as key reference points for that discussion.

Rhythm and Narrative

> What is rhythm? The answer, I am afraid, is, so far, just – a word: a word without a generally accepted meaning. Everybody believes himself entitled to usurp it for an arbitrary definition of his own.
> The confusion is terrifying indeed.[16]

In the face of this confusion identified by Curt Sachs and reiterated in Justin London's entry on 'Rhythm' in *Grove Music Online*, my

---

14   See Rushworth, *Discourses of Mourning in Dante, Petrarch, and Proust*, esp. 'Proust's *Recherche*, Derridean "demi-deuil", and Mimetic Mourning', pp. 91–125.

15   Kathleen Woodward, 'Freud and Barthes: Theorizing Mourning, Sustaining Grief', *Discourse: Journal for Theoretical Studies in Media and Culture* 13/1 (Fall-Winter 1990–1), 93–110 (p. 96). For a reading of Derridean *demi-deuil* in relation to Italian poetry, see Adele Bardazzi, 'Rethinking the Ends of Poetry: Elegy and "Demi-deuil" in Eugenio Montale's "La casa dei doganieri"', *California Italian Studies* 8/1 (2018), 1–19.

16   Curt Sachs, *Rhythm and Tempo: A Study in Music History* (London: J. M. Dent & Sons, 1953), p. 12, cited in Justin London, 'Rhythm', *Grove Music Online* <https://doi.org/10.1093/gmo/9781561592630.article.45963> [accessed 18 April 2019].

understanding of rhythm is shaped by three interconnected areas of consideration: the literary, the musical and the bodily.

Within literary studies, it is unsurprising that rhythm has typically been considered in relation to poetry rather than to prose.[17] Two edited volumes do, however, extend the scope of rhythm in literature to include prose.[18] From the plentiful studies of poetic rhythm, particularly helpful are Clive Scott's observations about, firstly, the links between rhythm and repetition and, secondly, rhythm as a matter of perception and interpretation:

> To describe rhythm as a principle of repetition or recurrence is to desemanticize and to displace it; rhythm is a perceptual experience not to be dissociated from the particularity of its context (in poetry, the verse-instance); it is part of the dynamic of perception and cognition, rather than an anterior or posterior hypostatization. Thus in Chatman's account (1965: 18–29), 'primary' rhythm ('simple periodic return of a given stimulus', p. 20) is not meaningfully rhythmic; only 'secondary' rhythm (the grouping, differential highlighting, 'interpretation', of 'primary' rhythm) is. The perception of rhythm is a psychological need, the means whereby phenomena are made sense of, and sensory stimuli are absorbed as subjective percepts. Rhythm

17   Clive Scott, 'Poetry and the Rhythmic', in *The Poetics of French Verse: Studies in Reading* (Oxford: Clarendon Press, 1998), pp. 182–217; David Evans, *Rhythm, Illusion and the Poetic Idea: Baudelaire, Rimbaud, Mallarmé* (Amsterdam: Rodopi, 2004). For a longer historical view, see also Roger Pensom, *Accent, Rhythm and Meaning in French Verse* (Oxford: Legenda, 2018).

18   See *Rhythms: Essays in French Literature, Thought and Culture*, ed. Elizabeth Lindley and Laura McMahon (Bern: Peter Lang, 2008), and *Rhythm in Literature after the Crisis in Verse*, ed. Peter Dayan and David Evans, special issue of *Paragraph*, 33/2 (July 2010). Both of these volumes are understandably weighted in favour of poetry. The first, *Rhythms*, is divided into five sections, each with three essays except for the section on 'Narrative Rhythms' which only has two: Brenda Garvey, 'Rhythms, Repetitions and Rewritings in *Passion Simple* by Annie Ernaux', pp. 75–85, and Luke Sunderland, 'The (Future) Perfect Knight: Repetition in the *Cycle de Guillaume d'Orange*', pp. 87–99. The second volume, *Rhythm in Literature after the Crisis in Verse*, includes two articles on narrative: Emma Sutton, ' "Putting Words on the Backs of Rhythm": Woolf, "Street Music", and *The Voyage Out*', pp. 176–96; Peter Dayan and Carolina Orloff, 'Finding Rhythm in Julio Cortázar's *Los Premios*', pp. 215–29.

compels the text to recover its status as enunciation (process), to resist being something which already exists, the enunciated (product).[19]

Scott's initial description of rhythm as 'a principle of repetition' points us to a particular tension in thinking about rhythm, namely the relationship between regularity and irregularity. In fact, generally repetitive rhythm in poetry might more accurately be spoken of as metre. Yet Scott is also suggesting that repetition may be not so much within the text objectively as, rather, a projection of the reader that is, to a certain extent, subjective. In order to understand something, we seek, both consciously and unconsciously, to impose form and structure – often involving some elements of repetition and regularity – onto the object of our perceptions.

Thus, for example, Swann listening to the Vinteuil sonata transforms it, through the power of memory, from indescribable musical motifs into a describable structure:

> Et cette impression continuerait à envelopper de sa liquidité et de son 'fondu' les motifs qui par instants en émergent, à peine discernables, pour plonger aussitôt et disparaître, connus seulement par le plaisir particulier qu'ils donnent, impossibles à décrire, à se rappeler, à nommer, ineffables – si la mémoire, comme un ouvrier qui travaille à établir des fondations durables au milieu des flots, en fabriquant pour nous des fac-similés de ces phrases fugitives, ne nous permettait de les comparer à celles qui leur succèdent et de les différencier. Ainsi à peine la sensation délicieuse que Swann avait ressentie était-elle expirée, que sa mémoire lui en avait fourni séance tenante une transcription sommaire et provisoire, mais sur laquelle il avait jeté les yeux tandis que le morceau continuait, si bien que, quand la même impression était tout d'un coup revenue, elle n'était déjà plus insaisissable. Il s'en représentait l'étendue, les groupements symétriques, la graphie, la valeur expressive; il avait devant lui cette chose qui n'est plus de la musique pure, qui est du dessin, de l'architecture, de la pensée, et qui permet de se rappeler la musique. (*ALR* I, 206)

> [And this impression would continue to envelop with its liquidity and its 'mellowness' the motifs that at times emerge from it, barely discernible, immediately to dive under and disappear, known only by the particular pleasure they give, impossible to describe, recall, name, ineffable – if memory, like a labourer working to put down lasting foundations in the midst of the waves, by fabricating for us facsimiles of these

---

19   Scott, 'Poetry and the Rhythmic', p. 182. In this passage Scott makes reference to
       Seymour Benjamin Chatman, *A Theory of Meter* (The Hague: Mouton, 1965).

fleeting phrases, did not allow us to compare them to those that follow them and to differentiate them. And so, scarcely had the delicious sensation which Swann had felt died away than his memory at once furnished him with a transcription that was summary and temporary but at which he could glance while the piece continued, so that already, when the same impression suddenly returned, it was no longer impossible to grasp. He could picture to himself its extent, its symmetrical groupings, its notation, its expressive value; he had before him this thing which is no longer pure music, which is drawing, architecture, thought, and which allows us to recall the music.] (*WS* 212)

In this passage, we witness a transition from a lack of perceptible rhythm ('flots') to an awareness and understanding of rhythm ('l'étendue, les groupements symétriques, la graphie') enabled by the work of memory.[20] To return to Chatman's terms highlighted by Scott, Swann learns to perceive rhythm through 'grouping, differential highlighting, "interpretation"'.[21] To think about rhythm necessitates, therefore, acknowledging a potential tension between a lack of regularity in the material itself versus a retrospective imposition of regularity by the listener or reader.

Thinking about rhythm has led us straight to one of the most famous musical experiences of Proust's novel. Of course, rhythm encourages consideration of music (a much-discussed Proustian theme), but it also has the capacity to render non-musical experiences and forms musical. Narrative is, then, arguably musical partly thanks to the extent to which it relies upon rhythm. Jean-Yves Tadié has written of Proust's novel that 'le récit tout entier est poétique, parce que rythme' [the whole narrative is poetic, because of rhythm], and I would replace the adjective 'poétique' here with the adjective 'musical'.[22] This reliance on rhythm may be manifested on a small scale in phrasing and syntax, or on a larger scale in overall form and structure. Both approaches have been productive within Proust studies. For example, Erika Fülöp has analysed the rhythm of the imperfect in Proust's prose, Lydia Davis writes about how the experience of translating

---

20 This is not to say that 'flots' have no rhythm, but rather that their rhythm is impossible to grasp, for Swann.
21 Scott, 'Poetry and the Rhythmic', p. 182.
22 Jean-Yves Tadié, *Proust et le roman: essai sur les formes et techniques du roman dans 'À la recherche du temps perdu'* (Paris: Gallimard, 1971), p. 434 (my translation).

the first volume of *À la recherche* led her to notice the rhythms of Proust's writing, and rhythm is one factor amongst others in Adam Piette's close reading of sound in Proust.[23] We might note here the narrator's observation that his mother's reading of George Sand's *François le Champi* bestows 'un rythme uniforme' [one uniform rhythm] on 'cette prose si commune' [this very common prose], 'tantôt pressant, tantôt ralentissant la marche des syllabes' [sometimes hurrying, sometimes slowing down the pace of the syllables] (*ALR* 1, 42; *WS* 45).[24] From this perspective, regularity is sweet and desirable, functioning even at the level of individual syllables, and crucially dependent on the particular reader's interpretation and performance of the text.

Malcolm Bowie, in contrast, takes a broader approach in his reading of Proust as structured according to a 'respiratory rhythm'. He writes:

> A majestic respiratory rhythm is at work in *A la recherche du temps perdu*. On the one hand, the narrator of the novel has a mania for multiplicity, wants the world to contain more things rather than fewer, and stands guard over an unstoppable transformational machine. [...]
>
> On the other hand, everything is connected to everything else in the remembering or fantasising mind, and the oceanic swell which seems to bear the voyager onwards to ever-new destinations can easily bring him home to his habitual tastes and his over-familiar emotional landmarks. Structure, limitation and fewness have a way of

23 Erika Fülöp, 'Proust's Imperfect: Rhythms of the *Recherche*', in Adam Watt, ed., *'Swann' at 100/'Swann' à 100 ans*, special edition of *Marcel Proust aujourd'hui*, 12 (2015), 197–212; Lydia Davis, 'Les Marteaux et les claquements des sabots: rythmes et motifs syntaxiques dans *Du côté de chez Swann*', trans. Naomi Toth, in *Marcel Proust, roman moderne: perspectives comparatistes*, Vincent Ferré and Raffaello Rossi, eds, special edition of *Marcel Proust aujourd'hui*, 14 (2018), 159–77; Adam Piette, *Remembering and the Sound of Words: Mallarmé, Proust, Joyce, Beckett* (Oxford: Clarendon Press, 1996), esp. 'Re-establishing Contacts: Prose Rhymes in *A la recherche du temps perdu*', pp. 81–141. Such studies also build on the earlier work of Jean Milly, *La Phrase de Proust: des phrases de Bergotte aux phrases de Vinteuil* (Paris: Librairie Larousse, 1975).

24 I have argued elsewhere that this rhythm resonates with Reynaldo Hahn's definition of rubato, heightening the musicality of this scene: Rushworth, 'Proust, Hahn, and the Art of Song', in *'Swann' at 100/'Swann' à 100 ans*, pp. 168–83 (pp. 172–5).

reasserting themselves even as the narrative seeks to be convinced that an indefinite plurality of worlds lies at his feet. [...]

The narrative breathes out, and the world is many. It breathes in again, and the world is one.[25]

This passage is a beautiful characterization of Proust's novel. It suggests how rhythm might work on a grand formal scale, across the novel, in a repetitive but varied, alternating manner. It also highlights a key connection between rhythm and the body.[26] Bowie focuses here on the rhythm of breathing, but his comments might also have been couched within the rhythm of the beating heart with its cycle of diastole (expansion) and systole (contraction).

From a related, medical perspective, regular rhythm is desirable and healthy, whereas irregularity – such as arrhythmia – is dangerous.[27] As much is evident from the narrative of the grandmother's death in *Le Côté de Guermantes* [*The Guermantes Way*]. At first, it sounds as if the grandmother is singing, thanks to the aid of extra oxygen: 'ma grand-mère semblait nous adresser un long chant heureux qui remplissait la chambre, rapide et musical' [my grandmother seemed to be singing us a long, happy song which filled the room, rapid and musical] (*ALR* ii, 635; *GW* 338). As she approaches the moment of death, however, her breathing becomes less regular:

> Par moments, il semblait que tout fût fini, le souffle s'arrêtait, soit par ces mêmes changements d'octaves qu'il y a dans la respiration d'un dormeur, soit par une intermittence naturelle, un effet de l'anesthésie, le progrès de l'asphyxie, quelque défaillance du cœur. (*ALR* ii, 639)

---

25   Malcolm Bowie, 'Preface', in *Proust Among the Stars* (London: Fontana Press, 1998), pp. xi–xix (pp. xiv–xvi).

26   On the latter, see Liza Gabaston, *Le Langage du corps dans 'À la recherche du temps perdu'* (Paris: Honoré Champion, 2011), and Michael R. Finn, *Proust, the Body and Literary Form* (Cambridge: Cambridge University Press, 1999).

27   Of the many studies of Proust from a medical perspective, see at least Serge Béhar, *L'Univers médical de Proust* (Paris: Gallimard, 1970), and David Wright, *Du discours médical dans 'À la recherche du temps perdu': science et souffrance* (Paris: Honoré Champion, 2007).

[At times it seemed as if it was all over: her breath stopped, either because of one of those shifts of octave that occur in the respiration of a sleeper or because of some natural interruption, an effect of anaesthesia, developing asphyxia, a failure of the heart.] (*GW* 342)

These lines suggest an intimate connection between breathing and the beating of the heart, while the passage as a whole traces a shift from regular breathing (enhanced by medical oxygen) to irregularities of breath and heart which lead, finally, to death.[28] It is, moreover, the narrator's mourning for his grandmother's death which I take as emblematic of the rhythm of Proustian mourning.

The Rhythm of Mourning

In his *Journal de deuil* written after the death of his mother, Barthes expresses the following desire: 'Non pas supprimer le deuil (le chagrin) (idée stupide du temps qui abolira) mais le changer, le transformer, le faire passer d'un état statique (stase, engorgement, récurrences répétitives de l'identique) à un état fluide' [Not to suppress mourning (suffering) (the stupid notion that time will do away with such a thing) but to change it, transform it, to shift it from a static stage (stasis, obstruction, recurrences of the same thing) to a fluid state].[29] Barthes is here seeking an alternative to both the stasis of melancholia and the teleological drive of the work of mourning. As I have suggested, Derridean *demi-deuil* represents one possible alternative, thanks to its ability to incorporate change without progress. *Demi-deuil* offers the possibility of introducing rhythm and variety into an experience that would otherwise be pure stasis and repetition, at the same time without moving towards any end or exit from that

28   I have noted elsewhere how the very terminology of this passage foreshadows the later episode of the 'intermittences du cœur': Rushworth, 'Mourning and Intermittence between Proust and Barthes', p. 273.

29   Barthes, *Journal de deuil*, p. 154; *Mourning Diary*, p. 142.

experience. *Demi-deuil* is both interminable and discontinuous or, to use a more Proustian word, intermittent.

What sort of rhythm might achieve the fluidity desired by Barthes? It is useful here to turn to Émile Benveniste's classic discussion of rhythm, in which he delineates a historical, etymological contrast between rhythm as the 'mouvement régulier des flots' [the regular movement of the waves of the sea] versus the continuous flow of a river.[30] As Benveniste points out, the latter is, in fact, not rhythmical at all. Barthes himself cites Benveniste on rhythm in his first lecture of *Comment vivre ensemble* [*How to Live Together*], on 12 January 1977.[31] This lecture series precedes the writing of *Journal de deuil*, and yet both are connected by a meditation on rhythm. In the former, Barthes presents his fantasy of 'idiorrythmie', a word formed by combining *idios* (one's own, private, personal, distinct) and its opposite, *rythme* [rhythm]. Barthes interprets rhythm as 'une cadence cassante, implacable de régularité' [an inflexible, implacably regular cadence] and explains that 'c'est parce que le rythme a pris le sens répressif […] qu'il a fallu lui adjoindre *idios*' [it's because rhythm acquired a repressive meaning […] that it was necessary to add the prefix *idios*].[32] Against the association of rhythm with regularity (and therefore regulation), Barthes celebrates rhythm for its particularity, explaining that in an idiorrhythmic space 'chaque sujet y a son rythme propre' [each subject lives according to his own

30   Émile Benveniste, 'La Notion de "rythme" dans son expression linguistique', in his *Problèmes de linguistique générale*, 2 vols (Paris: Gallimard, 1966–74), I, 327–35 (p. 328); 'The Notion of "Rhythm" in Its Linguistic Expression', in *Problems in General Linguistics*, trans. Mary Elizabeth Meek (Coral Gables, FL: University of Miami Press, 1971), pp. 281–8. Fülöp also summarizes this contrast in 'Proust's Imperfect', p. 210, arguing that it regulates the rhythm of the *Recherche*.

31   Roland Barthes, *Comment vivre ensemble: simulations romanesques de quelques espaces quotidiens: notes de cours et de séminaires au Collège de France, 1976–1977*, ed. Claude Coste (Paris: Seuil/IMEC, 2002), p. 38; *How to Live Together: Novelistic Simulations of Some Everyday Spaces: Notes for a Lecture Course and Seminar at the Collège de France (1976–1977)*, ed. Claude Coste and trans. Kate Briggs (New York: Columbia University Press, 2013), p. 7.

32   Ibid., p. 39; p. 8.

rhythm].[33] As he writes pithily in *Journal de deuil*: 'Chacun son rythme de chagrin' [To each his own rhythm of suffering].[34]

Grief is, in short, idiorrhythmic, and although this conclusion means a privileging of individual, particular experience, it is my contention that the rhythm of mourning is similar in Proust, Barthes and Derrida. Here, of course, it is important to remember the warning of Scott and Chatman that rhythm is always 'secondary' and 'interpretation'.[35] Yet, as we have seen, this interpretation takes place not only in reading but already within the text, through the work of memory and the self-analysis of characters (such as Swann listening to the Vinteuil sonata). Moreover, thinking of rhythm in this way allows us to experience the text 'as enunciation (process)'.[36] This type of engagement is dynamic and provisional, restoring to the text its vital rhythms. With these observations in mind, let us return to the 'fluid state' desired by Barthes.

Pursuing this liquid metaphor, while heeding Benveniste's reflections on rhythm, we can imagine mourning taking the form of an endless ebb and flow. Rhythmically, there would be strong and weak beats; metaphorically, the tide of grief would have high and low points, in succession but without diminution. What is essential is that this rhythm allows for change without a teleological forward drive towards an end to mourning. It also means that any apparent abatement of grief represents, rather, the necessary background from which mourning will one day re-emerge. Such a rhythm is amply observable in Proust's novel, which alternates between assertions of the end of mourning and resurgent moments of grief.[37] Indeed, it is perhaps no coincidence that the narrator's mourning for Albertine takes place partly in Venice, so that the ebb and flow of his grief is mirrored in his maritime surroundings.[38] For the purposes of this essay, however, I will

33   Ibid., p. 37; p. 6.
34   Barthes, *Journal de deuil*, p. 174; *Mourning Diary*, p. 162.
35   Scott, 'Poetry and the Rhythmic', p. 182.
36   Ibid.
37   I have already charted this movement in relation to Albertine in *Discourses of Mourning in Dante, Petrarch, and Proust*, pp. 92–5.
38   See Carles Besa, 'Proust du côté de Venise ou l'âme en deuil', *Bulletin Marcel Proust* 43 (1993), 103–11. Citing Proust, Besa writes that 'le temps proustien n'avance que par des mouvements en arrière, il baigne obsessivement dans l'itératif, à l'instar du

chart this rhythmical movement quite succinctly in relation to the narrator's mourning for his grandmother.

It is firstly striking that mourning for the grandmother precedes her death. Already, whilst on holiday in Balbec, the protagonist is caught up in worries about mortality that relate directly to the anticipated possibility of his grandmother's death and persist under the surface of his hopeful, if disingenuous, expression of belief in a happy afterlife: 'je dis que c'était curieux, qu'après les dernières découvertes de la science le matérialisme semblait ruiné, et que le plus probable était encore l'éternité des âmes et leur future réunion' [it was remarkable, I said, that the latest advances in science seemed to have made materialism untenable, and that the most likely outcome was still the eternal life of the soul and reunion beyond the grave] (*ALR* II, 87; *SYG* 307).[39] Later, at Doncières, speaking to his grandmother on the telephone makes the protagonist once more realize her mortality, this time without any hope of redemption or resurrection. She is present to him only as a distant, disembodied voice whose disappearance at the end of the phone call is lamented in Orphic terms: 'seul devant l'appareil, je continuais à répéter en vain: "Grand-mère, grand-mère", comme Orphée, resté seul, répète le nom de la morte' [standing there alone in front of the telephone I went on vainly calling: 'Grandmother! Grandmother!' like the abandoned Orpheus repeating the name of his dead wife] (*ALR* II, 434; *GW* 133).[40] It is fruitful to consider both these episodes

---

va-et-vient des flots vénitiens "où le flux et le reflux se font sentir deux fois par jour" ' [Proustian time advances only through movements backwards, it is steeped in the iterative, in the manner of the to-ing and fro-ing of the Venetian waves 'where the ebb and flow of the tide are perceptible twice a day']: 'Proust du côté de Venise', p. 106, citing from *ALR* IV, 208; English translation my own, with quotation from *PF* 594.

39 Stéphane Chaudier rightly notes that this is a 'discours menteur destiné à réconforter la grand-mère' [a deceptive speech designed to comfort the grandmother], and situates it within other comments on the afterlife, in his book *Proust et le langage religieux: la cathédrale profane* (Paris: Honoré Champion, 2004), p. 123.

40 This episode has been much discussed by critics in relation to the importance of myth and technology respectively in this scene. See Margaret Topping, *Proust's Gods: Christian and Mythological Figures of Speech in the Works of Marcel Proust* (Oxford: Oxford University Press, 2000), esp. pp. 69–75, and Sara Danius,

as instances of anticipated mourning as theorized by Derrida, who notes that: 'L'appréhension angoissée du deuil (sans laquelle l'acte d'amitié ne surgirait pas, dans son énergie même) s'insinue *a priori*, elle s'anticipe, elle hante, elle endeuille l'ami avant le deuil' [The anguished apprehension of mourning (without which the act of friendship would not spring forth in its very energy) insinuates itself a priori and anticipates itself; it haunts and plunges the friend, before mourning, into mourning].[41] While mourning thus precedes death, the actual moment of death is oddly unemotional in Proust. We have seen that the narrative of the grandmother's death is highly medicalized, with a particular focus on the grandmother's struggles for breath. Once it has occurred, however, there is a sudden sense of stasis, firstly in the description of the grandmother's dead body as peacefully youthful and statuesque and then in the blank space of the narrative break that follows, since this moment comes at the very end of the first chapter of *Le Côté de Guermantes*: 'Sur ce lit funèbre, la mort, comme le sculpteur du Moyen Âge, l'avait couchée sous l'apparence d'une jeune fille' [On that funeral couch, death, like a sculptor of the Middle Ages, had laid her to rest with the face of a young girl] (*ALR* II, 641; *GW* 343).[42] Here, death really means *requiescat in pace*. Grief is, accordingly, suspended, elided, perhaps repressed, only to return in full force a year later when the protagonist experiences a keen sense of her loss in the famous involuntary memory that occasions a 'bouleversement de toute [s]a personne' [a convulsion of [his] entire being] in the following volume, *Sodome et Gomorrhe* [*Sodom and Gomorrah*]. At this moment, the protagonist's physical discomfort – 'une crise de fatigue cardiaque' [an attack of cardiac fatigue], aggravated by bending down to unbutton his boots – is compounded by a different

---

'Orpheus and the Machine: Proust as Theorist of Technological Change, and the Case of Joyce', *Forum for Modern Language Studies* 37/2 (April 2001), 127–40.

41   Jacques Derrida, *Politiques de l'amitié suivi de L'Oreille de Heidegger* (Paris: Galilée, 1994), p. 31; *The Politics of Friendship*, trans. George Collins (London and New York: Verso, 2005), p. 14.

42   On the medievalism of this image see Richard Bales, *Proust and the Middle Ages* (Geneva: Droz, 1975), p. 107. See also Aude Le Roux-Kieken, *Imaginaire et écriture de la mort dans l'œuvre de Marcel Proust* (Paris: Honoré Champion, 2005), p. 370.

crisis of the heart, the experience of sudden and overwhelming grief for his grandmother (*ALR* III, 152; *SG* 158).

Thereafter, the protagonist may protest that he has forgotten his grandmother, but such declarations will be consistently undercut by subsequent admissions of enduring attachment, such as the following from the final volume of *À la recherche*: 'Il m'arrivait parfois de souhaiter que, par un miracle, entrassent auprès de moi, restées vivantes contrairement à ce que j'avais cru, ma grand-mère, Albertine. Je croyais les voir, mon cœur s'élançait vers elles' [I sometimes used to find myself wishing that, by a miracle, still alive to the contrary to what I had believed, my grandmother or Albertine might just walk into the room where I was. I imagined I could see them, my heart shot towards them] (*ALR* IV, 566; *FTA* 297). In this brief passage, the protagonist is again presented as not in control of his grief, while grief itself is framed as intermittent, temporary and prone to repetition through the adverb *parfois* [sometimes]. As elsewhere, the narrator encourages the reader to draw a parallel between his mourning for his grandmother and his mourning for Albertine, so that from two quite different and specific examples we witness the suggestion of a wider pattern in Proustian mourning. The protagonist's earlier desirous imagining of life after death also returns here in his hope for a miracle. This miracle, nonetheless, emerges both as hopelessly subjective, thanks to the repetition of the verb *croire* ('j'avais cru', 'Je croyais') and as regrettably impossible (as suggested by the imperfect subjunctive 'entrassent').

The preceding quotations have established that mourning in Proust is characterized by its periodic but unpredictable return. In other words, its rhythm is that of an alternation between forgetting and remembering, between an apparent lack of mourning and renewed mourning. But can we be more specific about the timing of this alternating pattern? Here again, the problem of interpretation is crucial. It is tempting, both for the narrator and his reader, to impose a semblance of regularity retrospectively on the experience of grief as it is narrated. As we have seen, such a process occurs in Swann's listening to Vinteuil's music as in the narrator's mother's reading of Sand's prose. Yet it is important to respect the unpredictable nature of Proustian involuntary memory, which means that while a return of grief is likely, its timing is unforeseeable. Proustian mourning is, as a result, paradoxically regular in its irregularity.

Conclusions

Perhaps most fundamentally, Proust, Barthes and Derrida share a suspicion about metalanguage, especially as regards grief. Instead, they argue that mourning has to be thought and written about within a particular framework, whether real (in the case of Derrida and Barthes) or imagined (in the case of Proust's novel). To return to Proust's maxim: 'c'est à la cime du particulier qu'éclot le général' [the general flourishes when the particular is at its height].[43] Accordingly, the writings of Proust, Barthes and Derrida suggest that theoretical reflections on mourning need to be formulated with reference to specific losses. This argument means not only recognizing the contribution that both autobiography and fiction can make to theoretical reflections on grief, but even calling into question the status and characteristics of theory. From this perspective, in order to function well theory requires inclusion of and attention to the particular and the personal.

Proust, Barthes and Derrida also share the belief that mourning has rhythm and that this rhythm is particular to each individual. To use Barthes's term, mourning is idiorrhythmic. For Derrida, mourning oscillates between infidelity and fidelity, between forgetting and remembering, between possibility and impossibility. His term for this experience, as we have seen, is *demi-deuil*. Derridean *demi-deuil* offers a way of understanding mourning as rhythmical but without progress. In this way, *demi-deuil* might be one answer to Barthes's call, in his *Journal de deuil*, not for an end to mourning but rather for the transformation of mourning from an 'état statique' [a static state] to an 'état fluide' [a fluid state].[44] It is, nonetheless, in Proust's *À la recherche* that I see the clearest manifestation of

43   Proust, *Correspondance*, XVIII, 334; *Selected Letters 1918–1922*, p. 86.
44   Barthes, *Journal de deuil*, p. 154; *Mourning Diary*, p. 142.

a form of Derridean *demi-deuil*, in the narrator's succeeding declarations of indifference and renewed grief. This consonance suggests that despite grief's noted idiorrhythmy, the particular rhythm of mourning explored in this essay has the potential to be shared by different writers. As Julian Barnes writes in *Levels of Life* – a striking example of a text that blends together autobiography, biography and theory – 'Griefs do not explain one another, but they may overlap. And so there is a complicity among the griefstruck.'[45] We see a similar complicity between Proust, Barthes and Derrida as regards their understanding of mourning as (idio)rhythmical.

Finally, what is important about this mourning rhythm is that it represents a way of living through, surviving and narrating grief, without in this process suppressing or leaving grief behind. In this case, rhythm enables the perpetuation of grief, life and narrative, just as, conversely, the end or absence of rhythm would represent the end of life and the end of narrative. The end of grief would not necessarily thereby be entailed, since certain forms of grief – for instance, Freudian melancholia – do suggest an absence of rhythm. Nonetheless, grief without rhythm poses a particular challenge to its narration (not to mention to the one who experiences such a stultifying grief). In contrast, the rhythm of grief in *À la recherche* gives to Proust's novel a recursive structure in which moments of intense suffering are interspersed with periods of temporary freedom from mourning. We might characterize the latter as breathing spaces, recalling Bowie's discussion of the 'respiratory rhythm' of *À la recherche*.[46] Certainly, mourning in Proust's novel encourages a somatic, almost medical reading of its rhythm, both in the attention to the grandmother's dying breath in *Le Côté de Guermantes* (which moves from regularity to irregularity to cessation) and in the emphasis on the suffering of the protagonist's grieving heart in the aptly named episode of the 'intermittences du cœur' [intermittences of the heart] in *Sodome et Gomorrhe*. In all these cases, as long as there is rhythm, there is life, narrative and a certain form of mourning.

---

45   Julian Barnes, *Levels of Life* (London: Jonathan Cape, 2013), p. 72.
46   Bowie, *Proust Among the Stars*, p. xiv.

HENRIETTE KORTHALS ALTES

Mourning Their Mothers: Roland Barthes, Jacques Derrida and the Gift of Tears

ABSTRACT

Since the late 1990s, melancholy has been defined as an ethical gesture, reflecting the ethics of Levinas and Derrida. No longer construed as a pathological form of mourning, as the classical Freudian opposition would have it, melancholy becomes a sustained devotion to the mourned. Roland Barthes and Jacques Derrida, when mourning their respective mothers, have an ambivalent position towards melancholy: it should be embraced while avoiding the pitfalls of complacent tearful egotism. The chapter not only traces how melancholy and its acute awareness of transience takes on a positive valence and becomes tinted with joy and a heightened receptivity to the present. Fleshing out the references to both Proust and St Augustine in Barthes's *Journal de deuil* [*Mourning Diary*] and Derrida's 'Circonfession' [Circumfession], I will show how tears herald a desire for not only a literary 'conversion', when authors turn away from an abstract, ethical language to an embodied form of writing. In this context, the chapterr analyses the meaning of tears as moments of truth (aletheia for Jacques Derrida) or moments of grace (satori for Roland Barthes) that allow for communion with the mourned mother.

> C'est peut-être ça qu'on cherche à travers la vie, rien que cela, le plus grand chagrin possible pour devenir soi-même avant de mourir.
> [That is perhaps what we seek throughout life, that and nothing more, the greatest possible grief so as to become fully ourselves before dying.]
>
> Louis Ferdinand Céline, *Voyage au bout de la nuit*

'Qui écrira l'histoire des larmes?' [Who will write the history of tears?] asked Roland Barthes.[1] Crying, he remarks, is a form of sensitivity no

---

1   Roland Barthes, 'Éloge des larmes', in *Fragments d'un discours amoureux*, in *Œuvres complètes* (Paris: Seuil, 2002), V, 223; 'In Praise of Tears', in *A Lover's Discourse: Fragments*, trans. Richard Howard (London: Vintage, 2002), p. 180 (hereafter referenced in main text as *FDA* and *LV*).

longer acceptable among men, and has progressively become associated
with sentimentality. He recalls:

> Les Grecs, les gens du XVIIe siècle pleuraient beaucoup au théâtre. Saint Louis, au
> dire de Michelet, souffrait de n'avoir pas reçu le don des pleurs; une fois qu'il sentit
> les larmes couler doucement sur sa figure, elles lui semblèrent si savoureuses et très
> douces, non pas seulement au coeur mais à la bouche. (*FDA* 233)

> [The Greeks as well as our audiences of the seventeenth century cried a great deal at
> the theatre. St. Louis, according to Michelet, suffered at not having received the gift of
> tears; on the one occasion that he felt tears running gently down his face, they seemed
> to him delectable and comforting, not only to the heart but to the tongue.] (*LV* 180)

In his *Journal de deuil*, which charts the daily business of grieving for his
late mother and trying to come to terms with her loss, Barthes admits
he suffers from repeated bouts of tearfulness.[2] So does Jacques Derrida,
who in 'Circonfession', an autobiographical text that forms an anticipated
piece of mourning for his mother, confesses to a 'ritualized effusion' made
of 'prayers and tears'.[3]

Both autobiographical texts have more in common than the grieving
for their respective mothers. As the death of the mother confronts both
authors with their own mortality, they seem to have a visceral need to redefine their writing and *raison d'être* in the light of this realization. What
is more, Barthes and Derrida seem to share an ethics of mourning: they
want to invent a language that does justice to the absolute singularity of
both their respective mothers and their own grief. Roland Barthes refuses
psychoanalytical categories, preferring to talk about his *chagrin* [grief]
rather than mourning: 'mon chagrin est chaotique, erratique, ce en quoi il
résiste à l'idée courante – et psychanalytique – d'un deuil soumis au temps,
qui se dialectise, s'use' [my distress is chaotic, erratic, whereby it resists the

2   Roland Barthes, *Journal de deuil: 26 octobre 1977–15 septembre 1979*, ed. Nathalie
     Léger (Paris: Seuil/IMEC, 2009); *Mourning Diary*, trans. Richard Howard
     (London: Notting Hill Editions, 2011) (hereafter referenced in main text as *JD*
     and *MD*).
3   Jacques Derrida, *Circonfession* (Paris: Seuil, 1991); *Circumfession*, trans. Geoffrey
     Bennington (Chicago: Chicago University Press, 1993), p. 38 (hereafter both refer-
     enced in main text as *C*).

accepted – and psychoanalytic – notion of a mourning subject to time, becoming dialectical, wearing out, 'adapting'] (*JD* 81; *MD* 71). Likewise, Derrida refuses the traditional Freudian opposition between mourning, that is, the acceptance of loss in favour of a new love-object, be it symbolic or real, and its clinical counterpart, melancholia, that is, the refusal of closure. He removes melancholy from the sphere of the pathological, bringing it into the sphere of the ethical. Both Barthes and Derrida construe mourning and its aim for closure as a betrayal of the lost object and melancholy as a continued devotion to its uniqueness and, to put it in Levinasian terms, to its absolute otherness.[4] Derrida and Barthes thus find themselves submitted to two irreconcilable imperatives: a continued devotion to the mourned at the risk of refusing to let go of him or her, which they see as narcissistic self-indulgence, or that of moving on and fixing their beloved mother into a reductive memory. Derrida pithily summarizes this double-bind in 'Le Goût des larmes' [The Taste of Tears]: 'On ne devrait pas prendre goût au deuil qu'*il faut* pourtant' [One should not develop a taste for mourning, and yet mourn we *must*].[5]

The Freudian opposition between mourning and melancholia has been discarded on the basis that propounding mourning as the norm reflects a utilitarian stance. By a dialectics of sorts, mourning transforms loss into a gain, be it into a new attachment – a new love-object or a sublimated one – the affective investment into a creative act or symbolical meaning assigned to the lost love. De-pathologizing melancholy and foregrounding its ethical component, however, has now gained wide currency. 'With regard to mourning and melancholy, the predominant opinion is the following: [...] Against Freud, one should assert the conceptual and ethical primacy of melancholy.'[6] Slavoj Žižek's article 'Melancholy and the Act'

---

4   Levinas defines subjectivity as the responsibility towards the Other, an Other that is irreducible to any totalizing concept. Emmanuel Levinas, *Otherwise than Being or Beyond Essence* (Pittsburgh, PA: Duquesne University Press, 1998).

5   Jacques Derrida, *Chaque fois unique la fin du monde* (Paris: Galilée, 2001), p. 141; *The Work of Mourning* (Chicago: Chicago University Press, 2001), p. 110 (hereafter referenced in main text as *CFU* and *WM*).

6   Slavoj Žižek, 'Melancholy and the Act', *Critical Inquiry* 26/4 (2000), 657–81 (p. 658).

aims to form a cautionary tale against the rehabilitation of melancholy, in particular in the form of nostalgia. Enlisting Lacan's opposition between loss and lack, he argues that melancholy is the idealization of a lost object that did not exist in the first place.[7]

This essay will not so much go against the grain of Žižek's argument as take it sideways. I will show how both Barthes's and Derrida's texts on mourning supersede the Freudian opposition between pathological and normal mourning and how this breakdown is an ethical breakthrough. The rehabilitation of melancholy as an ethical gesture has been part of the ethical turn that has marked the humanities and in particular mourning and trauma studies. Instead, I propose to look at how Barthes's and Derrida's texts of melancholy mourning can be interpreted in the light of an 'affective turn' that attends to the body and its emotions since affect can been seen as 'what straddle two divides: between the mind and body, and between actions and passions'.[8] If Fredric Jameson has argued that postmodernism is defined by a 'waning of affect', I would argue instead that affect finds expression in multiple ways.[9] Acedia, tearfulness, depression, sadness or humour and laughter are different manifestations of melancholy. The question I want to ask is what dialectic is at play in melancholy. Since it underpins the creative process in both Barthes's *Journal de deuil* and Derrida's 'Circonfession', is there not a labour of melancholy just as there is a work of mourning? Mourning their mothers, while bringing both the critic and philosopher to the limits of language, and back to his own embodied experience and the realm of affect, also triggers a transformational process. How can we understand the tears shed by Barthes and Derrida and the desire for a 'literary' or writerly conversion that comes with it? Augustine's

7   The *object a*, i.e. is what drives desire, and is already lacking in the object we desire. The melancholy mourning fails to identify the lacking *object a*, according to Lacan and therefore clings to the lost object. For a compelling account of how object a relates to lack and loss, see Malcolm Bowie, *Lacan* (London: HarperCollins, 1991), pp. 165–78.

8   Michael Hardt, 'Foreword: What Affects Are Good For', in Patricia Ticineto Clough and Jean O'Malley Halley, eds, *The Affective Turn: Theorizing the Social* (Durham, NC: Duke University Press, 2007), pp. ix–xii (p. xi).

9   Fredric Jameson, *Postmodernism or the Cultural Logic of Late Capitalism* (Durham, NC: Duke University Press, 1991), p. 11.

Confessions and his conversion provide an obvious intertextual reference to Barthes's and Derrida's texts. Barthes indeed spoke at the Cerisy-la-Salle colloquium in 1977 of his sense of elation that comes with the prospect of self-transformation, as he was finally 'entering into the "Novel", just as one enters into religion'.[10] This chapter will tease out in what ways and to what purpose both author's literary 'conversions' are differently clad in religious vocabulary and how they may be understood as a lay spiritual practice or, to use Michel Foucault's expression, a practice of the self that is a practice that leads to self-transformation.

Melancholy as Devotional Stance

Before taking my argument further I would like to make some prefatory remarks concerning Freud's seminal essay 'Mourning and Melancholia' (1917) since it represents a classic reference for mourning and trauma studies. Freud opposes normal mourning to its pathological counterpart, melancholia, arguing that mourning is the piecemeal relinquishing of a lost love-object in favour of a substitute, real or imaginary. In contrast, the melancholy mourner is not able to redirect his investment. Freud draws a further opposition: 'Melancholia is in some way related to an object-loss which is withdrawn from consciousness, in contradistinction to mourning, in which there is nothing about loss that is unconscious.'[11] For melancholia to be overcome and transmuted into mourning, the melancholic needs to make sense of his loss. Melancholia therefore is an enigma to be solved. Furthermore Freud concludes that 'in mourning it is the world which has become poor and empty; in melancholia it is the ego itself'. The refusal to let go of the mourned is pathological because

10   Diana Knight, 'What Turns the Writer into a Great Writer?: The Conversion Narrative of Barthes's "Vita nova"'; and see *Prétexte: Roland Barthes, colloque de Cerisy*, ed. Antoine Compagnon (Paris: Union Générale d'Éditions, 1978), p. 366.

11   Sigmund Freud, 'Mourning and Melancholia' [1917], in *The Standard Edition of the Complete Psychological Works of Sigmund Freud*, ed. and trans. James Strachey, 24 vols (London: Hogarth Press, 1953–74), XIV, 237–58 (p. 254).

it betrays an inability of the mourning subject to conceive of himself without the mourned, which Freud construes as none other than a narcissistic affliction.

It should be remembered however that Freud himself progressively abandoned this binary logic when he introduced the second topic and the death drive. As a drive towards regression to an initial state and compulsion to repeat, the end and ending of mourning, like those of analysis itself, became less likely to be closure. As Alessia Ricciardi has suggested, by the time he wrote 'Analysis Terminable and Interminable' (1937), the binary opposition dissolves, thus suggesting that analysis presupposes a work of mourning now conceived as the confrontation with an enigma that will never be fully resolved.[12]

This historical reminder helps us to understand how Derrida's 'Spéculer – sur "Freud"', a deconstructive reading of *Beyond the Pleasure Principle*, allows him to coin the notion of 'mid-mourning' (*demi-deuil*). Derrida analyses at length the *fort/da* episode, that is, Freud's grandson Ernst's compulsion to repeat the game by which he would master the absence of his mother. The compulsion to repeat the gesture of throwing away the reel allows him to conclude that the temporality of mourning is not as linear as working towards closure would suggest. Derrida also rejects Abraham and Torok's opposition between incorporation, the piecemeal remembering and internalizing of the lost love-object, and introjection, the magical assimilation of it at the detriment of its otherness. Located beyond the polarization between normal and pathological mourning, *demi-deuil* or mid-mourning, is defined by the collapse between introjection and incorporation, between mourning and melancholia: 'introjection et/ou incorporation, le demi-deuil étant ici représenté par la barre entre *et et/ou ou* qui pour des raisons structurelles me paraît aussi nécessaire que nécessairement impure' [introjection and/or incorporation, mid-mourning here being represented by the bar between and/or, which for structural

---

12   Sigmund Freud, 'Analysis Terminable and Interminable' [1937], in *The Standard Edition*, XXIII, 211–55. Alessia Ricciardi, *The Ends of Mourning: Psychoanalysis, Literature, Film* (Stanford, CA: Stanford University Press, 2003), p. 34.

reasons seems to me as necessary as necessarily impure].[13] Hence, there is a new temporality of mourning based on the oscillation between intro-jection and incorporation, mourning and melancholia. This refusal to assimilate the other 'corresponds to an ethical standpoint', according to Ricciardi: 'The impossibility of successfully mourning the Other clears a space for what Derrida defines as "hauntology": a domain inhabited by the *revenants* and *arrivants* of memory.'[14] Ultimately, Derrida's double in-junction to fail to mourn and yet not to, to be melancholic and yet not to, allows him to redefine a practice of mourning and a practice of remembering that paves the way for his ethics of 'hantologie' [hauntology], according to which the subject is hospitable to the ghosts of the past with whom s/he maintains a dialogue.

One can see how Derrida's ethics of melancholy corresponds to a devotional stance. The mourner lets himself be haunted by those he mourns and this hauntedness forms a silent dialogue with the dead.[15] This ongoing conversation is also constitutive of the mourner's individu-ation, for subjectivity is always intersubjective. Beyond the framework provided by psychoanalysis, one can see how melancholia can be inter-preted as both an act of devotion and a process of self-transformation, what Foucault would call 'une pratique de soi' [a practice of the self], that is, a lay spiritual practice that is premised on the belief that the self must undergo transformations in order to access a subjective truth about oneself.[16]

---

13   Jacques Derrida, *La Carte postale* (Paris: Flammarion, 1980), p. 356; *Post Card: From Socrates to Freud and Beyond*, trans. Alan Bass (Chicago: University of Chicago Press, 1987), p. 340.

14   Ricciardi, *The Ends of Mourning*, p. 37.

15   Colin Davis, 'Derrida's Haunted Subjects', in *Haunted Subjects: Deconstruction, Psychoanalysis and the Return of the Dead* (Basingstoke: Palgrave Macmillan, 2007), pp. 128–50 (p. 146).

16   Michel Foucault, *L'Herméneutique du sujet: cours au Collège de France (1981–1982)*, ed. François Ewald, Alessandro Fontana and Frédéric Gros (Paris: Seuil & Gallimard, 2001), p. 16.

Overcoming Acedia: Barthes' 'Conversion' to Literature

In what ways is Barthes's melancholy mourning a devotional and transformative process? *Journal de deuil*, which Barthes started writing the
day after his mother died on 25 October 1977, spans a period of two
years. The entries are made of sparse annotations that record his persistent grief, his sense of bereavement or his hopes that a literary 'conversion' will lift him out of his sadness and put a term to the process
of mourning. Barthes is a melancholy mourner and from the start, he
refuses to medicalize his own mourning. 'Irritation. Non, le deuil (la
depression) est bien autre chose qu'une maladie' [No, bereavement (depression) is different from sickness] (*JD* 18; *MD* 8), he explains, later
admitting that he cannot imagine taking any medication to alleviate
his depression. 'Impossibility – indignity, actually – of entrusting to a
drug – on the pretext of depression – my suffering, as if it were a disease,
a 'possession' – an alienation (something that estranges you) – whereas
it's an essential intimate part of yourself' (*MD* 163). The atypical notion
of 'indignity' gives Barthes's rejection of medication both a moral and
ascetic dimension. Not only does his grief have a positive valence; it also
defines him most intimately.

In the first six months covered by the diary, he admits to a state of
despondency, an ennui, a lack of interest in all his habitual pursuits, be
they professional or intellectual, social or erotic. If common consensus
holds that 'time soothes mourning', Barthes's experience goes against the
grain: 'Non le Temps ne fait rien passer; il fait seulement passer l'émotivité
du deuil' [No, Time makes nothing happen; it merely makes the *emotivity* of mourning pass] (*JD* 111; *MD* 101). By his own account, he suffers
from depression and is stuck in a mourning process that does not seem to
evolve. There is no gradual dissolution of his attachment to his mother and
Barthes cannot stand the idea of any substitute love: 'le trait commun de
mes dépressions [...]: que je ne supporte pas ce que je pourrais prendre
pour une substitution de mam' [the common feature of my depressions
would be this: (...) that I cannot bear what is on offer as a *substitute* for
maman] (*JD* 206; *MD* 193).

Barthes's melancholy also seems to stem from the inexpressible nature of his grief. Time and again Barthes questions the limits of narrative: 'true mourning [is] not susceptible to any narrative dialectic' (*MD* 50). In that respect, his experience finds resonance with Julia Kristeva's definition of melancholy. In *Soleil Noir*, she equates the capacity to mourn, and thus to avoid melancholy, with 'la capacité imaginaire de l'homme occidental [...] de transférer du sens au lieu même où il s'est perdu dans la mort et/ ou dans le non-sens' ['the capability to transfer meaning to the very place where it is lost to death and non-meaning'], this capability having long been entrusted to Christian narrative.[17] For her, the melancholy subject fails to work through and give meaning to loss, acting out his/her helplessness in sadness. Sadness is the mood associated with melancholy, and moods pertain to the realm of affect.[18] As affects are situated at the crossroads of the body and language, 'on the frontier between animality and symbol formation', they are irreducible to verbal or other coded expression.[19] They correspond to bodily encrypted energy that seeks to transmute into something else. She therefore proposes that creativity, and literature in particular, is: 'cette aventure du corps et des signes qui porte témoignage de l'affect' [that adventure of the body and signs that bears witness to affect].[20] Thus the melancholy mourner suffers from an inability to find either a meaningful narrative that would make sense of his or her loss or an outlet for affects impossible to articulate in language. With melancholy, grief does not find an outlet in sublimation. Suffering is compared to 'une pierre (à mon cou, au fond de moi)' [a stone ... around my neck, deep inside me] (*JD* 117; *MD* 106). Barthes thus expresses the very embodied nature of his grief, the downward pull of physical pain that resists transmuting into narrative.

His repeated bouts of tearfulness reflect that inability to transform grief and bodily pain into a meaningful narrative. In that respect, Barthes's fear lest literature be no longer consoling is telling: 'La dépression viendra quand,

17   Julia Kristeva, *Soleil noir: dépression et mélancolie* (Paris: Gallimard, 1982), p. 115; *Black Sun: Depression and Melancholia*, trans. Leon S. Roudiez (New York: Columbia University Press, 1989), p. 103.

18   Kristeva, *Soleil noir*; *Black Sun*, ibid.

19   Ibid., p. 24; *Black Sun*, p. 22.

20   Ibid., p. 32; p. 22.

du fond du chagrin, je ne pourrais même pas me raccrocher à l'écriture' [Depression comes when, in the depths of despair, I cannot manage to save myself by my attachment to writing] (*JD* 72; *MD* 62). And yet, even in the depth of sorrow, he still places his hope in literature, expecting writing to be a consoling and constructive process, which, to use his own words, would 'dialecticize the process of mourning' (*MD* 81). Looking forward to writing his book on photography, Barthes writes, 'Croyance et, semble-t-il, vérification que l'écriture transforme en moi les "stases" de l'affect, dialectise les "crises"' [Belief, and apparently, verification that writing transforms for me the various 'stases' of affect, dialectizes my 'crises'] (*JD* 115; *MD* 105). Barthes hopes that writing, besides providing a narrative that makes sense of the loss of his mother, will transform, affect and alleviate what he calls crises of grief. Barthes repeatedly states how he is in search of an art form that would do justice both to the singularity of his mother and the unique quality of his own grief: 'Je ne puis supporter qu'on réduise – qu'on généralise – Kierkegaard – mon chagrin: c'est comme si on me le volait' [I can't endure seeing my suffering being reduced – being generalized: it's as if it were being stolen from me] (*JD* 82; *MD* 71). His grief represents the ultimate vestige of the loving bond that he had with his mother and to be robbed of it would imply her second death.

Tellingly, Barthes repeatedly uses a medieval Latin religious term *acedia* to qualify his grief:

> Je n'abandonne aucun de mes égoismes, de mes petits attachements, je continue sans cesse à me préférer, mais encore je n'arrive pas à investir amoureusement en un être; tous me sont un peu indifférents, même les plus chers. J'éprouve – et c'est dur la « sécheresse de cœur » – l'acédie. (*JD* 129)

> [Not only do I abandon none of my egoisms, my little attachments, I continue to put myself first, to prefer myself at every turn, unable to invest lovingly in any other being; it is they who are indifferent to me, even the dearest among them. I suffer – and this is truly painful – hardness of heart – acedia.]. (*MD* 118)

In *Comment vivre ensemble* [*How to Live Together*], the seminar series he gave the year his mother was dying, he recalls how *acedia* is an affliction from which medieval monks living as hermits were suffering. It is a loss of faith, an *ennui*, a *tedium vitae*, a general loss of interest in others. In that respect, it is telling that he feels guilty over his incapacity to imitate his mother's kindness and 'generosity' as a homage to her: 'Je croyais, elle disparue, que je sublimerais cette disparition par une sorte de perfection de "bonté", l'abandon de toute mesquinerie, de toute jalousie, de tout narcissisme. Et je deviens de moins en moins "noble", "généreux" ' [I had supposed that once she was gone I would sublimate her absence by a sort of perfected 'kindness', the surrender of all nastiness, jealousy, narcissism. Yet I am becoming less and less 'noble', 'generous'] (*JD* 102; *MD* 92).

Barthes's desire to find a new genre of writing that would do justice to the singularity of his mother and his own grief, and thus sever the cycle of melancholy, is couched in spiritual terms. During a vacation in Morocco, on 15 April 1978, Barthes experiences an epiphany, what he calls, using a Buddhist concept, a satori, an illumination comparable to the one experienced at the end of Proust's *À la recherche du temps perdu*.[21] 'Une *vita nova*, comme un geste radical (discontinuer – nécessité de discontinuer ce qui marchait avant sur sa lancée)' [Vita nova, as a radical gesture: (discontinuous – necessity of discontinuing what previously continued on its own momentum)] (*JD* 84; *MD* 74). In *La Préparation du roman*, Barthes further defines this moment as no less than 'a "literary" conversion', which has been compared with that of Augustine.[22]

In 'Longtemps je me suis couché de bonne heure', Barthes associates this 'Vita nova' with a new style of writing, his 'Roman' [Novel], which would, like Proust's *À la recherche*, form a hybrid genre partaking both of fiction and essay, would be obliquely autobiographical yet with a general impersonal scope, and affect-driven yet avoiding sentimentalism. If his novel 'Vita nova' never developed beyond a projected outline because of Barthes's premature death, *La Chambre claire* [*Camera Lucida*] comes closest to embodying that hybrid genre.[23] The diary evokes how Barthes

21   Roland Barthes, *The Preparation of the Novel*, trans. Kate Briggs and ed. Nathalie Léger (New York: Columbia University Press, 2003), p. 8.

22   Ibid. Eric Marty, *Roland Barthes, la littérature et le droit à la mort* (Paris: Seuil, 2010), pp. 44–6. Dominique Carlat, *Témoins de l'inactuel: quatre écrivains contemporains face au deuil* (Paris: José Corti, 2007), pp. 96–100.

23   Roland Barthes, *La Chambre claire* (Paris: Gallimard & Seuil, 1980) (hereafter referenced in main text as *CC*); *Camera Lucida: Reflections on Photography*, trans. Richard Howard (London: Jonathan Cape, 1981) (hereafter referenced in main text as *CL*).

stakes his hopes high on this essay on photography, which also forms an oblique piece of mourning for his mother. Indeed *La Chambre claire* offers consolations of sorts. The Winter Garden photograph depicting his mother as a young child has the emotional power of Proust's *moments bienheureux*: it elicits a satori, which allows for an imaginary reunion with the mother. The photograph, thus, breaks the cycle of melancholy and ultimately can 'transform(s) his grief into mourning' (*CL* 90). Yves Hersant has compellingly shown how *Camera Lucida* subverts the opposition between a liberating work of mourning and unproductive melancholy, 'opening instead an *interminable process of mourning* and resulting in *creative melancholy*'.[24] That melancholy is productive can also be seen in the diary, when Barthes explains that his inconsolable grief makes him happy. His melancholy diary corresponds to a devotional gesture in which he dedicates all his thoughts to his mother and, like Derrida's mid-mourning, it is 'in-fini' and based on a positive identification with his mother. He invokes Proust's letter to André Baunier, written after the death of his mother, by way of saying that consolation may lie in the acceptance that mourning and remembering will never end and will only intensify love:

> Soyez inerte, attendez que la force incompréhensible […] qui vous a brisé, vous relève un peu […]. Dites-vous cela aussi car c'est une douceur de savoir qu'on n'aimera jamais moins, qu'on ne se consolera jamais, qu'on se souviendra de plus en plus. (*JD* 183)

> [Let yourself be inert, wait till the incomprehensible power […] that has broken you restores you a little […]. Tell yourself this, too, for it is a kind of pleasure to know that you will never love less, that you will never be consoled, that you will constantly remember more and more.] (*MD* 170–1)

And Barthes continues asserting the next day that he endorses his sadness: 'Tout m'est insupportable qui m'empêche d'habiter mon chagrin' [Anything that keeps me from living in my suffering is unbearable to me] (*JD* 185; *MD* 174). Melancholy grief, as a devotional and ethical stance,

---

24   Yves Hersant, 'Une sorte de mélancolie: notule sur *La Chambre claire* in Roland Barthes', in M. Di Maio, ed., *Teoria e scrittura*, Pubblicazioni dell'Università di Salerno 36 (Naples: *Edizioni Scientifiche Italiane*, 1992), pp. 49–58 (p. 4, my translation).

has its own transformational powers and leads to a more profound love of his mother. This devotional stance also translates into heightened identification with the mother, the will to imitate her and live like her. In that respect, tears have a sweet taste, as Barthes tellingly talks about his 'feminine emotivity'. Tearfulness, giving in to emotion and affect, brings him closer to the feminine and his mother. In that, tears bring temporary relief from his suffering: the transformation of pain grief into tears alleviates it.

Jacques Derrida's Impossible Confessions: Tears, Prayers and the Search for Embodied Writing

'Circonfession', Jacques Derrida's autobiographical text, forms a piece of anticipated mourning for his mother. Written between January 1989 and April 1990, it covers her protracted agony when she was suffering from terminal Alzheimer's. 'Circonfession' echoes many of Barthes's preoccupations concerning the ethical and emotional demands of mourning as well as the deconstruction of autobiographical writing. If Barthes described his autobiographical project as 'the book of [the] resistances to [his] own ideas' by way of saying that autobiographical unity is an illusion, Derrida is sceptical about the act of confessing and of attaining to a subjective truth.[25] At best, the title suggests, one can circle around it through oblique self-expression. He does so by recollecting the splintered episodes of his mother's life that form *biographèmes* of sorts, by identifying with episodes of Augustine's *Confessions*, by weaving in fragments of his own unpublished manuscript on circumcision. Lastly, the unusual format of 'Circonfession' suggests that autobiography is always written together with or against another text and emerges from this dialectic between self and other: Derrida's text occupies a seemingly ancillary position as it is printed under what he calls 'Derridabase', Geoffrey Bennington's critical interpretation of Derrida's work. Derrida's overt aim is thus to give the lie

---

25 *Roland Barthes by Roland Barthes*, trans. Richard Howard (New York: Farrar, Strauss & Giroux, 1977), p. 119.

to Bennington's abstract framework. 'Je ne suis, je ne pense, je ne retrouve mes esprits, car j'en ai plus d'un qui se partagent mon corps, qu'à multiplier en moi les contre-exemples et les contre-vérités que je suis' [There are more than one sharing my body multiplying in me the counterexamples and the countertruths that are in me] (*C* 236; 254), he writes, by way of saying that his own multiple selves remain secret and intractable even to himself.

What is more, just as Barthes is in a quest for a new genre of writing that would coincide 'absolument avec un arrachement émotif, un cri; à même le corps du lecteur qui vit' [literature coincides with an emotional wrench, a cry; a direct emanation of the reader's body, who experiences by proxy the faraway separation from the loved one, a form of transcendence], Derrida is in search of an affective, physical language.[26] 'Et toujours je rêve d'une plume qui soit seringue' [I always dream of a pen that would be a syringe] (*C* 13; 12) and, once the right vein found, 'no more toil, no more responsibility'. He thus dreams of a form of writing that would take on a life of his own. The effusion of blood forms a fantasy image of an inner self that has become externalized, tangible in 'le pouls d'une phrase contournante' [the pulse of an encircling phrase] (*C* 17; 15), of a form of writing that would carry not only his life story, his identity (biography) and the stuff and beat of his physical existence (zoography). It is as if the dying body of his aging mother not only points him to his own mortality but also triggers a renewed awareness of her and his own embodied presence in the world.

The body in all its varied states pervades the philosopher's autobiographical discourse: the dying mother whom he feeds like a child and who inadvertently exposed herself naked (*C* 24); Derrida's blood that carries life through his veins and beats to the unique pulse of his body; the blood of his circumcised sex and the clipped foreskin that bears *en creux* both his Jewish identity and the unique signature of his own lineage; Derrida nursing his mother, feeding her, turning her over, caressing, being confronted with her naked vulnerability. Her mortal body prompts him to

---

26　Roland Barthes, 'Longtemps je me suis couché de bonne heure', in *Le Bruissement de la langue* (Paris: Seuil, 1982), pp. 313–25 (p. 323; my translation).

write in hyper-affective mode. 'Car jamais l'écorché vif que je suis n'aura ainsi écrit' [Never will the man flayed alive that I am have written like this] (*C* 192; 206), he explains. And the very unpredictability of her death, albeit imminent, is what gives shape to his writing and 'give[s] it its form and its rhythm' (*C* 207): 'la mort de ma mère [...] viendrait sculpter l'écriture du dehors, lui donner sa forme et son rythme depuis une interruption incalculable' (*C* 192). His mother's imminent death also forces him to reconsider his own identity, all the more so because Alzheimer's has left her incapable of recognizing him: 'J'écris ici *pour* ma mère, [...] pour une mère vivante qui ne reconnaît pas son fils' [I am writing *for* my mother [...] who does not recognize her son] (*C* 26–7; 25). The italicized *pour* becomes the operative word with multiple connotations. The text – a splintered but lively portrait of his mother – is an address, a dedication and a homage to his mother.

The dying mother, who is ailing beyond recognition, also calls into question Derrida's own fragile identity, as her gaze, in which he has always existed, no longer recognizes him, is soon to be lost to death. This beckons him to reconsider his cultural inheritance, in particular his ambiguous Jewish roots, as he is a Jew without practicing Judaism, just as he is French and Francophone but as an outsider from his native Algeria. The question of mourning is inevitably bound up with both his mother's and his own identity for, Derrida argues, 'we are only ever ourselves from that place within us where the other, the mortal other, resonates'. Subjectivity for Derrida is inherently intersubjective; we exist in relation to others we cannot fully comprehend. This unknowable otherness we mourn as something unattainable during life and cherish upon the loved one's death or in anticipation of it, in 'la possibilité anticipée d'une mort' [the anticipated possibility of a death] to use Derrida's words.[27] The anticipation of the other's death heightens the awareness that others are unknowable. Yet, his mother's death also sends him back to his own mortality. Knowing he is 'the last Jew' ('le dernier juif') of his lineage, his writing is a conscious play of self-effacement: 'et je cherche à me désintéresser de moi pour me

---

27   Jacques Derrida, *Mémoires -Pour Paul de Man* (Paris : Galilée, 1988), p. 54; Jacques Derrida, *Mémoires -For Paul de Man* (New York : Columbia University Press, 1986), trans. Cecil Lindsay and Jonathan Culler, p. 34.

soustraire à la mort en faisant que peu à peu le "je" auquel la mort est censée arriver soit parti' [and I am trying to disinterest myself from myself to withdraw from death by making the 'I', to whom death is supposed to happen, gradually go away, no, to be destroyed before death come to meet it] (*C* 178; 190). Derrida's practices of self-effacement, through letting Augustine speak in his stead, through not revealing the personal secret that the confessional genre has the reader expect, thus form a game of hide-and-seek with death, as Derrida is well aware of the 'intense rapport à la survivance qu'est l'écriture' [intense relation to survival that writing is] (*C* 179; 191).

Derrida recalls how on 24 December 1988, his mother utters 'I want to kill myself', an utterance which, he claims, could only be his own, and represents his very own secret, a secret that Bennington's 'Derridabase' could never have guessed. Derrida admits to a depressive streak in himself. According to his mother he was a child 'qui ne pleure pour rien' (*C* 40) and 'Circonfession' also mentions the 'great depression' he suffered during his spell as a young teacher in Le Mans in 1960. 'J'ai envie de me tuer' [I want to kill myself] may be construed as a suicidal ideation yet not a suicidal impulse. This statement does not so much express a will to put an end to his life as an acute awareness of his own mortality, which takes on a new intensity with the imminent death of his mother. As Derrida explains, 'le retour incessant du "j'ai envie de me tuer" dit moins le désir de mettre fin à ma vie qu'une sorte de compulsion à doubler chaque seconde, comme une voiture l'autre' [a compulsion to overtake each second, like one car overtaking another] (*C* 40; 39). Pitting each second against his own death, Derrida associates melancholy with a fiction in which he overtakes each second by way of trumping transience and the fleeting nature of time, or seeing it with hindsight from the perspective of his own disappearance. Hence melancholy has a temporality of its own – that of fastness and retrospection from the perspective of death – which redefines it: it is tinged with the exhilaration of a heightened sense of transience, the pleasurable awareness that the present always already becomes the past.

This sensitivity to his own transience and mortality culminates when he anticipates his own sons mourning his death: 'Je me vois mourir, je me vois mort coupé de vous en vos mémoires que j'aime et je pleure comme mes propres enfants au bord de ma tombe' [I see myself dying [...] I weep like my own children at the edge of my grave, I weep not only for my children, but for all my children] (*C* 40/40). The melancholy feeling arises with that capacity to disappear and envisage one's life from the perspective of the loved ones who will mourn Derrida. This melancholy dissolution of the subject is thus in turn associated with the exhilaration of living life to the full, from the perspective of all his future mourners. And ultimately, this melancholy position is a joyful acceptance of his own transience. For Derrida's capacity for identification with his mother and sons is a disappearing act of sorts that is tinted with joy too and ultimately allows him to accept his own death, which he writes up as a confession to his reader Geoffrey Bennington:

> Je veux une seule chose me perdre dans l'orchestre que je formerais avec mes fils guérir bénir et séduire le monde en jouant divinement avec mes fils, produire avec eux l'extase musicale du monde, leur création, j'accepterai de mourir si c'est la descendre lentement, oui, jusqu'au fond de cette musique bien-aimée. (*C* 194)

> [I want one thing only, and that is to lose myself in the orchestra that I would form with my sons, heal, bless and seduce the whole world by playing divinely with my sons, producing with them the world's ecstasy, *their* creation, I will accept dying if dying is sinking slowly, yes, into the bottom of this beloved music.] (*C* 208)

Derrida's ultimate lyrical acceptance of his own death is described here as an orchestral moment where his own voice merges with that of his sons.

The Gift of Tears

Melancholy thus has variegated meanings: for Derrida, it corresponds to a heightened awareness of transience and a will to live life to the full; for Barthes, melancholy is associated with *acedia*, but also the suffering tinted with pleasure of devoting himself to his mother. For both, tears are no doubt the physiological expression of grief and melancholy, of affect that cannot find its way into words or narrative. What I want to examine is the ways in which tears herald a transformative process, since both in *Journal de deuil* and 'Circonfession', tears, prayers and a conversion of sorts go hand in hand.

Barthes, we have seen, is beset with melancholy, an inability to love that he calls *acedia* and defines as 'dryness of heart' ('sécheresse du coeur') (*JD* 190). Albeit translated as 'hardness of heart' (*MD* 118), 'dryness', Barthes's original choice of words, suggests that tears may well be able to counter *acedia*, restoring movement and flow into melancholy, a mood associated with paralysis. Both texts further capture a pivotal moment of conversion that refers, implicitly for Barthes and explicitly for Derrida, to Augustine. For Derrida, his *Confessions* are quintessentially 'the book of tears', since Augustine asks God 'why tears are so sweet to those in misery (*cur fluctus dulcis sit miseris*)?'.[28] As historian Piroska Nagy has foregrounded, Augustine's spiritual journey towards conversion is paved with tears, from pagan to Christian.[29] There are the pagan tears of compassion and identification; the tears his mother sheds over her son's sins and which Augustine sees as the embodiment of divine grace – tears being the intercessors between his mother and God. And finally there are the sweet tears that flow at the moment of his conversion when he parts with the secular pleasures of the world. The 'gift of tears' for him represents a moment of grace, of receptivity to the divine, which in turns leads towards conversion and faith. Nagy thus argues that what makes Augustine so compelling to the secular reader is that he places affectivity at the heart of human experience, thus overcoming the duality between body and soul, despite his conversion to Christianity.

For Augustine, grieving his dying mother is a key experience towards conversion. Likewise, for Barthes and Derrida, the tears of grief and mourning are a transformational process that inspires them to find renewed affective forms of writing. We have seen how Barthes's projected 'Novel' holds the promise of lifting him out of melancholy: 'Seule, par bouffées, l'image de l'écriture comme "chose qui fait envie", havre, "salut", bref "amour", joie suppose que la *dévote* sincère a les mêmes mouvements vers son "Dieu"' [Only, in snatches, the image of writing as 'something

28   Jacques Derrida, *Mémoires d'aveugles: l'autoportrait et autres ruines* (Paris: Réunion des musées nationaux, 1991); *Memoirs for the Blind: The Self-portrait and Other Ruins*, trans. Pascale-Anne Brault and Michael Naas (Chicago: Chicago University Press, 1993), p. 126 (hereafter referenced in main text as *MA* and *MB*).
29   Piroska Nagy, *Le Don des larmes* (Paris: Albin Michel, 2000), pp. 115–23.

desirable', haven, 'salvation', hope, in short, 'love', joy. I imagine a sincerely devout woman has the same impulses towards her God] (*JD* 69; *MD* 59). Writing thus holds the promise of a 'salvation' that is duly bracketed off by way of stripping it of its religious connotation. Comparing himself with a devout woman implicitly associates religion and literature as well as the writer and the feminine. He thus reasserts his identification with his mother, all the more so as he repeatedly associates his mother with non-dogmatic Christianity. Derrida's expectations of writing are no less ambitious:

> Si ce livre ne me transforme pas de fond en comble, s'il ne me donne pas le sourire divin devant la mort, la mienne et celle des aimés, s'il ne m'aide pas à aimer plus encore la vie, il aura échoué. (*C* 79)

> [If this 'book' does not transform me through and through, if it does not give me a divine smile in the face of death, my own and that of loved ones, if it does not help me to love life even more, it will have failed, whatever signs there may be of its success.] (*C* 77)

Writing is a transformational process or a practice of the self, to use Foucault's terminology. And ultimately, just as for Barthes, writing is a way to trump death with a 'sourire divin' [divine smile] and enhanced love of life.

As Bruno Clément remarks, prayers and tears are consubstantially bound for Derrida, just as they were for Augustine. Tears express a confused intuitive knowledge of a truth that cannot be pinned down, whereas a prayer gives meaning to it. 'As for the prayer, it is an address, it knows its recipient, it is also the truth, it gives tears a meaning that so far had remained unknown.'[30] Derrida's confession is impossible, in part because self-knowledge is never fully attainable in his view: 'Et pleurant l'inavouable vérité, autrement dit, vous aurez fini par comprendre, qu'une confession n'a rien à voir avec la vérité' [Weeping for the unavowable truth, in other words, you will have understood in the end, that a confession has nothing to do with the truth] (*C* 103; 107). Hence, Derrida continues to explain, a confession is not so much constative as performative; it brings about

---

30 Bruno Clément, *L'Invention du commentaire: Augustin, Jacques Derrida* (Paris: Presses Universitaires de France, 2000), p. 3.

change, a conversion, when the subject asks for forgiveness, repents, 'that is to improve, to transform my hatred into love, to transform myself, and to do so out of love. Confession is not a matter of knowledge, it is not a matter of making the other know what happened, but a matter of changing oneself, of transforming oneself. That's perhaps what St Augustine calls "making the truth". Not to *tell* the truth.'[31]

For each, this transformational process is triggered as they care for their dying mother. Both Derrida's and Barthes's mothers evoke the figure of the *pietà*, the embodiment of compassion who suffers for her dying son. But the *pietà* here would be of a special kind: it would point to the caring son but also the mother's compassion for her son's grief as he mourns her anticipated death. Derrida's mother lost two sons and Jackie has grown up with the guilt of knowing he is a substitute for the brother who died just a few months before he was born. Weeping is a transformative experience in that it reveals the capacity to identify with and be another. He cries out tears of compassion that are his own as much as his mother's: ' "je pleure sur moi" – mais comme un autre, un autre pleuré par un autre pleurant, je pleure depuis ma mère sur l'enfant dont je suis le substitut' ['I'm crying over myself' – but like another, another wept over by another weeper, I weep from my mother the child whose substitute I am] (*C* 114; 119). Similarly, Henriette Barthes is depicted as the ultimate figure of selflessness. 'That's what Sanctity is' (*MD* 209), he says about her. Her dying words, 'Mon Roland! Mon Roland!', reflect her compassion for her son's suffering in anticipation of her death. It is this benevolence and kindness mentioned earlier that he will seek to emulate as a way to overcome his grief.

Tears not only bring about a transformational process, they also express the unsayable of grief and loss. In his obituary for Jean-François Lyotard, Derrida conveys how he is lost for words, and how the unthinkable dimension of death finds only expression in tears: 'celui dont l'absence même me restera à jamais impensable: l'impensable même au fond des larmes', the absence of his dear friend 'will remain for me, I am certain, forever

---

31   Jacques Derrida, 'Composing « Circumfession »', in J. D. Caputo and Michael J. Scanlon, eds, *Augustine and Postmodernism: Confessions and Circumfession* (Bloomington: Indiana University Press, 2005), pp. 19–27 (p. 23).

unthinkable: the unthinkable itself in the depth of tears' (*CFU* 255; *WM* 214). And in *Mémoires d'aveugle*, Derrida then further extrapolates that tears reveal the true essence of the eye, that is, to weep rather than to see:

> Au moment même où elles voilent la vue, les larmes dévoileraient le propre de l'œil. Ce qu'elles font jaillir hors de l'oubli où le regard la garde en réserve, ce ne serait rien de moins que l'*aletheia*, la vérité des yeux dont elle révèleraient ainsi la destination suprême: avoir en vue l'imploration plutôt que la vision, adresser la prière, l'amour, la joie, la tristesse plutôt que le regard. Avant même d'illuminer, la révélation est le moment des 'pleurs de joie'. (*MA* 125)

> [For at the very moment they veil sight, tears would unveil what is proper to the eye. And what they cause to surge up out of forgetfulness [...] would be nothing less than *aletheia*, the truth of the eyes [...]: to have imploration rather than vision in sight, to address prayer, love, joy or sadness rather than a look or gaze. Even before it illuminates, revelation is the moment of the 'tears of joy'.] (*MB* 126)

When tears surge and cover the eyeball, this troubled moment of vision allows for a moment of truth resurrected from oblivion. Drawing on the notion of *aletheia*, he reactivates not only its pre-Socratic acceptation in order to exp n ress that tears reveal what was consigned to oblivion but also its Heideggerian connotation in order to foreground how tears are a moment of revelation and sense-making. Playing with *pleurs* and its cognate *implorer*, the supreme destination of eyes and tears becomes a prayer mixed with sadness and joy addressed to the loved and mourned. Derrida thus does away with the prevalent conception that sight is quintessentially the seat of knowledge; tears, to the contrary, lead to a moment of silent, apophatic knowledge and communion with the other, which Derrida summarizes with Andrew Marwell's line of poetry: 'Those weeping eyes, those seeing tears'. For Barthes too, tears send 'le plus vrai des messages, celui de mon corps, non celui de la langue' [the 'truest' of messages, that of my body, not that of my speech], making the body the ultimate seat of a subjective truth. Calling upon Schubert's in 'Praise of Tears', he foregrounds their affective power: ' "Words what are they? One tear will say more than all of them" '. What's more, if the crying subject accepted 'de retrouver le corps enfant' [accepts rediscovering the infant body], as he argued, Barthes's outbursts of tears may well be a way to re-enact and perpetuate the bond with his mother (*FDA* 225, 223; *LV* 182, 180).

One instantiation of how tears are a moment of revelation can be found in Barthes's *Journal de deuil*, when he is overwhelmed by one of the pictures representing his mother: 'Ce matin à grand peine, reprenant les photos, bouleversé par une où mam., petite fille, douce, discrete à côté de Philippe Binger (Jardin d'hiver de Chennevières) Je pleure. Pas même l'envie de me suicider' [This morning, painfully returning to the photographs, overwhelmed by one in which *maman*, a gentle discreet little girl beside Philippe Binger (the Winter Garden of Chennevières, 1898). I weep. Not even the desire to commit suicide] (*JD* 155; *MD* 143). A few days before, Barthes relates how, visiting Saint-Sulpice, he has an 'instinctive "prayer"': he prays that he will finish *La Chambre claire*, let go of 'childish Desire', that is, his egoism, and reach contentment: 'Un jour s'asseoir au même endroit, fermer les yeux et ne rien demander. Nietsche: ne pas prier, bénir' [to sit in the same place, to close my eyes and ask for nothing … Nietzsche: not to pray, to bless. It is not to this that mourning should lead to?] (*JD* 148; *MD* 136). Being able to bless would thus be the end of mourning.

If we read these two episodes against the description of the 'Winter Photograph' in *Camera Lucida* when the photograph elicits a satori, that is the Buddhist term for a wordless revelation, Barthes's tears and prayers acquire new meaning. Barthes indeed reflected how the *punctum*, the detail that is subjectively poignant to the viewer, represents 'une sorte de hors-champ subtil, comme si l'image lançait le désir au-delà de ce qu'elle donne à voir' [propels his desire, and launches him into a 'subtle beyond' of what the picture represents] (*CC* 93; *CL* 59). The Winter Garden picture, by the same token, not only reveals the true essence of his mother; it elicits a sudden awakening, 'un *satori* où les mots défaillent' [in which words fail] (*CC* 168; *CL* 109). And more importantly, the Winter Garden picture elicits on several occasions a moment of 'grace' or an 'act of grace' as the mother's singular essence is revealed by the *punctum*.

Tears then allow him to capture the true essence of his mother and commemorate her silently. But the tears shed also elicit a moment of communion:

j'entrais follement dans le spectacle, dans l'image, entourant de mes bras ce qui est mort, ce qui va mourir, comme le fit Nietzsche, lorsque le 3 janvier 1889, il se jeta en pleurant au cou d'un cheval martyrisé: devenu fou pour cause de Pitié. (*CC* 179)

[I entered crazily into the spectacle, into the image, taking into my arms what is dead, what is going to die, as Nietzsche did when, as Podach tells us, on January 3, 1889, he threw himself in tears on the neck of a beaten horse: gone mad for Pity's sake.] (*CL* 117)

Tears allow Barthes to see beyond the materiality of the picture, embrace the dead, thus accomplishing his own Orphic quest. Barthes and Derrida would agree that the eye comes into its own essence when tears reveal a subjective emotional truth consigned to oblivion: repressed pathos, pity, the essence of a loved one, a *je ne sais quoi* that cannot be captured by words. As Emma Mason has compellingly shown, tears, like the photographic *punctum*, trigger what she coins 'punctive grace', that is, a quasi-religious moment that inspires a will to change and overcome melancholy grief.[32] Mason's religious comparison has the merit of underlining the emotional power of tears and the conversion they herald, that is, the renewed capacity to hope, write and love again. Grace, Mason argues, is a temporary relief from suffering.[33] The believer is touched by divine intervention that allows for transformation, redemption and conversion in the believer. Compunction, the realization of guilt and the will to change, she further shows, is also a moment of grace for which tears are the expression: it is the awakening to the pleasure of acting on behalf of something greater than oneself. For Barthes and Derrida, the identification with his dying mother, whether we call it pity or compassion, triggers such a moment of grace and the will to turn to literature as an outlet for emotive embodied writing.

For Barthes this literary conversion translated into the writing of *Camera Lucida*. Whether it triggered a renewed capacity to love – the sombre last word of his diary would suggest otherwise? – is difficult to assess given Barthes's premature death and perhaps his 'desire for the novel', just

32   Emma Mason, 'Punctive Grace: Reading Religion in Barthes' *Mourning Diary*', *Textual Practice* 30/2 (2016), 327–43.

33   Ibid., p. 327.

as his melancholy mourning, was submitted to the same 'intermittences' as we find in *À la recherche*.[34] As for Derrida, his literary 'conversion' towards 'creative' and autobiographical writing is patent in 'Circonfession'. What's more, the address he asked his son to read at his funeral seems to point to an appeased experience of grief, melancholy and mourning, as it points to a renewed merging of generations and their voices. Like Roland Barthes imitating Nietzsche, he asks his son to 'bless' everyone, to implore everyone not to be sad. 'Préférez toujours la vie et affirmez sans cesse la survie … Je vous aime et vous souris d'où que je sois' [Do always prefer life and continue to assert the afterlife. I love you and smile at you from wherever I am].[35] And thus Derrida, the advocate of mid-mourning, ultimately finds consolation in such imaginative afterlife.

34   On the presence of Proust in *Mourning Diary* see Adam Watt, 'Reading Proust in Barthes's *Journal de deuil*', *Nottingham French Studies* 53/1 (2014), 102–12.
35   *Derridex: index des termes de l'œuvre de Jacques Derrida* <https://www.idixa.net/Pixa/pagixa-0505151017.html> [accessed 7 April 2020] (my translation).

KHALID LYAMLAHY

With Barthes and Derrida in 'the Margins of a Funereal Song': The Poetics of Maternal Mourning in the Work of Abdelkébir Khatibi

ABSTRACT

In *Par-dessus l'épaule* [*Over the Shoulder*] (1988), a composite work by Moroccan writer and intellectual Abdelkébir Khatibi, the section entitled 'Cendres et reliques' [Ashes and Relics] represents an attempt to come to terms with the grief for his mother through a fragmented and dynamic act of writing. By reading this section alongside Roland Barthes's *Journal de deuil* [*Mourning Diary*] and Jacques Derrida's 'Circonfession' [Circumfession], this essay demonstrates that writing the loss of the mother leads Khatibi, following these two authors he knew very well and whose works paralleled and shared affinities with his own, to a quest for a form of writing anchored in the poetics of the fragment. More than a simple healing or overcoming of a personal trauma, Khatibi's 'Ashes and Relics' uses transcription, translation and notation as a way to displace the writing of mourning towards the margins, where a counter-discourse opposes the *doxa* of mourning in its anticipation of loss, its refusal of melancholy and its rejection of narrative unity in favour of the open-ended shattering and regeneration of fragments.

In 'Circonfession', written between January 1989 and April 1990, Jacques Derrida evokes the remorse and guilt he feels at the idea of 'publier [la] fin' [publishing [the] end] of his dying mother, 'd'en exhiber les derniers souffles et pis encore, à des fins que d'aucuns pourraient juger littéraires' [of exposing her last breaths and worse still, of doing so for ends some could see as literary].[1] How can one write the death of a loved one without facing this ambivalent emotion which is almost inevitable in any

---

1   Jacques Derrida, 'Circonfession', in Jacques Derrida and Geoffrey Bennington, *Jacques Derrida* (Paris: Seuil, 1991), p. 38 (hereafter referenced in main text as *C*). Translations of French quotations are by Sara-Louise Cooper throughout, unless otherwise stated.

narration of mourning? How can one anticipate or prepare oneself for this death and then write in the wake of the enduring pain it causes? How to translate the 'deuil primaire et fondateur' [primary and foundational loss] which is the loss of the mother?[2]

Any reading of a mourning text requires taking into account this irreducible tension between the uniqueness or particularity of the loss and the transmission or generalization of its meaning, and this is probably all the more the case when the death of a parent or loved one is at stake. In another text written after the death of Roland Barthes, Derrida comments on the way Barthes analyses the death of his mother in *La Chambre claire* [*Camera Lucida*] (1980), referring to Barthes's work as simultaneously 'irremplaçable' [irreplaceable] and as carrying 'une force métonymique [qui] peut assurer encore une certaine généralité du discours, l'offrir à l'analyse, en proposer les concepts à une utilisation quasi instrumentale' [a metonymic force [which] can continue to assure a certain generality to the discourse and offer it to analysis by submitting its concepts to a quasi-instrumental use].[3] The mourning for Barthes's mother is the site of an insurmountable paradox: it does not open on to any possibility of repetition and yet at the same time is one of the most universal experiences.

Some years after the publication of *La Chambre claire* and just before the appearance of Derrida's text, the Moroccan writer Abdelkébir Khatibi grapples with maternal mourning in 'Cendres et reliques'.[4] This quasi simultaneous concern with mourning in the works of Barthes, Derrida and Khatibi is far from being fortuitous. The three men not only met and spent time together but also read and commented on each other's works. Barthes was one of the examiners of the doctorate in sociology which Khatibi received from the Sorbonne in 1965 and almost worked with him on a project dedicated to the semiology of the Moroccan garment. In his

2   Pierre-Louis Fort, *Ma mère, la morte: l'écriture du deuil au féminin chez Yourcenar, Beauvoir et Ernaux* (Paris: Editions Imago, 2007), p. 16.

3   Jacques Derrida, *Chaque fois unique, la fin du monde* (Paris: Galilée, 2003), pp. 87–8; *The Work of Mourning*, ed. Pascale-Anne Brault and Michael Naas (Chicago: The University of Chicago Press, 2001), p. 58.

4   Abdelkébir Khatibi, 'Cendres et reliques', in *Par-dessus l'épaule* (Paris: Aubier, 1988), pp. 137–49 (hereafter referenced in main text as *PDE*).

last autobiography, published a year before his death, Khatibi remembers Barthes as a 'sceptique modéré qui croyait et ne croyait pas à la vie' [moderate sceptic who believed and did not believe in life] and who 'cherchait *sous* la langue la révélation du silence à venir' [sought *beneath* language the revelation of the silence to come].[5] For Khatibi, Barthes's work is defined as much by its movement and singularity as by its tendency to transform silence into matter and an experience of meaning. This relationship to silence dominates Barthes's *Journal de deuil* (2009), written shortly after the death of his mother, and recurs simultaneously as part of mourning and as a reminder of the maternal bond: 'Mam.: peu de paroles entre nous, je restai silencieux [...], mais je me souviens du moindre de ses goûts, de ses jugements' [*Maman*: few words between us, I remained silent [...] but I remember every one of her tastes, of her judgments].[6] The writing of mourning requires handling this silence and translating it into the fragmented space of the diary. The writer in mourning is an apprentice translator who is working between the silence of death and the language of mourning.

This coming together of mourning, silence and translation resurfaces in the introduction of a work written by Khatibi in homage to his friend Derrida. The two writers, who met in 1974 in Paris, had a long intellectual and personal friendship which Khatibi describes in these terms:

L'amitié pensante ne se volatilise pas après le décès de l'un des amis. Elle continue, se réincarne régulièrement à travers le deuil, dans l'épreuve même de l'esprit et ses exorcismes [...]. Nous étions des amis qui vivions à distance; lui à côté de Paris; et moi, à côté de Rabat. Il voyageait et travaillait beaucoup à l'étranger. Son importance intellectuelle sur le plan international n'est plus à démontrer. Elle est même en devenir dans de nombreux pays. Elle voyage dans le temps, grâce à la traduction; et pour ma part, j'ai initié sa traduction en langue arabe.[7]

[An intellectual friendship does not vanish after the death of one of the friends. It continues, is reincarnated regularly through mourning, in the very ordeal of the

---

5   Abdelkébir Khatibi, *Le Scribe et son ombre* (Paris: La Différence, 2008), pp. 56, 57.
6   Roland Barthes, *Journal de deuil* (Paris: Seuil, 2009), p. 200; *Mourning Diary*, trans. Richard Howard (New York: Hill & Wang, 2010), p. 188 (hereafter referenced in main text as *JD* and *MD*).
7   Abdelkébir Khatibi, *Jacques Derrida, en effet* (Neuilly-sur-Seine: Al Manar, 2007), p. 7.

mind and its exorcisms […]. We were friends who lived at a distance; he near Paris, and I, near Rabat. He travelled and worked a lot abroad. His intellectual importance on the international scene is now beyond doubt. It is even still growing in many countries. It travels in time, thanks to translation; and for my part, I initiated his translation into Arabic.]

As Khatibi's words suggest, mourning is the shared site not only of a common experience but equally of an intellectual and writerly dynamic which, like translation, reduces distance, creates links between thoughts and renews, even re-introduces, the voice of the other beyond the borders of language and territory. By writing about the deaths of their respective mothers, Barthes, Khatibi and Derrida allow us to read the experience of a protean mourning which is always in motion and ceaselessly invites questioning of the relationship between the writing, reading and circulation of the mourning text. It is striking that each of the three writers often evokes both the death of his mother and that of an intellectual friend in a fragmentary mode. Khatibi's 'Cendres et reliques', Barthes's *Journal de deuil*, Derrida's 'Circonfession', like the text Khatibi writes in homage to Derrida or the text Derrida writes after the death of Barthes, are so many interwoven examples of the way in which mourning writing resists any kind of unity or uniformity by deploying the textual fragment to articulate the pain of loss and the quest for an open form of writing.

By taking Barthes's *Journal de deuil* and Derrida's 'Circonfession' as examples and landmarks of mourning writing, this chapter proposes a reading of the hybrid and fragmented form of Khatibi's text, focused around the concepts of the marginal and the detour. From the double exercise of transcription and translation, which keeps the mother's voice alive, to the practice of episodic notation, which investigates the signs and paradoxes of loss, this essay will demonstrate that writing the loss of the mother leads Khatibi, following Barthes and Derrida, to a quest for a form of writing anchored in the poetics of the fragment. More than a simple healing or overcoming of a personal trauma, Khatibi's 'Cendres et reliques' displaces the writing of mourning towards that indispensable – if fragile and unstable – margin where a fragmentary mode of thought anticipates loss, refuses melancholy and tends towards notation as the site where the work is both created and left incomplete.

In the Margins of Psychoanalysis and 'Lovence'

In the prolific and polymorphous œuvre of Khatibi, *Par-dessus l'épaule* is a unique work which stands out both for the diversity of its content and the variety of its form. Organized in six parts, the book opens and closes with 'notes de mémoire' [memory notes] around the concept of 'aimance' ('lovence') and includes a brief section entitled 'Socio-clips', 'note[s] aussi rapide[s] qu'un regard sur autrui' [notes as fleeting as a glance at other people] (*PDE* 156), as well as two other parts associated with the psychoanalysis the author undertook between 1982 and 1983, that is, a few years before the death of his mother.[8] These are composed of a diary, scattered notes and four studies of the relationship between psychoanalysis and the concepts of trauma and the sacred.

Two prefatory remarks are necessary here. On the one hand, and as the structure of Khatibi's work suggests, the experience of mourning the mother seems to be simultaneously separate from and linked to psychoanalysis. This remark is not surprising given that the loss of the mother, as Julia Kristeva points out, 'est une nécessité biologique et psychique, le jalon premier de l'autonomisation. Le matricide est notre nécessité vitale, condition *sine qua non* de notre individuation' [is a biological and psychological necessity, the first step on the path to becoming autonomous. Matricide is necessary for us to live, the necessary condition of our individuation].[9] However, Khatibi does not restrict his exploration of the loss of the mother to psychoanalytical jargon nor the cult of the individual. Psychoanalysis, which he approaches in *Par-dessus l'épaule* through the lens of his own experience and through theoretical reflection, permits above all a reconceptualization of the act of writing and its form. For Khatibi this is the central question: 'comment se résorbe la diglossie entre "l'association d'idées" et la parole de celui qui est en

8   Derrida's 'aimance' is translated by George Collins as 'lovence'. Jacques Derrida, *Politiques de l'amitié* (Paris: Galilée, 1994); *The Politics of Friendship*, trans. George Collins (London & New York: Verso, 1997).

9   Julia Kristeva, *Soleil noir: dépression et mélancolie* (Paris: Gallimard, 1987), p. 38.

analyse, dans la construction d'une forme et d'un style littéraires?' [how
does the construction of a literary style and form narrow the diglossic
gap between the 'free association of ideas' and the language of the an-
alysand?] (*PDE* 8). Mourning the mother thus becomes the space of a
fruitful dialogue between ideas associated with maternal loss and the
writer's developing style. If writing, as Khatibi notes elsewhere, is 'une
traduction du corps, de l'inconscient et du désir' [a translation of the
body, of the unconscious and of desire], to which is joined the bilin-
gualism of the francophone writer, mourning, as a form of bodily and
psychological rupture, directly calls into question the modalities and
practice of this translation.[10]

The distance introduced by Khatibi between mourning and psychoanalysis echoes the step Derrida takes in defining his text 'Circonfession'
as an 'aveu à la machine, au-delà des institutions, la psychanalyse comprise,
au-delà du savoir de la vérité' [a mechanical confession, beyond institutions, including psychoanalysis, beyond the knowledge of the truth] (*C*
85). Derrida's text is an exercise in radical unveiling around the wound of
circumcision and a confession woven around the second wound of the
inevitable loss of the mother. This act of moving the text beyond psychoanalysis also resonates with Barthes's work, where the author describes
the word *deuil* [mourning] as 'trop psychanalytique' [too psychoanalytic]
(*JD* 83; *MD* 73) and prefers the word *chagrin* [distress], which he under-
stands as 'chaotique, erratique, ce en quoi il résiste à l'idée courante – et
psychanalytique – d'un deuil soumis au temps, qui se dialectise, s'use,
"s'arrange"' [chaotic, erratic, whereby it resists the accepted – and psychoanalytic – notion of a mourning subject to time, becoming dialectical, wearing out, 'adapting'] (*JD* 81; *MD* 71). This dynamic approach to
mourning which pushes writing beyond the boundaries of psychoanalysis
to encounter the chaos and instability characteristic of the experience
of loss is common to Khatibi, Barthes and Derrida, whether this loss is

10   Abdelkébir Khatibi, 'Lettre-préface', in Marc Gontard, *La Violence du texte: études
      sur la littérature marocaine d'expression française* (Paris: L'Harmattan, 1981), pp. 7–9
      (p. 8).

imminent (Derrida), has already occurred (Barthes) or something of the two (Khatibi).

The other element that frames the text of 'Cendres et reliques' is the concept of 'lovence'. If Khatibi defines this elsewhere as 'une langue d'amour qui affirme une affinité plus active entre les êtres' [a love language which affirms a more active affinity between individuals], he adds that it prolongs love, fills silence, recognizes suffering and proposes 'un dialogue plus sensible entre corps et esprit' [a more sensitive dialogue between body and mind].[11] It is precisely this sensitive dialogue which informs the writing of mourning in the work of Khatibi: 'lovence' is the other name of the attempt not only to restore and respond to the language of the mother but also to share a relational ethics founded on dialogue, sharing and transmission. Here again, the move Khatibi makes echoes Barthes's call to 'ne pas *manifester* le deuil (ou du moins être indifférent à cela), mais *imposer* le droit *public* à la relation aimante qu'il implique' [not to *manifest* mourning (or at least to be indifferent to it) but to *impose* the *public* right to the loving relation it implies] (*JD* 81; *MD* 71; emphasis is in the original). This 'public' right to 'lovence', expressed by the double gesture of translation and notation, is the horizon towards which Khatibi's writing of mourning moves. In other words, Khatibi seeks to move beyond the individuation of mourning to make mourning the object of shared reading and collective thought.

Translating Ashes, Conceiving Relics

At first sight, Khatibi's writing about the loss of his mother seems to carry within it the signs of wounding and dissociation, as 'Cendres et reliques' is composed of two distinct parts. The first, entitled 'Ashes', is Khatibi's retranscription of the content of a series of interviews he recorded with his mother in 1980 and 1982, that is, six and four years respectively before

11   Abdelkébir Khatibi, *Le Livre de l'aimance* (Rabat: Marsam, 1995), p. 5.

her death, which occurred in 1986. The second part, entitled 'Relics', is a set of ten fragmentary notes written after the death of his mother. While the first part precedes and anticipates mourning, as in Derrida's 'Circonfession', the second is situated 'dans le sillage' [in the wake] (*PDE* 147) of mourning, as is the case in Barthes's *Journal de deuil*. In short, Khatibi's writing of mourning brings together the gesture of anticipation of Derrida and the post-traumatic notation of Barthes. Where ashes make legible what will remain of the mother after her death, relics point to a discontinuous philosophy of loss and mourning. Fragments of 'Reliques' can be read as an incomplete mourning diary, a liminal study of the possibility of writing *after* and *around* the mother's death. In this context, the generic and impersonal character of the two titles seems simultaneously to accentuate the theme of death and to invite a reading of Khatibi's text which goes beyond the mother and the particular experience of the author. In other terms, 'Ashes and Relics' appears from the beginning as less of a literary memorial *to* the mother than as a writing project *in the margins of* her death and of death in general.

The concept of the margin is directly linked to the text which Derrida writes during his mother's final illness and which he defines as 'cinquante-neuf périodes et périphrases *écrites dans une sorte de marge intérieure entre le livre de Geoffrey Bennington et un ouvrage en préparation*' [fifty-nine periods and periphrases *written in a kind of interior margin between Geoffrey Bennington's book and a work in preparation*] (*C* 6; emphasis is in the original). Not only is 'Circonfession' published as a series of numbered bands (fifty-nine is an allusion to the age of the author) and placed in the margins of the footnote section in Bennington's book, but the process of writing itself is undertaken in the margins of another project and of the anticipated mourning for the mother. The concept of the margin, which recurs in the works of Derrida, is linked to an exploration of the limit, a gesture of extension and appropriation which deconstructs any form of centrality or closure.[12] Therefore, like writing, the anticipated mourning is an open and decentred space which depends on notation as a mode of fragmentation and incursion. In Derrida's text, writing mourning is a process which

12   See, for example, Jacques Derrida, *Marges de la philosophie* (Paris: Minuit, 1972).

resists all borders as it creates a simultaneous dialogue with the text of the other (notably St Augustine), personal memory and the loss of the mother.

In Khatibi's work, this extension of the writing of mourning towards the margin of the text is reinforced by the intertextuality which arises around the concepts of 'ashes' and 'relics', as if the echo of mourning resonates through his work as a whole. In his novel *Un été à Stockholm* [*A Summer in Stockholm*], the narrator Gérard Namir, having accidentally entered a church in the Swedish capital, begins an unexpected prayer in which he mentions, among other things, the Scandinavian custom of cremation which he finds extraordinary before wondering:

> Seigneur, est-ce barbarie d'incinérer le corps et d'en disperser les cendres au gré du vent et des vagues? Puisque la mort est dissociation et oubli de la terre, pourquoi ne pas s'envoler avec ses cendres? […] Ornés de reliques vivantes, les humains oublient-ils la vie au seuil de leur disparition sans figure?[13]

> [Lord, is it barbaric to burn a body and to scatter the ashes where the wind and waves will take them? Since death is separation from and a forgetting of the earth, why not fly into the air along with one's ashes? […] Bedecked with living relics, do human beings forget their life on the threshold of their faceless death?]

While entering into an implicit dialogue with the law against cremation in Islam, the musings of Khatibi's narrator situate ashes and relics as a double sign of a kind of presence and of life which go beyond death. Dispersed ashes, like animate relics, create a link between the annihilation inflicted by death and the dream of regeneration expressed by the act of writing.

But beyond the cult of the dead, ashes and relics are also linked to the way in which the writer recreates, renews and maintains the fragmented material of his reading. When, in *Le Scribe et son ombre* [*The Scribe and His Shadow*] (2008), Khatibi discusses the way he was influenced by Mallarmé's dream of the 'Great Work', that ultimate book which crosses the boundaries of genre and symbolizes the final horizon of writing, he writes that his first autobiography, *La Mémoire tatouée* [*Tattooed Memory*]

---

13 Abdelkébir Khatibi, *Un été à Stockholm*, in *Œuvres d'Abdelkébir Khatibi*, 3 vols (Paris: La Différence, 2008), I, pp. 285–379 (p. 358).

'en garde la trace, et peut-être même quelques cendres' [has a trace of it and perhaps even some ashes].[14] More than the influence of the French poet, it is indeed the unattainable nature of Mallarmé's dream and the fragmentation of his work which inspire the Moroccan writer. A few lines later, Khatibi adds:

> Celui qui écrit en cheminant vers soi et vers l'autre, n'est pas que le gardien des reliques de celui qui fait le mort durant la vie. Au-delà de ce culte, le scribe qui se souvient est prêt au sacrifice, devant le témoin anonyme qu'est le lecteur. Il élève, en vue de cette lecture, un autel réversible, une sorte de paravent qui brille dans la nuit du langage.[15]

> [The one who writes while making his way towards himself and the other, is not only the guardian of the relics of the one who plays dead during his life. Beyond this worship, the scribe who remembers is ready for sacrifice before the anonymous witness who is the reader. He raises up, with this reading in mind, a reversible altar, a kind of screen which shines in the night of language.]

For Khatibi, writing is just as much a process of reproduction of textual ashes and a preservation of relics gathered through reading as a sacrificial movement towards the reader. In other words, writing is a kind of double worship given as much to the other's text as to the circulation and erasure of this same text through the act of reading, with this being by definition a confrontation with absence and the 'mise en œuvre d'une distance' [creation of a distance].[16] In his collection of poetry, *Dédicace à l'année qui vient* [*Dedication to the Coming Year*] (1986), Khatibi writes:

> La nostalgie n'est pas ma joie
> Mettez les reliques
> Dans des mots ciselés
> Et sous des clefs désenvoûtées
> Mettez-les dans la nuit furtive

---

14   Khatibi, *Le Scribe et son ombre*, p. 26.
15   Ibid., pp. 26–7.
16   Dominique Carlat, *Témoins de l'inactuel: quatre écrivains contemporains face au deuil* (Paris: José Corti, 2007), p. 17.

Que l'oubli favorise
Dans une main en cendres.[17]

[Nostalgia is not my joy
Put the relics
In chiselled words
And beneath disenchanted keys
Put them in the furtive night
Which forgetting favour
In the hand made of ashes.]

As these lines suggest, language is the site of renegotiation and recomposition of signs. In Khatibi's work, writing is the ambivalent process which allows the generation of new ashes as it revisits the relics of the past. The transfer of relics to the reader echoes the dispersal of ashes in the space of the text. Put another way, 'ashes and relics' is the twinned name of the writing process which recuperates and transforms, consumes and regenerates, erases and recreates.

The Scribe and the Mother's Voice

In 'Cendres', Khatibi's mourning writing works according to a dual process of translation and transcription, offering to the reader the written and Gallicized version of his mother's memories which he collected during his interviews with her. If the writing of mourning, in the words of Philippe Forest, 'conduit seulement au précipice où se perd toute parole' [leads only to the precipice where all words are lost], the fragmentary narration of 'Cendres' can be read as a way of avoiding this loss in a gesture of anticipation and transferral.[18] Here, it is not about writing mourning, but rather, anticipating its writing, decentring it and displacing it towards the margins of the mother's speech. As in Derrida's text, Khatibi creates a form of writing which turns both *towards* and *around* the mother. As Derrida

17 Abdelkébir Khatibi, *Dédicace à l'année qui vient* (Montpellier: Fata Morgana, 1986), p. 26.
18 Philippe Forest, *Le Roman infanticide: Dostoïevski, Faulkner, Camus. Essais sur la littérature et le deuil* (Nantes: Cécile Defaut, 2010), p. 116.

puts it, 'on confesse toujours l'autre, je me confesse veut dire je confesse ma mère veut dire j'avoue faire avouer ma mère, je la fais parler en moi, devant moi' [one always confesses the other, I confess means I confess my mother means I confess that I make my mother confess, I make her speak in me, before me] (*C* 139): in sum, it is about exorcizing the pain of loss by re-routing mourning towards the place and the margins of the loss to come.

The recording of the interviews with the mother is firstly a form of anticipation of mourning: 'Je m'attendais à une disparition plus ou moins rapide. Je m'étais préparé au deuil en enregistrant donc plusieurs cassettes, sans m'être demandé quel usage j'allais en faire' [I was expecting a death that would be quite sudden. I had therefore prepared for mourning by re-cording several cassettes, without having asked myself what use I would make of them] (*PDE* 139). The reader of 'Cendres' is therefore confronted with two forms of looking forward (the preparation for the death of the mother and the question of the use of the recordings) and of looking back (the mother's memories as they are revealed by the recordings). As Éric Benoit notes in relation to the poem 'Pour un tombeau d'Anatole' [A Tomb for Anatole] by Mallarmé, 'le temps pivote de part et d'autre du moment irreprésentable de la mort' [time pivots either side of the irrepresentable moment of loss]: translating and transcribing the mother's words allow the text to follow and reproduce this movement.[19] Therefore, the turn to audio recording is one of those 'formes inédites de ritualisation' [unusual forms of ritualization] whose technical aspect does not only 'renforce [le] face à face solitaire avec la mort' [reinforce [the] solitary standoff with death] but equally imposes 'la confrontation à ces nouvelles traces, signes dérisoires et atroces' [a confrontation with these new traces, derisory and atrocious signs].[20] From this point onwards, the work of translation and transcription is comparable to a search for meaning beyond death, to a beginning of the process of deciphering and reconstructing meaning.

At the same time, the uncertainty of Khatibi when it comes to the use of the recordings keeps open the possibility of writing a work from or at

---

19   Éric Benoit, 'Le Deuil des virtualités inaccomplies', in Pierre Glaudes and Dominique Rabaté, eds, *Deuil et littérature*, Modernités 21 (Bordeaux: Presses universitaires, 2005), pp. 177–93 (p. 181).

20   Carlat, *Témoins de l'inactuel*, pp. 13–14.

least in the wake of the loss of the mother. This possibility echoes Barthes's project in 'Vita nova', the novel he left unfinished but spent much time studying, notably in his lectures at the Collège de France on the preparation of the novel. In Khatibi's work, the audio recordings allow him to set in place both the last signs of a maternal world which is destined to disappear and the foundations of what could become a literary project. The recordings simultaneously anticipate the inevitable death and the hypothetical future work. In this context, *Par-dessus l'épaule*, a text which combines the genres of the theoretical essay, autobiographical writing and fragmentary notation, represents, in the words of Dominique Carlat on Barthes's *La Chambre claire*, 'le lieu de réalisation paradoxale' [the site of a paradoxical actualization] of a writing project which cannot be dissociated from the mourning for the mother, 'en même temps que le symptôme de son impossible accomplissement définitif' [as well as the symptom of its impossible final completion].[21] It is as if writing the loss of the mother requires formal experimentation, a search for meaning and structure, a slippage towards the margins of the text as in Derrida's 'Circonfession'.

The fruit of a shift from orality to writing and from the Moroccan Arabic to the French language, 'Cendres' is equally a double transferral which inscribes the writing of mourning in a linguistic dynamic, opens it up to meaning and to the idea of a community with the reader. Khatibi's approach consists of, as Blanchot puts it:

> Me maintenir présent dans la proximité d'autrui qui s'éloigne définitivement en mourant, prendre sur moi la mort d'autrui comme la seule mort qui me concerne, voilà ce qui me met hors de moi et est la seule séparation qui puisse m'ouvrir, dans son impossibilité, à l'Ouvert d'une communauté.[22]

> [Maintaining my presence near others who are definitively moving away from me by dying, taking on to myself the death of others as the only death which concerns me, this is what leads me outside of myself and is the only separation which can open me, in its impossibility, to the Openness of a community.]

The transcription of the mother's speech thus corresponds as much to a maintenance of the author's presence at his mother's side as to a sharing of

21   Ibid., p. 123.
22   Maurice Blanchot, *La Communauté inavouable* (Paris: Minuit, 1983), p. 21.

the event of her death. In other words, it is as much about sustaining the link with the mother beyond her loss as about inviting an appropriation of this same loss through the act of reading.

The mother's voice is at the heart of this double process: 'J'aimais sa voix, son grain de voix' [I loved her voice, the tenor of her voice] (*PDE* 139). The text of 'Cendres' is a continuation of the dialogue with the mother, a form of vocal resurrection through writing. Here, the task of the writer, as Forest emphasizes, 's'apparente à l'art du nécromancien' [is like the art of the necromancer]: he remembers the deceased, listens to her voice and reactivates her communication with the living.[23] For Khatibi, it is about resisting the fading of the mother's voice. It is precisely this absence of the voice that Barthes points to in his *Journal de deuil*: 'Chose bizarre, sa voix que je connaissais si bien, dont on dit qu'elle est le grain même du souvenir ('la chère inflexion …'), je ne l'entends pas. Comme une surdité localisée' [How strange: her voice, which I knew so well, and which is said to be the very texture of memory ('the dear inflection …'), I no longer hear. Like a localized deafness] (*JD* 24; *MD* 14). In Barthes's work, the irreparable loss of the mother's voice is a central element of mourning as it signifies the breaking down of the dialogue between mother and son and makes clear the impossibility of narration, as in his reflection on the snow falling in Paris: 'Je me dis et j'en souffre: elle ne sera jamais plus là pour le voir, pour que je le lui raconte' [I tell myself and suffer for it: she will never again be here to see it, or for me to describe it for her] (*JD* 103; *MD* 93). Avoiding this impossibility, the transcription of the mother's speech allows Khatibi to continue to be near the voice of his mother and to narrate his own life in its wake and from the vantage point of its loss.

The double transfer of the mother's speech, from orality to writing and from the Moroccan dialect to the language of the other, must be read in dialogue with the fact that the mother was illiterate. To transcribe the mother's words is also a way of giving her access to the closed sphere of writing. Khatibi explains that his mother was 'une conteuse analphabète' [an illiterate storyteller] (*PDE* 139): an evocative formulation where the act of narration evades the limits of illiteracy. Khatibi's text thus comes out of a gesture of extension and transmission: that of telling the story

23   Forest, *Le Roman infanticide*, p. 121.

of the deceased mother and of liberating her speech from its silence in society and its absence in the world of writing. The text of 'Cendres' is the diary that the mother was not able to write, the impossible narration of a storyteller from the margins who is saved by the gesture of translation and transcription. This question of access to writing as an inherent part of the mourning text once more resonates with a comment Barthes makes in his diary:

> Je vis sans aucun souci de la postérité, aucun désir d'être lu plus tard [...], la parfaite acceptation de disparaître complètement, aucune envie de 'monument' – mais je ne peux supporter qu'il en soit ainsi pour mam. (peut-être parce qu'elle n'a pas écrit et que son souvenir dépend entièrement de moi). (*JD* 246)

> [I live without any concern for posterity, no desire to be read later on [...], complete acceptance of vanishing utterly, no desire for a 'monument' but I cannot endure that this should be the case for *maman* (perhaps because she has not written and her memory depends entirely on me).] (*MD* 234)

To write the loss of the mother becomes equivalent to projecting her life beyond silence, offering her the posterity of the verb, the memory and the memorial of writing. Following Barthes's terminology, for Khatibi it is about liberating oneself from the 'méta-langage incessant' [incessant metalanguage] of the intellectual and about giving form to the sovereign 'non-langage' [non-language] (*JD* 222; *MD* 209) of the mother, which at once recalls childhood and resists the power of words and the hegemony of discourse and representations. By creating a monument to the mother who does not write, Khatibi seeks to preserve the non-language of his mother at the heart of his writer's language. As Valéry suggests, 'le langage doit *conserver* du non-langage [...]. Il doit conserver, au sens de possibilité de répétition; et transmettre, et avant tout à celui qui est émetteur, ou plutôt *produire l'émetteur*' [language must *preserve* non-language [...]. It must preserve it, in the sense of maintaining the possibility of repetition; and transmit, above all to the one who is the speaker, or rather *produce the speaker*].[24] Through the double process of

---

24   Paul Valéry, *Cahiers*, 29 vols (Paris: CNRS, 1957–61), XXIV, 262; cited in Jürgen Schmidt-Radefeldt, *Paul Valéry linguiste dans les Cahiers* (Paris: Klincksieck, 1970), p. 63. Emphasis is in the original.

translation and transcription, Khatibi reproduces his mother's speech as a narration and makes his mother the speaker-writer of the text. That said, the inability of the mother to read the transcription of her own words keeps her on the margins of the text: Khatibi does not write to be read by his mother. This same painful separation echoes in 'Circonfession' where Derrida notes in relation to his mother:

> Elle ignore tout de ce que j'écris, n'en ayant pu vouloir de sa vie lire la moindre phrase, ce qui donne à l'exercice auquel et dans lequel nous nous livrons, G. [Geoffrey Bennington] et moi, la juste dimension d'un chuchotement, l'aparté d'un confessionnal où nous ne sommes pour personne, changeant de peau à chaque instant pour *faire* la vérité, à chacun la sienne, pour confesser sans que personne le sache (*C* 216–17; emphasis is in the original)

> [She does not know any of my writing, having spent her whole life not having been able to want to read the slightest phrase, which gives the exercise in which G. [Geoffrey Bennington] and I are engaged the exact quality of whispering, an aside in a confessional where we have come for no one, shifting skins at each moment to *create* the truth, to each his own, to confess with no one knowing about it.]

If the anticipated writing of mourning the mother resists separation by following the final illness (in the case of Derrida) or by recording the voice (in the case of Khatibi), the passage into writing distances the mother once more and accelerates the project of the writer into the very solitude he seeks to ward off. To write in the margins of anticipated mourning is also to resolve to occupy this margin oneself by accepting writing as a form of rupture and separation.

That said, Khatibi does not limit himself to the twin process of transcription and translation but also takes on a form of editorial work which shapes the mother's narration. In fact, if the text of 'Cendres' appears at first sight as a homogeneous block, it is nonetheless defined by a logic of fragmentation and discontinuity as the accumulation of ellipses and comments in italics and parentheses makes clear. On this subject, Khatibi writes:

> Je n'ai pas reproduit les questions que je lui posais ou les commentaires les accompagnant, en me contentant de jouer le rôle d'un scribe. Les points de suspension marquent les coupes que j'ai dû faire, vu la longueur de ces entretiens. Les mots placés entre parenthèses sont des précisions ajoutées par moi pour faciliter la lecture. (*PDE* 139)

[I have not reproduced the questions that I asked her or the comments that accompanied them, limiting myself to the role of a scribe. The ellipses mark the cuts that I had to make, given the length of these interviews. The words in parentheses are explanations added by me to make reading the text easier.]

The erasure of the writer in favour of the 'scribe' who edits the mother's narration means that the writing of mourning is displaced towards that intermediary space where the author is simultaneously present in and absent from the text. For Khatibi, the work of the scribe is 'une bonne manière de gérer un deuil' [a good way of coping with mourning] (*PDE* 140). On the one hand, Khatibi's removal of his own questions and comments creates a 'written' text by his illiterate mother. The evocatory power of the mother's narration is reinforced by this: it is as if the mother took the place of the author and composed her own text. On the other hand, the addition by Khatibi of words in parentheses reintroduces the author into his mother's narration. The words in question give more information on the attitude of the mother ('elle rit sans terminer sa phrase') [she laughs without finishing her sentence], provide biographical details ('maternal' grandfather, 'paternal' grandfather, 'celle qui est morte' [the one who died]) or historical clarification ('fille du Prophète' [daughter of the Prophet]) or explain terms from classical or Moroccan Arabic ('alem', 'khrissa'). These words can therefore be read as an attempt at negotiating the following dilemma: to seek to usher the mother's speech into the world at the risk of drowning it out or to refrain from all commentary even at the price of abandoning the mother. In the text he writes in memory of Barthes, Derrida describes this dilemma by using the formula 'deux infidélités, un choix impossible' [two infidelities, an impossible choice] in reference to the author's sense of being torn between the need to erase his own voice in favour of the voice of his deceased friend and the need to avoid any form of citation or approximation of his friend's words which would risk re-enacting the latter's disappearance.[25] In 'Circonfession', Derrida creates a text where extracts of his notebooks, fragments of his mother's sentences and citations

25 Derrida, *Chaque fois unique, la fin du monde*, p. 71; *The Work of Mourning*, p. 45.

from and commentaries on Saint Augustine are reproduced: a hybrid structure where the mother's voice is simultaneously isolated and surrounded, as if a constant battle were necessary to find for her an impossible balance.

In the same way, caught between the risk of abandoning his mother's voice to its original solitude and that of enclosing it within the language of the writer, Khatibi chooses to reduce his editorial work to that which is strictly necessary. The elimination of the author's questions and the addition of several words to the mother's narration generate a subtext which emphasizes the inherent tension of mourning writing as defined by Derrida. This subtext is simultaneously a trace of the negotiation of this tension and the early form of a dialogue between Khatibi, his mother and the reader. Therefore, 'Cendres' is presented as a collage of fragments which articulate the pain of mourning and its circulation as a narrative and a text.

Orphic Variations

This logic of fragmentation continues into the second part, 'Reliques', whose notes, written after the death of the mother, initiate a dialogue with loss and with the mother's narrative ashes. The writing of mourning, as Pierre Glaudes observes, 'ne permet pas seulement à la douleur de se dire, elle lui *répond*: [il] tente de la sublimer, en la faisant entrer dans l'ordre des signes' [does not only permit pain to express itself, but also *responds* to it: it attempts to sublimate it, by bringing it into the order of signs].[26] Khatibi's notation becomes the incarnation of these signs, a memorial in fragments which responds to the mother's narration while also sketching out a more general reflection on the question of mourning.

---

26   Pierre Glaudes, ' "Nécropolis": les romantiques et le deuil', in Glaudes and Rabaté, eds, *Deuil et littérature*, pp. 15–40 (p. 35). Emphasis is in the original.

The choice of the term 'relics', which is linked to the register of the sacred and of worship, confirms Khatibi's wish to displace sorrow towards a semiology of mourning and to elevate notational writing to the level of ritual. The worship of the dead is a system of notation and valorization which works as well at an individual level as it does on a collective scale. In a note from *Par-dessus l'épaule*, Khatibi writes, for example, that 'les valeurs et leur auréole que se donne un pays on les trouve dans les noms des rues, c'est-à-dire dans le culte des morts' [the values and the atmosphere around them which a country gives itself can be found in the names of the streets, that is in the worship of the dead] (*PDE* 154). That is to say that this worship is in constant dialogue with movement through space and with the circulation of signs. After the death of his mother, Khatibi explains that he had 'géré systématiquement ce deuil pendant plusieurs mois en écrivant et en voyageant beaucoup, multipliant également plusieurs pôles d'activité' [managed the grief systematically for several months by writing and by travelling a lot, multiplying at the same time several forms of activity] (*PDE* 147). If the adverb 'systématiquement' confirms the repetition inherent in the idea of an attempt to manage grief over a lost loved one through ritual, the multiplication of writing projects, journeys and categories of activity can be compared to an attempt to scatter the sites of mourning. To the oneness of the loss answers the breaking up of daily activity, whether that is spatial, intellectual or authorly. The fragments of 'Reliques' are thus nothing but the translation of this fundamental correspondence between the space of mourning and the space of writing, between the voice of the mother and that of the author. The relatively reduced number of notes suggests that this correspondence does indeed remain incomplete but that this incompleteness is precisely that which creates the poetics of mourning in the work of Khatibi.

In a brief heading to 'Reliques', Khatibi describes his notes as 'les marges d'un chant funèbre' [the margins of a funereal song] and associates them with the 'regard orphique de la mémoire' [Orphic gaze of memory] (*PDE* 140). Khatibi's notes are thus part of the writing of loss and of indirectness: they are less about writing mourning than about recreating that which surrounds, accompanies or follows the experience of loss. This amounts to, in Derrida's words, 'écrire *à* la mort de [la] mère, de cette écriture ainsi *promise à la mort*' [writing *towards* the death of [the] mother, of this writing which is thus *destined to die*] (*C* 135). Faced with the elusive subject of death, the writer creates an oblique, decentred text which is condemned to be lost. The reference to the myth of Orpheus suggests that the text of mourning, the funereal song that is somehow still seductive, is the seat of an ineluctable paradox, as Blanchot explains:

> Il [Orphée] perd Eurydice, parce qu'il la désire par-delà les limites mesurées du chant et il se perd lui-même, mais ce désir et Eurydice perdue et Orphée dispersé sont nécessaires au chant comme est nécessaire à l'œuvre l'épreuve du désœuvrement éternel.

> [He [Orpheus] loses Eurydice because he desires her beyond the measured limits of the song, and he loses himself, but this desire, and Eurydice lost, and Orpheus dispersed are necessary to the song, just as the ordeal of eternal inertia is necessary to the work.][27]

The experience of loss is simultaneously the necessary condition and the inevitable horizon of the writing of mourning, as the latter is not able to come into being except through inactivity and repetition. Writing fragments in the margin of the maternal narration is one way of giving form to this impossibility. It is that, in the work of Khatibi as in that of Barthes, 'la dérobade ou le détour' [the evasion or detour] of which notation is one of the forms, 'est un écho de la poursuite orphique d'une vérité perdue dans son atteinte même' [is an echo of the Orphic pursuit of a truth which is lost just as you reach it].[28] The fragmented notes of 'Reliques' give form to this pursuit which, as it seeks to go beyond the death of the mother, only reproduces separation, dispersal and death.

27   Maurice Blanchot, *L'Espace littéraire* (Paris: Gallimard, 1955), p. 228; *The Space of Literature*, trans. Ann Smock (Lincoln: University of Nebraska Press, 1982), p. 172.
28   Evelyne Londyn, 'L'Orphique chez Blanchot: voir et dire', *French Forum* 5 (1980), 261–8 (p. 261).

Duplication and Diversion

In 'Cendres et reliques', the representation or evocation of death allows one to grasp the poetics of the margin and the detour which are at work in Khatibi's mourning writing. In fact, the event of death is subject to a systematic process of duplication, distancing and displacement. These three devices aim at the diversion of the experience of mourning through a disruption and variation in the ways in which it is presented.

While it anticipates mourning the mother and faces the death to come, the text does not sidestep exhuming the deaths of the past. In 'Circonfession', Derrida evokes the death of his father, of his two brothers, Paul and Norbert, and of his cousin, Jean-Pierre. The death of the mother is a final wound which re-awakens the experience of loss, prolonging and completing what Derrida calls 'un temps d'anéantissement dont tu n'es jamais ressuscité' [a time of annihilation from which you never recovered] (*C* 230). In the same way, as he refers in the heading of 'Cendres' to the death of his mother in January 1986, Khatibi immediately recalls the death of his father in 1947, as if the first loss reactivated the second. As well as this, in the narration of 'Cendres', death recurs several times, reminding the author of the loss of his brother, his sister, his grandmother and his aunt. The wound of the writer who is now an orphan is a double wrench which is prolonged through the memory of other deaths. It is as if the death of the mother leads to a loss of a family memory which the author seeks to preserve, albeit in a fragmented form. At the same time, this doubling of death is inherent to the encounter of mourning and writing. As Michel Picard underlines:

> Le deuil, dans son paroxysme de souffrance, a quelque chose d'emblématique, de générique. La 'mort' renvoie non à une perte, si douloureuse qu'elle soit, mais à *toutes les pertes* déjà vécues par le Sujet, à la fois concaténées, emboîtées, télescopées.[29]
>
> [Mourning, at its peak of suffering, is in a way emblematic and typical. 'Death' refers not to one loss, as painful as it might be, but to *all the losses* that have already been experienced by the Subject which are simultaneously concatenated, interlocking and telescoped.]

29   Michel Picard, *La Littérature et la mort* (Paris: Presses Universitaires de France, 1995), p. 146. Emphasis is in the original.

By referring to the memory of other deaths, the mother's narration, which is guided by the author's questions, prolongs the space of loss and thus requires a reading of mourning in the margins of the mother's death. Khatibi's text consequently records the mother's speech as a space where the experience of mourning simultaneously comes together and is scattered.

In addition, death is constantly distanced in the mother's narration in 'Cendres', which rejects, indirectly and implicitly, the pathos of mourning. From the first lines, the mother testifies: 'Tu ne fis pas attention à la mort du petit frère, ni à celle du père; aucune larme versée' [You did not pay attention to the death of your little brother, nor to that of your father; there was no tear shed] (*PDE* 140–1). This form of detachment in the young Khatibi seems to announce the poetics of the margin in the future writer: rejecting pathos is a way of avoiding the *doxa* of mourning and of inflecting it towards *chagrin*. This same dynamic is taken up in the fragmented notes of 'Reliques'. Thus, in the fourth note, Khatibi writes about the death of his mother: 'Aucune larme. Je revenais de voyage et je repartais déjà, vers mon au-delà terrestre. Mes carnets en suivent le sillage' [No tears. I was coming back from a journey and I was leaving again, towards my earthly beyond. My notebooks follow the wake of this] (*PDE* 148). There is here an attempt to transform death into a poetic motif: that of Orphic writing which re-establishes a link with the underworld, transforming pain into a rhythmic lyric and distancing mourning through the use of fragmented notation.

Finally, the third device which demonstrates Khatibi's poetics of the margin consists in displacing death to the spheres of popular culture and dream. In the narration of 'Cendres', the text offers, in the margins of the memories of the mother, a world which teems with popular beliefs and practices: ritual sacrifices, memories of fantasia, visits to holy men, stays with saints, a search for the 'baraka' … From the first lines, the mother recounts this anecdote about the deceased brother of the author:

> Ton père alla le chercher au cimetière, après sa mort. Ton jeune frère lui apparut, la tête au-dessus de la tombe. Ton père me dit: 'Cette tête me regarde. Ma nuque devint lourde'. Il récita des versets du Coran et quitta le cimetière. Il s'était dit: 'Je ne dois plus aller le revoir'. (*PDE* 140)

[Your father went to find him in the cemetery, after his death. Your young brother appeared to him, his head above the grave. Your father said to me: 'That head is watching me. The nape of my neck became heavy.' He recited verses from the Koran and left the cemetery. He had said to himself: 'I must not come to see him any more.']

Here, the space and practice of mourning seem to be vanquished by the fantastic appearance of the brother: the popular belief cancels out to an extent the work of mourning. The reality of death is diverted towards the sphere of the fantastic. By transmitting the mother's words with their dense web of religious and sociocultural references, Khatibi opposes to her death the capacity of popular culture to resist, through its power of evocation and its prophetic energy, all forms of inevitability and closure. In the same way, 'Reliques' displaces death towards the world of dreams. This displacement can be read as a response to the way in which mourning, in Barthes's words, 'frappe le monde, le mondain, d'irréalité, d'importunité' [affects the world – and the worldly – with unreality, with importunity] (*JD* 137; *MD* 126). The dream space allows the author to fight this very importunity by opposing the imaginative and interpretive knowledge of the dream to the banality of the everyday. Thinking again of the death of his mother, Khatibi asks himself: 'A-t-elle rêvé sa vie pour que je la traduise? Mais la vie est un rêve à interpréter, dit le grand mystique Ibn Arabi, que mon père admirait' [Did she dream her life so that I could translate it? But life is a dream to be interpreted, said the great mystic Ibn Arabi, whom my father admired] (*PDE* 148). Writing mourning requires a work of interpretation and a constant coming and going between lived experience and dreams. Faced with the latter, as he is when he contemplates the photograph of his mother, Barthes evokes 'le même effort, le même travail sisyphéen: remonter, tendu, vers l'essence, redescendre sans l'avoir contemplée, et recommencer' [the same effort, the same Sisyphean labor: to reascend, straining towards the essence, to climb back down without having seen it, and to begin all over again].[30] The dream is the site

---

30 Roland Barthes, *La Chambre claire*, in *Œuvres complètes*, 5 vols (Paris: Seuil, 2002), v, 785–892 (p. 843); *Camera Lucida: Reflections on Photography*, trans. Richard Howard (New York: Hill & Wang, 1981), p. 66.

of the disappointed but necessary quest for the lost person, the margin where the gesture of repetition inherent to mourning is translated. In Khatibi's work, the association between the dream and mysticism allows him not only to destabilize the religious dogma which surrounds death but also to reinforce the symbolism of the gap incarnated by the figure of the Sufi philosopher Ibn Arabi. The fragmentary writing of mourning is also a rite of passage, a displacement towards those limits where the sense of loss is revealed through contact with the occult. In the third note of 'Reliques', Khatibi writes:

> Ma naissance: à l'aube d'une fête sacrée du monothéisme. La mort de ma mère: au début d'une année grégorienne. Superstition de chiffres qui me revient parfois dans sa mémoire alchimique. Mais traduire les chiffres en lettres est ma tâche, mon don aux cendres. (*PDE* 148)

> [My birth: at the dawn of a sacred feast of monotheism. The death of my mother: at the beginning of a Gregorian year. Superstition around numbers which comes back to me at times in its alchemical memory. But translating numbers into letters is my task, my gift to the ashes.]

The birth of the author and the death of the mother are in line with both a ritual logic and a calendar of superstition, a circulation of magical signs which gravitate around mourning and which must be identified and translated. To the gift of life given by the mother, Khatibi offers this 'don aux cendres' which is the translation of mourning in the combined margins of the mother's language and the signs which surround or accompany the experience of loss.

Wounds of Language and of the Fragment

Following Barthes and Derrida, mourning the mother in the work of Khatibi is an encounter with the impossibility of narrating loss. If 'la mort, comme achèvement, pourrait être considérée comme l'horreur narrative, la fin de toute narration' [death, as an ending, could be considered as the enemy of narrative, the end of any possible narration] while 'le récit est au contraire, inévitablement, au Commencement' [narration is on the contrary and inevitably associated with the Beginning], how can this paradox be negotiated in the margins of the mother's speech?[31] If the notes from 'Reliques' open the possibility of rewriting loss by establishing a dialogue with the mother's narrative in 'Cendres', how can the practice of notation allow one to go beyond the impossibility of narration? To answer these questions, a detour through the question of language is necessary before one can examine the significance of the fragment in Khatibi's text.

The first note in 'Reliques' opens with the paradox brought about by the death of the mother and the survival of the recordings of her voice: 'Entendre sa voix sans l'entendre. Les cassettes tournaient dans un sous-silence, la froideur des anges' [Hearing her voice without hearing it. The cassettes spun in a silence beneath, an angelic cold] (*PDE* 147). The mother's narrative, retranscribed by the author, carries simultaneously the imprint of the mother's voice and the material proof of her absence. It is the ambivalent sign of the concomitant restitution and loss of the mother's language. Not simply a response to the mother's narration, the notes in 'Reliques' are the product of this ambivalence. As Derrida writes of his friend Khatibi in his work *Le Monolinguisme de l'autre* [*The Monolingualism of the Other*]: 'Celui qui parle à la première personne élève la voix depuis la langue de sa mère' [The one who speaks in the first person raises his voice from the language of his mother].[32] This mother's language, simultaneously materialized (through transcription) and erased (through translation) in 'Cendres', constitutes to a certain extent the ambivalent foundation or background to the writing of mourning which is developed in 'Reliques'. The paradoxical need to depend on the mother's language while keeping it at a distance resonates in the preface Derrida

31   Régis Bertrand, Anne Carol and Jean-Noël Pelen, 'Avant-propos: narrer la mort', in Régis Bertrand, Anne Carol and Jean-Noël Pelen, eds, *Les Narrations de la mort* (Aix-en-Provence: Publications de l'Université de Provence, 2005), pp. 5–14 (p. 7).

32   Jacques Derrida, *Le Monolinguisme de l'autre ou la prothèse de l'origine* (Paris: Galilée, 1996), p. 64; *Monolinguism of the Other; or, The Prosthesis of the Origin*, trans. Patrick Mensah (Stanford, CA: Stanford University Press, 1998), p. 36.

writes to the French edition of *Chaque fois unique, la fin du monde* [*The Work of Mourning*], first published in English:

> Je n'aurais jamais osé prendre l'initiative d'un tel recueil en France, dans 'mon' pays et dans 'ma' langue [...]. La position de survivant qu'un tel recueil semble exhiber me resterait dans 'ma' langue, tout autre que cette langue demeure encore pour moi, insupportable. Indécente, voire obscène.

> [I would never have dared to take the initiative of writing such a collection in France, in 'my' country and 'my' language [...]. The position of survivor that such a collection seems to display would have been for me in 'my own' language entirely different since this language remains for me unbearable, indecent and even obscene.][33]

The distancing of the mother's language (because of the historical alienation of Derrida and through the practice of translation in Khatibi's text) is the foundational act which echoes the topos of the detour through a displacement of the mourning text into the language of the other, which reproduces the wound of separation in the domain of language. There is in this a sign of a wrenching loss which only writing in fragments can allow the author to circumvent, or at least to face, through the ruptured form of the text.

According to Barthes, mourning is distinguished by its 'caractère *discontinu*' [*discontinuous* character] (*JD* 77; *MD* 67; emphasis is in the original): his mourning text is a succession of isolated paragraphs recalling the definitive loss of the mother. The discontinuity of mourning is indissociable from its irregularity: it is 'immuable et sporadique: *il ne s'use pas*, parce qu'il n'est pas continu' [immutable and sporadic: *it does not wear away*, because it is not continuous] (*JD* 105; *MD* 95; emphasis is in the original). In Barthes's thought, this discontinuity is simultaneously a source of fear and anxiety and a necessary condition for writing. The plan of the novel 'Vita nova' must be conceived 'comme geste radical' [as a radical gesture] motivated by the 'nécessité de discontinuer ce qui marchait avant sur sa lancée' [necessity of discontinuing what previously continued on its own momentum] (*JD* 84; *MD* 74). It is a question of shattering unity and of

33   Derrida, *Chaque fois unique la fin du monde*, pp. 9–10.

taking note of the rupture brought about by loss. Therefore, the discontinuity of mourning calls for a discontinuity of writing: fragmented notes allow the evocation of the 'brusques et fugitives vacillations, fadings très courts' [sudden and fugitive vacillations, brief fade-outs] (*JD* 127; *MD* 116) which characterize mourning. This poetics of the fragment resonates directly with the work of Khatibi. For the Moroccan writer, writing the loss of the mother in scattered notes allows him to 'gérer le deuil en dispersant poétiquement les cendres de la défunte' [cope with mourning through a poetic dispersal of the ashes of the deceased]: a form of 'exorcisme' [exorcism] but which is 'sans mélancolie' [without melancholy] (*PDE* 148). The ten notes of 'Reliques' are the echo of the discontinuity of memory and of the mourning for the mother. Each note, each relic, is the result of a transformation of the memories of the mother and of the loss of the mother through the unstable energy of the fragment.

In the book he writes in homage to Derrida, Khatibi admits: 'Que je souffre ou que je me console, je sais que mon deuil sera toujours fragmentaire. Une manière de parler à l'autre, au prochain qui soit vivant, me fera défaut' [Whether I suffer or console myself, I know that my mourning will always be fragmentary. I will lack a way of speaking to the other, to my neighbour who is alive].[34] If the fragment is the sign of a lack, of an absence of dialogue, of the death of this 'manière de parler' to the friend as to the mother, the fragmentary writing of mourning allows a salutary reversal: the transformation of the paralyzing shock of loss into a dynamic of multiplication and return. Khatibi explains that 'le travail du deuil' [the work of mourning] consists of 'réfléchir à la finitude qui immobilise, à la pétrification, au bruit sans écho en regardant de l'autre côté des yeux' [reflecting on the finitude which stills, on petrification, on the echoless noise of gazing from the other side of the eyes] (*PDE* 149). The closure and silence of death give way to the openness and resonance of the short form. It is a question of writing to oppose the lack of finality of the note to the finality of death. The second-last note of 'Cendres' confirms this strategy of inversion: 'Le mot 'mort': le laisser vivre en soi sans bruit' [The word 'death': to let it live within one

---

34   Khatibi, *Jacques Derrida, en effet*, pp. 77–8.

noiselessly] (*PDE* 149), writes Khatibi as if echoing Derrida who evokes 'la mort vivante de la mère' [the living death of the mother] (*C* 130). With both authors, each fragment makes death live again by shattering its scenes, by displacing its language and by appropriating its silence.

At the same time, the fragment is what allows Khatibi to grasp the eminently contradictory and searing character of mourning, as the last note suggests: 'Le paradoxe: communiquer de l'incommunicable. Une note étouffée. Ma mère est morte avec douceur, avec élégance: à peine un cri d'adieu, si discret que son entourage a été presque ébloui' [Paradox: to communicate what cannot be communicated. A stifled note. My mother died gently, elegantly: there was barely a call goodbye, she died so discreetly that those around her were almost in awe] (*PDE* 149). Simultaneously discreet and blinding, the fragmentary note translates the paradox of loss into the writing sphere, that is, the putting into words of the 'présence de l'absence' [presence of absence] (*JD* 79; *MD* 69) that Barthes speaks of. The fragment is the sign of speech that is simultaneously muffled and liberated, an attempt to speak the unspeakable, to reconcile the word and the ineffable. This attempt is the very sign of the division inherent in the writing of mourning. Khatibi writes that 'la fin de ces notes sera un exercice réconcilié avec ses reliques et ses cendres' [the end of these notes will be a form of reconciliation with her relics and ashes] (*PDE* 149). But how can one reconcile, unless it is through a fragmentary form, a mother's story saved from death and scattered notes on the return of that same death?

In 'Cendres', as in 'Reliques', the gap which separates each of the mother's anecdotes and each of Khatibi's notes from the next defines a suspended space of mourning, a silent margin where the reconciliation of the sites of life and death can be read. In the work of Derrida, this space carries the symbolic name of 'escarre' [bedsore] in reference to the wounds which cross the body of his dying mother. The bedsore is 'un archipel de volcans rouges et noirâtres, plaies enflammées [...] s'ouvrant ici, se fermant là' [an archipelago of red and blackish volcanoes, inflamed wounds [...] opening here, closing there] (*C* 79), exactly like the fifty-nine periphrases of 'Circonfession'. Derrida's fragments make visible the impact of the mourning to come on the text as it is being written. Convinced that the imminent death of his mother would come to 'sculpter l'écriture du dehors, lui donner sa forme et son rythme' [sculpt the writing from the outside, give it form and rhythm], Derrida explains:

> Jamais aucun de mes textes n'aura dépendu en son dedans le plus essentiel d'un dehors aussi coupant, accidentel et contingent, comme si chaque syllabe, et le milieu même de chaque périphrase se préparait à recevoir un coup de téléphone, la nouvelle de la mort d'une mourante (*C* 192–3)

> [Never will any of my texts have depended in its most essential inner content on an outer circumstance so sharp, accidental and contingent, as if each syllable, and the very context of each periphrasis were preparing to receive a telephone call, the news of the death of a dying woman.]

In the work of Khatibi, this interdependence of phenomena external to the text (the voice and death of the mother) and of the inside of the text (structure in fragments) is displayed in the underlying link between 'Cendres' and 'Reliques'. Each fragment of the second section carries within it the trace or 'escarre' of the first. The accumulation of these traces or unstable margins corresponds to a sketch of the writing as it is being constructed, the mobile horizon of a text to come.

Whether it is a question of a diary in fragments haunted by the plan for a novel (Barthes), of a series of fleeting periphrases defying death throes (Derrida), or of ten isolated notes written in the wake of the memories of the mother (Khatibi), writing of maternal loss always makes evident 'le retentissement solennel du deuil sur la possibilité de faire œuvre' [the solemn impact of mourning on the possibility of creating a work of any kind] (*JD* 249; *MD* 237). In the work of Khatibi, this possibility remains suspended, closed within the broken-up narrative of the mother and the incompletion of the fragments which follow it. In the introduction to *Pardessus l'épaule*, Khatibi admits: 'J'ai toujours rêvé, sans en connaître bien le secret, d'écrire un texte en pointillé' [I have always dreamed, without truly knowing how, of writing a text in dots] (*PDE* 9). In the margins of the funereal song which accompanies the death of the mother, the dream of the writer retains its mystery, postponing a little further the shared horizon of mourning and writing.

– Translated from the French by Sara-Louise Cooper

SARA-LOUISE COOPER

Mourning the Mother, Mourning the World: Patrick Chamoiseau's *La Matière de l'absence*

ABSTRACT

Since the death of Patrick Chamoiseau's mother in 1999, mourning has taken on particular prominence in his work. This essay will examine the ways in which the experience of mourning the mother imbricates the personal, the historical and the literary in Chamoiseau's 2016 work, *La Matière de l'absence* [*The Matter of Absence*]. For Chamoiseau, the bereaved person's encounter with 'l'abîme insensé de la mort' [the senseless chasm of death], or what Chamoiseau calls 'l'en-dehors' [the without], recapitulates the rupture of consciousness provoked by the radical negation of life which reigned in the hold of the slave ship and in the Nazi camps. Chamoiseau presents this contact with *l'en-dehors* as a universal human experience which is nonetheless at the root of cultural difference, as each society tells itself different stories to keep *l'en-dehors* at bay. This essay offers a series of close readings of *La Matière de l'absence* to illustrate the ways in which Chamoiseau portrays mourning as a route into a globalized historical and artistic consciousness which is nonetheless attentive to the particular.

Mourning is a persistent concern in the writing of Patrick Chamoiseau, whose early work laments the loss of Creole culture. In the 1988 novel *Solibo Magnifique*, the passing of Creole culture is represented by the death of the eponymous hero, who is strangled by his own words.[1] To grieve this loss in its full enormity is to run counter to a colonial mentality which dismisses Creole culture as irrational and base. Understanding and striving to do justice to the death of Solibo thus becomes a question of freeing oneself from the insidious psychological domination of France in late twentieth-century Martinique. In this way mourning does not only concern the past, but can become the crucible in which a better ethics and politics is forged. The call for such productive forms of mourning is a key element of the 1989 *Éloge de la créolité*, where Chamoiseau and his

---

1   Patrick Chamoiseau, *Solibo Magnifique* (Paris: Gallimard, 1988).

co-authors call for recognition of the syncretic qualities of Caribbean culture.[2] Maeve McCusker has observed that this early phase of Chamoiseau's work possesses a 'confused temporality, an ambivalent mix of projection and retrospection, of prophetic proclamation and nostalgic regret', as Chamoiseau and his co-authors seek to '[reclaim] for the future the culture of the past'.[3]

This temporal dynamic resonates with Édouard Glissant's vision of Caribbean time. Glissant writes in the 1961 preface to his play *Monsieur Toussaint* of seeking a 'prophetic vision of the past', a task he characterizes as 'a poetic endeavour'.[4] Chamoiseau inherits Glissant's view of mourning as ethical, political and aesthetic. The younger author's exploration of good ways of inheriting the past goes hand in hand with the complex question of his relationship to Glissant. In its imbrication of narratives, the structure of Chamoiseau's writing often raises questions about relating to the voices of forebears, literal or literary. These include fellow Caribbean writers, such as Aimé Césaire and Frankétienne, canonical French authors such as Montaigne and Baudelaire and authors who write in different languages such as Gabriel García Márquez and Lewis Carroll. Glissant is however one of the most prominent literary forebears in Chamoiseau's work, leading one critic to refer to Chamoiseau as Glissant's 'fils spirituel' [spiritual son].[5]

Born in 1928, twenty-five years before the younger author, Glissant appears as a tutelary figure in Chamoiseau's work who inspires him to multiple conversions. In the 1997 *Écrire en pays dominé*, an essay which blurs the boundaries between literary history, theory and autobiography, Chamoiseau recounts the transformation of his understanding brought

2   Patrick Chamoiseau, Jean Bernabé and Raphaël Confiant, *Éloge de la créolité* (Paris: Gallimard, 1989).

3   Maeve McCusker, *Patrick Chamoiseau: Recovering Memory* (Liverpool: Liverpool University Press, 2007), p. 11.

4   Édouard Glissant, *Monsieur Toussaint: A Play*, trans. J. Michael Dash (Boulder, CO: Rienner, 2005), pp. 15–16, quoted in John E. Drabinski, 'Sites of Relation and "Tout-monde": Reflections on Glissant's Late Work', *Angelaki* 24 (2019), 157–72 (pp. 161–2).

5   Jean-Louis Cornille, *Chamoiseau … fils* (Paris: Hermann, 2014), p. 5.

about by reading Glissant's 1975 novel: '*Malemort* explosait la coquille du "Monde noir" pour solliciter ces êtres qui s'étaient emmêlés dans ces bateaux, dans ces cales, dans ces plantations, dans ces îles' [*Malemort* blew up the shell of the 'Black World' to call up those beings who had tangled together in those ships, those holds, those plantations, those islands].[6] Glissant is here situated as inspiring a turn away from a quest for African roots towards attention to the particularities of intercultural contact from the Middle Passage onwards. I wish to examine a second Glissantian movement in Chamoiseau's thought: the shift from a primary concern with Martinique and the Caribbean towards more global concerns.

This shift can be discerned in Chamoiseau's attention to issues such as ecology, Buddhist theories of consciousness and contemporary migration from Africa to Europe.[7] Chamoiseau's engagement with such themes is influenced by Glissant's concept of the 'tout-monde', laid out in the 1997 *Traité du tout-monde* [*Treatise on the Whole-World*]. In the *tout-monde*, each individual, no matter which culture, language or country s/he belongs to, is exposed to all the cultures and all the languages of the world, which interact with each other in a chaotic swirl.[8] Critics such as Chris Bongie and Peter Hallward see Glissant's concept of the *tout-monde* as a shift away from his earlier anti-colonial politics to a quietist, apolitical celebration of cultural mixing.[9] Chamoiseau's comparable shift from the local to the global has not been immune from such criticisms either. On this subject, Jean-Louis Cornille asks: '[S]ous couvert de "diversalité", voire de "multiversalité", n'en revient-on pas aux bons vieux universaux?' [In sum, beneath the cover of

---

6   Patrick Chamoiseau, *Écrire en pays dominé* (Paris: Gallimard, 1997), p. 101.

7   Chamoiseau explores ecological questions and Buddhism in *Les Neuf Consciences du Malfini* (Paris: Gallimard, 2009). Migration from Africa to Europe is the subject of *Frères migrants* (Paris: Seuil, 2017) and an edited collection, *Osons la fraternité: les écrivains aux côtés des migrants*, ed. Patrick Chamoiseau and Michel Le Bris (Paris: Rey, 2018).

8   Édouard Glissant, *Traité du tout-monde* (Paris: Gallimard, 1997).

9   Peter Hallward, *Absolutely Postcolonial: Writing between the Singular and the Specific* (Manchester: Manchester University Press, 2001); Chris Bongie, *Friends and Enemies: The Scribal Politics of Post/Colonial Literature* (Liverpool: Liverpool University Press, 2008).

'diversality', or indeed of 'multiversality', are we not simply coming back to the good old universals?].[10] Both the doubt raised by Cornille and the criticisms of Glissant's later work are tied to the potentially irresolvable difficulties of engaging simultaneously with the total and the particular.

As many essays in this volume have brought out, this question is fundamental to the writing of mourning. To narrate the experience of mourning, the author must articulate his or her own particular loss as well as grapple with the shattering reality of loss itself. If the writers of mourning texts tilt towards addressing their own bereavement as an example of the general phenomenon of loss, the specificity of the lost loved one is submerged, meaning that the deceased is effectively erased a second time in the space of the literary text. Yet if the writer of a mourning text focuses exclusively on the specificity of the loss, he or she risks neglecting the open-ended infinity of grief. A more minor point is that the author is creating a text for a public who does not know the lost loved one, and so is presumably in search of something broader and more general to take away from the text. An author's commitment to create a faithful literary memorial can thus be understood through a Derridean understanding of the promise as caught between possibility and impossibility, doubt and certainty.[11] To create a mourning text is to engage simultaneously with the infinity of the loss and the specificity of the lost loved one, but the completion of the text ends this dual engagement and so risks infidelity to the loved one.

Since this is a dilemma which can never be fully resolved, much writing on mourning is characterized by its open-ended form and by multiple returns to the inexhaustible subject of the loss. As briefly explored above, mourning is also a political gesture, and so a return to mourning can also occur when an author's politics have shifted. In this essay, I examine Chamoiseau's practice of return in his writing on the loss of his mother. Firstly, I compare his treatment of this subject in his autobiographical trilogy and in a recent essay of 2016, *La Matière de l'absence*. Secondly, I show how his return to the mother's death in the later work is also a

10   Cornille, *Chamoiseau … fils*, p. 120.
11   Jacques Derrida explores this notion of the promise in 'Avances', preface to Serge Marcel, *Le Tombeau du dieu artisan: sur Platon* (Paris: Minuit, 1995), pp. 7–43.

return to the 1902 eruption of Martinican volcano Mont Pelée, and to the Caribbean literary canon, via the writing of Aimé Césaire. This return to the Caribbean canon is also a return to the French canon, since *La Matière de l'absence* self-consciously echoes the digressive form of Montaigne's 'Des Coches' [Of Coaches]. This layered revisiting of Mont Pelée and 'Des Coches' becomes an experiment in negotiating the tension between the particular and the total as Chamoiseau simultaneously writes the loss of his mother and seeks a literary form for writing the world. Through the deployment of the essay form and a volcanic metaphor, Chamoiseau holds together a multi-perspectival imagination of the wholeness of the world while at the same time maintaining a strand of anti-colonial thought. Reading Chamoiseau's writing in this way suggests that 'world literature' can be francophone as well as anglophone, essayistic as well as novelistic, and early modern or, rather, 'eerily modern' as well as modern.[12]

From the Local to the Global: *Une enfance créole to La Matière de l'absence*

To make this argument we must first demonstrate that a shift from the local to the global does indeed occur in Chamoiseau's work. Such a shift becomes apparent through an examination of Chamoiseau's earlier and later writing on the loss of his mother. He first approaches this subject in *Une enfance créole* [*A Creole Childhood*], a trilogy composed of *Antan d'enfance* [*Childhood*] (1990), *Chemin-d'école* [*School Days*] (1994) and *À bout d'enfance* [*Out of Childhood*] (2005).[13] Although Chamoiseau's mother is still living at the time of the publication of the first two volumes,

12   I am grateful to Professor Wes Williams for the term 'eerily modern' as an expression for the uncanny recurrence of the early modern in the contemporary.

13   Patrick Chamoiseau, *Antan d'enfance* (Paris: Hatier, 1990), republished as *Une enfance créole I, Antan d'enfance* (Paris: Gallimard, 1996); *Chemin d'école* (Paris: Gallimard, 1994), republished as *Une enfance créole II, Chemin d'école* (Paris: Gallimard, 1996); *À bout d'enfance* (Paris: Gallimard, 2005), republished as *Une enfance créole III, À Bout d'enfance* (Paris: Gallimard 2006). Further references

the trilogy as a whole deals with the theme of maternal loss, as this begins to occur as the child grows up and leaves the domestic environment, and is hastened when the colonial education system alienates him from his mother's Creole speech and culture. All three volumes of the trilogy experiment with autobiographical form by incorporating elements of the fantastic, referring to the author in the third person as 'le négrillon' [little Black boy] and evading linear chronology through an absence of dates and a layering and fusing of child and adult perspectives.

La Matière de l'absence is an essay published sixteen years after the mother's death. The text begins as the author and his older sister cross the threshold of the cemetery to begin the yearly ritual of tending to the mother's grave on All Saints Day. The body of the text is formed by the dialogue between the two siblings at the cemetery as they grapple with the meaning of the mother's death and with the human encounter with absence more broadly. The author's voice predominates with the older sister playing the role of a foil who occasionally interjects to question or reject the conclusions of the author, or to prompt him to further clarification. The text draws on the flexibility of the essay form to weave together elements of autobiography, ethnography, evolutionary history, music criticism and poetry, among many other genres. The form of the text thus enacts one of the arguments put forward about loss: the devastation it wreaks has an eruptive and paradoxically creative force.

As is evident in the titles of *Une enfance créole* and *La Matière de l'absence*, in both texts mourning the mother offers a way into other subjects. *Antan d'enfance* was published the year after the 1989 *Éloge de la créolité* and can be seen as an illustration and defence of Creole origins. Through its lament for the loss of the mother and the language and culture she represents, it calls for recognition of the value of her world. These elements are still present when Chamoiseau returns to the subject in 2016, but now they are set within a strikingly comparative, transnational framework, reflecting an increasing engagement with the Glissantian *tout-monde*. To

---

to these works in the main text are to the republished versions, abbreviated as *A* (*Antan d'enfance*), *C* (*Chemin d'école*) and *B* (*À bout d'enfance*). All translations of quotations in this chapter are mine unless otherwise stated.

revisit the mother's death is also to revisit the cultural and political meanings ascribed to the maternal. Where *Une enfance créole* is a return to origins, *La Matière de l'absence* is a 'retour à l'origine des origines' [a return to the origin of origins] as the mother's death becomes a way of thinking about the birth of culture, art and consciousness in human history as a whole.[14]

This shift away from focus on a particular culture to a dual focus on Martinique and the history of human culture as a whole is discernible in slight contrasts between the earlier and later work's treatment of two themes: death and Creole customs. In both texts, death is portrayed as an ever-present thread in everyday life which is nonetheless difficult to perceive and articulate. Both texts express ideas about death and mourning present elsewhere in Chamoiseau's work: mourning structures the relationship to the everyday, because death, like a ravaging swarm of ants, runs through life, as catastrophic as it is imperceptible. To mourn is to become conscious of the destructive forces present in the world normally obscured by conventional habits of perception, which lull us into acceptance of the slow deaths imposed by hostile political forces and our own tendencies to self-destruction. Although both texts express these ideas, the hostile political forces in question in *Une enfance créole* are those of neo-colonialism, while those at work in *La Matière de l'absence* are those of neo-liberal globalization. Although these forces are by no means mutually exclusive in Chamoiseau's thought or elsewhere, he explores neo-colonialism primarily from a Martinican perspective whereas the images used to evoke neo-liberal globalization are suggestive of networks of communication which imprison the whole world.

This shift becomes apparent through an examination of the different metaphors used in the two texts to evoke the mother's death. In *À bout d'enfance*, Chamoiseau deploys the metaphor of a tree which dies while remaining intact to convey the nature of his mother's slow decline into dementia and her eventual death (*B* 283–4). Dispersed rather than unitary, the temporality of the death of the mother and the tree is confused. Its beginning is only visible in retrospect and its end is also difficult to date. As

14   Patrick Chamoiseau, *La Matière de l'absence* (Paris: Seuil, 2016), pp. 308–9 (hereafter referenced in main text as *LM*).

the destruction of the mother's mind begins to takes its course, there are small perturbations in everyday life – a saucepan of milk forgotten on the stove, a vague look in his mother's eyes – which in retrospect appear as the beginning of the end (*B* 226, 242–3). Like the few dead leaves which signal the beginning of the tree's decline, such signs pass unnoticed at the time. The children lose their relationship with their mother when she ceases to recognize them, but her physical life continues after this point (*B* 288). The metaphor of the dying tree thus evokes a slow, invisible but irrevocable form of destruction, difficult to perceive but nonetheless devastating.

These aspects of the loss of the mother resonate with Chamoiseau's depiction of the psychological death which occurs under neo-colonialism. In theoretical work published in this period, he uses oxymoronic phrases such as 'silencieux tocsin' [silent alarm] to evoke the invasion of Martinican minds by neo-colonial ways of thinking.[15] Like the ants which kill the tree or the mother's dementia, this is a form of death which begins from the inside and can leave the physical body intact long after mental life has been thoroughly colonized. It, too, is only visible in retrospect, as the middle-aged author contemplates details of his childhood, like his identification with white characters in films or his drawing of a house with a chimney in primary school. Although Chamoiseau's exploration of such neo-colonial culture does make some comparative gestures, it is primarily focused on his own Martinican childhood. The dying tree, the mother slowly losing her memory and Martinican children drawing chimneys are all suffering from damage done to roots, to connections with the past, to Martinican culture.

In *La Matière de l'absence*, by contrast, Chamoiseau deploys the image of a rhizome rather than a root to evoke the invasive but invisible presence of death in everyday life:

> À croire qu'à la manière de pêcheurs clandestins les cimetières envoyaient vers la vie des lignes chargées d'hameçons, et en ramenaient des trâlées de victimes. Mais, contrairement à nos pêcheurs, les cimetières n'étaient jamais bredouilles. Ils n'en finissaient pas de siphonner les ruines de la vie, d'accumuler des os, d'entasser des souvenirs, d'accueillir des cortèges de tristesses et de larmes. (*LM* 35)

15   Chamoiseau, *Écrire en pays dominé*, p. 19.

[It was as if the cemeteries, like clandestine fishermen, sent lines weighted down with bait into life, and brought back from it heaps of victims. But, unlike our fishermen, the cemeteries were never empty-handed. They kept siphoning off the ruins of life, accumulating bones, piling up memories, welcoming processions of sadnesses and tears.]

In a possible reimagination of the Baudelairean pun on 'vers' (worms and lines of poetry), the polysemy of 'lignes' [lines] as both fishing lines and lines written by an author suggest the omnipresence of the tentacles of death in the world of the living and the world of the text. Unlike the tree roots which reach down into the ground, reminiscent of the depth/surface metaphors of *créolité*, the fishing lines reach outwards in many directions, recalling images elsewhere in Chamoiseau's work of 'mailles' [chains, links, stitches or mesh]. These 'mailles' choke ocean life, evoke the chains of the enslaved who died in the Atlantic and also come to stand for the digital networks which entrap free human beings.[16] Whereas in the metaphor of the dying tree, it is death which eats up the person from the inside, here the victims are unwittingly complicit in their own destruction. Death comes about specifically through a perverted form of consumption, a parody of eating where hooked bait replaces food. This, too recalls the deployment of fast food as an image of neo-liberal globalization elsewhere in Chamoiseau's work; a form of nourishment which seems to satisfy desire but is in fact slow poison.[17] Death makes itself visible not only in the zombified life of someone who is physically alive but mentally colonized, but also in material accumulation, as signalled by the list in the last sentence. The exploration of death here thus resonates with images of neo-liberal globalization, with its accumulation of dead goods, slow poisoning of bodies and its invisible but imprisoning networks.

The second way in which a shift from the local to the global can be discerned between *Une enfance créole* and *La Matière de l'absence* is through comparing the presentation of Creole customs. In *Une enfance créole*, Chamoiseau's narration of his childhood includes an evocation of his mother's daily rhythms. These, in turn, are a way into portraying Creole cultural practices. In *La Matière de l'absence*, Chamoiseau returns

---

16   Chamoiseau, *Frères migrants*, pp. 19–23.
17   Patrick Chamoiseau, *Le Papillon et la lumière* (Paris: Gallimard, 2013), p. 70.

to this material: his family's Sunday customs; his mother's creation of a garden and a chicken coop in Fort-de-France; her use of herbs as medicine for herself but not for her children (*LM* 168–72, 173, 186). He foregrounds the connection between his earlier narrations of childhood and the later text through playful allusions to the first volume of the trilogy, referring to his 'antan[s] d'enfance' [yesteryears of childhood] or simply his 'antans' [yesteryears] (*LM* 34, 301, 328–9). Yet where in the older work there was a sense that many of these episodes afforded the author a tenuous but vital connection to Martinican culture, in *La Matière de l'absence* the enchantment of these elements of Creole life seems to have been exhausted and the avenue they offered both to the past and to the future is now closed off. The description of the conch shells is typical in this respect:

> L'espèce des lambis défaille. Leurs conques persistent parmi nous sans beaucoup d'enchantement, dans un vide de folklore qui les use sur elles-mêmes. Celles que l'on voit proclament leur propre disparition. Chère Baronne, regarde bien chaque conque: elle porte en elle un monde sans audience et quelques siècles devenus silencieux. (*LM* 77)

> [The species of the *lambis* is dying out. Their conch shells persist among us without much enchantment, in an emptiness of folklore which wears them out. Those that we see proclaim their own disappearance. Dear *Baronne*, look closely at each conch shell: it carries within it a world without an audience and several centuries that have become silent.]

Where *Une enfance créole*, alongside *Éloge de la créolité*, seemed to argue for renewed attention to the world within the conch shells, here there seems to be regretful acceptance of the lack of such attention.

This is also evident to an extent in the linguistic differences between *Une enfance créole* and *La Matière de l'absence*. The autobiography is written in creolized French; the essay almost entirely in standard French. This linguistic shift at times seems to bring with it a kind of cultural erasure too. In both texts, the night is portrayed as a time of mystery, when the boundaries between the real and the fantastic begin to tremble. When Chamoiseau writes about his memories of the night in *Antan d'enfance*, he weaves figures from Creole folk tales into the narration. He creolizes the genres of autobiography and the folk tale, and in doing so creates a linguistic fusion of Creole and French. The French text is punctuated by oral, creolized interjections such as 'hébin!' or 'flap', and includes distinctively Caribbean words, such as 'cheval-trois-pattes' [horse with three hooves] and 'zombi' [zombie] (*A* 175). In *La Matière de l'absence*, the night is still a time of mystery when daylight certainties begin to tremble, but now it is presented with no reference to Creole folklore and in entirely standard French: 'La nuit qui efface tout rendait ce tout mille fois bien plus palpable, dans des amplitudes sans limites et des configurations pour le moins détestables' [The night which erases everything made this everything a thousand times more palpable, in limitless breadths and configurations which were, to say the least, foul] (*LM* 26–7). There is also an element of *tout-monde* consciousness in the author's summing up of his view of the night through a non-Caribbean perspective: 'Les nuits sont toujours enceintes, nous disent les Arabes' [Nights are always pregnant, the Arabs tell us] (*LM* 34).

This approach to childhood vision through the perspective of others is also present in the return to the memory of the crib his oldest sister would make at Christmas. The *Baronne*'s Nativity figures, evoked vividly from the child-self's perspective in *Antan d'enfance*, are now seen through the eyes of her grandchildren, who gaze at them 'comme nous la regardions dans nos antans perdus' [as we would gaze at them in our lost yesteryears] (*LM* 328–9). By ending this episode with 'perdus', Chamoiseau moves away from an attempt to bring his childhood to life. Instead, its disappearance is emphasized. Returns to this way of seeing must now take place through indirect routes, such as watching his sister's grandchildren watch the figures he remembers. In Chamoiseau's thought, reality is elusive and slippery, and perceiving it is a feat of the liberated poetic imagination and not merely a routine part of everyday life. In *Antan d'enfance*, returning to the child's vision of the world acts as a kind of detour which exposes the falseness of conventional 'reality' (in fact a neo-colonial construction) and reveals the rich poetic real it cloaks.[18] In *La Matière de l'absence*, by contrast, it is loss which disconcerts and disrupts and so has the power to reveal what normally escapes our vision (*LM* 359). The literary text, rather than enabling a

---

18   Chamoiseau outlines this distinction between reality and the real in *Antan d'enfance* (*A* 93–4).

recreation of the poetic richness of the narrator's childhood, instead enables
a series of displaced and deferred returns to the paradoxically ungraspable
immediacy of absence.

L'en-dehors and the Volcanic Real

Having shown that there is a shift from the local to the global in
Chamoiseau's work, the question remains: what devices does he use to
engage simultaneously with the total and the particular? The concept of
l'en-dehors, which Chamoiseau develops in *La Matière de l'absence*, is key
to this. For Chamoiseau, *l'en-dehors* is 'le surgissement de l'impensable'
[the sudden appearance of the unthinkable] (*LM* 308). It is what lies
beyond the bounds of human consciousness and has the paradoxical
effect of both devastating the mind and stimulating creativity. It can be
experienced in many ways: through beauty, scientific discovery and also
through an unmediated encounter with death, which is the focus of *La
Matière de l'absence* (*LM* 310). For Chamoiseau, the encounter with death
and absence is at the origin of consciousness and art. He offers an imagined account of the first human experience of another's death, positing
that this must have triggered the creation of myth, ritual and story. Such
rituals and stories serve to express some understanding of the force of a
sudden absence, but also function to protect human societies from an unmediated encounter with it. Although *l'en-dehors* can never be held at bay
entirely, Chamoiseau suggests that in the pre-modern era culture in its
broadest sense was generally successful in allowing human beings to perceive death's radical negation of sense only through a protective weave of
imagined meaning. However, when the walls of ritual and culture begin
to crumble, *l'en-dehors* is re-experienced in all its terrifying immediacy
(*LM* 306–8).

   L'en-dehors is an inherently comparative concept, as it does not belong
to any one culture, place or time, but can appear in any place or time and
is at the origin of culture itself. Since it is something which exists beyond
human consciousness and to which there are multiple points of entry, it

also allows comparison of phenomena very different in magnitude and origin. Chamoiseau, for example, compares the shattering of protective cultural narratives that occurs in the hold of the slave ship to the 'puissance relationnelle' [relational power] of the *tout-monde* (*LM* 358–9). For Chamoiseau, both phenomena rent the veil of culture which protects individuals from *l'en-dehors*. Instead, they are exposed to 'la grand-scène du monde' [the whole stage of the world] and must improvise individual responses to it. Chamoiseau's theoretical framework is explicitly comparative when he draws parallels between the Middle Passage and the consciousness of *tout-monde*, but it is also implicitly comparative, when, for example, he refers to the African heritage of people in the Caribbean as 'un passé dépassé, repassé, trépassé, qui pourtant ne passe pas' [a past we have gone beyond, gone over and which has passed away, and yet which does not pass] (*LM* 69). Here Chamoiseau rewrites the title of Henry Rousso's foundational study of repression in French national memory, *Vichy, un passé qui ne passe pas* [*Vichy: A Past which Does Not Pass*]. In doing so, he enacts in miniature the project of the whole essay: delving into repressed national memory to draw out its transnational dimensions; illuminating the complexity of a past which both eludes memory and overwhelms it; creating layered connections between different modes of personal, national and transnational trauma.

To give tangible form to the concept of *l'en-dehors* and to convey the impact of his mother's death, Chamoiseau deploys the metaphor of the volcanic eruption, and specifically the 1902 eruption of Mont Pelée. Like the concept of *l'en-dehors*, the volcanic metaphor allows Chamoiseau to move between the particular and the global and to explore destructive forms of creation and creative forms of destruction. Volcanoes are particular to the Caribbean and to Martinique, but they are also one of the foundations of the global in the sense that every piece of earth has been formed by volcanic activity. The volcano thus offers a fitting metaphor for Martinican closeness to a source of radical negation which is nonetheless at the root of every human culture. In ways we will go on to examine, the volcanic metaphor allows a triple-layered return to the Martinican canon, the French canon and the idea of discovering the world.

The May 1902 eruption of Mont Pelée was a cataclysmic event in Martinican history; in three minutes it killed a quarter of the island's population and almost entirely destroyed the city of Saint-Pierre. On the eve of the eruption, Saint-Pierre was the principal city of Martinique, and a major world port, known as the 'capitale mondiale du rhum' [world capital of rum].[19] The eruption left only two survivors and one intact structure, the Pont Roche.[20] The scale of the event eclipsed all other twentieth-century natural disasters in Martinique and is referred to simply as 'LA catastrophe'.[21] Since almost all inhabitants of the city were killed, the eruption could only be perceived from a distance, for example, by the two survivors who heard it but did not see it since they were buried in an underground prison, or by the captain who saw it from his ship off the coast of Martinique, or by the scientists who returned to study the event by examining the ashes it left.[22] This parallels the way Chamoiseau conceives of *l'en-dehors* and approaches writing the loss of his mother; the moment he learned of this loss overwhelms his mind and can only be understood indirectly, through multiple returns from different perspectives. This is evident across the body of Chamoiseau's autobiographical work, as he returns to the subject ten years after treating it in *À bout d'enfance*. It is also evident within *La Matière de l'absence* itself. The structure of the text is highly digressive, as the author repeatedly approaches, then retreats from, the moment he learns of his mother's death. The indirect approach to the mother's death through the metaphor of the volcano is simultaneously a multi-layered and multi-perspectival return to the Martinican canon, the French canon and the early modern genre of the essay. Together these

19   Fanny Benitez, 'La Catastrophe de la Montagne Pelée le 8 mai 1902 en Martinique: Saint-Pierre, une ville résiliente ou un exemple archétypal de bifurcation', *Physio-Géo* 14 (2019), 227–52 (§ 18) <https://journals.openedition.org/physio-geo/9338> [accessed 24 August 2020].

20   Ibid., § 7. Chamoiseau tells the story of the two survivors in his novel *Texaco* (Paris: Gallimard, 1992).

21   Benitez, 'La Catastrophe de la Montagne Pelée le 8 mai 1902 en Martinique', § 36.

22   The testimony of the captain who witnessed the eruption from his ship is reproduced in Alfred Lacroix, *La Montagne Pelée et ses éruptions* (Paris: Masson, 2004), pp. 243–4, quoted in Benitez, 'La Catastrophe de la Montagne Pelée le 8 mai 1902 en Martinique', § 21.

many-layered returns contribute to a decolonized concept of 'discovering the world' which holds in tension multiple situated perspectives and the idea of an elusive totality.

Returning to the Volcano, to the Essay, to the World

To return to Mont Pelée is also to revisit the Martinican canon. The volcano is a key metaphor in the work of Aimé Césaire, referred to by Chamoiseau and his co-authors in the *Éloge de la créolité* as a father figure for modern Martinican writing.[23] This metaphor depends on a sense of the paradoxically creative force of the 1902 eruption. In a 2013 work of homage to Aimé Césaire, Guadeloupean author Daniel Maximin draws a link between the material, political effects of the eruption and its role as a metaphor for poetry in Césaire's work. Maximin points out that the 1902 eruption can be read through Amerindian beliefs that natural disasters destroy that which should not exist. The destruction of Saint-Pierre thus appears as nature seeking vengeance on an oppressive colonial capital.[24] Volcanoes have long been associated with the disruptive force of revolutions, but in the case of the May 1902 disaster there are specific reasons to see a kind of antagonism between the smooth running of the colony and the force of the volcano.[25] Elections were due to take place in Saint-Pierre around the time of the eruption, and, eager that these go ahead, the city authorities had commissioned scientists to study the increasing volcanic activity of the mountain. The scientific commission had assured the population that it was safe to remain in the city, so the devastation of the eruption can be seen as a dramatic illumination of the limits of colonial knowledge. Those who fled the city in spite of official instructions to stay in retrospect appear as possessing a subversive form

23   Chamoiseau, Bernabé and Confiant, *Éloge de la créolité*, p. 19.
24   Daniel Maximin, *Aimé Césaire: frère volcan* (Paris: Seuil, 2013), pp. 22–3.
25   David McCallam, 'The Volcano: From Enlightenment to Revolution', *Nottingham French Studies* 45 (2006), 52–68.

of counter-knowledge, a subject to which we will return below. The only survivors were imprisoned Black men; paradoxically punishment for supposedly threatening the colony shielded them from harm.

The destruction of the city is thus tied to questions of knowledge and counter-knowledge, the sudden illumination of the provisional quality of meanings which seem oppressively fixed. These resonances are at work when Césaire describes his poetry as 'péléen' [volcanic], evoking its destructively creative character, as well as its spontaneous, unpredictable and uncontainable qualities.[26] Maximin writes: 'La découverte de ton écriture m'a bien fait comprendre ce que tu as toujours appelé la dimension péléenne de notre poésie: *que tout s'enflamme soudain d'un sens inaperçu*' [The discovery of your writing led me to understand what you have always called the volcanic dimension of our poetry: *that everything is ignited suddenly by an unnoticed meaning*].[27] By returning to Mont Pelée as a metaphor, Chamoiseau aligns himself with the modern Martinican poetic tradition. In *La Matière de l'absence*, however, the illumination of sense which takes place is not only of the provisional quality of seemingly fixed colonial hierarchies, but also of previously unsuspected connections between the times and places where consciousness of the world comes into being.

One such connection is the link between Montaigne and Chamoiseau as writers of the world. The Martinican author foregrounds echoes between the digressive structure of his essay and Montaigne's 'Des Coches' through rewriting Montaigne's 'Mais retombons à nos coches' [But let us go back to our coaches].[28] At several points, Chamoiseau appears to wander away from his subject, only to draw his reader back with a phrase such as 'Mais revenons à nos fameux zombis' [But let us come back to our famous zombies] (*LM* 26). Chamoiseau thus creates echoes between his 2016 exploration of the worldly, and Montaigne's questioning of the new

---

26   Jacqueline Leiner, 'Entretien avec Aimé Césaire', in *Tropiques: 1941–1945* (Paris: Jean-Michel Place, 1978), p. xvii, quoted in Gary Wilder, *The French Imperial Nation-State: Négritude and Colonial Humanism Between the Two World Wars* (Chicago: University of Chicago Press, 2005), p. 280.

27   Maximin, *Aimé Césaire*, p. 22.

28   Michel de Montaigne, *Essais de Michel de Montaigne, avec des notes de tous les commentateurs* (Paris: Lefèvre, 1834), p. 538.

relationship between the two hemispheres. In the replacement of 'coches' by 'zombis', Chamoiseau signals his return to an 'eerily modern', undead essay form whose openness remains a valuable vehicle for grappling with the encounter between worlds old and new. Although most recent studies of 'world literature' focus on the novel form, *La Matière de l'absence* is an argument for the value of the essay form for registering the encounter with the global.[29] This is tied to the temporal location of 'world literature'. If 'world literature' is seen as one form of the literature of modernity, and the novel as the quintessentially modern literary form, it makes sense to focus on the ways in which the global entanglements of a modern world are expressed in the novel form.[30] However, from a Caribbean perspective, global entanglements are an early modern rather than a modern development, as it is in the early modern period that the Caribbean becomes a site of encounter between people from three continents (European colonizers, indigenous Caribbean peoples and transported and enslaved Africans) and a site of production of global commodities such as coffee and sugar. In this context, it makes sense for an early modern genre to become the space of exploration of the ongoing legacy and uncanny resonances of the coming into being of a global world.

Drawing Chamoiseau's own comments on form into dialogue with studies of the early modern essay as a genre demonstrates the congruence of the two. This is how Chamoiseau describes his view of form: '*chaque forme non comme un commencement mais comme incommencement. Offrir la sen-sation que quelque chose commence, jamais que quelque chose s'achève, ni que quelque chose s'est installé* [*each form not as a beginning but as an unbeginning. To offer the sensation that something is beginning, never that something is ending, nor that something has taken hold*] (*LM* 69, italics in original). The essay offers a promising vehicle for such a poetics. Scott Black, writing of the prominence of the essay in early modern England (whence

29 See, for example, Warwick Research Collective, *Combined and Uneven Development: Towards a New Theory of World-Literature* (Liverpool: Liverpool University Press, 2015); Pheng Cheah, *What Is a World? On Postcolonial Literature as World Literature* (Durham, NC: Duke University Press, 2016).

30 This link between the novel, modernity and 'world literature' is made in Warwick Research Collective, *Combined and Uneven Development*, p. 16.

it arrived via translations of Montaigne's *Essais*) characterizes the form as 'writing in the shape of reading, offering first thoughts instead of final words'. He adds: 'Remnants of response, not engines of production, such works disclaim authority and even authorship.'[31] In returning to this aspect of the early modern genre, Chamoiseau expresses the diminished view of the author which characterizes his work and here is put in the service of a portrayal of 'worldedness' as a phenomenon which, like death, can only ever be incompletely registered and expressed. The return to the nineteenth-century eruption is thus both a return to the twentieth-century Martinican poetic tradition and to early modern French literature.

This temporal layering is further enriched by the addition of a prehistoric strand. The author's experience of his mother's death echoes the eruption because it is destructively creative in ways which can be compared to the nineteenth-century reproof to colonial pride, to Montaigne's essay and to the prehistoric birth of consciousness. It leads the author to grapple with 'l'informulable et l'indicible, vrais amis des poètes' [the unformulable and the ineffable, true friends of poets] (*LM* 212). The writing hand of the poet who grapples with absence is compared to the hands of the first hominid creatures to walk on their hind legs, whose hands also found themselves moving through empty air (*LM* 212–13). Human consciousness is imagined as co-extensive with the encounter with the 'indicible' (*LM* 222). Through the volcanic metaphor, the mother's death is layered with the creation of the earth and the birth of artistic consciousness, which are both written of in terms of eruption (*LM* 57). The traditionally postcolonial rewriting of a French canonical text and alignment with a cannibalistic literary forebear like Césaire is thus layered with a movement further back in time and further outwards towards the concept of the human than is traditionally emphasized in postcolonial criticism.

Although it is just such moves towards the total which risk abandonment of anti-colonial politics, Chamoiseau negotiates this risk by presenting the human and the world as, like death, eluding the mind's capacity for comprehension. He compares intuition of the coming explosion to the

31   Scott Black, 'Introduction', in *Of Essays and Reading in Early Modern Britain* (London: Palgrave Macmillan, 2006), p. 2.

dawning consciousness of the *tout-monde*. As noted above, those who fled the city before the eruption in retrospect seem to possess a subversive and life-sustaining form of counter-knowledge. Just as the volcanic explosion is a metaphor for the mother's death, so the foreknowledge of it becomes a metaphor for his sister's sense that her mother's death was imminent. Such forms of intuition are in turn compared to four early prefigurations of global consciousness. These involve human beings rooted in particular places who nonetheless intuit phenomena beyond the boundaries of their own culture. They include the first people to migrate to Australia, the first Amerindian to see a European vessel, the African king who declared war on slave ships in the sixteenth century and the writers of the Manden Constitution, a thirteenth-century African document which is the earliest known written defence of human rights (*LM* 66). These can all be seen as early versions of a *tout-monde* consciousness because they involve awareness of connections between different peoples which open on to a consciousness of the complex oneness of the human race. Chamoiseau's language in this passage enacts his own version of such a consciousness through his use of phrases such as 'ce premier groupe de Sapiens' [this first group of Sapiens] or 'droits de la personne' [rights of the person], not 'droits de l'homme' [rights of man] as in the 1789 French declaration. This subtle rewriting of a canonical European formulation of human rights is an example of counter-colonial political thought remaining present within what could be seen as a move away from concrete contestation of colonial power into abstract defences of the human. Although Chamoiseau's series of examples neither obviously contests any one colonial power, nor asserts the rights of one colonized group against their aggressor, it remains counter-colonial in the way it takes up of the signs of a supposed Western superiority and subverts them.

What emerges from the volcanic event of the mother's death is a consciousness which tremors with awareness of elusive totalities: the force of absence, the oneness of the human, the uncanny recurrence of the past in the present. Faced with the ungraspable event of the death of the mother, the author is thrown back to his past, to his childhood and his writing on childhood. The personal past and the past of the species are fused as his own experience of bereavement leads him to imagine the first human experience of a loved one's death. This, in turn, offers a way into layered connections between the prehistoric dawning of consciousness, the birth of modernity in the hold of the slave ship and our own era, with its disenchantment and crumbling of grand narratives. The volcano offers a way of holding in tension these various encounters with *l'en-dehors*; seen from the earth's core the seas which divide the land belie a common origin in the creative destruction and destructive creation of magma in motion. This volcanic vision of the world is 'eerily modern' in its return to a time when consciousness of the world as a globe was new and disconcerting. To return to Montaigne and Césaire through a return to Mont Pelée is to hold in tension the canonical and the subversive, the total and the particular, the local and the global. Writing the death of the mother and the birth of the *tout-monde* through rewriting an early modern essay is to forget the common acceptance of the global as an anglophone category and to remember the literary as a mode of expression of a new astonishment at the unsuspected breadth and the fraught oneness of the world and the human.

PART III

Poéthique: Between New Elegy and Anti-Elegy

ARIANE MILDENBERG

'The Door Pushed Back the Light': On a Phenomenology of Mourning in Maurice Merleau-Ponty and Jacques Roubaud

ABSTRACT

In Maurice Merleau-Ponty's phenomenology, 'the body-subject's comportment toward the world'[1] and the idea of a chiasmatic crossing of the body and the world speak of a deep-rooted 'intimacy as close as between the sea and the strand'[2] which can help shed light on the experience of mourning.[3] The failing of language in Jacques Roubaud's *Some Thing Black* (1986), a collection of prose poems written after the death of the poet's wife, reflects a lived experience of absence, a comportment toward the world which is no longer open. This chapter shows how Roubaud's poetry presents writing itself as a chiasmatic crossing of hesitance and healing.

'There is a sort of invisible blanket between the world and me', C. S. Lewis writes in *A Grief Observed* (1961) when mourning the death of his wife.[4] Due to the disappearance of his wife's bodily presence, Lewis is unable to engage

---

1   See Jacques Reynolds, *Merleau-Ponty and Derrida: Intertwining Embodiment and Alterity* (Athens: Ohio University Press, 2004), pp. 173–95 (p. 180).

2   Maurice Merleau-Ponty, *The Visible and the Invisible*, ed. Claude Lefort and trans. Alphonso Lingis (Evanston, IL: Northwestern University Press, 1968), pp. 130–1 (hereafter referenced in main text as *VI*).

3   As Stefan Kristensen writes, 'Somehow the motif of mourning haunts the philosophy of the late Merleau-Ponty', it 'point[s] to the centrality of the work of mourning for properly understanding the structure of subjectivity in Merleau-Ponty (and in general)'. Stefan Kristensen, 'Flesh as the Space of Mourning', in Kirsten Jacobsen and John Russon, eds, *Perception and Its Development in Merleau-Ponty's Phenomenology* (Toronto: University of Toronto Press, 2017), pp. 272–82 (p. 278). For another excellent phenomenological approach to grief and mourning that draws upon the work of Merleau-Ponty, see J. Todd Dubose, 'The Phenomenology of Grief, Bereavement and Mourning', *Journal of Religion and Health* 36/4 (Winter 1997), 367–76.

4   C. S. Lewis, *A Grief Observed* (London: Faber & Faber, 1961), p. 5.

with the world around him. What Lewis experiences is 'life transformed as irreversibly and immemorially out of joint'.[5] The failing of language itself in Jacques Roubaud's *Quelque chose noir* [*Some Thing Black*] (1986), a collection of prose poems written in response to the death of the poet's wife, the photographer Alix Cléo Roubaud, reflects this being out of joint. In a compelling analysis of Roubaud's poetic form, Mairéad Hanrahan writes on 'the silencing effect that [Alix Cléo's] disappearance has had on [the poet]' and how 'this silencing affects above all his capacity for poetry'.[6] The struggling of Roubaud's words to make it onto the page and the unusual use of spaces and punctuation express a changed embodied engagement with the world, a grief-stricken lived experience of absence and loss. 'Tes couleurs m'échappent l'une par l'autre. comme tes phrases' [Your colours escape me one by one. like your words], writes the poet in 'Tu m'échappes' [You Escape Me].[7] Throughout *Quelque chose noir*, 'black lines being pushed across the paper' (*QCN* 86; *STB* 82) mirror the way in which 'la porte repoussait de la lumière' [the door pushed back the light] (*QCN* 13; *STB* 11) so that his wife's 'état, hors lumière, ne peut pas être pensé' [state, outside the light, cannot be thought] (*QCN* 111; *STB* 109) and cannot be written. Yet, the poet persists: 'De débris de poèmes je fais ces phrases' [Out of the wreckage of poems I fashion these phrases' (*QCN* 127; *STB* 124). Although raw, stumbling and full of visible gaps on the page, Roubaud's prose poems express the process of writing itself as both hesitant and healing.

The work of mourning is first and foremost bodily work. As the 'body is lived-through, is phenomenal, is experienced from the inside as it opens to the outside', the importance of the body must also be

5   Galen A. Johnson, 'Merleau-Ponty and Kant's *Third Critique*: The Beautiful and the Sublime', in Kascha Semonovitch and Neal DeRoo, eds, *Merleau-Ponty and the Limits of Art, Religion, and Perception* (London: Continuum, 2010), pp. 41–59 (p. 55).

6   Mairéad Hanrahan, 'Going On, or Achieving Interruption: Jacques Roubaud's *Quelque chose noir*', in Patrick Crowley and Shirley Jordan, eds, *What Forms Can Do: The Work of Form in 20th- and 21st-Century Literature and Thought* (Liverpool: Liverpool University Press, 2020), pp. 81–94 (p. 82).

7   Jacques Roubaud, *Quelque chose noir* (Paris: Gallimard, 1986), p. 127; *Some Thing Black*, trans. Rosmarie Waldrop (Champaign, IL: Dalkey Archive Press, 1990), p. 124 (hereafter abbreviated in main text as *QCN* and *STB*).

emphasized in understanding the mourning process.[8] J. Todd Dubose, Laura Tanner, Suzanne Laba Cataldi and Stefan Kristensen are among the scholars who have brought into dialogue Merleau-Ponty's philosophy, including the notion of the chiasm, with the experience of loss and the process of mourning from different perspectives.[9] Complementing these scholarly efforts, this chapter contributes to the field of the phenomenology of mourning by focusing on and exploring the phenomenological notion of chiasmatic 'crossing' in Roubaud's *Quelque chose noir*, which brings to the fore the bodiliness of mourning and the difficulty of expression following the loss of a loved one. The poetry of Roubaud, a mathematician and keen scholar of Wittgenstein, has previously been studied in relation to mathematical logic and Wittgenstein's philosophy.[10] Both preoccupied with 'restor[ing] meaning to human life in the face of indefensible scientism',[11] Wittgenstein and Merleau-Ponty agree that 'bodily expressions are communicative. […] To recognise expressive content is to grasp that expression is woven into a pattern of *intersubjective life*'.[12] Both are aware that the expression of art is

8   Douglas Beck Low, *Merleau-Ponty's Last Vision: A Proposal for the Completion of 'The Visible and the Invisible'* (Evanston, IL: Northwestern University Press, 2000), p. 25. As Reynolds also puts it, 'Merleau-Ponty would affirm the importance of the body to any process of grieving' (p. 190).

9   See Dubose, 'The Phenomenology of Grief, Bereavement and Mourning', pp. 367–74; Kristensen, 'Flesh as the Space of Mourning'; Laura E. Tanner, *Lost Bodies: Inhabiting the Borders of Life and Death* (Ithaca, NY: Cornell University Press, 2006); Suzanna Laba Cataldi, 'Embodying Perceptions of Death: Emotional Apprehension and Reversibilities of Flesh', in Fred Evans and Leonard Lawlor, eds, *Chiasms: Merleau-Ponty's Notion of Flesh* (New York: State University of New York Press, 2000), pp. 189–201.

10 See Greg Kinzer, 'Possible Words: Trans-word Travel, Haecceity and Grief in Jacques Roubaud's *The Plurality of Worlds of Lewis*', *Journal of Modern Literature* 34/3 (Spring 2011), 162–81; and Maria Rusanda Muresan, 'Wittgenstein in Recent French Poetics: Henri Meschonnic and Jacques Roubaud', *Paragraph* 34/3 (2011), 423–30.

11 Komarine Romdenh-Romluc, 'Introduction', in Komarine Romdenh-Romluc, ed., *Wittgenstein and Merleau-Ponty* (New York: Routledge, 2017), pp. 1–10 (p. 3).

12 Kathleen Lennon, 'Expression', in Romdenh-Romluc, ed., *Wittgenstein and Merleau-Ponty*, pp. 31–48 (p. 36).

grounded in these bodily expressions. However, whereas Wittgenstein is primarily interested in language, language games and 'linguistic behaviour', Merleau-Ponty is concerned with 'experience'.[13] For the latter, the grasping of intersubjective life relies on the chiasmatic intertwining and reversibility between an embodied self and other bodies, and as Cataldi notes, in her work on Merleau-Ponty, Roubaud's poetry is 'rich in intercorporeal and reversible imagery'.[14]

While Merleau-Ponty writes most fully about reversibility and chiasmatic crossing in the chapter 'L'entrelacs-le chiasme' [The Intertwining – The Chiasm] in *Le Visible et l'invisible* [*The Visible and the Invisible*] (1964), in the earlier 1953 course notes from the Collège de France, later published in *The Sensible World and the World of Expression* (2011), he had already explored the crossing of the perceived world and the world of expression.[15] The goals of the course notes were to 'deepen the analysis of the perceived world by showing that it already presupposes the expressive function'[16] and that expression always involves 'a crossing of sensation and language'.[17] The chiasm itself is a cross like the Greek letter *chi* (X) or a crossover. In Merleau-Ponty's late work the term expresses a 'carnal intertwining through difference' and is used for exploring the crossing over of the active body and the world that encroaches upon it, perception and language, the invisible and the visible, the experience of touching and being touched;[18] Merleau-Ponty refers to it as a 'double and crossed situating of the visible in the tangible and of the tangible in the visible' (*VI* 134). Others cross over into our lives and vice

13   Romdenh-Romluc, 'Introduction', p. 1.
14   Cataldi, 'Embodying Perceptions of Death', p. 194.
15   See Richard Kearney, 'The Wager of Carnal Hermeneutics', in Richard Kearney and Brian Treanor, eds, *Carnal Hermeneutics* (New York: Fordham University Press, 2015), pp. 15–56 (pp. 42–5).
16   Brian Smyth, 'Translator's Introduction', in Maurice Merleau-Ponty, *The Sensible World and the World of Expression: Course Notes from the Collège de France*, trans. and intr. Bryan Smyth (Evanston, IL: Northwestern University Press, 2020), pp. xi–xlii** (pp. xv, 9).
17   Kearney, 'The Wager of Carnal Hermeneutics', p. 42.
18   Lawrence Hass, *Merleau-Ponty's Philosophy* (Bloomington: Indiana University Press, 2008), p. 227, n. 13.

versa. In fact, living itself consists of 'a series of crossings and recrossings of flesh',[19] an '*Ineinander*' [in-each-other] (*VI* 174) or 'connective tissue' (*VI* 174) of subject and object that is both 'enveloping-enveloped' (*VI* 267), stressing the perpetual folding into each other of the body and the world as well as words and meaning.[20] It is important to stress, however, that this crossing of the flesh *precedes* distinctions (*VI* 27) (such as the separate categories of subject and object) and is 'never complete' in that the perceiver and the perceived, like the imagery of the sea and the strand, are at once overlapping and divergent, unified and differentiated, meaning that they can never completely coincide – there is always a 'fundamental fission' (*VI* 143) between them. Sensation is diacritical in that it moves across such fissions and folds: 'there must be a slippage, a displacement, a distance that separates the perceiver and the perceived' for meaning to be produced at all.[21]

In *The Visible and the Invisible*, Merleau-Ponty describes this as 'two circles, or two vortexes or two spheres [...] the one slightly decentered with respect to the other' (*VI* 138). This differentiation is what Merleau-Ponty thought of as *écart* (*VI* 197, 198, 201), a fission or 'dehiscence' that points to 'a constitutive difference in the fabric of experience', a difference that is 'not an opposition' but rather a mutual openness and this is 'what opens, for example, the seer to the seen, but it is an opening that isn't so severe that the two aspects are divorced from one another'.[22] Just as 'the visible itself has an invisible inner framework (*membrure*)' (*VI* 215–16), language has a silent centre, a 'core of primary meaning round which the acts of naming and expression take shape'.[23] Although we seek to capture meaning through acts of expression, the gap between immediate experience and our speaking about it can never be closed, for 'between experience and its own [*propre*] truth, there is always a certain [...] temporal displacement, [...] an *écart*,

---

19   David Farrell Krell, *Architecture: Ecstasies of Space, Time, and the Human Body* (New York: State University of New York Press, 1997), p. 170.

20   See Low, *Merleau-Ponty's Last Vision*, p. 34.

21   Ibid.

22   Hass, *Merleau-Ponty's Philosophy*, p. 129. In fact, as Lawrence Hass stresses, *écart* is 'an expressive device [...] that Merleau-Ponty uses to gesture toward the subtle differentiation in experience that is not an opposition'.

23   Maurice Merleau-Ponty, *Phenomenology of Perception*, trans. Donald A. Landes (Abingdon: Routledge, 2012), p. xv.

or "spacing", of a temporal nature, this distantiation being itself a necessary condition for the production of meaning'.[24] In other words, all our acts and expressions arise from this divergence, slippage or displacement. Although 'this *separation* (écart) […] forms meaning' (*VI* 216), we do not perceive it as it is prior to our ability to reflect on and speak *about* experience.[25] In what follows, I show how Roubaud's poems of mourning shine a painfully self-aware spotlight on the usually unperceived separation (*écart*) and the reversibility central to the chiasm, the simultaneous connection with and separateness from others that characterizes living experience and the formation of meaning.

Crossing Over

Douglas Low writes:

> The lived-through body actively opens upon a world that includes it. The active body and the world cross into each other to form meaning. Where the active body meets the world that impinges upon it, there meaning is formed. As we have seen, perception already stylizes. It meets the world actively and helps to create meaning. It is already a meaningful gesture.[26]

But how can perception even begin to 'stylize' when a loved one dies? 'How can I write, married to a dead (wo)man' (*QCN* 63; *STB* 61), writes Roubaud.[27] Roubaud's wife, Alix Cléo Roubaud, passed away in 1983. She was 31-year old. How is it possible for the active body and the world to cross into each other as normal when a piece of the fabric

---

24   G. B. Madison, 'Merleau-Ponty and Derrida: La différEnce', in M. C. Dillon, ed., *Écart and différance: Merleau-Ponty and Derrida on Seeing and Writing* (Atlantic Heights, NJ: Humanities Press, 1997), p. 104.

25   Jerrold Seigel, 'A Unique Way of Existing: Merleau-Ponty and the Subject', *Journal of the History of Philosophy* 29/1 (January 1991), 455–80 (p. 475).

26   Douglas Low, *In Defense of Phenomenology: Merleau-Ponty's Philosophy* (New Brunswick, NJ: Transaction Publishers, 2016), p. 40.

27   'Impossible d'écrire, mariée à une morte' (*QCN* 63).

of everyday existence is missing, when, as J. Todd Dubose puts it, 'the chiasmatic structure of self and other is drowned in the reversibility of dis-appearance' or,[28] as Stefan Kristensen writes, mourning becomes 'a process of restructuring the body's spatiality'?[29] What happens to meaning-making? *Quelque chose noir* is the product of the shock of death reflected in a kind of aphasia and a contempt for structured sentences that have nothing to do with the brokenness of the mourner's experience. In Roubaud's poems, perceptions no longer simply cross into linguistic expression, thus shedding light on the chiasmatic notions of intertwining and encroachment which, in the words of Laura E. Tanner, have become chiasmatic 'entangle[ments] with a missing body the inaccessibility of which shapes the contours of our grief'.[30] 'Go on talk' (*QCN* 12; *STB* 10), writes Roubaud in 'Meditation of 5/12/85', 'just don't expect too much from words' (*STB* 10).[31] And in 'En moi régnait la désolation' [Desolation Reigned in My Heart]: 'Mais les paroles n'avaient pas la force de franchir. De franchir seulement. car il n'y avait pas quoi' [But the words not strong enough to come across. Come across simply. there was no what to cross] (*QCN* 18; *STB* 16).[32] *There was no what to cross.* The fluid crossing over of his words onto the page seems impossible, just as the poet cannot cross into the world: 'Je m'éloigne peu souvent de cet endroit comme si l'enfermement dans un espace minime te restituait de la réalité, puisque tu y vivais avec moi' [I rarely go out as if locking myself in the minimal space could make you real again because you lived here with me] (*QCN* 36; *STB* 34). As he has not incorporated his loss into the continuity of everyday life, entering back into the world outside his door and simply carrying on will only be a reminder of his wife's absence.[33] The poet only 'laisse

---

28   Dubose, 'The Phenomenology of Grief, Bereavement and Mourning', p. 373.
29   Tanner, *Lost Bodies*, p. 87.
30   Ibid.
31   'parle et attend une seule chose de la parole' (*QCN* 12).
32   Editor's note: the transitivity and polysemy of the French verb *franchir* is impossible to replicate in English.
33   As Dubose puts it, 'Mourning is the process of incorporating the loss into our ongoing life-worlds': 'The Phenomenology of Bereavement, Grief, and Mourning', p. 368.

le soleil s'approcher' [lets in the sun under the door] (*QCN* 37; *STB* 36). 'To me, what is most interesting, profound, and painful about the grieving process', Cataldi writes, 'is the way in which it reveals how intimately woven, incorporated others are, into the fabric of our lives.'[34] Due to a sudden loosening of this fabric, being in mourning means that one experiences an altered bodily engagement with the world, a lived experience of absence that cannot be easily expressed.[35] Galen Johnson highlights how apt the idea of 'the fabric of the world' is when commenting on Merleau-Ponty's notion of flesh: 'Fabric has some life and movement as it folds, rustles, and moves together with the actions of the body.' As he stresses, fabric implies movement and 'progression, a development [...] from human flesh to the more general meaning of the flesh of things'.[36] It is exactly this development that is stifled for Roubaud: a strip has been torn from the fabric or 'connective tissue' of the poet's existence and the result is a harrowing poetry of loneliness and bewilderment, a 'violence la plus grande au principe de réalité' [violence to the principle of reality] (*QCN* 116; *STB* 114) as he calls it. 'Textile', another word for 'fabric', and the word 'text' (also a 'fabrication') share the Latin origin *texere*, which can mean both 'to braid' or 'to weave'.[37] As the textile of Roubaud's life loosens, the texture of his text too becomes looser as the recipient of his monologue, the 'you' he addresses throughout, can no longer speak back: Alix Cléo can no longer help tighten the braid of their connection, what used to be their 'toile de la ressemblance. ses fils croisés et recroisés' [weave of likeness, threads crossed and recrossed] (*QCN* 17; *STB* 15).

---

34   Cataldi, 'Embodying Perceptions of Death', p. 197.
35   In the words of Dubose, while 'grief takes place inside the body [...] mourning takes place inside the body as it reacts to the outside world': 'The Phenomenology of Grief, Bereavement and Mourning', p. 369.
36   Galen A. Johnson, *The Retrieval of the Beautiful: Thinking through Merleau-Ponty's Aesthetics* (Evanston, IL: Northwestern University Press, 2010), p. 32.
37   For more on the difference between weaving and braiding and the notion of what Edmund Husserl, the founding father of phenomenology, called *Verflechtung*, see Ariane Mildenberg, *Modernism and Phenomenology: Literature, Philosophy, Art* (London: Palgrave Macmillan, 2017), pp. 1–39.

It is not just selves and others that cross over into each other's lives. Importantly, as Low puts it, just as the body and the word cross over into each other, 'perceptual expressions cross (chiasm) into linguistic expressions that fold back upon the perceived to help stabilize them, yet perception still remains the primary term, for language would mean little without it'.[38] Merleau-Ponty's notion of flesh, then, which 'is not matter, is not mind, is not substance' but an ' "element", in the sense it was used to speak of water, air, earth, and fire, that is, in the sense of a *general thing*, midway between the spatio-temporal individual and the idea' (*VI* 139; see also 147), is *also* an element of language:[39] 'Yet this flesh that one sees and touches is not all there is to flesh, not this massive corporeity all there is to the body. The reversibility that defines the flesh exists in other fields' (*VI* 144). Indeed, Merleau-Ponty continues a few pages later, just as there is a chiasmatic overlapping and reversibility of the seeing and the seen, the touching and the touched, 'so also there is a reversibility of the speech and what it signifies; the signification is what comes to seal, to close, to gather up the multiplicity of the physical, physiological, linguistic meaning of elocution' (*VI* 154). In other words, sign and signification should not be kept apart, Merleau-Ponty stresses, but are chiasmatically intertwined and criss-crossed. However, 'sans le redoublement de réel qui supportait la désignation' [without the doubling of reality which underpinned the sign] (*QCN* 68; *STB* 66), as there is 'no what to cross' and no 'weave of likeness', no signification 'comes to seal, to close, to gather up' in Roubaud's poetry of mourning. Instead, what we are faced with is a raw poetry that cannot seal, cannot close, cannot console, and Roubaud refuses to pretend that it can. His poetry is painfully aware and accepting of its own imperfection and framelessness in the face of death, and of the insufficiency of pre-established significations.

---

38   Douglas Low, *Merleau-Ponty in Contemporary Contexts: Philosophy and Politics in the Twenty-First Century* (New Brunswick, NJ: Transaction Publishers, 2013), p. 96.

39   Merleau-Ponty writes: 'We must not think the flesh starting from substances, from body and spirit – the concrete emblem of a general manner of being' (*VI* 147).

In *Quelque chose noir*, the poet's body is no longer open in its comportment towards the world, a comportment that is needed to express oneself in written and spoken language; rather, the body is like an open wound. 'I imagine grief as an injury', writes Cataldi, 'as a type of open wound: torn tissue' or torn fabric, adding how Jewish people rip their clothes after the death of a loved one.[40] Symbolically, the tear in the clothes stands for the torn connection with the deceased, the tearing of the very life of its fabric, of its folding and rustling movement as discussed by Johnson. In Roubaud's poems there is a tear in the taken-for-granted 'progression […] from human flesh to the more general meaning of the flesh of things',[41] from 'sens', as Merleau-Ponty would call it, that is, the meaning and direction (*VI* 65) of the lived body that is the condition *for* language, to signification.[42] As 'la moindre distance devient infranchissable' [the least distance becomes insurmountable] (*QCN* 81; *STB* 79) for Roubaud in life and on the page, this tear is marked by the gaps or visible pauses in the middle of lines. Hanrahan associates these gaps or marks of loss with 'interruptions' and refers to them as 'the necessary gap or failure at the heart of poetic speech'.[43] Focusing on the chiasmatic relationship between embodied experience and expression, I propose to read the gaps as intervals of hesitation that lay bare the usually unperceived divergence that Merleau-Ponty calls *écart*, which is the necessary condition for any aesthetic practice including the process of writing. Consider Roubaud's 'Meditation of 5/12/85': 'Je me trouvai devant ce silence   inarticulé   un peu comme le bois' [There before this silence   inarticulate   a little like wood] (*QCN* 11; *STB* 9); and 'parle et attend une seule chose de la parole   elle ne sera pas pensée' [go on talk just don't expect too much from words   they won't be thoughts] (*QCN* 12; *STB* 10). The poet writes in 'Énigme' [Riddle]: 'Sans être maintenant   sans lieu   sans poids'

40   Cataldi, 'Embodying Perceptions of Death', p. 199.
41   Johnson, *The Retrieval of the Beautiful*, p. 32.
42   M. C. Dillon writes: 'Note also that meaning is founded, that worldly *sens* remains the foundation of the significations of language'. In fact, 'it is worldly *sens* which is reflected in the signification of both body and language': *Merleau-Ponty's Ontology* (Evanston, IL: Northwestern University Press, 1988), pp. 217, 219.
43   Hanrahan, 'Going On, or Achieving Interruption', p. 91.

[Without being now   without weight   without words] (*QCN* 97; *STB* 95). And in 'Au matin' [In the Morning]: 'Je suis habitant de la mort idiote   la tête comme un porridge' [I inhabit an idiotic death   my head like porridge] (*QCN* 35; *STB* 33). A 'head like porridge' is a head 'without weight' and 'without words' incapable of conceptualizing. Language does not exist without the lived body.

Spewing Out Words

What Merleau-Ponty called 'the flesh of the world' (*VI* 144) underlies the ongoing crossing and recrossing of perceiver and perceived. Each one of us is at once a sensing/touching subject and a sensed/touched object who is interlaced into the thicker braid, the textile or text of life. Thus, embodied consciousness both projects and receives meaning.[44] But what if this reversibility is ruptured due to the disappearance of a loved one? Responding to the sudden death of her 25-year-old son Carl Emil, Danish author Naja Marie Aidt writes: 'My body still doesn't understand that you don't exist'; 'You are singing in me.'[45] The work of mourning is first and foremost bodily work. As she 'cannot form a sentence' and as her 'language is all dried up',[46] Aidt gains strength from reading and citing Roubaud's fragmentary work, the *debris* [wreckage] of *Quelque chose noir*:

> Most of what I read about raw grief and lamentation is fragmentary. It's chaotic, not artistic. Often, the writer doesn't have the strength to use capital letters after full stops. Often, the writer doesn't have the strength to complete the fragment. It *can't* be completed.[47]

---

44   Kearney, 'The Wager of Carnal Hermeneutics', p. 28.
45   Naja Marie Aidt, *When Death Takes Something from You Give It Back*, trans. Denise Newman (London: Quercus, 2019), pp. 18, 26.
46   Ibid., p. 14.
47   Ibid., p. 115.

What the grief-stricken Aidt expresses is that language is *not* transparent, but that it has a 'mute' and 'silent' dimension. Treating painting as 'a language' that discloses 'a *perceptual* meaning' is helpful, writes Merleau-Ponty in *The Prose of the World*, as

> It will enable us to detect beneath the spoken language, whose sounds and sentences are cleverly suited to ready-made significations, an operant or speaking language, whose words have a silent life like the animals at the bottom of the ocean and come together or separate according to the needs of their lateral or indirect signification.[48]

Merleau-Ponty returns again and again in his work to the paintings of Paul Cézanne in that they rupture the 'habits of thought' that present meaning as always ready-made and complete, and art as ordered and finished.[49] The philosopher also speaks of 'the recognition of a mode of communication which does not pass through objective evidence' and which is not a formal construct.[50] He speaks of a 'living use of language' which 'is the opposite of both formalism and "thematic" literature' and which 'presupposes a general communication, however vague and unarticulated'.[51] It is this prelinguistic mode of communication that characterizes Roubaud's as well as Aidt's work of impossible mourning, their 'path for the disrupted heart', to borrow from David L. Uhlin, a path on which the poets 'engage with language not to salve or re-create but to clear a space'.[52] Writing through their incomprehensible and all-consuming places of mourning, both seem to address what Merleau-Ponty stresses: 'One does not love by means of principles.'[53]

---

48   Maurice Merleau-Ponty, *The Prose of the World*, trans. John O'Neill (Evanston, IL: Northwestern University Press, 1973), p. 87.

49   Maurice Merleau-Ponty, *Sense and Non-sense*, trans. Hubert L. Dreyfus and Patricia Allen Dreyfus (Evanston, IL: Northwestern University Press, 1964), p. 16.

50   Merleau-Ponty, *The Prose of the World*, p. 56.

51   Ibid., p. 103.

52   David L. Uhlin, 'The Unthinkable: Writing about the Death of Children', *The Yale Review* 108/2 (Summer 2020), 173–85 (p. 184).

53   Merleau-Ponty, *The Prose of the World*, p. 111.

A certain logic of unfinishedness also pertains to the process of mourning. In fact, 'the idea of sorrow as a project completely disgusts me', stresses Aidt; rather, 'the language gasps, falls to the ground, flat and useless. Language's mourning clothes are ugly and stinky' and punctuation becomes redundant: 'no language possible language dies with my child could not be artistic could not be art did not want to be fucking art I vomit art over syntax'.[54] Aidt's words recall Roubaud:

> Je suis devant les mots avec mécontentement
> Très longtemps je n'ai même pas pu m'en approcher
> Maintenant, je les entends et je les crache. (*QCN* 126)

> [I face words with discontent
> For a long time I couldn't go near them
> Now, I hear, and spew them out.] (*STB* 123)

To Roubaud, an admirer of Gertrude Stein's interrogation of 'language's elements' and what he has called the 'Stein-sentence' – 'Nothing but words and the typographical spaces between the words. Nothing else. No punctuation'[55] – neither the principles of punctuation nor capitalization are essential elements in 'ces phrases de neuf que je nomme poèmes' [these new sentences that I call poems] (*QCN* 85; *STB* 82):[56] 'Ponctuation vide. il y a des fleurs ou il n'y a pas de fleurs. Il pleut ou il ne pleut pas. c'est un trajet long, le métro, un autobus' [Empty punctuation. there are flowers or there are no flowers. it rains or it doesn't. it's a long ride, metro and bus] (*QCN* 122; *STB* 120). Clearly influenced by David Lewis's philosophical

54   Aidt, *When Death Takes Something*, pp. 56, 115, 3.
55   Jacques Roubaud, 'Gertrude Stein Grammaticus', trans. ean-Jacques Poucel, in Sarah Posman and Laura Luise Schultz, eds, *Gertrude Stein in Europe: Reconfigurations Across Media, Disciplines, and Traditions* (London: Bloomsbury, 201), pp. 273–85 (p. 276).
56   Editor's note: the punning expression 'de neuf' is, alas, lost in translation.

logic, the punctuation here seems forced, silly, inadequate.[57] Roubaud's work of mourning resists the structure of such logic. In the same way, colours become redundant: 'Dans tout souvenir se perdent les couleurs, là tu es claire ou sombre, c'est tout ce dont mon langage peut jouer' [Always, in memory, the colors get lost. here you are light or dark. it's all my language can muster] (*QCN* 127; *STB* 124). In the 1945 essay 'Le Doute de Cézanne' [Cézanne's Doubt], Merleau-Ponty discusses the relationship between outline and colour in creative composition: 'Cézanne follows the swelling of the object in modulated colors and indicates *several* outlines in blue. Rebounding among these, one's glance captures a shape that emerges from among them all, just as it does in perception'. Any 'outline', Merleau-Ponty goes on to explain, 'should [...] be the result of the colours if the world is to be given in its true density'.[58] Also citing Paul Cézanne (citing Paul Klee) in 'Œil et esprit' [Eye and Mind], the philosopher writes: 'color is "the place where our brain and the universe meet" '; in fact, 'the return to color has the merit of getting us closer to the heart of things'.[59] The outline or external form, in other words, is caused *from* the colours: as colours are the merging of brain and universe, self and world, it is the gradual 'swelling' or emerging of the object(s) in colours that give shape *to* the artwork. The fact that Roubaud's poems do not have recognizable outlines in terms of form – we are presented with half-thoughts and fragments of sentences – is due to a loss of meaning of embodied colours and words, the very 'color in living perception'.[60]

---

57   Dorothy Edgington, 'On Conditionals', in Dov M. Gabbay and Franz Guenthner, eds, *Handbook of Philosophical Logic: Volume 14* (Dordrecht: Springer, 2007), p. 172. Edgington cites Lewis: 'If it rains or snows tomorrow, then if it doesn't rain tomorrow, it will snow'.

58   Merleau-Ponty, 'Cézanne's Doubt', in *Sense and Non-sense*, pp. 9–25 (p. 15).

59   Maurice Merleau-Ponty, 'Eye and Mind', in James M. Edie, ed., *The Primacy of Perception and Other Essays* (Evanston, IL: Northwestern University Press, 1964), pp. 159–90 (pp. 180, 181).

60   Merleau-Ponty, *Phenomenology of Perception*, p. 319.

Carnal Knowledge

How can language be written back into existence when it is all 'dried up' and colourless, when there seems to be a loss of the living perception inhabiting ready-made significations, the accepted 'frames' of words and syntax? As Frances Gillespie writes in a review of *Some Thing Black*, Roubaud wrote only one poem just after Alix Cléo's death, 'Rien' [Nothing],[61] before being unable to utter a word for more than two years, as expressed in the prose poem 'Aphasie' [Aphasia]:

> Devant ta mort je suis resté entièrement silencieux.
> Je n'ai pas pu parler pendant presque trente mois.
> Je ne pouvais plus parler selon ma manière de dire qui
> est la poésie. (*QCN* 131)
>
> [Faced with your death I remained stone silent.
> I could not speak for nearly thirty months.
> I could no longer speak in my way of speaking, I mean
> poetry.] (*STB* 128)

Paradoxically, as Hanrahan puts it, 'the material existence of the poems manifestly attests to the fact that the interruption of poetry (the thirty months during which he could not speak) has itself now been interrupted' by the possibility of writing itself.[62] Aphasia is what Merleau-Ponty in *The Sensible World and the World of Expression* calls an 'an apraxia of language'.[63] Commenting upon the aphasia of a patient by the name of Johann Schneider, in *Phenomenology of Perception*, Merleau-Ponty notes that '[w]hat the patient had lost, and what the normal person possessed, was

---

61   For Frances Gillespie's review of *Some Thing Black*, see <https://metapsychology. net/index.php/book-review/some-thing-black/> [accessed 23 July 2020].

62   Hanrahan, 'Going On, or Achieving Interruption', p. 83.

63   Merleau-Ponty, *The Sensible World and the World of Expression*, p. 105.

not a certain stock of words, but rather a certain manner of using them.'[64] It is the awareness of the limitation of words, or rather the poet's indifference to the 'framing' properties of words and grammar, when working through the experience of loss that is central to Roubaud's *Quelque chose noir*: 'Le registre rythmique de la parole me fait horreur' [The rhythmic range of words fills me with horror], he writes, 'Je ne parviens pas à ouvrir un seul livre contenant de la poésie' [I can't bring myself to open a single book of poems] (*QCN* 33; *STB* 31). And yet, 'de débris de poèmes je fais ces phrases. de couleurs devenues négligeables. de jours troubles' [out of the wreckage of poems I fashion these phrases. out of colours become unimportant. out of troubled days] (*QCN* 127; *STB* 124). Although aware of its limitations, writing remains his only path, a path that cannot seal, cannot close, cannot console as it gravitates around that which remains unspeakable: 'Quelque chose noir qui se referme. et se boucle. une déposition pure, inaccomplie' [Some thing black which closes in. locks shut. Pure, un-accomplished de-position] (*QCN* 76; *STB* 74). While writing remains a struggle, Roubaud is acutely aware of his own bodily reactions to Alix Cléo's death: 'Les autres traces, venues des autres sens, ne sont qu'en moi. Quand je trébuche dessus, j'étouffe' [Other traces of you, come through my other senses, are only inside me. These I stumble on and choke] (*QCN* 34; *STB* 32). But 'avec tout le mécontentement formel dont je suis capable au regard de la poésie' [with all the formal discontent that I can muster against poetry] (*QCN* 85; *STB* 82), he cannot write *about* them, like he cannot write 'about' Alix in the usual sense (*STB* 119); 'Je ne pourrai pas aller au-delà' [I'll write about you only on my level] (*QCN* 121; *STB* 119), for the experience of mourning is not 'like' any word. There is no mimetic agreement between the mourning process and its representation: 'Tout se suspend au point où surgit *un dissemblable*. et de là quelque chose, mais quelque chose noir' [Everything depends on the point when the *unlike* appears. and thence something, but some thing black] (*QCN* 76; *STB* 73, my emphasis); 'Je ne te nomme plus que comme incolore' [I do not name you any more except colorless] (*QCN* 68; *STB* 66). In 'Dans cette lumière, II' [In This Light, II], Roubaud writes: 'Ton état, hors lumière, ne peut pas être pensé cela veut dire que je ne

---

64   Merleau-Ponty, *Phenomenology of Perception*, p. 180.

peux pas penser sa trace en moi-même' [Your state, outside the life, cannot be thought which also means I cannot think its trace within me] (*QCN* 111; *STB* 109). As it 'cannot be thought', the work of mourning continues within the poet. Roubaud writes of a purely physical experience prior to signification, a signification that depends on a bodily openness unto the world. But as the mutual openness between the mourning poet's body and the world has been curbed in the face of death, the chiasm manifested in the crossing of lived experience and language is inhibited or, in the words of Dubose, 'drowned in the reversibility of dis-appearance':[65]

> Mais ta mort en moi progresse   lente   incompré-
> hensiblement.
>   Je me réveille toujours dans ta voix   ta main   ton
> odeur.
>   Je dis toujours ton nom ton nom en moi   comme
> si tu étais. (*QCN* 136)

> [But inside me your death proceeds   slowly   incom-
> prehensibly.
>   I always wake up in your voice   your hand   your
> smell.
>   I always say your name   your name inside me   as if
> you were.] (*STB* 132)

Once again, the visible spaces on the page, marks of loss and intervals of hesitation, express the physicality of the work of mourning 'proceeding' inside the poet.[66] Indeed, what the poet keeps of his loved one is bodily: 'Toucher de genoux à front, goût de bière sur la langue, parfum aux bras, dessous, vue et voix, de loin, m'embrasent: circuits qui ne s'oblitéreront pas. pas encore' [Knees touching forehead, taste of beer on your tongue, perfumed armpits, look and voices, at a distance, igniting me: circuits that can't be erased, not yet] (*QCN* 121; *STB* 119). This process of writing

---

65   Dubose, 'The Phenomenology of Grief, Bereavement and Mourning', p. 373.
66   Gillespie writes about Roubaud's punctuation: 'The unusual use of punctuation –
     full-stops mid sentence – draws me into the jaggedness of feeling and the disjoint-
     edness of thought that traumatic shock engenders' <https://metapsychology.net/
     index.php/book-review/some-thing-black/> [accessed 23 July 2020].

through mourning, which is really what Roubaud does as he cannot possibly write *about* it, is not cognitive but carnal. 'This state is physically raw', writes the English poet Denise Riley, 'and has nothing whatever to do with thinking sad thoughts of "mourning". It thuds into you. Inexorable carnal knowledge.'[67] Riley wrote *Time Lived, Without Its Flow* (2012) after the untimely death of her adult son Jacob in 2008. 'Your altered temporality is not to do with any kind of *taking thought*', she writes, 'it is prior to that, and supremely indifferent to lament and to cogitation alike. Instead it feels foundational: to do with a change in the entire structure of cognition.'[68] Riley cites Merleau-Ponty who 'assigned primacy to carnal knowledge as the rich *fond* from which conceptuality draws in its process of clarification and refinement' and whose notion of flesh expresses carnal mutuality and reversibility,[69] the 'crossing' of which 'precedes all analytic and transcendental divisions between subject and object, consciousness and thing'.[70] It also *precedes* all facts and objective notions. And because it precedes them, it is different from cogitation and neat linguistic expression. The authenticity of *Quelque chose noir* lies in the fact that it makes reference to the primacy of such carnal intelligence which can only translate as whispers:

> Où ton inexistence était si forte. elle était devenue forme d'être.
> En moi régnait la désolation. comme conversant à voix basse.
> Mais les paroles n'avaient pas la force de franchir. (*QCN* 18)

> [Where your nonexistence was so strong. it had become a form of being.
> Desolation reigned in my heart. as if talking in whispers.
> But the words not strong enough to come across.] (*STB* 16)

67   Denise Riley, *Time Lived, Without Its Flow*, intr. Max Porter (London: Picador, 2012), p. 28.
68   Ibid., p. 59.
69   M. C. Dillon, *Beyond Romance* (New York: Stage University of New York Press, 2001), p. 125.
70   Kearney, 'The Wager of Carnal Hermeneutics', p. 37.

Hesitance, Healing

Greg Kinzer has argued that Roubaud, who is also a mathematician, in the volume of poetry that followed *Some Thing Black*, *The Plurality of Worlds of Lewis* (1995), 'shows us something important about the mathematical way in which words work' and that in *Some Thing Black*, by contrast, 'Roubaud is resigned to [a] contradiction of reference, and to the contradiction of the being of [Alix Cléo's] nonbeing.'[71] Thus, Kinzer concludes: 'It is in this sense that I describe this first attempt to adequately respond to his wife's death as a failure: aesthetically and emotionally moving yet logically and mathematically inconsistent.'[72] In *The Plurality of Worlds of Lewis*, Kinzer points out, Roubaud 'refuses to allow this contradiction [of *Some Thing Black*] to continue'.[73] What we have learnt from Merleau-Ponty, however, is that the language reflecting the mourning process cannot but be inconsistent and halting if it is to authentically embody the absence experienced by the mourner. Just as the *incomplete* crossings and recrossings of Merleau-Ponty's notion of flesh are not a failure but a sign of the continual rebirth of experience and the unfinished articulation of that experience, the inconsistent nature of Roubaud's words crossed with the possibility of writing itself is not a sign of failure but of welcoming one's own incompleteness in the face of the incomprehensible. In this way, the tangible hesitance and inconsistence are a surprisingly exact capturing of the pain of grief. Incompleteness, hesitance and inconsistence are necessary for what Low calls a new path of 'quest and acquisition'[74] and this is where hesitance becomes chiasmatically entangled with a gradual process of healing. In 'Cézanne's Doubt', Merleau-Ponty tells us that one of Cézanne's strength was that he was able to create *with* doubt, with hesitance: 'Cézanne is an example of how precariously expression and communication are achieved. Expression is like a step taken

---

71   Kinzer, 'Possible Words', pp. 179, 167.
72   Ibid., p. 167.
73   Ibid.
74   Low, *Merleau-Ponty's Last Vision*, p. 114.

in the fog – no one can say where, if anywhere, it will lead.'[75] Healing, I want to argue, should not be understood as closure or completion of the mourning process; rather, hesitance merely offers the possibility of healing. Roubaud's poems make it clear that the work of mourning is not a question of simply 'get[ting] beyond the brute facts of death' and the pain of loss.[76] Healing demands hesitance or intervals of hesitation, mute pauses or gaps experienced directly through the senses that do not rush towards recovery from pain: 'Quelque chose va sortir   du silence, de la punctuation, du blanc   remonter jusqu'à moi' [Something is going to arise   out of the silence, the punctuation, the blank space   going to surface for me] (*QCN* 124; *STB* 122). Roubaud's elegiac poems hesitantly work through what Riley calls 'an altered condition of life':

> It's as if any death causes collapse of the simplest referring syntax. As if the grammatical subject of the sentence and the human subject have been felled together by one blow. Yet at the same time, *the continuing possibilities for discussing the no longer existing person induce a curious linguistic quasi-resurrection.*[77]

Interestingly, Alix Cléo Roubaud, in her *Journal, 1979–1983*, written during the last years of her life, writes of 'language's inability to convey the truth'.[78] Poignantly, *Si quelque chose noir* [*If Some Thing Black*] (1980), the young photographer's series of black and white self-portraits of her deteriorating body, added as an appendix of sorts at the end of Roubaud's *Some Thing Black*, conveys the very 'truth' the poet is struggling to express in his poems. His words' lack of solidity echoes the lack of solidity of Alix Cléo's body or the several doubles, shadows or echoes of her body that appear in the photographs. 'Oscillating between subjective and objective views', writes Kathleen Morris, in Alix Cléo Roubaud's haunting

---

75 Merleau-Ponty, 'Cézanne's Doubt', p. 3.

76 John Taylor, 'The Composition of Mourning (Jacques Roubaud)', in *Paths to Contemporary French Literature*, Vol. 1 (New Brunswick, NJ: Transaction Publishers, 2004), p. 142.

77 Riley, *Time Lived, Without Its Flow*, pp. 13, 62 (my emphasis).

78 Alix Cléo Roubaud, as cited in Kathleen Morris, 'Illness, Photography, and Exile: The Photography of Alix Cléo Roubaud', *Canadian Art Review* 36/2 (2011), 41–51 (p. 43).

self-portraits, 'the light penetrates the corporeal at the same time that the corporeal releases the light, thereby complicating the boundary between interior and exterior and becoming a kind of symbol of air and breath.'[79] The doubling up of body into both inside and outside, subject and object, like the doubling up of the young photographer as both photographer and photographed, viewer and viewed, is the very 'turning point' of Merleau-Ponty's chiasm: 'the application of the inside and the outside to one an-other' (*VI* 264). Much like inhalation and exhalation, like the heart-beat cycle, Alix Cléo's photographs are silently folded into 'the pulsation of […] existence […], its systole and its diastole', the fabric of the world.[80] Roubaud writes: 'Je ne peux pas écrire de toi plus véridiquement que toi-même. Ce n'est pas que j'en sois incapable par nature, mais la vérité de toi, tu l'as écrite' [I cannot write about you with more truth than you have done. It's not that I'm incapable by nature, but your truth has been written down by you] (*QCN* 121; *STB* 119). It has been written down in Alix Cléo's *Journal* and in her photographs. Roubaud's elegiac poetry 'n'est pas de l'ordre de la vérité mais de la physique' [is not on the order of truth but of the body]: 'Ce que je détiens de toi, et qui me concerne seul' [This is mine alone, and for good reason] (*QCN* 121; *STB* 119). His process of mourning too is his alone. And it is from inside its gaps and marks of loss, its intervals of hesitation, that language is written back into a new form of existence.

79   Ibid., pp. 48, 47.
80   Merleau-Ponty, *Phenomenology of Perception*, p. 298.

DAISY SAINSBURY

The Ends and Beginnings of Language in Valérie Rouzeau's *Pas revoir*

ABSTRACT

Valérie Rouzeau's *Pas revoir* (1999) is a collection of poetry written shortly after the death of her father. Like other works of mourning, it depicts the silence ushered in by grief, and the deficiency of the linguistic conventions that surround the experience of death in both everyday life and literature. Throughout the collection, Rouzeau develops her own idiosyncratic language of mourning, what she describes as 'une sorte de langue paternelle' generated by fragments of childhood conversations between a young Valérie and her father. In so doing, she elaborates a mode of expression poised between its disintegration into disordered, aphasic speech and its construction, in an idiolect inflected with the lexical, syntactic and phonetic forms of child language. This idiolect offers her both a means to go on, in poetry, when it seems like such a continuation is an impossibility, and a space to explore the paradoxical proximity between the pre- and postlinguistic, the beginnings and ends of language.

Born in 1967 in Burgundy, the contemporary French poet Valérie Rouzeau lives what Stephen Romer describes as a 'vie de poésie' [life of poetry].[1] Alongside her writing, she gives readings and workshops in bookshops and local schools, and has translated a number of English-language poets such as Sylvia Plath, Ted Hughes, William Carlos Williams and Emily Dickinson. Mary Noonan talks about Rouzeau's 'poetic idiolect', which captures both the resolutely idiosyncratic nature of her voice, and its subsequent resistance to the conventional categories that carve up the

---

1   Stephen Romer, 'Introduction', in Valérie Rouzeau, *Cold Spring in Winter*, trans. Susan Wicks (Todmorden: Arc Publications, 2009), pp. 15–18 (p. 17). All English quotations of *Pas revoir* are taken from this translation (hereafter referenced in main text as *CSW*); these translations have occasionally been amended when analysis of the passage in question requires a more literal translation.

contemporary field.[2] Rouzeau's work might be described as occupying a middle ground between formally experimental, linguistically subversive poetry and a lyric tradition with its conventions of voice and subject matter, but such a description would nonetheless reduce its richness and complexity according to the trends and tribes of our times. In collections such as *Pas revoir* [*Cold Spring in Winter*] (1999), *Neige rien* [*Snow Nothing*] (2000), *Va où* [*Goes Where*] (2002), *Quand je me deux* [*When I Am Too*] (2009), *Vrouz* [*Talking Vrouz*] (2012) and *Sens averse* [*Meaning Shower*] (2018), what strikes the reader above all is Rouzeau's desire to find a flexibility within the French language, to fashion in simple and accessible ways new modes of expression for those most fundamental concerns of human existence: everyday life, relationships, love, death and grief.

The success of *Pas revoir*, published in 1999 by *Le Dé bleu* and later reissued in 2010 by *La Table ronde*, brought Rouzeau's work to the attention of a wider readership.[3] The collection is a *livre de deuil* [book of mourning], written in the wake of her father's death. It contains page-length poems, written in *vers libre* [free verse], without titles and without sections, that bear many of the markers of a work of mourning. It unites memories of her father, André, and their time spent together, with the everyday experience of grief, played out in the poet's daily life after his death. It explores themes of absence and presence, loss and negation, and language and silence. Nature holds a significant role in the collection, as the title of Susan Wicks's excellent English translation, *Cold Spring in Winter*, would suggest. The interior cadences of the poet's mourning are interwoven with the circadian rhythms and seasonal cycles of the exterior world. The imagery of the collection is etched in black and white: the pages are filled with snow and oil, magpies and swallows. Colour becomes a prominent motif, introducing a thematic exploration of sensory experience and memory. Alongside these more conventional features of a *livre de deuil*, *Pas revoir* bears the personal imprint of Valérie and her father. Rouzeau constructs a *tombeau* [tomb/poetic epigraph] for André,

2   Mary Noonan, 'Dismantling, Sifting, Sorting: Valérie Rouzeau's Poetics of Scrappage', *Irish Journal of French Studies* 12 (2012), 113–37 (p. 124).
3   Valérie Rouzeau, *Pas revoir, suivi de Neige rien* (Paris: La Table Ronde, 2010) (hereafter referenced in main text as *PR*).

a scrap merchant by trade, populating the poems with corrugated iron, rusting lorries and cranes. The collection's language, imagery and formal features are often determined by its starting point, by André himself. As Rouzeau suggests, when she began writing *Pas revoir* she assumed the role of 'récupérateur' from her father:

> En hommage à mon père, j'avais écrit dans une sorte de langue paternelle … Mon père était récupérateur, son travail consistait donc à 'récupérer': ferrailles, papiers, chiffons, métaux, pneus usagés etc. et pour les voitures vieilles ou accidentées, le carton en vrac il les pressait avant de les livrer sous forme de dés à jouer de cinq cents kilos aux usines de recyclage. J'avais fait cela avec les mots, quasimodo![4]

> [As a tribute to my father, I wrote in a sort of paternal language … My father was a scrap merchant, so his work involved salvaging: scrap, paper, rags, metal, worn-out tyres etc. and for old or damaged cars, loose cardboard, he would compress them before delivering them to recycling plants in the form of five-hundred-kilo dice. That's pretty much what I did with words!][5]

Using her father's work as a conceptual model, Rouzeau revisits Baudelaire's notion of the poet-ragpicker, collecting scraps of language, images and memories, converting these base materials into the poem so that it forms an archive, one that bears the imprint of her father, not only in the words themselves, but in the very poetic practice that has assembled them. As André Velter writes in the preface to *Pas revoir*: 'Comme son père qui récupérait cartons, casseroles, cuivre rouge, aluminium ou nickel, Valérie Rouzeau recycle par bribes des lambeaux de mélodies, des miettes de souvenirs, des bris d'émotions: elle ferraille dans l'or du temps' [Just as her father salvaged cardboard, pots and pans, red copper, aluminium or nickel, Valérie Rouzeau recycles bit by bit scraps of memories, fragments of emotions: she sifts through the gold of time].[6]

---

4   Valérie Rouzeau, cited in Serge Martin, 'Chronique poésie Valérie Rouzeau ou le poème libre', *Le Français aujourd'hui* 149 (2005), 105–10 (p. 107).
5   All translations my own unless otherwise stated.
6   André Velter, 'Ferrailler dans l'or du temps', in Rouzeau, *Pas revoir*, pp. 7–10 (p. 8).

The Impasse of Grief

Like other *livres de deuil*, *Pas revoir* depicts how death ushers in a silence: the silence of the deceased father, the silence imposed on the
grieving family, and the difficulty, or even impossibility, of expression
when language is tasked with comprehending the enormity of loss. The
collection is filled with allusions to the father's now-silent state: 'toi qui
ne dis plus rien ton | silence' [you who don't say anything anymore your
| silence] (*PR* 20; *CSW* 29), 'c'est de la haute fidélité ton silence' [yours
is a hi-fi silence] (*PR* 40; *CSW* 55). This is mirrored by the silence of the
family left behind: Valérie's brothers ('ils se taisent' [they keep quiet],
PR 81; *CSW* 113, adapted), her grandmother ('elle [ne] jase plus' [her
tongue no longer wags], *PR* 79; *CSW* 111) and, of course, Valérie herself. In one poem, the poet describes how the letter that she wrote to
her father on the morning of his death is buried with him, unopened:

> La carte postale du lundi elle
> est restée dans l'enveloppe dans ta poche
> dans le cercueil dans le caveau dans la
> terre, père gigogne. (*PR* 77)

> [But as for Monday's card it stayed in the
> envelope in your pocket in the coffin in the
> vault in the earth, my Russian doll daddy.] (*CSW* 107)

As *Pas revoir* unfolds, it enacts the end point of Valérie's communication
with her father, and the conclusion of their dialogue. The collection opens
with an apostrophe to André in the hours before his death. The opening
lines address him directly, 'Toi mourant' [You dying], beseeching him to
go on living: 'Pas mouranrir désespérir père infinir | lever courir' [Not
deadying not desperish father everlast | get up run fast] (*PR* 13; *CSW*
21). Rouzeau sustains this direct address throughout the collection, long
after her father's death is announced at the end of the first poem. She
uses the second-person pronouns *tu* and *toi* until the concluding pages
of the book, where a marked transition takes place. The final use of the
second person pronoun *tu* appears in the second-from-last poem of the

collection, where Rouzeau describes taking flowers to André's grave. She writes:

> Maintenant je m'en vais.
> Tu avais de beaux yeux mon père mais
> J'ai à voir ailleurs.
> Tu as mes fleurs j'ai ton sourire on est
> quittes. (*PR* 89)

> [I'm leaving now.
> You had beautiful eyes my father but
> I have things to see to elsewhere.
> You've got my flowers, I've got your smile
> we're quits.] (*CSW* 123, adapted)

Having announced this moment of closure, in the two remaining poems that follow, André is no longer addressed directly, but rather described in the third person. In the penultimate poem of the collection, Rouzeau commits explicitly to the conclusion of their communication: 'je n'écrirai plus à mon père | dessous la terre comme un oignon' [I won't write any more | to my father underneath the earth like an | onion] (*PR* 90; *CSW* 123). In such a way, Rouzeau traces in *Pas revoir* the successive stages of her grief: the desire to sustain a dialogue with her father; the temptation to do so through the elegiac tradition of apostrophizing the deceased; and the subsequent rejection of the illusion of continuation that this might offer. It is fitting that in her rejection of the poetic trope of apostrophe, Rouzeau uses a resolutely un-poetic image: the onion – bitter, foul-smelling and without promise of new life. This contrasts with the elaborate network of flowers found in the preceding poems, each forming part of the distinct colour-scape of *Pas revoir*, and each hinting at personal and universal symbolisms that might be ascribed. In this penultimate poem, the brutal symbolism of the onion stands in stark contrast, suggesting a resistance to the easy aestheticizing of death. In conjunction with the rejection of apostrophe, we find in *Pas revoir* an implicit criticism, and subsequent revision, of some of the common tropes employed in the treatment of mourning in lyric poetry.

Throughout *Pas revoir*, Rouzeau depicts a sustained disruption of normal communication, and the impending threat of an absolute silence.

This unites *Pas revoir* with the three *livres de deuil* that Dominique Rabaté discusses in his article 'Maintenant sans ressemblance' [Now Without Likeness], namely, Paul Éluard's *Le Temps déborde* [*Time Overflows*] (1947), Jacques Roubaud's *Quelque chose noir* [*Some Thing Black*] (1986) and Michel Deguy's *A ce qui n'en finit pas* [*To That Which Is Never-ending*] (1995).[7] Rabaté observes that these three poets are all involved in a quest to combat, or overcome, in poetry, the impossibility of language after death. He writes: 'C'est ce qui fait toute la force d'émotion des trois recueils que j'ai réunis: ils luttent tous, à leur manière, contre la tentation et la menace d'un effondrement du langage, une aphasie définitive' [This is what constitutes the strength of emotion in the three books I've assembled: in their various ways, they all fight against the temptation and threat of language collapsing, of definitive aphasia].[8] Discussing Roubaud's collection, which was written after the death of the poet's wife, Alix Cléo, Rabaté remarks: '*Quelque chose noir* est la survie de la poésie, son chant défait mais continué' [*Quelque chose noir* is the survival of poetry, its disordered but sustained song].[9] This is precisely what we witness in Rouzeau's *Pas revoir*: the continuation of poetry when grief threatens to silence it indefinitely. Throughout the collection, the poet presents a number of different forms of language that surround the experience of death, in everyday life, as in literature: from the deficient conventions of elegiac poetry to the clumsy inadequacy of euphemisms uttered by well-intentioned friends, and the disjointed sterility of medical descriptions of her father's illness. In response to the insufficiency of the linguistic forms at her disposal, she develops her own language of mourning, one that is generated by fragments of childhood conversations between a young Valérie and her father. By adopting a poetic idiolect inflected with the syntactic, prosodic and linguistic features of child speech, Rouzeau identifies a way to go on, in language, when it seems like such a continuation is an impossibility.

7   Dominique Rabaté, '"Maintenant sans ressemblance": le temps du deuil et du poème (Deguy, Eluard, Roubaud)', in Pierre Glaudes and Dominique Rabaté, eds, *Deuil et littérature*, Modernités 21 (Bordeaux: Presses universitaires de Bordeaux, 2005), pp. 319–32.
8   Ibid., p. 330.
9   Ibid., p. 327.

When Words Fail

Throughout *Pas revoir*, Rouzeau depicts how even the words for death itself involve a degree of impersonality or abstraction that render them insufficient to convey the singularity of any one instance of death. In one poem, she reprises the words of the nurses in the hospital where her father died: 'Vous ne savez pas? Monsieur Rouzeau est […] "décédé"' [Don't you know? Mr Rouzeau has […] 'passed away'] (*PR* 55; *CSW* 73, adapted). From the syllables of the formal term *décédé*, left in quotation marks to signal her distance from them, the poet teases out 'dédé', André's familial name:

> Toi c'est Dédé ton nom d'ami de paternel
> papa Dédé.
>   Les trois syllabes dans le désordre des
> infirmières toutes en chœur et bouleversées
> que c'est Dédé lui si gentiment si malade. (*PR* 55)

> [You that is Dédé with your friendly
> name of fatherly daddy Dédé.
>   Three syllables in chaos nurses all in
> chorus stunned that Dédé's dead and him
> so kind so ill.] (*CSW* 73)

The three syllables of *décédé* are reconfigured as 'c'est dédé'; the euphemistic adjective, 'passed away' or 'deceased', often used in administrative, legal and medical settings, is transformed into the declarative construction *c'est*, that encloses the referential nominal phrase, 'dédé'. In the passage from adjective to noun, there is a transition from the description of a property to the identification of a person. In a slight but no less tangible way, Rouzeau rejects the abstraction of the nurses' terminology, and through her subsequent revision distils the personal from the impersonal. Elsewhere, it is the term *disparition*, meaning both 'death' and 'disappearance', that Rouzeau takes issues with. She writes: 'Dans le journal on a parlé de ta disparition' [In the paper they spoke about your passing] (*PR* 47; *CSW* 63), yet, as she reflects, he has not disappeared or gone on the run or left for a foreign land. The indirectness of the euphemism renders the word absurd; it sits at odds with reality.

In another poem, it is everyday conversations with friends that prompt a reflection on the inadequacy of language in the context of mourning:

> Ça va quand on demande moi je dis
> bien surtout s'il y a du monde je prends sur
> moi très bien. (*PR* 42)

> [Okay when people ask I tell them
> fine especially when there are people round
> me yes I'm coping fine.] (*CSW* 57)

A couple of poems later, in a shift from reported speech that depicts Rouzeau's conversation with others, to a direct address to her father, the *ça va* of social politeness is transformed into an altogether more distressing refrain:

> Papa ça va pas dis comme ça va plus
> comme ça va pas plus.
> [...]
> Ça va pas sans dire je vais pas comme
> toi ça va pas papa.
> Ça va pas la tête ça va
> pas le foie ça va pas comme ça. (*PR* 46)

> [Daddy how goes it tell me no it doesn't
> any more like this it doesn't go no more.
> [...]
> It doesn't go without saying I don't go
> like you daddy it doesn't go.
> The head won't go the liver doesn't go it
> doesn't go like this.] (*CSW* 63)

The repetition of the central motif, 'ça va pas', which in itself marks a transition from the affirmative 'ça va' of the earlier poem to the negated form found here, evokes the desperate speech of a child addressing her father. The austerity of the language, accompanied by the simple gesture of repetition, has a quiet force to it that is characteristic of Rouzeau's language in *Pas revoir*.

One prominent set of linguistic conventions presented in the collection are those of romantic poetry and elegiac verse. As already suggested, if Rouzeau appears to have retained a number of features traditionally employed in poetic representations of mourning, such as the use of apostrophe and imagery drawn from the natural world, she is just as quick to subvert them. In one poem, we read 'Ça rime à rien ta mort intérieurement | pauvre chant' [It makes no sense your dying inwardly | poor song] (*PR* 42; *CSW* 57), which encloses a metapoetic reflection on the language of the collection as a whole. The double meaning of *ne rimer à rien* expresses not only the senselessness of her father's death, but also the poet's rejection of traditional verse forms and rhyme schemes, and with that, her refusal to impose conventional forms of order or structure onto the chaos of loss. Rouzeau appears to resist the temptation to use poetry as a corrective to reality; as we see throughout *Pas revoir*, the meaninglessness of death merits the impoverished verse, and the disintegrating, disorientating language of the poetry that evokes it. From the first page, the reader is presented with the disjunctive effects of Rouzeau's own idiolect of mourning, which forms a patchwork of heterogeneous linguistic forms. Antiquated lexis, 'pernocter' [last the night] (*PR* 13; *CSW* 21), appears alongside neologisms and portmanteaus: 'désespérir' [desperish], 'mouranrir' [deadying], 'chiardemment' [kidly], 'infinir' [everlast] (*PR* 13, 69; *CSW* 21, 95). Macaronic puns that blend French and English, 'Golden jusqu'au trognon' [Golden to the core] (*PR* 38; *CSW* 51), are juxtaposed with transcriptions of spoken language: 'Pas mourir steu plaît' [Not die oh please] (*PR* 13; *CSW* 21). Homophonic play generates sequences of words whose simplicity serves to reinforce the emotional intensity of an unanswered address:

> Papa dire papa dear dada pire: tu te
> souviens de mon petit cheval?
> [...]
> Comme ça valsait les boîtes à thé les
> casseroles belles comme ça y allait à dada
> rire oh papa rear à tout casser pas dire? (*PR* 29)

[Tell me, daddy dear, dadarling, daddy poorling:
do you remember my little horse?
[…]
        How the tins of tea the saucepans danced
so fine as how we went for it to dada laughing
daddy rear until it all breaks up not say no getting away.] (*CSW* 39)

This type of wordplay often appears in the parts of the collection that evoke the most troubling aspects of Rouzeau's father's death. In a poem that describes the details of his illness, Rouzeau writes:

        'C'est une colle' a dit le chirurgien
que la bile dans son corps.
        Tout le sang poison à cause de la bile
qui poisse maintenant laratélefoie – une
colle a-t-il dit.
        Six à huit semaines et c'est très beau-
coup pas mort pas croyable déjà déjà.
        Une fois sur cent mille mais ça ne par-
donne pas – une foie sur sang bile bê ça de
rate pas qu'il a expliqué que ma mère m'a
dit même temps qu'elle pleurait
[…]. (*PR* 32)

        ['It's a sticky one' the surgeon said the bile
inside his body.
        All the blood poison from the clogging
bile has now ruinedhisliver – sticky he said.
        Six to eight weeks that's a long long time
and not yet dead it's amazing to have come
so far so far.
        One in a hundred thousand but it's
unforgiving – wud id a hudred bilion it's
undfailig as he explained my mother told
me while she cried […].] (*CSW* 45)

Here, the linguistic play, which stresses the materiality of the words themselves, might be interpreted as an attempt to soften, or hold at a distance, the horror of the anatomical facts, timeframes and statistics that are presented. At the same time, the ludic nature of the language heightens the contrast between the stark reality of the father's condition and the insufficiency of the words themselves to describe it. This juxtaposition of the levity of the language and the gravity of the subject matter occurs throughout the collection. The following poem offers a further example:

> Prenant chez mémé café moulu bouillu
> foutu parlant de ça ta mort bientôt […].
>   Café bêtu ventru couru j'arrêtai d'en
> avoir trop bu.
> […]
>   Café vieillu marc noir repu j'en reprends
> chez grand-mère rendue toi mort ta mort
> elle n'en jase plus. (*PR* 79)

> [Coffee at gran's her groundup boiledup
> fuckedup coffee talking about it all your
> dying soon […].
>   Coffees wallowed bellied run away I
> stopped having drunk too much.
> […]
>   Oldened coffee blackened dregs full up
> I'll have another cup worn out turned up at
> gran's now that you're dead your death her
> tongue no longer wags.] (*CSW* 111)

Prosodically, the assonance of the repeated /u/, which is generated by the original adjective 'moulu', and which transforms verbs and adjectives into the neologistic forms, 'bouillu', 'bêtu', is juxtaposed by the intrusion of the repeated vowel /ɔ/ of 'ta mort', 'toi mort ta mort'. This acoustic contrast reflects a broader distinction between the ludic character of the language, and the thinly veiled omnipresence of André's death. The repeated refrain, 'café moulu […] café bêtu […] café vieillu', which structures the poem, framing its beginning, middle and end, is reminiscent of the structure and rhythm of nursery rhymes, an impression which is reinforced by the playful revision of words and the child-like language found throughout. So while Rouzeau's poetry might represent a *chant pauvre* in so far as it resists some of the more typical forms of traditional versification, these prosodic and metrical conventions are supplanted by abundant internal rhyme that spills out in unusual patterns, lending it its own idiosyncratic musicality.

The domestic scene that Rouzeau depicts here recalls a poem in Roubaud's *Quelque chose noir*, where he describes the intricate details of his daily life, following the death of his wife, Alix Cléo. He writes: 'Je verse un fond de café en poudre, de la marque ZAMA filtre, que j'achète en grands verres de 200 grammes au supermarché FRANPRIX, en face du métro Saint Paul' [I pour in some Zama Filter instant coffee which I buy in large 200 gram jars at the Franprix supermarket opposite métro Saint-Paul].[10] In *Quelque chose noir*, Roubaud describes the tunnel-vision or myopia of grief, and in both *Pas revoir* and *Quelque chose noir*, the poets depict a tendency to get bogged down in the trivial details and daily routines of everyday life. In *Pas revoir*, it is scenes such as the one described in the passage above that dominate the narrative: cups of coffee, trips to the *boulangerie* and conversations with the postman. In a similar vein, we might read in this passage a further form of escapism; temporary relief is sought in the possibility of losing oneself in the *ritournelles* of prosodic play.

Stuttered Ends and the Babbling of Beginnings

The most striking feature of Rouzeau's poetic language in *Pas revoir*, and one that has no doubt been apparent in the passages presented so far, is the incorporation of child speech. Rouzeau's ludic refrains recall playground chants and nursery rhymes, and the simplicity of her expression is accompanied by frequent references to the 'stuff' of childhood: dolls, a tea party set and buttered *tartines* (*PR* 31, 35). Memories of childhood conversations, phrases exchanged between father and child, resurface throughout. We find games of hide-and-seek, 'tu fermes bien les yeux | et bouh' [you've got your eyes tight | shut and boo] (*PR* 60; *CSW* 81), meal times, 'Une cuillère pour papa dédé' [A spoonful for daddy Dédé] (*PR* 31; *CSW* 43) and a young Valérie learning to count, 'ça fait deux facile' [that makes two, easy-peasy] (*PR* 43; *CSW* 59, adapted). In one poem,

10   Jacques Roubaud, *Quelque chose noir* (Paris: Gallimard, 1986), p. 27; *Some Thing Black*, trans. Rosmarie Waldrop (Champaign, IL: Dalkey Archive Press, 1990), p. 25.

Rouzeau revisits her early memories of episodes from the kitchen table, describing 'la vieille sensation de dire paa la bou- | che pleine de midi les mains pas bien lavées' [The way we used to feel saying Daa no | not with your mouth full at dinner-time you | haven't washed your hands] (*PR* 64; *CSW* 87). In the following stanza she writes:

> Moi paa se laisse pousser les ongles et
> les cheveux et ne déjeune plus et ne répond
> plus de rien. (*PR* 64)
>
> [Not me my daa lets his nails and
> hair grow long and doesn't eat his dinner any more
> and doesn't speak for anything ever again.] (*CSW* 87, adapted)

Here, two temporalities – the past and the present – are collapsed. Death renders the once important domestic rules of childhood redundant and absurd, as the significance of table etiquette or hygiene rituals translates awkwardly into the present tense.

In the absence of the continuation of dialogue between an adult Valérie and her father, linguistic memories from childhood serve to generate the language of the collection more broadly. Features of child speech penetrate the text, and are particularly apparent in the opening poem:

> Toi mourant man au téléphone pernoc-
> tera pas voir papa.
> Le train foncé sous la pluie dure pas
> mourir mon père oh steu plaît tends-moi
> me dépêche d'arriver
> Pas mouranrir désespérir père infinir
> lever courir –
> Main montre l'heure sommes à Vierzon
> dehors ça tombe des grêlons.
> Nous nous loupons ça je l'ignore pas-
> sant Vierzon que tu es mort en cet horaire.
> Pas mourir steu plaît infinir jusqu'au
> couloir blanc d'infirmières.
> Jusqu'à ton lit comme la loco poursuit
> vite vers Lyon la Part-Dieu.
> Jusqu'à ton front c'est terminé tout le
> monde dans la petite chambre rien oublier. (*PR* 13)

[You dying on the phone my mum he will
not last the night see dad.
          The train a dark rush under rain not last
not die my father please oh please give me
the get there soon.
          Not deadying oh not desperish father
everlast get up run fast –
          Hand watch the time we've got to
Vierzon outside it's tipping hail.
          We miss each other I have no idea passing
through Vierzon that in these train arrival
times you've died.
          Not die oh please but everlast until the
nurses' corridor of white.
Until your bed as fast the engine into
Lyon la Part-Dieu.
          Until your forehead over now and all
together in the little room and not
forget.] (*CSW* 21)

The poem contains a number of linguistic forms that evoke the acquisition of language in childhood: infinitives in place of conjugated verbs, the
absence of the personal pronoun *je* where it would usually appear in adult
language, and elided speech, transcribed here phonetically, 'oh steu plaît
tends-moi'. The presence of child language in the collection frequently
enacts a stripping down of language, reducing communication to its bare
essentials. Adjectives and adverbs are used sparingly, and nouns and verbs
are the predominant parts of speech. When verbs are conjugated they
tend to appear in the present tense, either as exhortations or commands;
they almost always involve a direct addressee. In the initial stages of language acquisition, rather than narrating past events or abstract ideas,
language is grounded in an immediate present: nouns describe objects
in the child's surroundings, verbs perform requests and commands to
an immediately available interlocutor. For Rouzeau, faced with the prospect that her father will now be forever inscribed in the past tense, these
properties of child language offer the possibility of a sustained immediacy. The frequent use of infinitives in *Pas revoir* mimics the develop-
mental stage of early language acquisition where children, rather than

conjugating verbs as in adult language, use what linguists call 'root in-finitives'.[11] Temporality is unexpressed in this acquisitional stage because the tense is usually recoverable from context. The reprisal of these root infinitives in Rouzeau's poetry conveys a desire for ongoing actions and states without end. Rouzeau grapples with the possibility of an infinite tense to contain her father, an idea that is conveyed in the repeated neologism that she employs to address him as she travels to his death bed: 'père infinir', 'steu plaît infinir'. The use of infinitives which, depending on the context, might refer to either future, present or past events, involves a further collapsing of time into one single, verbal particle, a fitting metaphor for the disruption of temporalities in the experience of mourning. Thus, in the passage above, the final words 'rien oublier' are deliberately ambiguous. Is Rouzeau alluding to the fact that she has forgotten nothing of these final moments of her father's life, or is she committing or promising never to forget them? The infinitive form allows the possibility of both temporalities.

The absence of the personal pronoun *je*, which imitates the acquisitional stage of 'subject dropping', is also significant.[12] It might be read, on the one hand, as expressing Rouzeau's impression of the complete eradication of self in her experience of mourning. Conversely, framed within the context of child language, it might express the exact opposite: an absolute certainty of the presence of the child speaker, who is free to drop the subject pronoun precisely because their presence is felt to be immediately secure, and therefore unnecessarily over-expressed through the use of the pronoun. Indeed, this certainty around the speaker's presence is felt all the more strongly, precisely through its contrast to the now absent addressee. I would argue that the symbolism of the absent *je* is left deliberately ambiguous in *Pas revoir*; it is deliberately pitched between the two opposing poles. This ambiguity fits well with Mary Noonan's analysis of the *je* in Rouzeau's poetry, which she describes as a site of constant uncertainty. She writes: 'The personal

---

11   See, for example, Luigi Rizzi, 'Some Notes on Linguistic Theory and Language Development: The Case of Root Infinitives', *Language Acquisition* 3/4 (1993), 371–93.
12   For an overview of this phenomenon, see Kate Scott, 'Child Null Subjects', *UCL Working Papers in Linguistics* 17 (2005), 1–25.

pronoun is always mobile in Rouzeau's poetry, "je" being the source of doubt and hesitation'; and goes on to cite Rouzeau's own reflection: 'Il y a ce "j'euh ..." magnifique d'Antoine Emaz entre les lignes, je lui aurais bien volé' [There is Antoine Emaz's magnificent 'j'euh' somewhere between the lines, I'd have very much stolen it from him].[13] In such a way, child language in *Pas revoir* enacts two parallel but somewhat contradictory movements. On the one hand, it has a disorientating effect, it involves a process of Deleuzian deterritorialization rendering the mother tongue strange and unfamiliar, destabilizing the security of personhood and temporality that underpins adult communication.[14] In this respect, it corresponds with Julia Kristeva's reflections on language and mourning in *Soleil noir*, where she writes: 'le mélancolique est un étranger dans sa langue maternelle. Il a perdu le sens – la valeur – de sa langue maternelle, faute de perdre sa mère' [The melancholic person is a foreigner in his mother tongue. He has lost the meaning – the value – of his mother tongue, because he has lost his mother].[15] At the same time, the incorporation of child language suggests an aspiration towards a utopic state of communication, an idealized mother tongue reclaimed from childhood – or, to return to Rouzeau's own formulation, 'une sorte de langue paternelle' – where language is firmly rooted in a present state, and words are securely attached to a materially present world, exchanged between a materially present speaker and interlocutor.

A further feature of child language that appears throughout *Pas revoir* is the use of 'reduplication' where syllables are repeated, as in 'papa', 'dédé',

---

13   Noonan, 'Dismantling, Sifting, Sorting', p. 124. Thierry Guichard, 'Valérie Rouzeau in Conversation with Thierry Guichard', *Dossier Valérie Rouzeau*, special issue of *La Matricule des anges* 131 (2012), 18–27 (p. 24).

14   On this point, see Michael G. Kelly's analysis of the Deleuzian 'bégaiement' in *Pas revoir*. Michael G. Kelly, 'De l'exposition poétique: œuvre, Lêthé et précarité chez Guy Viarre et Valérie Rouzeau', in Michael Brophy, ed., *Ineffacer: l'œuvre et ses fins: esthétiques et poétiques des XXe et XXIe siècles* (Paris: Hermann, 2015), pp. 71–89.

15   Julia Kristeva, *Soleil noir: dépression et mélancolie* (Paris: Gallimard, 1989), p. 64. Noonan presents an extended analysis of how the linguistic play in Rouzeau's poetry relates to Kristeva's account of the pre-verbal, arguing that the poet 'inhabits the threshold between the Kristevan semiotic – the pre-verbal – and the symbolic'. See Noonan, 'Dismantling, Sifting, Sorting', p. 137.

'mémé' (the English equivalents would be words like 'dada', 'mama' and 'nana').[16] This practice extends to repetition of entire words: 'les lilas là là' [the lilacs there there] (*PR* 14; *CSW* 23), 'Tes mains sur le drap blanc jaunissaient | jaunissaient' [Your hands on the white sheet were growing yellow | yellow] (*PR* 36; *CSW* 49). As the collection continues, the *pa* of 'papa' becomes a parasitic tic that resurfaces, as in the following example:

> Te parler papa j'ai pu te paparler un peu
> un petit peu paparce que nous n'avions plus
> tout le temps. (*PR* 36)

> [Talk to you dad I managed a bit
> of daddychat a chitter 'cause we didn't have
> that much time.] (*CSW* 49)

Throughout *Pas revoir*, Rouzeau plays on the homophony of *pas* as a particle of negation and *pa* as a noun evoking her father. In the title of the collection itself, Rouzeau captures a duality between the father's presence and his absence, which is sustained throughout the subsequent poems. The word *pa* is also significant because, like *ma* or *da*, it constitutes one of the earliest phonemic configurations that a child acquires during the babbling stage of language acquisition.[17] Its repetition throughout *Pas revoir*, alongside the 'reduplications' described here, constitutes a form of *babil enfantin* [infant babbling]. There is a certain resonance to the incorporation of *babil enfantin* in poetry, as in both instances, in contrast to ordinary communication, language use is motivated as much by sound as it is by meaning. The incorporation of babbling, a protolinguistic form of expression where words exist as pure sound, not yet affixed to referents, might suggest a broader reflection on the non-signification of language tasked with comprehending death. At the same time, babble might communicate a desire for a certain materiality, for a language that, in all its acoustic or graphic physicality, is reassuring, offering the possibility of

---

16   See Charles A. Ferguson, 'Reduplication in Child Phonology', *Journal of Child Language* 10/1 (1983), 239–43.

17   See Maria Teresa Guasti, *Language Acquisition: The Growth of Grammar* (Cambridge, MA: MIT Press, 2002), pp. 23–54.

some form of corporeality, if not in the father himself, then in the language that describes him.

Alongside the repetition of *papa*, often it is the syllables of André's name, 'dédé', that reappear, elsewhere it is the word *père*: 'Mon père mon père mon père […] je te répète | perroquet mon père mon père' [My father my father my father […] I repeat you | parrot my father my father] (*PR* 63; *CSW* 85, adapted). Here, Rouzeau identifies the practice of repetition that occurs throughout *Pas revoir*, an attempt perhaps at a continuation, that is reinforced by her reflection of the abrupt discontinuity of her father's daily routines. She describes his hammers lying untouched on the worktop, his boots left at the door, and in some small way, the gesture of repeating his name constitutes a desire for him to 'infinir'. We might also read in Rouzeau's repetition of *père* and *papa* a dialogue with Sylvia Plath's famous poem 'Daddy', written to her father, which involves similar refrains that alternate around that word.[18] Rouzeau has translated a number of Plath's works, including *Ariel*, which contains this poem, and in 2003, published *Un galop infatigable* [*The Indefatigable Hoof-taps*], a monograph on the American writer. At the time of writing *Pas revoir*, Rouzeau was working on a translation of Plath's 'Crossing the Water', and as Stephen Romer points out, 'there is something of Plath's "indefatigable hoofbeat" in the syncopated, broken rhythms of *Pas revoir*'.[19] Alongside a number of tangible similarities between the two poets, such as the motif of the shoe, or the absence left behind by the father, the obsessive refrains of Plath's work find their way into Rouzeau's, suggesting the manic repetition and revisions of language poised at the brink of disorder. In *Pas revoir*, Rouzeau writes:

> Nous n'irons pas nous n'irons plus pas
> plus que nous n'irons que nous ne rirons
> pas que nous ne rirons plus que nous ne
> rirons ronds. (*PR* 25)

> [We will not go we will go no more no
> more will we not go than we

18   Sylvia Plath, 'Daddy', in Ted Hughes, ed., *The Collected Poems* (New York: Harper Perennial, 1992), p. 222.
19   Romer, 'Introduction', p. 16.

will not laugh than we will laugh no more than we
will laugh rat-arsed.] (*CSW* 35)[20]

This passage, like others in the collection, captures the way language des-
cends into disorder, losing itself in its own vertiginous refrains. At the
same time, taken alongside the incorporation of child speech, and the
pervasive practice of repetition in *Pas revoir*, we are also prompted to
think about the processes of repetition and reproduction that constitute
an essential part of the acquisition of language in childhood.

In *Pas revoir*, Rouzeau depicts language as poised between its own
disintegration and its very construction, between an end and a beginning
of language. This link between the end and beginnings of language has
been explored by Michel de Certeau in an essay on glossolalia, where he
writes the following:

> Comment se met-on à parler ? 'Glossolalie' signifie 'babiller', voire bafouiller, bégayer
> (*lalein*) dans la langue (*glossè*). […] Mais la question de la fin ou du *lapsus* de la
> parole se trouve jointe à celle du commencement. Comment le parler se défait-
> il ? La passion de la chute redouble celle de la naissance. L'une peut être d'ailleurs
> le lieu même de l'autre. Aussi les deux figures se mêlent-elles souvent. En chaque
> glossolalie se combinent d'ailleurs quelque chose de pré-langagier, relatif à une origine
> silencieuse ou à l'attaque' de la parole, et quelque chose de post-langagier, fait d'excès,
> de débordements ou de déchets de langue.

> [How does one start to speak? The term *glossolalia* signifies to babble, to jibber-jabber,
> or to stutter (Greek: *lalein*) in the tongue (Greek: *glossè*). […] But bound to the ques-
> tion of the beginnings of the spoken word [*la parole*] is the question of its *lapsus* or its
> end. How does speaking come undone? The passion of the fall redoubles the passion
> of the birth. Each, moreover, can be the very site of the other, and accordingly the two
> figures frequently mix. Every glossolalia combines something prelinguistic, related

20   This passage might also evoke the concluding poem of Éluard's *Le Temps
     déborde*: 'Nous n'irons pas au but un par un mais par deux | Nous connaîtrons par
     deux nous nous connaîtrons tous | Nous nous aimerons tous et nos enfants riront |
     De la légende noire où pleure un solitaire' [We will not get to the point one by one
     but two by two | Knowing ourselves by twos we all know each other too | We will all
     love each other and our children will laugh | At the sombre legend where the lonely
     man weeps]: 'Notre vie', in *Derniers poèmes d'amour* (Paris: Seghers, 1951), p. 88.

to a silent origin or to the 'attack' of the spoken word, and something postlinguistic, made from the excesses, the overflows, and the wastes of language.][21]

The glossolalia of Rouzeau's poetry appears to exemplify this intersection of the prelinguistic and the postlinguistic that Certeau evokes. We might return here to the earlier example of the parasitic *pa*:

Te parler papa j'ai pu te paparler un peu
un petit peu paparce que nous n'avions plus
tout le temps. (*PR* 36)

This line embodies rather well that meeting point of disordered language, with its stuttered 'paparler', 'paparce que', and the nascent possibility of child babble, where the rudimentary consonant-vowel combination, *pa*, forms one of the phonetic building blocks of a language to come.

Returning to the original starting point of this chapter, we will recall Rabaté's assertion that the *livre de deuil* might resist the aphasia of grief through the renovation of language within the poem. In Rouzeau's own idiolect of mourning both impulses are simultaneously present – the possibility of language's disintegration, and the possibility of its renewal. Intriguingly, in *Quelque chose noir* Roubaud makes a passing reference to the relationship between language disorder and language acquisition. In the poem 'Aphasie', where the poet describes the period of silence that followed Alix Cléo's death and the disassembling of his poetic verse that ensued, he writes the following: 'Jakobson dit que l'aphasie mange la langue à l'envers de son acquisition. Les articulations les plus récentes partent les premières. | Une bouche qui se défait commence par les lèvres' [Jakobson says aphasia devours language in reverse order to its acquisition. The most recent articulations going first. A mouth coming undone starts at the lips].[22] Here, Roubaud refers to Roman Jakobson's theory that, structurally, language

21   Michel de Certeau, 'Utopies vocales: glossolalies', *Traverses* 20 (1980), 26–37 (pp. 28–9); 'Vocal Utopias: Glossolalias', trans. Daniel Rosenberg, *Representations*, 56 (1996), 29–47 (p. 33).

22   Roubaud, *Quelque chose noir*, p. 131; *Some Thing Black*, p. 128. Roman Jakobson, *Child Language, Aphasia, and Phonological Universals*, trans. Allan R. Keiler (The Hague: Mouton, 1968).

development and language disorder mark two inverse, mirroring processes. For Rouzeau, death has dismantled the language at her disposal, and has undone the previously stable notions of signification and address. The conventional forms of language that surround the experience of mourning offer no possible means of continuation. The return to child language offers an alternative linguistic mode, an inverse process to aphasia, with its novel syntactic and temporal possibilities. If, as Rabaté suggested of *Quelque chose noir*, the *livre de deuil* can represent 'la survie de la poésie, son chant défait mais continué', then for Rouzeau it is the return to this language of childhood that offers a means to reconstruct, and to acquire language afresh in the face of death's silence.

CAROLE BOURNE-TAYLOR

Poethic Justice: *Re-incarnations* in Emmanuel Merle's Poetry

ABSTRACT

Echoes, traces and ghosts configure an isotopy of loss and exile in Emmanuel Merle's poetic universe, in which the entwined motifs of evocation, invocation and incarnation[1] reveal an ethical project. Like many of his contemporaries, Merle grounds his writings in Baudelaire, who is credited by Yves Bonnefoy for fusing poetry and death: 'Baudelaire a fait ce pas improbable. Il a nommé la mort' [Baudelaire took this improbable step. He named death].[2] A filiation[3] from the nineteen-century poet – whose main

---

1   'L'Incarnation, ce dehors du rêve, est un bien proche. Présence, oui, et cette fois plénière autant qu'immanente, et avec des mots à sa disposition: mots quotidiens, de parole.' [Incarnation, that exists outside of dream, is a resource close by. It is Presence, yes, and this time fully manifest as well as immanent, with words at its disposal: everyday words, the common speech], *Le Nuage rouge* (Paris: Mercure de France, 1977), p. 279; trans. Stephen Romer. In Bonnefoy's lexicon, incarnation is a synonym for 'Présence', which, rooted in immanence, is an awareness of death and the antidote to the illusory and perfect enclosure of image; it prompts a spiritual – in a secular sense – experience, which the poet sees as his duty to express, despite its ineffability.

2   Yves Bonnefoy, 'Les Fleurs du Mal' (1955), *L'Improbable et autres essais* (Paris: Gallimard, 1983), p. 34.

3   A sense of relational ethics underlies the motif of filiation – whether biological or intellectual (alongside Baudelaire, Apollinaire and Bonnefoy, American authors, such as Jim Harrison, Richard Hugo, Raymond Carver, Richard Brautigan are constant sources of inspiration) – which hinges upon a polymorphous alterity in the construction of the mourning subject. Intertextuality brings the ethical aspect into sharp relief with its staging of a dynamic entanglement: it was his 're-acquaintance' with Bonnefoy that mediated Merle's 're-acquaintance' with his father, Louis. A complex web of literal and metaphorical meanings, textu(r)ality and orality, 'filiation' promotes an 'ethics of restitution' in the sense of reconstituting *and* giving back, of speaking for the other, but perhaps more importantly, letting them speak. An orphan and heir, the poet is also a '*passeur*' (a term encompassing transmission

accomplishment is existential rather than merely poetic – to Merle sketches the elaboration of an artistically versatile *poéthique*.[4] The influence of Bonnefoy, particularly, permeates Merle's œuvre which is haunted by death – his father's, primarily, but his ongoing quest for a grieving sincerity extends to collective traumas. Mourning is endlessly, ethically figured, configured, transfigured, often articulating interrelated concerns within a staunch humanistic agenda.

> il faut des phrases, puisque ces personnes qu'on aime et qui mourront ou déjà sont mortes ne s'établiront dans la mémoire que par ce qu'on aura pu en dire: en dire pour en penser. La parole naît avec le savoir du hasard, du non-être.
> [There is now a world where sentences are necessary, because the people we love and who will die, or who have died, can only establish themselves in the memory because we can speak of them – we speak of them in order to think of them. Language comes to birth with our experience of chance, or of non-being ...][5]

A cluster of experiential, aesthetic and ethical concerns, mourning pervades Merle's œuvre from the travelogue-testimony *Un Homme à la mer* [*Man Overboard*] (2007)[6] – published four years after the death of his

---

and translation, which is an integral part of Bonnefoy and Merle's literary practice) and '*donateur*'. The concept of 'ethics of restitution' has been theorized by Dominique Viart, in Dominique Viart and Bruno Vercier, eds, *La Littérature française au présent. Héritage, modernité, mutation* (Paris: Bordas, 2005), 'Récits de filiation', p. 79–101. Merle also taps into the highly symbolic hypertextuality of myths (Orpheus, Percival, Icarus and Daedalus), which enacts the paradox of 'retour' through detour'. With its dialectic of identity and alterity, *rapprochement* and distance, it is an alternative discourse with maximal allegorical potential, thus amplifying language's poetic quality.

4   Defined as commitment with its emphasis on existence. Cf. Jean-Claude Pinson, *Poéthique. Une autothéorie* (Seyssel: Champ Vallon, 2013), p. 8.

5   Yves Bonnefoy, *Le Lieu d'herbes* (*le lac au loin*; suivi de mes souvenirs d'Arménie) (Paris: Galilée, 2010), p. 40; *The Place of Grasses*, trans. Stephen Romer (Calcutta & Chicago: Seagull Books, 2012), p. 187. From *Pierre Écrite* (1965) and *Dans Le leurre du seuil* (1975) onwards, death and alterity have become gradually more entwined. With *L'Arrière-pays* (1972), Bonnefoy's poetic writing took on a memorializing dimension.

6   *Un Homme à la mer* (Paris : Gallimard, 2007, prix Rhône-Alpes du Livre 2008); hereafter referenced in main text as *UHM*. All translations of Merle's works are by Stephen Romer.

father, to whom it is dedicated – to *Démembrements*[7] [*Dismemberments*] (2018): a trajectory that reveals an ongoing attempt at subduing pathos, dismissed as self-indulgent and complacent and an illusion of communion. A vision of space inflected by a ghostly paternal and ancestral presence is being sketched out, composing a vast echo chamber. Written in 2005, in just three months, *Un Homme à la mer* began as a collection of poems inspired by the Saint-Laurent whale, alternating with *tombeaux* for the father. Appearing, disappearing, reappearing, the solitary whale is a universal image of melancholia: it soon became an image of the deceased father, who is conflated with Ahab's ghost (*UHM* 20) – in keeping with the Melvillian hypotext. A looming presence of absence, it metaphorizes human unknowingness and exilic helplessness, in congruence with the ubiquitous trope of the orphan, reminiscent of Baudelaire's 'Le Cygne'.[8] Merle revisits, rather reinvents, his relationship with his father partly through the mediation of *Moby Dick* – whose prominence in Georges Perec's *La Disparition* [*A Void*] also interpellates the reader. Abysmal and awe-inspiring, Moby Dick is symbolically exemplary and notoriously inexhaustible. With its exploration of death and madness, the fatal confrontation with nature, the experience of the abyss and inconsolable mourning, the great environmentalist epic and ghost story allows sufficient distance for the autobiographical endeavour to be launched. The mythical, archetypal, Biblical and allegorical trigger a process of universalizing autobiographical experience, as in the inaugural poem, 'Moby Dick', with its interweaving of the personal, the impersonal, the transpersonal and the interpersonal. The speaker takes on the persona of Ishmael, the paradigmatic survivor, who, clinging to the remains of the wreckage, undertakes to tell Ahab's tragic fate, implicating the reader by his direct addressivity in the opening distich: 'Appelez-moi Ismaël./Achab est le surnom de tous les pères' [Call me Ishmael./Ahab is the name of every father] (*UHM* 13), which resonates with the ambivalence of fascination and intimidation.

---

7   *Démembrements* (Montélimar: Éditions Voix d'encre, 2018); hereafter referenced in main text as *D*.
8   Charles Baudelaire, 'Le Cygne', *Fleurs du Mal* (Paris: Garnier, 1961), p. 96.

With its punning title ('man overboard') and homophonic ambiguity, *Un Homme à la mer* points to the enigma of loss and the condition of being at a loss, adrift. The truth of the late father lies in the gap between the two sets of poems: therein is re-enacted a relationship of estrangement and reconciliation. Poetry was the natural choice to pursue the dialogue with the autodidactic father who had a partiality for the genre. How bitterly ironic though, that Louis died before his son embarked on poetry. It is tempting to approach *Un Homme à la mer* – laden with regrets about unexpressed love – as a compensatory and reparatory endeavour: 'Branches chargées des mots que je n'ai pas/Prononcés, gestes mal esquissés' [Branches loaded with words I have not//Uttered, incomplete actions] (*UHM* 23). Emmanuel's recourse to poetry only imposed itself in the aftermath of Louis's death. He contemporaneously wrote a poetic travelogue-cum-lyric diary, *Amère Indienne* [*Elsewhere on Earth*], consisting in a tribute to the Amerindians – with the eponymous poem, 'Amère Indienne', exploiting the trope of the violated mother[9] – and all the emigrants to America, including his own ancestors. It also encloses a homage to the poet-traveller Blaise Cendrars (*AI* 68), who, like the poet-translator, has a vocation for otherness. If the speaker is very much present – albeit as a self-effacing persona – he lets the memory of all those others unfold. There is some fluidity between the earlier collection with a poem entitled 'Louis' – with its cathartic anaphora, 'Il est mort' (*AI* 70) – whilst *Un Homme à la mer* also bears witness to the Amerindians' tragic fate which haunts all the ghostly villages of the Western United States. Further irony lies in the son's sorrowful retrospective deciphering of his filial love and the father's fatherhood, poignantly conveyed by the refrain of the eponymous ballad/nursery rhyme, 'Un père et manque' (*UHM* 14): forever gone, '[a]lors vraiment il devient un père/ Et manque' [Then he truly becomes a father/And I miss him] (*UHM* 15). A bond cemented by the laconic, elliptic and shaky reverberation of unmournable loss. Hence Merle's fondness for the first line of Apollinaire's elegiac 'Le Voyageur': 'Open the door, please; I am knocking and in tears'

9   Emmanuel Merle, 'Amère Indienne. Âme indienne, mère violée.' [Bitter Amerindian. Indian Soul, Ravaged/Violated Mother], in *Amère Indienne* (Paris: Gallimard, 2006. Prix Kowalski 2007; Prix Théophile Gautier de l'Académie Française, 2007), p. 95; hereafter referenced in main text as *AI*.

('Ouvrez-moi cette porte où je frappe en pleurant'[10]). From this archaic memory, only errant traces remain, which though inaccessible to intelligibility, solicit recollection: the leitmotifs, 'Do you remember?' ('te souviens-tu?') and 'I can remember, I can still remember' ('Je m'en souviens, je m'en souviens encore') sound like repeated knocks on that locked door, the irrepressibility of a past haunting the present, as in Yves Bonnefoy's 'Dans le leurre du seuil', shrouded in the same sense of loss: 'Heurte,/Heurte à jamais./ Dans le leurre du seuil.// À la porte, scellée ... À la phrase, vide' ['Knock,/ Knock forever// In the lure of the threshold.// A the sealed door ... At the empty phrase'].[11] The door that opens onto the past is forever shut while that leading to death is not yet open: in-between there are poetic visitations ('affleurements', which is one of Merle's pet-words). The 'je' strives to recapture fragments of memory, mobilizing the vocative, alternatively 'tu' and 'vous', which dents the poetic with the full force of the intrusive discourse it enacts: the identity – albeit ethereal and contingent – of the absent interlocutor takes precedence. The diffuse presence of the father, cropping up in *biographèmes* scattered about the collection, is addressed alternatively in the second and third persons. The systematic use of the pronoun 'vous' – which ambiguously brings back the father from the dead and interpellates the reader – in the first stanza in 'Lucide' (*UHM*, 30) encloses as well as it generalizes the father's experience of gazing at a mountain and falling dead, whereas the shorter second stanza switches to the eponymous 'homme'. Often the paternal voice can be heard, as in the opening poem of *Ici en exil* [*Here in Exile*]: 'Il faudra l'abattre me dit-il/ Il a la maladie' [It must be felled he said to me/It has got the disease],[12] echoing an earlier poem (*UHM* 23) haunted by the father through the deploring mantra, 'mauvaise année, tu sais, mauvaise année' [It was a bad

10   Guillaume Apollinaire, 'Le Voyageur', *Alcools*, *Œuvres poétiques*, préface par André Billy, texte établi et annoté par Marcel Adéma et Michel Décaudin (Paris: Gallimard, 1959), p. 78. My translation.

11   Yves Bonnefoy, 'Dans le leurre du seuil' (1975), *Poèmes* (Paris: Gallimard, 1982), p. 257. Tr. John Naughton in Anthony Rudolf, John Naughton, Stephen Romer, eds, *Yves Bonnefoy: Poems* (Manchester: Carcanet Press, 2017), p. 79.

12   Emmanuel Merle, *Ici en exil* (Chauvigny: L'Escampette, 2012), p. 7; hereafter referenced in main text as *IE*.

year, you know, a bad year]. The father's 'langue de la pierre' [language of stone] (*IE* 65) resonates across Merle's œuvre as an 'empreinte' [imprint] as if to compensate for the words that were never uttered in his lifetime. When the only recourse is a rhetorical, yet taunting, question (without a question mark) – 'lui ai-je assez parlé/lui ai-je dit je t'aime une fois au moins' [did I ever really talk to him/ did I tell him, just once, that I loved him] (*D* 71) – regret does not get stuck in the rut of *ressassement*: the direct style is a marker of performativity and commitment to the father in this interlocutory poetry. An emanation of corporeality, the phenomenology of vocality is distilled into apostrophic and prosopopoeic addresses – movingly exemplified by '1922' (*AI* 21), in which the poet adopts the persona of his ancestor, a fearful migrant to Idaho. Evocation and invocation chiasmatically converge in this ambiguous operation of spectral incarnation.

Despite memory being deaf to our appeals[13] – memory is but the memory of loss – poetry is conducive to re-capturing something of the concrete uniqueness of each being – whether human or non-human – while giving it an archetypal value and making it coincide with a universal experience; it aspires to the preservation of emotion – etymologically defined as a corporeal and existential exteriorization, emotion propels itself into motion – in the minimal mediation of 'matter-emotion'.[14] With its faith in existence against the background of absence, the Bonnefoyan ideal of 'truth of speech'[15] informs Merle's *poethical* practice intent on recovering original intuitions and emotions that precede any conceptualization and exemplified by a language pared down to its most elemental, like the unforgiving landscape of his native Alps. Nature is seen in its fundamental ambivalence: a source of exhilarating *and* harrowing experiences, scattered with persistent reminders of our fate, such as those ubiquitous

13   Emmanuel Merle *Schiste* (Thonon-les-Bains: Alidades, 2013), p. 8; hereafter referenced in main text as *S*.

14   Cf. Michel Collot, *La matière-émotion* (Paris: Presses Universitaires de France, 1997).

15   'vérité de parole' is defined by Bonnefoy as a fight against image in favour of 'la Présence', in *Lieux et destins de l'image* (Paris: Seuil, 1999), p. 35. Similarly, Philippe Jaccottet advocates 'justesse de ton' to refer to death, in *Observations et autres notes anciennes* 1947–62 (Paris : Gallimard, 1998), p. 37; p. 75.

abysses ('gouffres' and its polyptotonic variations, especially the dramatic 'engouffrement'[engulfment]), which figure the dark underside of this landscape tunnelled by coal mines, where Merle's father worked. Alongside those intractable elemental realities, more humble ones also evince mourning: the story of trees and stones is the story of death. This sudden encounter with death provides a vocation for poetry as the only possibility that is available to us to fulfil our being-in-the-world, and therefore the necessity to share with others a meaning to be invented in each stylistic choice.

The point of junction between the subject and whatever lies within their field of perception,[16] the landscape is the site of a dynamic interaction in the sense of connection and transgenerational continuity. Nature often mediates the fraught relationship with the father. Majestic summits, weeds, birds, trees, etc. all coexist within a habitat that fosters a sense of human and non-human interrelatedness. The wilderness of Merle's native mountains or their North-American counterparts is no mere scenery: in the *géopoétique*[17] of the so-called 'landscape poets',[18] vibrant signs of life are intimations of mortality. A Bachelardian poetics of presence underlies Merle's œuvre, in which mourning is staged as a continued dialogue with the father – whose presence is refracted into innumerable memories – symbiotically expressed through atavistically telluric images. In *Olan*,[19] the magnitude of the forbidding eponymous peak (recalling the whale in *Un Homme à la mer*) is dynamically inseparable from a very personal meaning within a dense dramaturgy of death. The desolation of the mountainscape is a *tombeau*, literally and figuratively: 'l'Olan, la mort dans son habit de pierre' [The Olan, death in its habit of stone] (*O* 8).

16   Michel Collot, *Paysage et poésie : du romantisme à nos jours* (Paris : Corti, 2005), p. 12.

17   Cf. M. Collot, *Pour une géographie littéraire* (Paris : Corti, 2014). Broadly defined as the encounter between experience and the language of that experience (109) – it flaunts its ethical agenda in the neologism *géopoéthique*, theorized by Michel Deguy as poetic resistance to both genocide and 'geocide', a world swiftly disappearing. Cf. *Ecologiques* (Paris: Hermann, 2012), *La fin dans le monde* (Paris: Hermann, 2009) and, in its wake, Christian Doumet and Michaël Ferrier, eds, *Penser avec Fukushima* (Paris: Éditions Cécile Defaut, 2016).

18   Most notably Bonnefoy and Jaccottet.

19   *Olan* (Châteauroux-les-Alpes: Éditions Gros Textes, 2014); hereafter referenced in main text as *O*.

The scarcity of toponyms highlights their emotional charge: spurring the writing process, they force their significance onto the reader, a poetico-phenomenological significance that has as much to do with the signi-fier (or *signifiance*) as with the associations triggered by their geological referentiality. With its particularizing effect and numinous sonorities, yet resisting any sublimating symbolism, Olan articulates the world and words – 'Olan, iambe de roche […] Olan, iambe hors souffle' [Olan, rocky iamb (…) Olan, breathless iamb] (*O* 7) – weaving its memorial quality and poetic potential in a process of phantasmatic re-enactment of Louis's heart attack – 'hors souffle' meaning (literally) breath-less – in an incantatory performative utterance: 'Olan violent, l'écume des nuages/est sur ta vague Abats-toi! Abats-toi/une seconde fois,//que je voie ce qu'il a vu'[20] [Turbulent Olan, the froth of cloud/ is upon your wave Flatten yourself!/ Flatten down/ once more//so I can see what he saw] (*O* 13). The homage is contained in the imploration to see 'what he will have seen' (*O* 8) in his final moments: another reminder of our fundamentally split and flawed condition, the future anterior underscores a commitment to memorability. The upward and downward thrust of those awe-inspiring mountains turns them into the allegorical stage of an arduous ascent and abrupt death. The romantically inspired Icarian motif[21] embodies the quest for some mighty goal; by reinventing the traditional myth of the poet as Icarus, Merle honours his father's own poetic aspirations, while seeking to untangle their ambivalent bond. Myth dramatizes the tension between an uncompromising world and poetry's powers.

Here is life with all its contradictions, in perpetual motion 'til it meets its fate, carried along by the erratic energy of poetry. The 'élan'[22] – an echo

20   It is tempting to spot an effect of diaeresis in 'violent'. There is much to unpack in the verb 's'abattre', with its connotations of falling down and collapsing (which ap-plies to both the mountain and the father), crashing down on, tumbling down on, subsiding, raining on, swooping down on, striking, descending upon – not to men-tion its enshrining 'abattre' (to fell, to bring down, to shoot down and to devastate).
21   As the mythical subtext of *Olan*, the Icarian motif expresses the conflictual rela-tionship between father and son.
22   *Élan* is a richly untranslatable word: thrust, jump, momentum, surge, vigour, etc. and impulse (talking about the heart), which evokes another symptomatic pet-word: 'élancement' [shooting pain].

of Olan … – of the rock seems to precipitate 'la dernière crispation, le dernier élan des/ viscères' [the last spasm, the final kick of the/viscera] (*O* 8). The combined tropes of descent and death will culminate in the polysemic image of the 'dernier battement' [beat, beating, flapping, fluttering, palpitation] with its resounding sense of tragic finality, enhanced by the hallucinatory image of an electrocardiogram gone mad ['fou', *O* 9], triggered by a sudden 'emballement du cœur' (which metaphorizes a pounding heart whilst hinting at the father's flashes of anger), with the all too familiar paronomasia amour/mort it allows.

That Louis died in the very spot where he wanted to die seems to turn him into a fictional character, which Emmanuel construes as a sign from beyond the grave, a confirmation of the mystery of the world; as if the father was entreating the son to attend to those material realities; as if, ultimately, his death was a confirmation of the son's artistic choices, although the poet is anxious that it be not recuperated by literature, or that language revert to its lyrical pretensions, hence the need to devise a language attuned to materiality and mortality, through discipline, dis-embellishment and simplification. *Olan* is an exercise in toning down elegy – pathetic grandiloquence being the tempting default that risks overpowering the expression of emotion. Merle remembers Baudelaire: the tighter, the more intense.

Poeticity encompasses sound effects – the blunt rhymes that typify a staccato style aimed at minimizing pathos – and rhythm, which brings together presence – of which it retains the temporality and the corporeality – and sense (meaning). Far from aspiring to the condition of music, this jerkily delineated free verse favours raucousness,[23] typified by the shrill or throaty cries of birds. The incipient monostich in *Schiste* sets the tone: 'C'est une langue étrange qu'un chemin de pierres' [A stony track is a strange kind of language] (*S* 7). Emulating his father's 'langue de la pierre', Merle's poetic ideal of 'chant rugueux' [rugged song] (*IE* 64) – 'immense/rude et douloureux' [vast/hard and painful] (*IE* 67) – emblematizes his stylistic quest for honesty. Mourning harnesses the power of the orphic myth

---

23   In this 'geology of sound', disharmony is a guarantee of truthfulness. Cf. Michèle Finck, *Épiphanies musicales en poésie moderne, de Rilke à Bonnefoy: le musicien panseur* (Paris: Champion, 2014), p. 292.

whose universalizing interpretation can be adapted to the singularity of personal loss. The foundational myth and allegory of poetic language pervading poetry from Romanticism to Bonnefoy, via Apollinaire, Orpheus features prominently in *Ici en exil*: the isocolon 'Orphée lapidé lacéré à mort' [Orpheus stoned lacerated to death] (*IE* 71) creates an onomatopoeically beating rhythm of harsh alliterations and curt assonances compelling to both ear and eye. Orpheus is out of tune – 'désaccordé' (*IE* 71) – everything dies out, including his song, but the world bears that imprint – 'en-creux' being a variation on the inscriptional metaphor exemplified by 'empreintes' (imprints and footsteps), although it also refers to what is unsaid.

Stones and rocks delineate a harsh topography, whose materiality imposes itself on the reader: the seemingly simple designation refers to the stubborn density of a presence endowed with a Rimbaldian and Bonnefoyan quality of 'réalité rugueuse' [rugged reality]. Carried along by the rhythmic and phonetic materiality of the recurring rugged 'fracas' [crashing, roaring, pattering], lexicality hinges upon 'pierre' endowed with a 'poetic coefficient', namely a heightening quality[24] that counteracts stylistic affectation, therefore the logical aesthetic choice of the sceptical lyricism of the aftermath of the Second World War.[25] The omnipresent hyperonym 'pierre' (so central to Bonnefoy's ascetic poetics) ramifies into all kinds of hyponyms ('schiste', 'phonolite', 'mica', 'silex', 'galet' [pebble], 'granit', 'roche', 'rocher', 'roc', etc.) composing the background against which existence and mortality are imbricated and transforming the world into a mausoleum. Clusters of words and piles of stones merge as boundaries blur between the linguistic and extralinguistic realms. The poetic potential of the phoneme 'pierre' unfurls, propagating subjective connotations as well as a more general meaning, skimming the water's surface. A tangible and humble signifier of reality, 'pierre' is, paradoxically, eminently poetic and emotional. The confluence of sound and memory produces, through an effect of paronomasia, a

---

24   Yves Bonnefoy establishes an analogy between the anfractuosity of stones that
       remain beneath signification and sounds, in 'Georges Poulet et la poésie', Stéphanie
       Cudré-Mauroux and Olivier Pot, eds, *Georges Poulet parmi nous* (Geneva &
       Berne: Éditions Slatkine/Archives littéraires suisses, 2004), p. 112.
25   Cf. Anne Gourio's analysis of an imaginary of minerality in twentieth-century
       poetry, in *Chants de pierres* (Grenoble: Ellug, 2005).

reversibility between 'père' and 'pierre', the latter memorializing the former, reverberating with its power of conjuration. Phonetic proximity is double edged: a miraculous coincidence *and* a symptom of the slippery nature of language. It is the usual conundrum: a mistrust of the naming power of language, yet the necessity of poetry rooted in a belief in its transformative power. Immanence secretes imminence, a sense of things lost or soon to be lost. In a poetry stripped of its consolatory tropes, pathetic fallacy is made to expose its fallacy: nature does not offer any refuge for the poet, nor does it mourn with him. A symbol of indisputable presence forcing us to confront death, minerality may be antithetic to language, but Merle is deft at capturing its cragginess. As language is cleansed of its superfluities, so the world takes on greater reality within the poem: signs are being filled with presence, yet presence is precisely that which can only be apprehended as lack and must contend with gaps and lapses. Mourning reality, language seeks to retain something of the opaque and resistant muteness of minerality, whose mystery is *our* mystery, which rhyming echoes seem to hint at that.

Poetic image is haunted by the lack from which it originates: at the very moment when it seems to presentify presence, it points to its absence: after all, it merely represents. Merle shares Bonnefoy's suspicion of language as 'une perte, un exil' [a loss, an exile][26] and emulates his attempt at overcoming its conceptual slant – which causes our estrangement from the world – by injecting a power of incarnation and presentification into poetry in keeping with Bonnefoy's re-semantization of the verb 'dé-signer' to define poetry[27] in the sense of freeing language from the prison of signs to replenish it with some substance. This privilege of poetry is inseparable from its duty, the two being folded into the polysemic near-neologism 'dé-signer' – it designates insofar as it 'unsigns' or 'undoes' the closure of signs so that presence may take precedence. To designate is, after all, to refer back to reality.

26   Yves Bonnefoy, 'Il reste à faire le négatif' (1988), *Entretiens sur la poésie. 1972–1990* (Paris: Mercure de France, 1990), p. 241.

27   Yves Bonnefoy, 'La poésie est dessin : ce qui dé-signe', in *Remarques sur le dessin* (Paris: Mercure de France, 1993), p. 36.

The semic characteristics of 'pierre' produce an effect of concreteness and immediacy: the sign and referent are textually and ontologically consubstantial and morphologically enhanced by enjambment, which embodies, beyond a rhetoric of discontinuity, the defiant spirit of poetry. Merle hails the 'verticality' of poetry as an ability to explore the enigma of death and loss: the arresting ubiquitous image of 'éboulement' [crumbling or collapsing rocks] seems to conflate the re-enactment of the fatal scene of the father being struck down, combined with those ricocheting or rebounding rocks with their telescoping of the 'no longer' and the 'always' and the 'again and again', which all coexist in the elongated temporality of mourning. Crushed by lexical density, lines cascade down the page, sweeping away neat boundaries and smooth syntactic order to unleash the force of emotion, rhythmically and often phonetically spilling over to more echoing. The concept of a 'complexe rythmique signifiant'[28] [a rhythmical complex of signifiers] pinpoints the process of sound enhancing image working towards lessening its abstractness and augmenting its intensity. Merle is anxious not to let recurrence tip into musicality, to which he prefers *signifiance*. Repeating is retaining in one's memory, rescuing from oblivion. Operating at a deep level of language, poetry is 'un ressouvenir, dans le discours, de la présence même que le discours conceptuel abolit' [a memory, within discourse, of presence itself, that conceptual discourse abolishes].[29] The title, *Ici en exil* impressed itself upon the poet's consciousness first and foremost as a signifier before its meaning took hold. The lucid confrontation with a past overshadowed by violence, yet unmournable, demands uncompromising lexical choices, such as 'vacarme' [racket, din], 'bruits' [noises] and 'coups' [knocks, blows] – soon to linger as echoes (*S* 12). Forced to confront a 'sick' and 'violent' past (*UHM* 24), the mourner is visited by memories that are 'like anxious dogs' ('chiens inquiets'). Hammered out, intensifying meaning though the sheer substance of sonorities, harsh words remembered from Merle's childhood are 'jets de pierres'[30] – those

28   Henri Maldiney, *L'art, l'éclair de l'être* (CERF, 2012), p. 86.
29   Yves Bonnefoy, *Le siècle où la parole a été victime*, trans. Stephen Romer (Paris: Mercure de France, 2010), p. 134.
30   Emmanuel Merle et Anne Tourmen, *La Pierre se lève – Un écho des sculptures* (Cannes et Clairan: Encre et Lumière, 2017), p. 14.

stones being thrown are painful reminders of the father's violence and its lingering trauma – but the polysemic 'jet' also conjures up the spurting or gushing of blood and the 'premier jet' [the first draft, ink-blots on the page]. Boundaries between reality and language blur: 'L'élancement des mots comme un jet de pierres,/d'armes blanches,/d'oiseaux craintifs,/de balles sorties du canon de la gorge,/c'est la voix adressée, la parole qui enjambe' [The pang of words like a skitter of stones,/of blades,/of frightened birds,/of shot from the barrel of the gorge,/it is the voice addressed, the speech that enjoins] (*D* 27). All those scattered words rushing forward and thrusting both upwards and downward, and the shooting pain they cause, figure the dynamic, infra-semantic sonorous expressivity of the so-called 'energy of despair', which can be described as 'the dislocating energy of poetry'[31] that eschews transitions and connectors, thus playing out the drama of a presence haunted by absence and suffused with a vivid sense of the past – real, unrealized or imagined.

Hurled by disjointed rhythmical balance – in keeping with a predilection for irregular lines, blanks and enjambment – a poetics of lacerated syntax and phonetic discordance, tears language apart; swift perceptions and fleeting sensations disrupt the thrust of lines, bringing to the fore the obsessional memory of being abandoned – re-enacted by the father's death – and a sense of implacable fate. Instantiated by innumerable 'fragments' or 'morceaux' [pieces], dispossession is the overarching motif. The polysemic image of 'éclats' [splinters, fragments, the father's outbursts and parental strife] is persistent enough to convey a sense of suffering, yet redeemed by an eruptive and irruptive force that sharpens language's interrogative edge. Merle seems to be emulating Bonnefoy in his uncovering of the stigmata of a suffering world, performing anatomical dismemberment linguistically through atomized words and sounds, monosyllabic utterances, the recourse to an alliterative web of encrusted plosives and gutturals, and polyptoton. If the Baudelairean phobia of dismemberment, which pervades Merle's poetry – from Ahab's amputation in *UHM* to the *disjecta membra* of *Démembrements* via the familiar figure of Orpheus – is symptomatic of

---

31   René Char, 'Pour un Prométhée saxifrage. En touchant la main éolienne de Hölderlin', in *La Parole en archipel* (Paris: Gallimard, 1962), p. 125.

decrepitude and death, it is also an insidious effect of absence, to which the nasal assonance lends a lingering effect: '[l]'absence démembre' [absence dismembers] (D 29). Pluralized – 'membres épars' [dispersed limbs] (D 20) amidst 'signes disjoints' [disjointed signs] – the motif extends to the dispersed members of deceased bodies, revealing a *correspondance* between the horror of mutilation and the fierce ridges of the landscape. The adjective 'épars' is a leitmotif. The more physical grazes, snags and scars – 'Cicatrices' is the title of a poem in *Démembrements* – are everywhere. Scratches abound, drawing attention to an inscription that is phenomenologically motivated. Recurring metaphors of the inscription of pain and poignancy into the flesh include 'incise', 'écharde' [splinter] and 'entaille' [cut, gash]. Bodily synecdoche reveals the prevalence of 'lambeau'[32] – which significantly culminates in the post-Holocaust collection, *Pierres de folie*[33] [*Stones of Madness*] – and 'bribes de chair désassemblées' ['shreds of dismantled flesh'] (D 39), that metapoetically compose 'an obscure' and 'incomplete' collection of members/limbs (D 39), 'scattered' (épars) fragments. This intertwining of the poetic and phenomenological registers is inherent in 'bribes' (snatches) and the exilic 'feuille [leaf and sheet of paper] détachée' (D 45). Self-reflexive tropes of inscription signify an allegiance to the ontology of the *hic et nunc*, symbolized by the omnipresent and phenomenologically resonant 'sang d'encre' (not just 'worried sick', but more literally, written/writing in blood).[34] There is reciprocity between writing and the world in some kind of calligraphic trans-figuration. The poet can feel the asperities on the wall turn into an alphabet, a grey Braille, a parchment 'as hard as death' (IE 22), with its secrets and wounds. The acoustic virtualities of some words turn them into incisive gestures, carved in space and tearing through memory: 'Il

32 *Lambeau* translates as strips of flesh, scaps of conversation, fragments or remnants of the past; surgical flap of skin; anything that is torn to shreds or bits or tattered.
33 Emmanuel Merle, *Pierres de folie* (Genouilleux: La passe du vent, 2010); hereafter referenced in main text as *PF*.
34 Cf. Laurent Demanze, 'Sang d'encre. Filiation et mélancolie dans la littérature contemporaine', in Sylviane Coyault, Christine Jerusalem, Gaspard Turin, eds, *La Revue des lettres modernes, Écritures contemporaines 12. Le Romain contemporain de la famille* (Paris: Minard, 2015), pp. 37–49.

y a des gestes incisifs, cris du corps,/ des paroles de peau et d'os'[35] [There are trenchant actions, body cries,// words of skin and bone]. The etymology of 'incisive' [slash, cut, gash, engrave] impinges upon the world through a phenomenological vision of language as gestural, that is, kinesthetically engaged with the world.

The all-encompassing motif of fragmentation ramifies endlessly: ruins, shavings of slate or slab, crystals, scoria, scraps and rags, dust, ruins, débris, marks of erosion, pieces of chalk, splinters, shreds and shards of corporeality. The ubiquitous metaphors of chipping, chapping and flaking are modalities of appearance haunted by disappearance, by a past that never was synonymous with completion, a present very tangibly present, yet bearing witness to an absence. A jagged language espouses the rugged outlines of the landscape, such as the phonetic echo produced by 'mots et copeaux' [words and shavings] (*PS* 13). Through its reminders of the raw reality of suffering, the metaphorizing process of flakiness and friability – poignantly exemplified in *Schiste* and more so in *Pierres de folie*, where it conjures the victims of the Shoah – seeks to pull semiosis into ever greater and grimmer mimesis – albeit highly figuratively. The metaphorization of memory – whether personal or collective – relies on pulverization (*S* 16), exemplified by crumbling mica and schist, squames or dead skin (*S* 9): 'Le schiste terne sous mes doigts,/pulvérulent parfois, souvent squames//de la terre, peaux mortes comme souvenirs' [The dull shale of the earth under my fingers,/ powdery sometimes, often in scales/ dead skins like memories] (*S* 9). *Ici en exil* revisits the death of the father, hauntingly conveyed through images of pulverization blowing errantly across the collection, enacting a diasporisation. Marks and wounds ('écorcher') and signs of erosion – cracks ('fissure', 'brèche') and rock falls ('éboulis'/'éboulements') – all exchange their idiosyncrasies within a multifarious metaphorization premised on microcosmic and macrocosmic interconnectedness. Wreckage, breakage and rifts bear witness to the alteration brought about by death (both its anticipation and recollection). The privative prefixes 'dé' and 'dis'

---

35   Emmanuel Merle, *Écarlates*, monotypes Jackie Plaetevoet (Malaucène: Sang d'encre, 2011), p. 18; hereafter referenced in main text as *E*.

are ubiquitous,[36] most notably in 'désolation' and 'déshérence' (escheat and its concomitant 'errance', which ties phonetics to semantics), which struggle to contain the destruction of the Amerindians (*AI* 95); the loaded notion of an unspeakable 'désastre' (*D* 20) will always reverberate with ample connotational value. Alongside the more generic 'détacher/détachement' (which also appear in italicized and pluralized form), one finds a multitude of varyingly poignant and dramatic counterparts – such as 'déperdition', bringing together the consubstantial 'perte' (loss) and 'perdition' in the description of childhood (*S* 11); without mentioning the equally momentous 'désordre' and 'désespoir'.

The quest for a language on the 'threshold' between 'parole' and presence' – [c]onceptuellement au plus vide, sensoriellement au plus plein' [at its emptiest conceptually, at its fullest sensorially][37] – relies on a palette of red, black and white to let presence and its invisible lining of death resonate. Chromatic visuality starkly conveys the raw emotion of errant words echoing and glowing red like embers, which is a recurring image: 'les mots errent comme des échos/dans le corps des autres/et rougeoient encore' [words wander like echoes/through the bodies of others/red and smouldering yet.] (*D* 27) With its incarnating power, red is a metonymy for the drama of deeply buried violence, its intensity exploding in the tomb-like *Les mots du peintre*.[38] Blood gushes from the body across the pages of *Écarlates*[39] (with its double-entendre: it is both the colour and the scarlet tanager), which revisits blood-stained haunting memories in a poem entitled 'Amer' (*UHM* 24) within a vaster 'haemophiliac' memory (*UHM* 31). The

---

36 This is exemplified by a spectrum of recurring verbs (most of which in the past participle, thus conveying an inexorable fate), 'démembrer', 'déliter' (to cleave), 'désassembler', 'dépareiller' (to make incomplete), 'découdre' (to unpick), 'désolidariser', 'désagréger', 'décentrer', 'déraciner' (to uproot), 'déshériter', 'désarticuler', etc. Alongside 'disloquer', 'disjoindre', 'inhabiter', 'inaccéder', as well as 'informulé', 'indicible' (unsayable, unnameable), etc. Last but not least, the neologistic 'déperlées' oysters (*PF* 13) to refer to the victims of the Shoah.
37 Yves Bonnefoy, 'Il reste à faire le négatif' (1988), in *Entretiens sur la poésie*. 1972–1990, p. 243. Tr. Stephen Romer.
38 Emmanuel Merle, *Les Mots du peintre*, illus. George Badin (Cannes-et-Clairan: Encre et lumière, 2016).
39 Emmanuel Merle, *Écarlates*, illus. Jackie Plaetevoet.

Amerindians' memory consists in bloodied tales (*AI* 93). Symptomatically, the post-Holocaust sun is haemophiliac (*PF* 7) in *Pierres de folie*, where red is the visual equivalent of the scream, hence its juxtaposition with birds' cries (*PF* 11). The raven's squawk betokening exile (*IE* 67), synesthetically red (*E* 35) or scarlet (*E* 46), hints at an 'écartèlement' [quartering, tearing apart], against a haemorrhaging horizon. Harking back to Chrétien de Troyes and optimally exploited by Bonnefoy via Baudelaire – Delacroix's 'lac de sang' in 'Les Phares' is transposed into *Démembrements* (*D* 49) – red substantializes the existential mission of poetry. When blood coagulates, it verges on black (*O* 53), the hyperbolic black of clots that come to symbolize a blackened life (*O* 54). In *Olan*, the blackness of coal – with its fatality of 'mal noir' (*O* 51) and Baudelairean pun (evil/illness) – metonymically encapsulates Merle's tribute to his father in 'Le choix du noir' (*O* 50): Hobson's choice if ever there was! The poet's own illustrations not only reinforce linguistic terseness, but also lend spectrality and foreboding to deepening shades of grey, outlining the summit, and a circling raven, which balefully materialize a grief without pathos. Here the ephemerality of ekphrastic gestures converts reading into an experiential process. In *Schistes*, black skeleton trees sketching 'an alphabet of lack' (*S* 15) against a wintry background that is just like the white page, configure the entanglement between words and world: reduced to its purest lines, the landscape strikes us less for its beauty than for the truth it evinces about mortality. Death, the ultimate enigma, is one of those 'things' that 'alter' words by virtue of the horror and awe they generate, making words recoil and resist. When enhanced by stark chromaticity, poetry is an optimal *alter*ation of language, striving to catch a glimpse of that radical and irreducible alterity that is death, always beyond any conceptualization; in the *alter*ation that affects the word, one gets a sense that presence is already, always already absence: this is our paradoxical condition. The typically Bonnefoyan image of snow delineates a landscape of loss and unending mourning in *Dernières paroles de Perceval*[40] [*Percival's Last Words*], where Merle reworks another founding myth to revisit the motif of the dead father and the crisis of language against the background

---

40 Emmanuel Merle, *Dernières paroles de Perceval* (Chauvigny: L'Escampette, 2015); hereafter referenced in main text as *DPP*.

of a wasteland – 'la terre veuve' [bereft and bereaved] (*DPP* 9), with its metonymic association with the devastated mother: 'terre' conjures up 'mère', phonetically and through the hypallage.

In this dramaturgical emulation of both mortality and impossible mourning, familiar images of dispossession, dissemination and pulveriza-tion unleash unsettling violence when they are transferred to an historic-ally singular context: this is the case in *Pierres de folie*, which, framed by an epigraph by Paul Celan (whose dialogical conception of poetry inspired Merle) and a reference to Primo Levi – takes on a more obviously ethical dimension: 'death was Jewish' (*PF* 9). Enclosed within 'disseminated verse' (*PF* 7), 'tossed about' on an incredible and unprecedented[41] refrain (*PF* 7), the paradigm of the 'pas'/'sans'/'rien' is accompanied by synecdoches of dehumanization and folded into an imaginary of traces and ashes (*PF* 19). Assonance and consonance create an elongated effect, tightening the elastic band of time to the limit, which almost materializes as a tongue twister, before releasing the inevitable break: 'Le temps s'est tendu lentement,/ Puis déchiré' ['Time grew tense, little by little//Then tore'] (*PF* 7). Clouds above Berlin are seen 'stretching their shrouds' (*PF* 12) – across a sky that is all infinity and despair, yet incongruously blue – that are 'like an armful ('brassée d'oublis') of oblivions' (*PF* 13), which conjure up a sense of erratic, centrifugal dispersion. The recurring 'brassées' are torn away from their customary usage, exiled and alienated, unexpectedly cropping up in images of dispersion and turmoil, limning the despairing sky above Berlin: in the same way as the speaker is unhinged – oscillating between different pos-tures and grammatical pronouns – language is struggling to make sense of the horror that haunts Berlin. Taken out of its context, the term 'brassée' (etymologically, a measure of land and which significantly crops up in *Ici en exil*) not only disrupts any chronology, but also unbalances any stability. Typographically uneven with its various fonts, performing an act of tearing and ripping of the text, *Pierres de folie* charts a temporality gone mad, hi-jacked by entropic and centrifucal forces: 'Ce n'est pas vrai que les jours passent/L'un suivant l'autre. Non c'est plutôt par brassées/Brutales qu'un

41 The French 'inouï' conflates all these nuances, including extraordinary, unheard and unheard-of.

vent les arrache' [It isn't true that the days pass/One after the other. No, a wind tears them off//in brutal armfuls.] (*PF* 14) – or petrified in moments that are adulterated or corrupted (*PF* 15). With each single moment being detached from its telos, disorientation is metaphorized as madness (*PF* 15). The verb 'passer' seems to have been hijacked by the Holocaust death trains ('le train est passé', *PF* 21), radicalizing the fatality of the past participle. We are left with the terror of the Shoah as the enduring emblem for the complete disintegration of human history. The motif of fragmentation is aggravated by the sun incongruously reduced to crumbs (*PF* 10); and, more eerily perhaps, by the image of perforating rain (*PF* 12), echoed by that of the map of Poland (*PF* 24) being 'perforated/By boots' heels and naked toes' (*PF* 24) and chests riddled with bullets (*PF* 13). The lexical field is dominated by 'trouer'/'trou', 'forer' and 'entaille' (gash) – the ship scything through the waves (*PF* 15).

Composed as a triptych – Berlin-Suppliques-Pierres – *Pierres de folie* channels the memorializing impulse through a self-decentering subject. A displacement, which, combined with the approximate sparseness of his language, corroborates poetry's status as an appropriate medium for the cultivation of vigilance. The alternation of the first and second person pronouns marks the oscillation between the speaker and the poet in a paradoxical effort to strike a balance between historical awareness and poetic creation whilst drawing attention to the unbridgeable gap and limitations of language. The dissociative enunciation of the self-addressing 'tu' enclosed within an alexandrine, signals the self-questioning stance of a perplexed poetic subject, who, abjuring the first person, devolves into empathy by repositioning himself within alterity – 'Tu te perds dans le Mémorial Juif à Berlin' [You get lost in the Holocaust Memorial in Berlin] (*PF* 17) – desperately tracking a glimmer of understanding in this 'labyrinth without its Daedalus' (*PF* 17) or 'theatre of shadows' (*PF* 21) of 'morts fantômes' (*PF* 31). If one is hit by the full force of self-interpellation – 'Tu ne sauras jamais/Ce qui a été éprouvé ni ce que tu aurais crié' [You will never know/ What was gone through nor what you would have cried out] (*PF* 17) – it is surely because the searching demand made by the poet to himself implicates us. Flaunting its agrammaticality, the figure of *enallage* draws attention to the failure of intellection and the violence of tearing apart, wrenching and devastation. Faced with the unrepresentability of the Shoah and symbols of irredeemable loss, transcendence vacillates in favour of the 'tu' of self-othering as the operator of a consciousness of responsibility and vigilance through the homonymy of 'tu'/tue [kill].

That poetry is all too aware of its precariousness is clear in the rhetorical question: 'Comment puis-je continuer à être un homme après ça?' ['How could I possibly be human after that?'] (*PF* 88), which betrays something of the survivor's guilt in literary reworkings of the testimonial act: we have here an echo of Primo Levi's treatment of the concept of the *Muselmann*[42] (musselman) – the radical Other experiencing absolute suffering and absolute dehumanization: 'Morts sans présent que la mort/Morts volés à votre propre mort' [Deaths whose only present was death/ Deaths stolen from your own death] (*PF* 31). The mission of the 'poète-justicier'[43] [poet-vigilante] is to pay honour to those who have been deprived not just of their lives, but also of their death, to enact the interminable mourning of the Shoah's interminable legacy. The anaphoric supplication – 'do not say': a martyr, a hecatomb, death, sacrifice for neither of these words is suitable, then the volta 'say', which consists in the capitulation of comprehension – reveals the conundrum of the poetry of the aftermath: 'Dites je ne sais pas/Dites que cela fut. […] // Quand j'entends le mot fosse/Je n'ai plus rien en commun/avec l'humanité […]//Dites je ne sais pas/Dites que cela fut' ['Say I do not know/Say that it happened' (…) 'When I hear the word pit/I have nothing more in common/with humanity// Say I do not know/ Say that it happened'] (*PF* 29). The exhortation to remember opens onto a broad ethical project, summed up as 'mes devoirs et ma mémoire' [my duties and my memory] to seal off 'le trou de ma mémoire' [the gap (hole) in my memory] (*PF* 20) – a pun on 'trou de mémoire' (memory lapse, blank), but also a warning to a humanity all too prone to amnesia.

---

42   Cf. Primo Levi, *The Drowned and the Saved*, trans. Raymond Rosenthal (New York: Random House, 1989). Sharon B. Oster offers an analysis of the denomination in 'Impossible Holocaust Metaphors: The Muselmann', *Prooftexts* 34/3 (Fall 2014), Indiana University Press, p. 302–48.

43   Roger Pearson enlists Bonnefoy (in the wake of Rimbaud) as an example of the power of poetry as legislation, in *Unacknowledged Legislators: The Poet as Lawgiver in Post-Revolutionary France*, p. 4.

The vocation of poetry, as conceived by Bonnefoy and Merle, is to re-member – with its innumerable variants from 'rapatrier' to the domestic 'ravauder'/'raccommoder' [to darn, to mend, to repair] – the 'disaster', to strive to restore what *might* have been. With its power of incarnation, poetic image can renegotiate (post)memorial grappling, but the search for proper diction is trapped in the unresolvable quandary of the necessity to preserve memory whilst foregrounding the fraught nature of figuration. Tentatively described as testimonial acts ('*comme* des témoins', *PF* 89) of the unnameable – in the wake of Primo Levi – the poems might return some of the humanity that we, humans, took away from them. With its optimal use of ambiguity, poetry is possibly the nearest to testimonial truth.

Merle's recent collection, *Démembrements*, encloses the imperative to *re-member* in the anaphoric injunction 'souvenons-nous' (*D* 14) and in the vocative gesture of reaching out in a poem entitled 'Remembrer' (*D* 16). In keeping with Bonnefoy's equation of poetry and hope – after all, Orpheus's tragic and symbolic trajectory, enmeshed in existence, heralds hope, too – Merle rehabilitates humanism insofar as it may reinvent its faith in humanity. His ongoing ethical attention to all victims of geno-cide, all those who suffer an irreparable loss – Amerindians, Jews, Irish,[44] migrants[45] – contributes to promoting a poetics of relationality that places its faith in compassion rather than consolation.[46] Baudelaire's dolorist brand is transcended by Bonnefoy's ethics of universal compassion, which is mapped onto the humanistic paradigm of *ensemble encore*[47] tentatively reconceptualized as 'l'étrange possibilité du partage' ['the startling possi-bility of sharing'] (*D* 40). With its intertwining of offering and othering, the foundational experience of loss is transmuted into a gift – 'Le don' is the last poem in *Démembrements* – which is the raison d'être of the poetic

---

44 Cf. *Tourbe* (Thonon-les-Bains: Alidades, 2018).

45 'La longue marche', cited in Patrick Chamoiseau's *Frères migrants* (Paris: Seuil, 2017), p. 58, before it was published in Merle, *Tourbe*.

46 As advocated by Jean-Claude Pinson, in *À Piatigorsk, sur la poésie* (Nantes: Editions Cécile Defaut, 2008), p. 68.

47 The title of his testamentary collection, *Ensemble encore* suivi de *Perambulans in noctem* (Paris: Mercure de France, 2016), from which Merle derives his epigraph to *Démembrements*.

endeavour: 'Ces gens, ce qui les aurait rendus heureux,/je voudrais pouvoir le formuler pour eux' [What would have made these people happy,/ is what I should like to articulate for them] (*S* 9). If poetry is an exercise in intergenerational trans-mission,[48] it is best defined as 'poétique du texte offert'[49] [*poetics of the text as gift*]; it is also the locus of a transfiguration into 'ressaisissement'[50] (a vigorous act of re-grasping in the sense of recol- lection, recomposure and recomposition), which 'dé-signe' in the sense, ultimately, of 'faire signe'[51] [to gesture], within the uncertain coincidence of sense and sign. Poetry's true power lies in its vigilance, in its humble philosophizing: it is not an end, just a means[52] to that improbable end …: '[d]ire cela, des paroles tutoyées,/des éclats de verbe' [To say that, words that are intimate,/fragments of language] (*DPP* 83).

48 Cf. 'Fils/Père' (*UHM* 91) and 'Mes enfants' (*D* 79).
49 Cf. Jean-Michel Maulpoix, ed., *Poétique du texte offert* (Fontenay & St Cloud, MN: E.N.S. Éditions, 1996).
50 Jean-Michel Maulpoix, *du lyrisme* (Paris: Corti, 2000), p. 190.
51 In keeping with Jean-Claude Pinson's view that 'une poétique fait toujours signe vers une poéthique', *Habiter en poète. Essai sur la poésie contemporaine* (Seyssel: Champ Vallon, 1995), p. 135.
52 In 'L'acte et le lieu de la poésie', Bonnefoy writes that, 'La poésie doit être un moyen et non une fin', *L'Improbable*, p. 117.

SARA-LOUISE COOPER

Conclusion: Mourning in Motion from Ireland to the Caribbean

As many contributors to this volume have noted, there is an ethical and aesthetic value to grief which resists closure, love which resists ending. Since mourning is linked to the infinite, and so to perpetual return to the new, in what follows I return to the ideas explored in this volume to show how they can illuminate a new literary subject: writing on the so-called 'European migration crisis' of 2015 onwards.[1] I focus in particular on what is at stake in Patrick Chamoiseau's quotation of a poem by Emmanuel Merle in his 2017 essay, *Frères migrants* [*Brother Migrants*]. Chamoiseau becomes interested in the migration crisis from 2015 onwards, first mentioning it in passing in the 2016 *La Matière de l'absence* [*The Matter of Absence*], before devoting a whole work to it in 2017 with the publication of *Frères migrants*, then co-editing a collection of short stories, poems and essays on the subject with Breton writer Michel Le Bris, *Osons la fraternité: les écrivains aux côtés des migrants* [*Let's Dare Fraternity: Writers at the Side of Migrants*] (2019). This last volume emerged out of the Étonnants Voyageurs literary festival, which also gave rise to the manifesto 'Pour une "littérature-monde" en français' [For a 'World Literature' in French] (2007).[2] Chamoiseau's interest in

---

1   Although the term 'migration crisis' is the most common way of referring to the surge in the number of people seeking entry to Europe from 2015 to 2019, it is open to question, as 'crisis' suggests a punctual event. Although migrant crossings and deaths did rise in this period, largely due to conflict in Syria and Afghanistan, the issue is also longstanding and ongoing, since it is not possible to apply for asylum in Europe from outside its borders.

2   This was first published by Michel Le Bris and others as 'Pour une "littérature-monde" en français', *Le Monde*, 15 March 2007. A book-length volume, *Pour une*

this topic is thus tied to experimentation with ways of moving between the local, the national and the worldly explored earlier in this volume. It is also tied to his quest to re-imagine the lives seen as worthy or unworthy of mourning, and his search for literary forms which could inspire a better ethics and a better politics.

The 'migration crisis' which began in 2015 raises the question of mourning in that at least 18,500 people lost their lives seeking entry to Europe between 2014 and 2019. The representation of these deaths is tied to questions explored in other ways in the volume by Benjamin Thurston, Rachel Benoît and Khalid Lyamlahy about the way mourning practices, or their suppression or revival, are linked to the constitution of the nation state. Whether negotiating the exhumed and re-mourned body of the king, the body of a child who was never born, or the disembodied voice of an illiterate, story-telling mother, Thurston, Benoît and Lyamlahy demonstrate the decisive relationship between the mourned body and the body politic. In different ways, these three scholars illustrate the way the mournable body emerges from a complex intertwining of the geographical, historical and political borders of France. In seeking to represent migrant deaths as both mournable and inadequately mourned, Chamoiseau establishes a tension between the current constitution of France and its unrealized possibility as a revolutionary *terre d'asile*.

There are also less obvious resonances between the attempt to write migrant trajectories and the creation of mourning texts. To begin to write a mourning text or to attempt to discuss the 'migration crisis' is to be perplexed by the inadequacy of language to articulate the value and otherness of other people's lives. As noted in the Introduction, Patrick Marot, in an essay on mourning and metaphor, writes that both processes necessitate 'travail sur les signes' [work on signs] and we can say the same of the attempt to articulate what occurs when people seek entry to Europe by crossing the Mediterranean.[3] In a radio interview on the writing of her

_____

littérature-monde, ed. Michel Le Bris and Jean Rouaud (Paris: Gallimard, 2007), a collection of essays by the signatories of the original manifesto, followed.

3   Patrick Marot, 'Deuil et métaphore', in Pierre Glaudes and Dominique Rabaté, eds, *Deuil et littérature*, Modernités 21 (Paris: Presses universitaires de Bordeaux, 2005), pp. 107–30 (p. 107).

2019 novel on the crisis, *La Mer à l'envers* [*The Sea Upside Down*], Marie Darrieussecq speaks of the difficulty she had embodying the migrant in her novel, and of the vexed question of how to name those who seek entry to Europe from other countries.[4] The linguistic stumblings of the novel's protagonist as she corrects her son for using the term 'migrants' suggest this: 'd'ailleurs il faut dire réfugiés, ou exilés […]. Pourquoi pas dire émigrés comme de mon temps, et les laisser atterrir deux secondes?' [by the way you should say refugees or exiles […]. Why not say emigrant as we did in my time, and let them land for two seconds?].[5] In this moment, the attempt to name migrants ethically necessitates a detour through a tussle with the available terms and also a shift between the contemporary moment and the past in the hope that older names might afford a better articulation of the reality of the present. There are resonances between this experience of the strange unwieldiness of language in relation to migration and the mourners' oft-expressed sense of the inadequacy of language to convey the magnitude and specificity of loss.

Chamoiseau and Le Bris see the difficulty and flux surrounding terms for the events of the summer of 2015 and after as occasion for some hope about the role of artistic vision. In the introduction to the volume they co-edit on the migration crisis, they argue that the response to the photograph of Aylan Kurdi is a reminder of the potential of 'un seul geste artistique' [a single artistic gesture] to change perception.[6] They point out that there had been many other photographs of people who had drowned crossing the Mediterranean, including photographs of drowned children (*OF* 10). The photograph of Aylan Kurdi, while representing the death of a unique individual, did not convey any qualitatively new information about the dangers faced by migrants crossing by sea. However, something about the form of the image, 'terrible mais nimbée d'une incompréhensible grâce,

---

4   <https://www.franceculture.fr/emissions/la-grande-table-culture/marie-darrieussecq-et-le-cours-de-nos-vies> [accessed 16 September 2020].

5   Marie Darrieussecq, *La Mer à l'envers* (Paris: P.O.L, 2019), p. 63. This and all translations in what follows are my own.

6   Patrick Chamoiseau and Michel Le Bris, 'Là où littérature ne peut', in Patrick Chamoiseau and Michel Le Bris, eds, *Osons la fraternité* (Paris: Philippe Rey, 2018), pp. 9–14 (p. 10) (hereafter referenced in main text as *OF*).

constituant à elle seule un vaste réquisitoire sans aucun hurlement, où le sommeil, le paisible, l'insolite et la mort se nouaient dans un seul bloc de perception' [terrible but with a halo of incomprehensible grace, constituting in itself a vast if silent indictment, where sleep, peace, the strange and the deathly are all wrapped together in one block of perception] (*OF* 10), led to a newly compassionate, albeit short-lived, response to information that had been widely available for some time.

Just as he approaches the death of the mother through multiple digressions and retreats, Chamoiseau first approaches the subject of migrants crossing the Mediterranean through a kind of aside as he offers three ways of thinking about the Atlantic Ocean in *La Matière de l'absence*:

> Il y a trois manières de contempler cet océan.
> On peut y voir une jonction entre l'Afrique et les Amériques.
> On peut y voir un des mieux oubliés des cimetières du monde.
> On peut aussi y voir un monde de plaines, de silences montagneux et de vies inconnues, tout aussi intense que celui qui se tient au soleil, et déjà fécondé d'un tragique qui aurait dû nous obliger à être meilleurs. Hélas, en ce moment même, ce qui se passe en Méditerranée, où déjà se creuse un énorme cimetière dessous le flot des migrations, nous montre que l'"expérience atlantique' est restée lettre morte … Les modalités et le contexte sont bien sûr d'une tout autre nature, mais, dans l'éclat d'une conscience mondiale de niveau similaire, l'indifférence est identique …
> Mais parlons de ces morts africains en Atlantique.[7]

> [There are three ways of contemplating this ocean.
> You can see it as a junction between Africa and the Americas.
> You can also see it as one of the most forgotten cemeteries of the world.
> You can also see it as a world of plains, mountainous silences and unknown lives, as intense as the one which is in the sun, and already fertilized by a tragedy which should have obliged us to be better. Alas, in this very moment, what is occurring in the Mediterranean, where already an enormous cemetery is being dug beneath the flow of the migrations, shows us that the 'Atlantic experience' has gone unheeded … The modalities and context are of course of an entirely different nature, but in the brilliance of global consciousness of a similar level, the indifference is identical …
> But let's speak about these African deaths in the Atlantic.]

7   Patrick Chamoiseau, *La Matière de l'absence* (Paris: Seuil, 2016), pp. 145–6.

In the perfect conditional of 'aurait dû' [should have], we find an echo of the Flaubertian tense use analysed by Rachel Benoît. Here Chamoiseau suggests that the fact that the deaths of captive Africans in the Atlantic have never been fully acknowledged or mourned continues to influence our difficulty in seeing and mourning the lives of those who die in the Mediterranean today. His use of a metaphor of light ('éclat' [brilliance]) for contemporary global consciousness resonates with passages in the later essay *Frères migrants*, where light is associated with the unblinking stare of the computer monitor or the border post floodlights as technologies of control which see human beings as targets. Chamoiseau draws on the work of Pier Paolo Pasolini, Georges Didi-Hubermann, Aimé Césaire and Antoine de Saint-Exupéry to oppose to the light of technological control the glimmerings of glow worms.[8] The invasive lucidity of globalization seeks to harness the human desire for an encounter with newness, reducing it to manageable fuel for the engines of consumption. The flickering of glow worms in the dark becomes an image for the unpredictable and intermittent illuminations of art which stimulate new thought and hope by suggesting a range of futures rather than wholly illuminating one (*FM* 124–6). The theoretical framework Chamoiseau sets up for understanding the movements and deaths of migrants thus resonates with the value placed on the marginal, the intermittent and the blurring of vision analysed in this volume by Lyamlahy, Rushworth and Korthals-Altes.

In the passage quoted above Chamoiseau enacts the value of the intermittent by briefly layering the factual junction of Africa and the Americas with a counterfactual superimposition of the Atlantic and the Mediterranean, before moving on. Equally, in *Frères migrants*, apparently marginal comments are essential to the project of approaching the subject of migrant crossings of the Mediterranean. This is the case when he includes a footnote to a stanza by a poem by Emmanuel Merle. The footnote appears in a chapter entitled 'Mondialité' [Globality], a concept first developed by Édouard Glissant and deployed here by Chamoiseau as a way of understanding the duality of migration into

---

8   Patrick Chamoiseau, *Frères migrants* (Paris: Seuil, 2017), p. 9 (hereafter referenced in main text as *FM*).

Europe.⁹ *Mondialité* is opposed to *mondialisation* [globalization], a homogenizing and oppressive force which seeks to reduce all human life to its economic dimensions. *Mondialité* arises in the context of *mondialisation* but is a positive term, referring to those unpredictable moments of genuine intercultural encounter and solidarity that can arise in a globalized world. In the passage in question, migrants' footsteps become engines of duality, generating 'des remparts multiformes, zones de non-droit, terres interdites et lignes rouges, blockhaus posés comme des horizons' [multifaceted bulwarks, no-rights zones, forbidden lands and red lines, blockhouses which set themselves up as horizons], but also expressing 'une force, venue du loin, venue d'un autre monde déjà au coeur de celui-ci' [a strength which has come far, from another world which is already at the heart of this one] (*FM* 57–8). Against the containing force of globalization, which has no interest in seeing migrants move, their footsteps affirm the precarious but tenacious freedom to defy imposed immobility and imagine the world otherwise.

To this passage, Chamoiseau adds a footnote to a stanza from Merle's poem 'La Longue Marche' [The Long Walk]. This poem was unpublished when *Frères migrants* came out, but has since appeared in the volume *Tourbe* [*Turf*] (2018), where Merle explores his encounters with Irish poetry and with the Irish landscape.¹⁰ 'La Longue Marche' commemorates an event of 1849 known as the 'Doolough Tragedy'. Chamoiseau's deployment of a French author's poem on the Irish famine to think about the deaths of migrants in the Mediterranean demonstrates the worldly energy of literary mourning. Just as Darrieussecqu's protagonist stumbles through 'réfugiés', 'exilés' and 'émigrés' as she attempts to name people seeking entry to Europe, the writing of Merle and Chamoiseau approaches migrants' journeys by going on complex journeys of its own. A few details about the Doolough Tragedy are necessary before exploring the ways in which it resonates with Chamoiseau's concern with lucidity and luciolity, and Merle's concern

---

9   Glissant outlines the distinction between *mondialisation* and *mondialité* in *La Cohée du Lamentin* (Paris: Gallimard, 2005), p. 15.

10   Emmanual Merle, *Tourbe* (Paris: Alidades, 2018) (hereafter referenced in main text as *T*).

with mourning the unmourned whose traces are present in post-imperial landscapes.[11]

The Doolough Tragedy occurred in County Mayo during the Irish Famine. Before receiving famine relief, those seeking it had to be inspected by the Poor Law Guardians to prove they were really in need. In March 1849, hundreds of people seeking famine relief had gathered at the town of Louisburg to be inspected. They were asked to walk ten miles away to Delphi Lodge, the hotel where the Guardians were staying. When they arrived at the hotel, they were given nothing. The weather conditions were harsh, and many died as they made the journey to and from Delphi Lodge. The exact number of people who died is disputed; the number ranges from twenty to four hundred.[12] The death-dealing consequences of the requirement to appear within the imperial gaze resonate with Chamoiseau's suggestion of the hostile qualities of the light of surveillance on migrant bodies. Against this demand for clear vision, Merle's poem affirms instead a form of memory which, like the Irish weather, rarely resolves into clarity. Instead, in 'La Longue Marche', memory is always in the process of emerging to consciousness through the lyric speaker's exposure to the landscape, which speaks of the presence of the dead in a language which is foreign yet tantalizingly translatable.

This sense of memory as a process of translation is in keeping with the memorial practices that have arisen at Doo Lough more broadly. The tragedy emerged partly in the context of imperial connections between Great Britain, Ireland and India, as the grain the famine victims had been promised had been imported to Ireland from India. The memorial practices around the event have equally had a transnational character, drawing connections both between Ireland and other places colonized by Great Britain and between the Famine and the hunger of the dispossessed more broadly. One of the memorials to the Famine at Doo Lough bears an inscription from Mahatma Gandhi, 'How can men feel themselves honoured by the

11 I am borrowing the term 'luciolity' to refer to glow worms and their resonances in the work of Pasolini and Didi-Hubermann from Thomas Baldwin, *Roland Barthes: The Proust Variations* (Oxford: Oxford University Press, 2019), p. 166.
12 The historical information in this paragraph is drawn from Charlie Connelly, 'The Black Lake's Secret', *New Statesman*, 7 May 2009, § 16 <https://www.newstatesman.com/travel/2009/05/ireland-louisburgh-night> [accessed 14 September 2020].

humiliation of their fellow beings?'.[13] Here the imperial connection between
Ireland and India is redeployed in the service of a resistant memory. Like
Chamoiseau's remark about migrant footsteps expressing a strength from
another world which is already at the heart of this world, this question situates imperial aggression as a supplementary gesture which destructively but
unsuccessfully seeks to mask an always already existing common dignity.

The annual memorial walk between Doo Lough and Delphi Lodge has
also been led by Waylon Gary White Deer, an Oklahoma Choctaw artist
and author. The Choctaws donated money to aid the victims of the Irish
Famine in 1847, and in 1995 made Mary Robinson, a former President of
Ireland, an honorary Choctaw chieftain, in recognition of the solidarity of
the Irish and Choctaw people.[14] As well as commemorating such historic
forms of identification between those who suffered at the hands of empire,
the Doo Lough memorial walk continues to forge new connections between Irish history and contemporary forms of famine, prejudice and war.
The walk has been attended by Archbishop Desmond Tutu, Chernobyl
children, Kim Phúc (the Vietnamese child pictured fleeing naked from a
napalm bomb) and Juan Contreras, a Guatemalan community leader cam-
paigning for food sovereignty.[15] The Doolough Tragedy thus becomes a way
into thinking both about connections between formerly colonized places
in the now-anglophone world, and broader echoes between experiences
of suffering, famine and dispossession across the globe.

Merle's poem partakes of the resonances of Doo Lough as a site of
transnational memory and solidarity, and, as Bourne-Taylor writes of the
poem 'Moby Dick' in her essay in this volume, it is an 'interweaving of
the personal, the impersonal, the transpersonal and the interpersonal'. 'La
Longue Marche' of the title is both the walk of the starving people seeking
relief and the walk of the writer and others who follow in their footsteps
centuries later. Like the Atlantic and the Mediterranean in Chamoiseau's
writing, for Merle, County Mayo is a kind of unacknowledged graveyard,

13   Ibid., § 17.
14   It also has to be said that many of the American politicians and government officials
      who imposed the displacement of the Choctaw nation from their ancestral lands
      were born in Ireland. See Turtle Bunbury, 'What the Irish Did For – and To – the
      Choctaw Tribe', *Irish Times*, 12 March 2018.
15   Connelly, 'The Black Lake's Secret', § 21.

haunted by '*l'engloutissement des noms, l'absence des tombes*' [*the swallowing up of names, the absence of tombs*] (*T* 18).[16] The speaker seeks to come into contact with the suffering which occurred at Doo Lough, but there is a sense of belatedness about this quest. As he walks, he encounters '*l'horizon toujours déjà peint*' [*the always already painted horizon*] (*T* 9). This evokes a skyscape which is both open and already criss-crossed by multiple memories, painted over by many artists. The belatedness is wistful in its sense of distance from the experience the speaker seeks to encounter, yet also enabling in the sense of immersion in a rich palimpsest of art and memory.

The ground is a major source of this multiplicitous otherness, and, like the horizon, it has been written over before. A translated stanza from Seamus Heaney's 'Digging' acts as an epigraph to the volume:

> L'odeur froide de la terre remuée, le gargouillis
> De la tourbe détrempée, les courtes entailles d'une lame
> Au travers de racines vivantes s'éveillent dans ma tête. (*T* 5)

> [The cold smell of potato mould, the squelch and slap
> Of soggy peat, the curt cuts of an edge
> Through living roots awaken in my head].[17]

Heaney's poem is a triple exploration of ways of relating to paternal ancestors, to writing, and to the land, which itself expresses a form of belatedness and inadequacy in relation to those who have come before, but also a determination to transpose the forebears' craft into the new medium of writing. Merle's poem can be seen as a displaced and translated engagement with these questions in a transnational context. As Bourne-Taylor points out in her essay in this volume, in Merle's *tombeaux* for his father, space is 'a vast echo chamber', 'inflected by a ghostly paternal and ancestral presence'. These tropes recur in Merle's exploration of the Irish landscape and the Doolough Tragedy.

Merle creates echoes between the engulfing moistness of turf and snow so that each footstep draws him into a landscape of suffering and internal

---

16   The poem is written almost entirely in italics; all italics in quotations are therefore original.

17   Seamus Heaney, *Opened Ground: Poems 1966–1996* (London: Faber & Faber, 1998), p. 3.

exile which could be either Irish or Alpine (*T* 19).[18] This is not simply a uni-directional process of translation from the foreign to the native, however; to be drawn into the land is to be taken on a journey with an open ending, as is suggested in Merle's rhizomatic evocation of tree roots: 'Les arbres plantés, qui sait jusqu'où vont leurs racines?' [Trees once planted, who knows how far their roots go?] (*T* 10). There is something about Merle's Irish landscape which is constitutively open, expressive of a submarine unity between land, sky and lake in County Mayo, the snowdrifts of Merle's native Alps and many other unnamed but present landscapes haunted by the suffering of the unrecorded dead, like that of the Americas which Merle explores elsewhere in his poetry. The practice of mourning here thus resonates with Lyamlahy's analysis of Abdelkebir Khatibi's conception of mourning which, 'like trans-lation, reduces distance, creates links between thoughts and renews, even re-introduces, the voice of the other beyond the borders of language and territory'. In his encounter with the Irish landscape and the memories it holds, Merle seeks not roots but routes. He walks in the hope of finding:

> le détail *qui révèlera l'ancien passage d'herbe*
> *et de pierres concassées qu'empruntaient*
> *les caravanes d'exil, des hommes*
> *poussés dans le dos par la vie,*
> *corps et âmes marchant, espérant.* (*T* 12)

> [*the* detail *which will reveal the ancient passage of grass*
> *and of crushed stones taken*
> *by the caravans of exile, men*
> *pushed on by life*
> *bodies and souls walking, hoping.*]

This stanza speaks of a quest for detail which will reveal passage rather than rootedness, openness rather than closure. In this volume, Sainsbury ana-lyses the role of 'root infinitives' in the poetry of Valérie Rouzeau, bringing out their capacity to express simultaneously a desire for ongoing states and the disrupted, uprooted temporality of mourning. Although Merle seeks to evoke the lives of unknown others here rather than a late father as is the case in Rouzeau's poetry, this same duality is at work in the tenseless gerunds

18   Merle was born in a town at the edge of the Alps.

which appear at the end of the stanza. 'Marchant, espérant' [walking, hoping] recreates the movement and emotion of the 1849 walkers, resonating with Chamoiseau's concept of the footsteps of migrants as expressive of hope for another possible world. Yet, this recreation of hope and movement is undermined by the brief note at the beginning of the poem which tells us that most of those who walked along Doo Lough in March 1849 died.

Sainsbury also explores the duality of the absence of subject pronouns in Rouzeau's work, which evokes both the 'eradication of self' in the experience of mourning, and the fullness of self of early childhood, so immediate that 'I' seems superfluous. Together Rouzeau's use of root infinitives and absence of subject pronouns contribute to a paradoxical effect where the mother tongue comes to seem both 'strange and unfamiliar' and 'firmly rooted in a present state'. This same duality is present in this stanza which evokes both the foreignness of the landscape and the immediacy of its presence; as language reaches out to express the journeys taken along Doo Lough, it expresses the material presence of the world but in the process becomes 'strange and unfamiliar', its meanings uncertain and difficult to pin down.

In keeping with the spirit of the memorial walk, there is a recurring ambiguity about whose movements are being evoked in the poem. In the following lines, the 'nous' could be the people who have gathered for the commemorative walk or the starving walkers of 1849:

> *Nous sommes partis,*
> *nos noms sont restés en arrière,*
> *arrimés aux maisons vides.* (*T* 13)

> [*We have left,*
> *our names have stayed behind,*
> *fastened to the empty houses.*]

The loss of identity expressed could thus be the dehumanization that occurs in the imperial gaze, or the prelude to the contemporary walkers' openness to another country's history, another people's suffering. Equally, when we read '*Je n'emporte pas mes outils, les mains | ont des souvenirs*' [*I do not take my tools with me, hands | have memories*] (*T* 10), we assume this is the voice of the speaker on the twenty-first-century walk who leaves without a pen, hoping to encounter the landscape through his body and to draw on this memory later to write. As before though, through the *je* of the lyric voice resonates the *je* of the desperate person leaving home to seek famine relief. This ambiguity about whether the absent tools are for writing or working the land is reinforced by the parallel in Heaney's 'Digging' between the spade and the pen, and by the open space after 'mains', which emphasizes both the emptiness of the hands and their plurality.

In the final stanza of the poem, which Chamoiseau quotes in *Frères migrants*, the shifting between the ambiguous *je* and *nous* resolves into the third-person designation of *celui* [the one], as the poem and the walk reach a kind of ending:

> *Celui qui marche déplie le monde,*
> *un horizon manqué après l'autre.*
>
> *Tout ce qui lui reste.*
>
> *Un pas est-il encore un nom?*
> *Je n'appartiens plus qu'à mon pas.*
>
> *La lumière, la parole du monde,*
> *prononce nos ombres passantes*
> *et nous identifie.*[19]
>
> [*The one who walks unfolds the world,*
> *One missed horizon after another.*
>
> *All that remains to him.*
>
> *Is a step still a name?*
> *I no longer belong to anything but my step.*
>
> *The light, the word abroad,*
> *pronounces our passing shadows*
> *and identifies us.*]

In keeping with the rest of the poem, this is a form of ending which resists closure. The present tense of 'marche' expresses ongoing action, but is also a present tense of a general truth which could apply to people in many different times and places. 'Celui' with its potential to refer to any number of walkers reinforces this. The unfolding of the world accomplished by the walker-writer

19   Emmanuel Merle, 'La Longue Marche', in *Tourbe* (Paris: Alidades, 2018), pp. 9–13, previously quoted in Patrick Chamoiseau, *Frères migrants* (Paris: Seuil, 2017), p. 58. Merle's poem was unpublished at the time of its appearance in Chamoiseau's text.

resonates with Bonnefoy's concept of poetry as 'dé-signation' or 'un-signing', 'un-doing' explored in Bourne-Taylor's essay on Merle.[20] The world is opened out here both in the sense that the speaker translates the language of rock, grass and lake into a form of verbal memory, and in the sense that the borders between Ireland and other landscapes of suffering are undone. Yet this does not resolve into a positive sense of shared identity, but is instead a paradoxically negative encounter with a horizon which is always missed.

This sense of the negative resonating through a generative process is reinforced by the irregular rhythm and grammar of the first three lines of the stanza. As this is the last stanza, it evokes both the culmination of the twenty-first-century encounter with otherness in the landscape and the hobbled motion of dying bodies in 1849. Rushworth notes in her exploration of intermittent grief in Proust's novel that the perception of rhythm is a process of discerning sense and pattern amid flux, and a way of thinking about disappearance and return. In particular, it is linked to disappearance and reappearance within the body, what Merleau-Ponty calls 'the pulsation of […] existence […], its systole and its diastole', the corporeal sense of breathing lungs and beating heart.[21] In the first three lines of nine, nine and five syllables, and the end-stopped third line, we hear the erratic, subsiding rhythm of expiration. The slight exceeding and falling short of octosyllables and hemistichs evokes a rhythm which struggles and fails to sustain itself, suggesting both the last motions of the expiring body and the poem's inability to express this expiration in regular poetic form. As Rushworth writes, 'rhythm compels the text to recover its status as enunciation (process)'; an effect of this is that the articulation of death as cessation of process lies beyond poetic expression. This moment is thus both an incarnation of a dying body and a withdrawal from such an incarnation, a recognition that the moment where life becomes death lies beyond the empathy and cognition of the speaker. It can be read through Mildenberg's evocation of living in Merleau-Ponty's thought as 'a series of crossings and recrossings of flesh', where 'the perceiver and the perceived, like the imagery

---

20   Yves Bonnefoy, 'La Poésie est dessin: ce qui dé-signe', in *Remarques sur le dessin* (Paris: Mercure de France, 1993), p. 36.

21   Maurice Merleau-Ponty, *Phenomenology of Perception*, trans. Donald A. Landes (Abingdon: Routledge, 2012), p. 298.

of the sea and the strand, are at once overlapping and divergent, unified and differentiated, meaning that they can never completely coincide'.[22] In this stanza, both the body and the world are crossed and recrossed as the speaker's voice approaches, re-imagines and retreats from their boundaries.

This fusion of the negative and the creative continues with '*Un pas est-il encore un nom?* | *Je n'appartiens plus qu'à mon pas*' [*Is a step still a name?* | *I no longer belong to anything but by step.*]. The double meaning of *pas* as both 'step' and 'not' marries forward motion with the energy of negation. The homophony of *nom* and *non* layers the emergence of identity with its disappearance, echoing the loss of identity and encounter with otherness explored earlier. As in Rouzeau's work, the *pas* also suggests the French children's word for father, *papa*, itself an ambivalent resonance here, as for Merle the paternal is tied to the theme of loss but childhood vision is associated with a rich relationship to the surrounding world.[23] The recurrence of *pas* in the fourth and fifth lines in the stanza evokes the regular intermittence of walking, where progress is achieved through the iterative making and unmaking of each step. The recurrence of *pas* in *parole* [word] and *passantes* [passing] reinforces this as *parole* suggests articulation where *passantes* suggests disappearance. In the image of the 'ombres passantes' [passing shadows], we can see both the moving shadows of the twenty-first-century walkers and the elusive presence of the nineteenth-century dead and all those who haunt post-imperial landscapes. The image of light pronouncing passing shadows and so generating a form of collective identity coalesce the sense present throughout the poem of the landscape as a speaker of a foreign language of memory, experience and presence, which the lyric voice might just be able to translate.

As the poem ends with the image of light edging the walkers' shadows, it seems fitting to return to Chamoiseau's suggestion that the flickering of glow worms offers a way of thinking about the relationship between art and death, politics and hope. Just as Chamoiseau argues in favour of

22   David Farrell Krell, *Architecture: Ecstasies of Space, Time, and the Human Body* (New York: State University of New York Press, 1997), p. 170.

23   This association is expressed earlier in the poem, albeit in a negative form, with the lines: '*Lorsque s'éteint l'oeil de l'enfance, là* | *disparaît le monde*' [*When the eye of childhood dies, there* | *the world disappears*].

fragile, flickering lights which do not obliterate the darkness, so the essays in this volume approach mourning texts as a form of writing which seeks to articulate the proximate otherness of the deceased without denying either their closeness or their alterity. Merle's image of light edging the moving shadows of the walkers suggests the paradoxical quest present in the writing of mourning to come as close as possible to the gap left by an absent body, to articulate that which one is not and cannot be. Though this quest for proximity can neither erase nor fully articulate the absence it seeks to speak, by seeking to touch it, it creates a responsive border around it which suggests the shifting, palpable life left by the loss of others, known and unknown, unloved and loved.

Notes on Contributors

RACHEL BENOÎT is a doctoral candidate at New College, Oxford. She holds a BA from Brown University in Comparative Literature, a Maîtrise from the Université Paris-Sorbonne, Paris IV, and an MSt in French and English from Brasenose College, Oxford. Her research draws into conversation the work of Gustave Flaubert and William Faulkner, with particular attention paid to their treatment of history.

CAROLE BOURNE-TAYLOR is Associate Professor of French, Fellow and Tutor at Brasenose College, Oxford, where she teaches modern literature in French and supervises doctoral research in comparative studies. Her PhD from Grenoble was published as *L'Univers imaginaire de Virginia Woolf* (Éditions du Temps, 2001, with a preface by Jean Guiguet and a postface by Gilbert Durand). The bulk of her research is devoted to literature in English, including the introductions to Charles Morgan, *Three Plays*, and *Dramatic Critic: Selected Reviews* (Oberon Press, 2013). She co-edited, with Ariane Mildenberg, *Phenomenology, Modernism and Beyond* (Peter Lang, 2010, with a preface by Kevin Hart) and is currently writing a biography of Alice Sapritch (to be published by Éditions Garnier, Paris).

SARA-LOUISE COOPER is Lecturer in French at the University of Kent. She is the author of *Memory Across Borders: Nabokov, Perec, Chamoiseau* (Legenda, 2017). She is writing a second monograph, *Where Word Meets World: Caribbean Writing in French and 'World Literature'* and has published articles on cross-cultural memory in *Francosphères*, *Wasafiri* and the *Journal of Modern Literature*.

HENRIETTE KORTHALS ALTES is currently a research fellow at the Maison Française d'Oxford. Her research interests are in contemporary French and comparative literature as well as in contemporary French thought. More specifically, she has written on the cultural construction of melancholy in contemporary French fiction and thought. She also has a special interest in the intersections between literature and dance and literature and music and has published on intermediality in the works of Roland Barthes and Pascal Quignard. Her current project looks at the writing and rewriting of history in relation to surveillance and self-surveillance.

KHALID LYAMLAHY is Assistant Professor of French and Francophone Studies at the University of Chicago. His research interests include North African studies, Francophone fiction and poetry, literary theory and translation. He recently wrote the preface to the complete poetic works of Moroccan poet Abdellatif Laâbi, republished in a special Moroccan edition by Editions du Sirocco in Casablanca, and is the co-editor, with Jane Hiddleston, of *Abdelkébir Khatibi: Postcolonialism, Transnationalism, and Culture in the Maghreb and Beyond* (Liverpool University Press, 2020). In addition to his academic work, he is a regular contributor to literary magazines and platforms including *En Attendant Nadeau*, *World Literature Today*, *Non-Fiction.fr*, *Africa at LSE* and *Zone Critique*. His first novel, *Un roman étranger*, was published in January 2017 in Paris by Présence Africaine Editions.

ARIANE MILDENBERG is Senior Lecturer in Modernism in the School of English, University of Kent. She is the author of *Modernism and Phenomenology: Literature, Philosophy, Art* (Palgrave Macmillan, 2017) and the editor of *Understanding Merleau-Ponty, Understanding Modernism* (Bloomsbury, 2018). She has co-edited two volumes: with Patricia Novillo-Corvalán, *Virginia Woolf, Europe and Peace: Transnational Circulations* (Clemson University Press, 2020), and with Carole Bourne-Taylor, *Phenomenology, Modernism and Beyond* (Peter Lang, 2010). Her current book project investigates the dialogues between, and postcritical aspects of, modernist and postcolonial literature, focusing on the ways in which selected authors dismantle the hierarchical binaries within language to counteract imperialist and colonial discourse. She also translates Danish poetry.

DOMINIQUE RABATÉ is Professor of Modern and Contemporary French Literature at the University of Paris, where he is president of the CERILAC – Centre d'Études et de Recherches Interdisciplinaires de l'UFR LAC (Lettres Arts Cinéma). A leading expert on narrative, he has published numerous essays of distinction, amongst which *Vers une littérature de l'épuisement* (1991), *Le Roman français depuis 1900* (1998), *Poétiques de la voix* (1999), *Le Chaudron fêlé. Écarts de la littérature* (2006), *Le Roman et le sens de la vie* (2009), *Gestes lyriques* (2013), *Désirs de disparaître: une traversée du roman français contemporain* (2015), *La Passion de l'impossible. Une histoire du récit au XXème siècle* (2018), *Petite physique du roman* (2019), and major studies of writers (Louis-René des Forêts, Marie Ndiaye, Pascal Quignard, etc.). He is also an editor of the collection 'Modernités' (based at Bordeaux University).

STEPHEN ROMER, who had a career as a Senior Lecturer at Tours University, has held Visiting Fellowships at All Souls, Christ Church, St Anne's, Oxford; he is currently Lecturer in French at Brasenose College. A specialist in Franco-British Modernism (his Cambridge PhD was on T. S. Eliot), he has translated widely from contemporary French poetry, notably Yves Bonnefoy. His most recent publications include *Set Thy Love in Order* (new and selected poems, 2017), *Le Fauteuil jaune* (2021) and *Julian Malpas. A Day of Unusual Measure* (2021). He was elected FRSL in 2011 and he features in the Pléiade *Anthologie bilingue de la poésie anglaise* (2005).

JENNIFER RUSHWORTH is Associate Professor in French and Comparative Literature at University College London. She has published two books, *Discourses of Mourning in Dante, Petrarch, and Proust* (Oxford University Press, 2016) and *Petrarch and the Literary Culture of Nineteenth-century France* (Boydell Press, 2017). She was the recipient of the Society for French Studies's Malcolm Bowie Prize 2015, for her article 'Proust, Derrida, and the Promise of Writing'. Her article on 'Mourning and Intermittence between Proust and Barthes' won the *Paragraph* Essay Prize 2016, awarded that year for the best essay on the topic of 'Mourning'.

DAISY SAINSBURY is an independent scholar based in Paris. Her monograph, *Contemporary French Poetry: Towards a Minor Poetics*, is forthcoming with Legenda in 2021. Her research has appeared in *French Studies*, *Comparative Literature*, *Paragraph*, *French Cultural Studies*, *Formes Poétiques Contemporaines* and *Modern Languages Open*.

BENJAMIN THURSTON completed a D.Phil. thesis on Joseph de Maistre's theory of language at the University of Oxford, upon which he was awarded a Leverhulme grant to do postdoctoral research at Paris IV into biblical discourses in early nineteenth-century French literature. He has published studies of apocalyptic literature during the Consulate and Empire, the evolution of biblical rhetoric between 1815 and 1830, and Chateaubriand's use of biblical language and ideas in *Le Génie du christianisme*. His current research is into regicide and memory during the Restoration. He is Head of Modern Languages at Magdalen College School, Oxford.

Index

Modern French Identities
Edited by Jean Khalfa

This series aims to publish monographs, editions or collections of papers based on recent research into modern French Literature. It welcomes contributions from academics, researchers and writers worldwide and in British and Irish universities in particular.

Modern French Identities focuses on the French and Francophone writing of the twentieth and twenty-first centuries, whose formal experiments and revisions of genre have combined to create an entirely new set of literary forms, from the the- matic autobiographies of Michel Leiris and Bernard Noël to the magic realism of French Caribbean writers.

The idea that identities are constructed rather than found, and that the self is an area to explore rather than a given pretext, runs through much of modern French literature, from Proust, Gide, Apollinaire and Césaire to Barthes, Duras, Kristeva, Glissant, Germain and Roubaud.

This series explores the turmoil in ideas and values expressed in the works of theorists like Lacan, Irigaray, Foucault, Fanon, Deleuze and Bourdieu and traces the impact of current theoretical approaches – such as gender and sexuality studies, de/coloniality, intersectionality, and ecocriticism – on the literary and cultural interpretation of the self.

The series publishes studies of individual authors and artists, comparative studies, and interdisciplinary projects and welcomes research on autobiography, cinema, fiction, poetry and performance art and/or the intersections between them.

Volume 25   Steve Wharton: Screening Reality.
            French Documentary Film during the German Occupation.
            252 pages. 2006. ISBN 3–03910-066-1 / US-ISBN 0–8204-6882-7

Volume 26   Frédéric Royall (ed.): Contemporary French Cultures and Societies.
            421 pages. 2004. ISBN 3–03910-074-2 / US-ISBN 0–8204-6890-8

Volume 27   Tom Genrich: Authentic Fictions.
            Cosmopolitan Writing of the Troisième République, 1908–1940.
            288 pages. 2004. ISBN 3–03910-285-0 / US-ISBN 0–8204-7212-3

Volume 28   Maeve Conrick & Vera Regan: French in Canada.
            Language Issues.
            186 pages. 2007. ISBN 978–3-03-910142-9

Volume 29   Kathryn Banks & Joseph Harris (eds): Exposure.
            Revealing Bodies, Unveiling Representations.
            194 pages. 2004. ISBN 3–03910-163-3 / US-ISBN 0–8204-6973-4

Volume 30   Emma Gilby & Katja Haustein (eds): Space.
            New Dimensions in French Studies.
            169 pages. 2005. ISBN 3–03910-178-1 / US-ISBN 0–8204-6988-2

Volume 31   Rachel Killick (ed.): Uncertain Relations.
            Some Configurations of the 'Third Space' in Francophone
            Writings of the Americas and of Europe.
            258 pages. 2005. ISBN 3–03910-189-7 / US-ISBN 0–8204-6999-8

Volume 32   Sarah F. Donachie & Kim Harrison (eds): Love and Sexuality.
            New Approaches in French Studies.
            194 pages. 2005. ISBN 3–03910-249-4 / US-ISBN 0–8204-7178-X

Volume 33   Michaël Abecassis: The Representation of Parisian Speech in the
            Cinema of the 1930s.
            409 pages. 2005. ISBN 3–03910-260-5 / US-ISBN 0–8204-7189-5

Volume 34   Benedict O'Donohoe: Sartre's Theatre: Acts for Life.
            301 pages. 2005. ISBN 3–03910-250-X / US-ISBN 0–8204-7207-7

Volume 35   Moya Longstaffe: The Fiction of Albert Camus. A Complex
            Simplicity.
            300 pages. 2007. ISBN 3–03910-304-0 / US-ISBN 0–8204-7229-8

Volume 36   Arnaud Beaujeu: Matière et lumière dans le théâtre de Samuel
            Beckett: Autour des notions de trivialité, de spiritualité et d'
            « autre-là ».
            377 pages. 2010. ISBN 978–3-0343-0206-8

www.ingramcontent.com/pod-product-compliance
Lightning Source LLC
Chambersburg PA
CBHW071530110726
47908CB00007B/1824